# Outrage in the Age of Reform

In the 1830s, as Britain navigated political reform to stave off instability and social unrest, Ireland became increasingly influential in determining British politics. This book is the first to chart the importance that Irish agrarian violence – instances of which were known as 'outrages' – played in shaping how the 'decade of reform' unfolded. It argues that while Whig politicians attempted to incorporate Ireland fully into the political union to address long-standing grievances, Conservative politicians and media outlets focussed on Irish outrages to stymie political change. Jay R. Roszman brings to light the ways that a wing of the Conservative Party, which included many Anglo-Irish, set Irish violence in the context of a wider imperial framework, stressing the ways in which outrages threatened the Union and with it the wider empire. Using underutilised sources, the book also reassesses the ways in which Irish people interpreted 'everyday' agrarian violence in pre-Famine society, suggesting that many people perpetuated outrages to assert popularly conceived notions of justice against the imposition of British sovereignty.

Jay R. Roszman completed his PhD in History at Carnegie Mellon University, for which he was awarded the Adele Dalsimer Prize for Distinguished Dissertation from the American Conference of Irish Studies. He has published articles in *Historical Journal* and *Historical Research*. He was appointed Lecturer in Nineteenth-Century Irish and British History at University College Cork in 2018. A native Vermonter, Jay earned his MA in Irish Studies at Queen's University Belfast and his BA in History and Political Science at Gettysburg College. He lives in Cork with his wife and daughter.

T0371245

*Modern British Histories*

Series Editors

Deborah Cohen, Northwestern University
Margot Finn, University College London
Peter Mandler, University of Cambridge

'Modern British Histories' publishes original research monographs drawn from the full spectrum of a large and lively community of modern historians of Britain. Its goal is to keep metropolitan and national histories of Britain fresh and vital in an intellectual atmosphere increasingly attuned to, and enriched by, the transnational, the international and the comparative. It will include books that focus on British histories within the UK and that tackle the subject of Britain and the world inside and outside the boundaries of formal empire from 1750 to the present. An indicative – not exclusive – list of approaches and topics that the series welcomes includes material culture studies, modern intellectual history, gender, race and class histories, histories of modern science and histories of British capitalism within a global framework. Open and wide-ranging, the series will publish books by authoritative scholars, at all stages of their career, with something genuinely new to say.

A complete list of titles in the series can be found at:
www.cambridge.org/modernbritishhistories

# Outrage in the Age of Reform

*Irish Agrarian Violence, Imperial Insecurity,
and British Governing Policy, 1830–1845*

Jay R. Roszman

*University College Cork*

CAMBRIDGE
UNIVERSITY PRESS

CAMBRIDGE
UNIVERSITY PRESS

Shaftesbury Road, Cambridge CB2 8EA, United Kingdom

One Liberty Plaza, 20th Floor, New York, NY 10006, USA

477 Williamstown Road, Port Melbourne, VIC 3207, Australia

314–321, 3rd Floor, Plot 3, Splendor Forum, Jasola District Centre, New Delhi – 110025, India

103 Penang Road, #05–06/07, Visioncrest Commercial, Singapore 238467

Cambridge University Press is part of Cambridge University Press & Assessment, a department of the University of Cambridge.

We share the University's mission to contribute to society through the pursuit of education, learning and research at the highest international levels of excellence.

www.cambridge.org
Information on this title: www.cambridge.org/9781009186766

DOI: 10.1017/9781009186773

First published 2022
First paperback edition 2024

*A catalogue record for this publication is available from the British Library*

ISBN   978-1-009-18678-0   Hardback
ISBN   978-1-009-18676-6   Paperback

Cambridge University Press & Assessment has no responsibility for the persistence or accuracy of URLs for external or third-party internet websites referred to in this publication and does not guarantee that any content on such websites is, or will remain, accurate or appropriate.

*For Rachel and Aubrey: My loves, forever*

# Contents

# Figures

# Tables

# Acknowledgements

You are reading my favourite part of any book I read. Acknowledgements are where the reader learns how the book in their hands came together: not simply through the sheer force of individual will but also with the support of dozens of relationships, both personal and professional, undergirded by the quiet work of people at a myriad of institutions and archives. This book is no different and reflects the profound impact that relationships that stretched across roughly a decade and over the Atlantic Ocean have had on me as I completed my work.

This project began when my doctoral supervisor, the late David W. Miller, gave me an old box of microfilm from his basement that he had collected in the 1990s for a project on collective action with Charles Tilly. David's project never materialised, but his generous spirit imbues this book, and the microfilmed 'Reports of Outrage' are the cornerstone upon which this scholarly edifice is built. Katherine Lynch provided detailed feedback and unfettered support along the way, caring about me as an individual and not simply a graduate student. When David became ill towards the end of my graduate career, I naively sent an email to a Cambridge academic I knew next to nothing about other than that he had written a book on some of the Whig aristocrats I was studying. I will never know exactly why Peter Mandler responded to my email, offering his advice on how to gain access to the private papers of a prominent Whig family (graciously including the information that I had misspelled the family's title!), as well as to read my dissertation, offer his constructive feedback, and provide his support after I had completed my PhD. What I do know is that I am forever in his debt and hope my academic career can (in some small way) mirror his scholarly generosity.

Academic conferences can get a bad rap for being too cliquish – I am lucky that the American Conference of Irish Studies bucked that trend. I have learned so much from scholars who welcomed me to their panels and out for pints: too many to list, but especially Jill Bender, Jason Knirk, Tim McMahon, Michael de Nie, Matt O'Brien, Anna Teekell, Paul Townend, and Nick Wolf. Cian McMahon, who finished his PhD at

Carnegie Mellon under David's direction a few years before I did, deserves special acknowledgement. When I was a cash-strapped graduate student attending my first 'big' conference in Chicago, Cian sacrificed his privacy and let me stay with him, making the trip possible. He always wanted to know not just about my project but also about me and offered his wisdom and humour over pints of Guinness and cups of coffee as a more experienced traveller further on the academic journey. Thanks, too, to all those from the North American Conference of British Studies who encouraged my research at critical junctures through their questions and conversations, especially Karl Gunther, Phil Harling, Seth Koven, and Richard N. Price. Even when an ocean away, friends from my undergraduate days kept my skills of argumentation attuned via our shared 'Politics' text thread, as we debated the political insanity unfolding from 2016 to the present. In Pittsburgh, I benefitted from a rich network of colleagues, friends, and teachers. Reflecting on that city and that time makes me nostalgic for the mix of intellectual stimulation and camaraderie, as well as the experience of sharing in the travails of everyday life, that that network provided. Thanks go to Caroline Acker, James and Sarah Bohnhoff, Dan and Lara Croce, Matt and Christine Croce, Kaylynn DeFusco, Paul Eiss, Wendy Goldman, François and Joy Guilleux, Dan Harding, Donna Hirsch, Rob Hutchings, Ricky Law, Jincheng Liu, Cassie Miller, Josh Moyer, Rachel Myers, Avigail Oren, Andrew Ramey, John Soluri, Alex Shuttleworth, Amund Tallaksen, Bea and Karl Thomas, Gaea and Phil Thompson, and Melissa and Zach Wilson.

The move across the Atlantic to take up my position at University College Cork has also incurred many debts. I am particularly grateful to John Borgonovo, Claire Connolly, David Fitzgerald, Dónal Hassett, Heather Laird, Andrew McCarthy, Hiram Morgan, Donal O Drisceoil, Mervyn O'Driscoll, Clare O'Halloran, Maeve O'Riordan, David Ryan, Diarmuid Scully, and Chris Williams for laying out the welcome mat. Peter Hession and Richard Butler (who read large chunks of this book!), both in their own ways, have shown me the ropes and best watering holes in Cork. Thanks to Ciaran O'Neill for helping me navigate what a job offer in Ireland looks like, for his early interest in my work, and for reading large parts of this book at various points. I appreciate Michael Brown and Colin Barr for inviting me to present my work at the University of Aberdeen's Research Institute of Irish and Scottish Studies, as well as Rose Luminiello for her friendship and interest in my work. Thanks to Lauren Arrington, who has always been encouraging of this book and sent off a few inquiring emails when things appeared to have stalled. Similarly, I am grateful to Ian McBride for his encouragement and help – including taking my Skype call while on research leave in Rome and offering encouragement to stay on the job market when I was about to give up. I have had many formative conversations along the way over coffee in random archives, across loud conference dinner tables, on the pavement of a busy Dublin street, or during thrilling (failed) job interviews, but I specifically want to acknowledge scholars who may hardly remember them, including Aidan Beatty, Guy Beiner, Marie Coleman, Sophie Cooper, David Dickson, David Gordon, Peter Gray, Matthew Kelly, Breandán Mac Suibhne, Stephanie McCurry, Fearghal McGarry, Mary Mullen, Susan Pedersen, Olwen Purdue, Sarah Roddy, Maggie Scull, Michael Silvestri, and Patrick Walsh.

This book would not have been possible without the assistance of a number of institutions and archives that financially supported this project and allowed me access to their materials. I am grateful for the financial support and warm hospitality I received from Boston College as its William B. Neenan Fellow during the summer of 2018, especially from Mike Cronin. When the project was nearing completion, I was awarded the Eoin O'Mahony Bursary in Irish History from the Royal Irish Academy, which allowed for a last archival research trip. I also acknowledge the support I received from UCC's College of Arts, Celtic Studies and Social Sciences; UCC's School of History; Carnegie Mellon University's Department of History; and the American Conference of Irish Studies (ACIS). I am indebted to numerous archival staff across England and Ireland. I want to thank the owners of private papers who permitted me to consult and quote from their archives: the Hon. Simon Howard, the Marquess of Normanby, and Thomas Pakenham of Tullynally Castle. I am also indebted to Sue Collins, the History Librarian at Carnegie Mellon University's Hunt Library, who tracked down books for me via interlibrary loans and fought to keep digital databases she knew I used. My thanks also go to Cambridge University Press, and to the series editors for supporting this book and helping make it a reality. Special thanks to editor Liz Friend-Smith for fielding all my questions and ultimately navigating this rookie author through the murky waters of academic publishing. This book would not have been possible without the assistance of content manager Melissa Ward, and the Herculean efforts of copy-editor Frances Tye. I am also deeply indebted to both of the anonymous readers of the manuscript, who provided more thoughtful and engaged feedback than I have ever received – the book is better because of their critique, and all errors and dubious historical interpretations remain my own.

Finally, I want to acknowledge the continued support of my parents, Doug and Kathy, who sacrificed so much for me to achieve my goals and whose unconditional love has been a balm during all of life's vicissitudes.

Above all, to Rachel, my wife and co-adventurer – thank you for saying 'yes' to a life together, whether in moving as a young married couple to a new city where we knew no one or relocating our shared life across the Atlantic Ocean with all the concomitant sacrifices. Here's to a lifetime of other adventures together. Aubrey, you make life infinitely brighter with your light – never stop.

# Abbreviations

| | |
|---|---|
| BARS | Bedfordshire Archives and Records Service, Bedford |
| BEM | *Blackwood's Edinburgh Magazine* |
| BL | British Library, London |
| BNL | *Belfast News-Letter* |
| CH | Castle Howard, York |
| DCRO | Durham County Record Office, Durham |
| DUM | Dublin University Magazine |
| ECL | Exeter Cathedral Library, Exeter |
| EHR | *English Historical Review* |
| FJ | *Freeman's Journal* |
| HJ | *The Historical Journal* |
| IHS | *Irish Historical Studies* |
| JBS | *Journal of British Studies* |
| LPL | Liverpool Public Library |
| MC | Mulgrave Castle, Whitby |
| NAI | National Archive Ireland, Dublin |
| NLI | National Library of Ireland, Dublin |
| PRONI | Public Record Office of Northern Ireland, Belfast |
| P. P. | Parliamentary Papers |
| P & P | *Past & Present* |
| RCBL | Representative Church Body Library, Dublin |
| TC | Tullynally Castle, Castlepollard |
| TCD | Trinity College Dublin, Dublin |
| TNA | The National Archives, Kew |
| UCL | University College London, London |
| UNSC | University of Nottingham Special Collections, Nottingham |
| USSC | University of Southampton Special Collections, Southampton |
| WSRO | West Sussex Record Office, Chichester |

# Introduction

Across 1839 and early 1840 a series of letters addressed to Britain's Protestants, entitled 'Popery – the Duties of Protestants', appeared in provincial newspapers across England.[1] Written by the Rev. James Dixon, a Wesleyan minister who would go on to be elected President of the Methodist Conference in 1841, the letters offer a window into the fear and anxiety evinced by many Protestants at the rapid social, religious, and political changes they witnessed in the 1830s. Dixon, who gained prominence as one of 'the most powerful, popular, and active anti-popish lecturers and speaker', equated the United Kingdom's political stability and geopolitical dominance with Protestantism.[2] He worried that those in power, the Whig government led by Lord Melbourne, were animated by a commitment to 'liberal principles' that threatened to unmoor the country from its foundation of freedom and liberty and imperil the wider empire. 'For ages the empire, reposing under the peaceful influence of Protestant institutions, appeared like the blue ocean beneath the bright sunshine of heaven', wrote Dixon, 'whilst the setting in of Popery, has been like a mountain deluge, rendering muddy and turbid the pure and tranquil waters'.[3] The struggle between the Conservative Party and the Whig Party was not one based on political principles; rather, it was about 'Protestantism on the one side, and Popery on the other'. Dixon stressed that '[i]n this as in other things England has been assimilated to Ireland', before asking his readers: 'Then, from all these facts and circumstances, it may be asked, is it *safe*, is it *rational*, is it *English*, is it *Christian*, to confide the religious destinies of the country to such hands as these?'[4]

It is questionable whether a few letters printed in provincial newspapers by a Methodist pastor in 1840 are worthy of historical memory. Reading

---

[1] These letters were later collected into pamphlet form, published in 1840. See Rev. James Dixon, *Letters of the Duties of Protestants with Regard to Popery* (Sheffield: G. Chaloner, 1840).
[2] Richard Watson Dixon, *The Life of James Dixon, D. D., Wesleyan Minister* (London: Watson and Hazell, 1874), 222.
[3] Dixon, *Letters*, 18.    [4] Dixon, *Letters*, 19, 24.

them is to plunge oneself into a litany of anti-Catholic stereotypes meant to jar mid-nineteenth-century sensibilities, to say nothing of today's. Nevertheless, they serve as a useful starting point for this book for two reasons. First, Dixon's writing was simply one example among dozens, if not hundreds, on similar themes of anti-Catholic sentiment that linked 'popery' with foreign tyranny, embroiling the Irish politician Daniel O'Connell and the supposed 'barbaric' state of Ireland into its narrative: 'The fond aim of these parties [the Whigs] is to make us all brother Papists with themselves. . . . Would this advance our freedom? . . . Let the present enslaved, ignorant, barbarous, and wretched state of the Irish peasantry answer this question.'[5] Other controversialists, offering riffs in the same key, promised 'the righteous judgment of God' would 'overtake the British empire', or stressed that the calamity of the Famine was a consequence of the British Parliament passing 'anti-Christian laws' that provided a permanent state endowment for the Catholic seminary at Maynooth College.[6] The variety of tracts, newspapers, poems, and magazines produced on anti-Catholic/anti-Irish themes in the 1830s and 1840s became political fodder for audiences, as Dixon and others of his ilk used stereotypes about Irish backwardness and violence toward political ends and suggested that if Catholicism was allowed to flourish, Great Britain might devolve into another Ireland.

Dixon's letters, and the countless other works of anti-Catholicism, also underscore another salient feature of political realities in the 1830s and 1840s – that Ireland, and Irish issues, did not function as a parochial backwater (even if many perceived Ireland as such) but stood instead at the crux of British politics during the 'age of reform', constraining its actions and shaping its outcomes. Ireland's role in shaping British politics is a fact that historians have often highlighted. One of the most exciting and enduring examples is George Dangerfield's *The Strange Death of Liberal England*, which despite its parochial title, advocated with witty vigour how the 'Ulster Question' offered one *casus belli* in a civil war that never happened but that nevertheless destroyed a particular cultural formation – 'Liberal England' – and a political party.[7] In the late nineteenth century the reoccurring question of Home Rule ensured that Irish questions were never far from parliamentary business. Eugenio Biagini

---

[5] Dixon, *Letters*, 18.
[6] Robert James M'Ghee, *A Sermon Preached in Harold's Cross Church [. . .]* (Dublin: Grant and Bolton, 1843), 24; Anon., *Popery in Power, and Britain Betrayed [. . .]* (London, J. F. Shaw, 1854), 50.
[7] George Dangerfield, *The Strange Death of Liberal England*, 20th ed. (New York: Perigee Books, 1980). Dangerfield would return to the Irish theme in his *The Damnable Question: A Study of Anglo-Irish Relations* (London: Little, Brown, 1976).

has noted that Irish mass immigration to Britain, along with Irish MPs making nearly one-sixth of the Westminster Parliament's membership, ensured that between 1876 and 1906, 'Ireland was *the* pressing question of the day and was treated as such by both Liberals and Unionists'.[8] But Irish MPs also showed up in unexpected places to exert political influence, much to the chagrin of their British counterparts, such as at critical moments of imperial interventions or on questions of fiscal policy and taxation.[9]

This book continues in this scholarly tradition by demonstrating the ways that Ireland shaped the crucial decade of reform – a period of monumental change in the United Kingdom that saw the end of the confessional state, with the passage of Catholic Emancipation in 1829 and the Great Reform Act of 1832, but also the growing remit of the central state to enumerate and tackle problems that had previously been handled by localities in a rising 'reform' agenda.[10] This book puts Ireland, especially the fundamental threat of Irish agrarian violence (known as 'outrages'), front and centre in the political narrative of the 1830s and 1840s. It argues that Irish 'problems' shaped British political culture in the 1830s, motivated politicians to apply their reformist vision in new ways, and profoundly influenced political outcomes in ways that heretofore have been underappreciated.[11] In short, if we fail to incorporate the Irish dimension of the 1830s, we run the risk of missing an important piece of the story of the 'age of reform'; one, I will add, that is hiding in plain sight, as a cursory glance at newspapers and the periodical press confirms.

The book advances three interrelated arguments that have implications for our understanding of the political history of Great Britain and Ireland,

---

[8] Eugenio F. Biagini, *British Democracy and Irish Nationalism, 1876–1906* (Cambridge: Cambridge University Press, 2007), 2.

[9] Paul A. Townend, *The Road to Home Rule: Anti-Imperialism and the Irish National Movement*, History of Ireland and the Irish Diaspora (Madison: The University of Wisconsin Press, 2016); Douglas Kanter, 'The Politics of Irish Taxation, 1842–53', EHR 127, no. 528 (1 October 2012): 1121–55; Douglas Kanter, 'The Campaign Against Over-Taxation, 1863–65: A Reappraisal', in *Taxation, Politics, and Protest in Ireland, 1662–2016*, ed. Douglas Kanter and Patrick Walsh (Cham: Springer, 2019), 227–52, https://doi.org/10.1007/978-3-030-04309-4_9.

[10] J. C. D. Clark, *English Society 1688–1832: Ideology, Social Structure and Political Practice During the Ancien Regime* (Cambridge: Cambridge University Press, 1985); Arthur Burns and Joanna Innes, 'Introduction', in *Rethinking the Age of Reform: Britain 1780–1850*, eds. Arthur Burns and Joanna Innes (Cambridge: Cambridge University Press, 2003), 1–70, at 47.

[11] Shunsuke Katsuta has recently highlighted the way the Rockite Rebellions of the early 1820s influenced political debate in Westminster. See Shunsuke Katsuta, *Rockites, Magistrates and Parliamentarians: Governance and Disturbances in Pre-Famine Rural Munster* (Abingdon: Routledge, 2020), ch. 4.

as well as the meaning of agrarian violence in the Irish countryside prior to the Famine. First, the book argues that the reforming agenda of the 1830s found its expression in a group of relatively young, aristocratic Whig politicians who believed that government had a positive and active role to play in solving social wrongs and who approached governing Ireland in novel ways between 1835 to 1841. This group of politicians sought to solve Ireland's innumerable problems, including Irish agrarian violence, by offering a number of legislative reforms from Westminster in an effort to win Irish hearts and minds to the reality of British rule – a policy they identified as 'justice to Ireland'. This policy differed from those of previous governments because the Whigs in power scorned coercive legislation against Ireland and instead sought remedial legislation for that country. At a more localised level, their governing strategy included attempts to make the mechanics of Irish law and order a popular instrument by opening positions in the state bureaucracy, including the constabulary, law offices, and positions in Dublin Castle, to Catholics. Whigs intended these measures to alleviate the conditions that in their minds had bred agrarian violence, which in turn would more fully incorporate Ireland into their political union and create stability throughout the British Empire. This argument builds on, and seeks to complicate, the structure laid out in K. T. Hoppen's magisterial *Governing Hibernia*, which charted British governing strategy during the Union on a spectrum between 'policies of differentiation' and 'policies deliberately conceived to assimilate Ireland into the norms and behaviour patterns of a larger metropolitan (that is, British) centre'.[12] On the one hand, the discussion that follows, especially concerning Whig government intentions, underscores how governing policy shifted towards assimilation extremes in the late 1830s. On the other hand, this shift was predicated on an existing structure in the apparatus of state control that treated Ireland separately and employed powerful coercive and surveillance powers to legitimise its control.

The election of Daniel O'Connell as an MP in 1828, and the subsequent passage of Catholic Emancipation, irrevocably altered the contours of the British state. Politics in pre-Famine Ireland operated on a zero-sum basis, and Protestant peers and gentry members saw Emancipation as an apocryphal event with grave portent for their political power – that Catholic Emancipation was identified with ideas like 'reform' or was encompassed in the 'spirit of the age' made it that much more threatening to a Protestant sociopolitical order. As a result, Protestants began an active campaign to undermine the effects of Catholic Emancipation

---

[12] K. Theodore Hoppen, *Governing Hibernia: British Politicians and Ireland, 1800–1921* (Oxford: Oxford University Press, 2016), 2.

through organising Protestant communities in Ireland and Great Britain and publishing anti-Catholic/anti-Irish propaganda in influential periodicals and the popular press. The second argument of this book focuses on this reaction to Catholic Emancipation and to the active inclusion of Catholics in the apparatus of the state. It suggests that Protestants on both sides of the Irish Sea used fears around agrarian violence and the alleged role in its organisation played by the Catholic Church's hierarchy as a political tool to stir latent anti-Catholic/anti-Irish feeling in Great Britain. This strategy included casting Irish violence in wider imperial contexts, suggesting either the potential inspiration Irish violence might offer in other colonial spaces or the potential for connection between revolutionary organisations. The book traces how this strategy was implemented successfully in the overwhelming Tory electoral victory of 1841, as well as the role that the aftermath of these sentiments played on the eve of the Famine.

Irish agrarian violence was an endemic feature of pre-Famine society, and many identified it (along with widespread poverty) as the chief inhibitor to Ireland's development as an integral part of the United Kingdom. In the eyes of propertied interests, Irish outrages threatened the free exercise of legal rights over private property and thus created a hostile environment for capital investment. For others, outrages signified the social fissures of class and religious background. The meaning of agrarian violence among those that perpetrated the violence, or suffered from it, has been a source of considerable debate in historiography, which I will discuss in greater detail below. However, I argue that for many among Ireland's underclass, the Whig efforts at 'justice for Ireland', which included the opening up of some professions in the state's apparatus, were not sufficient to satisfy their long-standing grievances. Instead, the rural poor often enacted justice on a local level defined by communal understandings of 'what was right'. This was interpreted by many government officials as a form of popular sovereignty that challenged the expanding sovereignty of the state. In short, I argue that Irish agrarian violence was an attempt to maintain a form of sovereignty exercised by Irish people over a range of social, economic, religious, and political relationships, thus resisting the encroachment of British institutions that were in the process (through 'reform') of seeking to gain legitimacy among Ireland's population.

## Ireland and Great Britain: Four Nations, One Union

This book examines Ireland and Great Britain after its political union in 1801, and therefore, it builds on the assumption that a proper historical understanding of Ireland must start with its relationship with the larger, more powerful, and politically dominant island across the Irish Sea – Great Britain. Although this assumption seems like common sense (and it is), it is also building on a larger historiographical tradition that has asserted the need to reclaim a contested, pluralist, and varied history of the British Isles from the standard Anglocentric history that too often has passed for British history. Indeed, one need look no further than the constitutional crisis surrounding Brexit to see the historical legacy that the four nations played in shaping the complexities of the United Kingdom as a multinational, multi-ethnic state. Therefore, Ireland in the nineteenth century (to say nothing of the seventeenth, eighteenth, or twentieth centuries) simply cannot be understood without placing it within the context of an expanding, increasingly powerful polity that had absorbed Ireland into its sphere and created a brand-new political entity – the United Kingdom.

In 1973, the year of Britain and Ireland's entrance into the European Economic Community (EEC), the historian J. G. A. Pocock delivered remarks at the inaugural Beaglehole memorial lecture in New Zealand that subsequently became a seminal turn in British historiography. The address called for a new 'British history' that embraced the complex, plural, contested histories of what Pocock termed the 'Atlantic archipelago'. Pocock argued that what often passed in textbooks for British history was really only the history of English actors that included Scots, Welsh, or Irish as 'peripheral peoples ... disturb[ing] the tenor of English politics'. Furthermore, the histories produced by scholars in Scotland, Ireland, or Wales tended to scorn Anglocentric accounts and create nationalist alternatives that further fractured scholarship, and created segregated audiences.[13] Pocock suggested investing new meaning into 'British history' by exploring the 'plural history of a group of cultures situated along an Anglo-Celtic frontier and marked by an increasing English political and cultural domination'.[14] Inspired in part by Queen's University Belfast historian J. C. Beckett's reinterpretation of the English Civil War into the now paradigmatic Wars of the Three Kingdoms, Pocock recognised the overlapping narratives that contributed to how events unfolded in Britain and Ireland, which historians who were determined to recount an English story largely ignored.[15]

Coming on the heels of Britain's entrance into the European community, Pocock's project had a certain present-mindedness worth exploring.

[13] J. G. A. Pocock, 'British History: A Plea for a New Subject', *Journal of Modern History* 47, no. 4 (December 1975): 603–4.
[14] Ibid., 605.
[15] J. C. Beckett, *The Making of Modern Ireland: 1603–1923* (London: Faber, 1966), ch. 4.

While on the one hand Pocock's model embraced the plural, diverse, and contested histories across the British Isles, its emphasis on sovereignty and empire underscored his profound unease with Britain's entrance into the EEC. Central to this uneasiness was Pocock's assertion that a nation needed to exercise sovereignty in order for it to have a history and national identity; by ceding its sovereignty to a supranational European state, he feared Britain would surrender its collective past. Pocock grounded this British identity crisis in the abrupt end of the British Empire after two world wars, coupled with the loss of the 'capacity to act' on the world stage with the country's reduced capability as an oceanic and imperial power.[16] Interrogating exactly what was meant by 'European', Pocock feared that in Britain's eagerness to cede its national sovereignty to the EEC it risked rewriting its distinctly insular, oceanic, and Atlantic past.[17] As a man who had grown up in New Zealand, Pocock also feared what Britain's turn towards Europe meant for the identities of many Commonwealth nations whose history and identity (to say nothing of their economy) centred on their relationship with Britain.[18]

In addition to his concern regarding Britain's sovereignty, and therefore the nation's history, Pocock's call for a new British history came a few years after conflict erupted in Northern Ireland in 1969, and nearly concurrently with the imposition of Direct Rule from Westminster, which led to an attempt at a power-sharing government embodied in the Sunningdale Agreement of December 1973 and its rapid demise in May 1974. The seeming intractability of the Ulster question, the multitude of identities associated with Northern Ireland, and the contestation over sovereignty offered a present-day problem that could be understood by means of Pocock's emphasis on the plurality of experiences and attempt to understand historically what being 'British' actually meant. The Troubles also pointed to the fact that Irish history could not be understood in isolation, or even as the antithesis of British imperialism, but rather needed to be incorporated within 'the processes of politicisation ... the formation and disruption of state structures ... and the reactions against that attempt and its consequences',[19] an acknowledgement that dovetailed nicely with

---

[16] J. G. A. Pocock, 'History and Sovereignty: The Historiographical Response to Europeanization in Two British Cultures', JBS 31, no. 4 (October 1992): 362–3. On Pocock's critique of Europe, see J. G. A. Pocock, 'Deconstructing Europe', in *The Discovery of Islands: Essays in British History* (Cambridge: Cambridge University Press, 2005), 269–88.

[17] Pocock, 'History and Sovereignty', 365, 377–8.

[18] Ibid., 361; J. G. A. Pocock, 'The New British History in Atlantic Perspective: An Antipodean Commentary', *The American Historical Review* 104, no. 2 (April 1999): 492.

[19] J. G. A. Pocock, 'The Limits and Divisions of British History: In Search of the Unknown Subject', *The American Historical Review* 87, no. 2 (April 1982): 318.

contemporaneous trends within Irish historiography among 'revisionists' attempting to reclaim Ireland's history from nationalist myth and hagiography.[20] Pocock himself acknowledged Ireland's profound importance in his historiographic endeavour, reframing the 'modern' period of British history as one defined by the 1801 Act of Union and the establishment of the Irish Free State in 1922.[21]

Pocock's call garnered mixed reactions among British and Irish academics. Some historians argued that this polycentric approach posed more questions than it could answer, that an archipelagic model failed to properly take into account Atlantic dimensions, or that Pocock's emphasis on sovereignty and the state was too present-minded, or too exclusive.[22] Others worried an archipelagic model underappreciated Ireland's continual connections with continental Europe. *The Irish in Europe 1580–1815*, an edited volume following a 1999 conference at NUI Maynooth, stressed Ireland's continual continental connections throughout the early modern period, causing one reviewer to dismiss the 'alleged uniqueness of "The British Isles"' and praise the volume for persuasively arguing that 'Irish culture was not, and could not be, contained by the island's surrounding waters'.[23] Other scholars wondered if the new British history was not justh another way to 'perpetuate the Anglocentricism characteristic of the study of early modern English history', comparing it to a 'poisoned chalice', and in any event stressing early modern Ireland's ambiguous ability to fit into either a strictly Old World or New World paradigm.[24] Those suspicious of 'Irish revisionism' also argued persuasively for a narrative in tension with the new British history

---

[20] On revisionism in Irish historiography, and its controversy, see Ciaran Brady, *Interpreting Irish History: The Debate on Historical Revisionism 1938–1994* (Dublin: Irish Academic Press, 1994); D. George Boyce and Alan O'Day, eds., *The Making of Modern Irish History: Revisionism and the Revisionist Controversy* (London: Routledge, 1996); Kevin Whelan, 'The Revisionist Debate in Ireland', *Boundary 2* 31, no. 1 (2004): 179–205; Ian McBride, 'The Shadow of the Gunman: Irish Historians and the IRA', *Journal of Contemporary History* 46, no. 3 (July 2011): 686–710.

[21] Pocock, 'Limits and Divisions', 331.

[22] Raphael Samuel, 'British Dimensions: "Four Nations History"', *History Workshop Journal*, no. 40 (Autumn 1995): iii–xxii; David Armitage, 'Greater Britain: A Useful Category of Historical Analysis?', *The American Historical Review* 104, no. 2 (April 1999): 427–45; Richard Bourke, 'Pocock and the Presuppositions of the New British History', *The Historical Journal* 53, no. 3 (August 2010): 747–70; Dana Simmons, 'The Weight of the Moment: J. G. A. Pocock's Politics of History', *History of European Ideas* 38, no. 2 (June 2012): 288–306.

[23] Karl S. Bottigheimer, review of *The Irish in Europe, 1580–1815*, Thomas O'Connor, ed., *The Sixteenth Century Journal* 33, no. 1 (Spring 2002): 264–6.

[24] Jane Ohlmeyer, 'Seventeenth-Century Ireland and the New British and Atlantic Histories', *The American Historical Review* 104, no. 2 (April 1999): 448; Armitage, 'Greater Britain', 433. Armitage quotes Raymond Gillespie's 'Explorers, Exploiters and Entrepreneurs: Early Modern Ireland and Its Context, 1500–1700', in *An*

advocated by Pocock, especially regarding Ireland's colonial past. According to revisionism's critics, rather than understanding the resurgence in sectarian violence in the north of Ireland as a product of British colonialism, revisionists simply ignored this process and focused on the internal nature of Ireland's difficulties, doing so in a clinical style unable to engage with parts of Ireland's traumatic past.[25] Ambiguities in Ireland's position and role in the British Empire were also highlighted, making it difficult to determine how best to understand the Irish experience within the history of the British Isles.[26]

While ambiguities may exist that make it difficult to categorise Ireland's place within the British Empire, or even with the British Isles, the political union of 1801 stands as a concrete event that attempted to integrate Ireland politically with its larger neighbour. The Union fundamentally transformed Ireland and Great Britain's relationship, resulting in the absorption of Ireland's subordinate parliament, the expansion of British sovereignty, and the unhinging of Protestant privilege across both islands with Catholic Emancipation in 1829. Born out of violent revolution and in the wider context of European war, the Union produced violent reactions among segments of Ireland's population and violent counter-reactions from the state defending its claim to the monopoly of the use of legitimate physical force. At the heart of this process of integration are a number of interrelated questions that this book explores, all of which are inspired in part by Pocock's suggestion to 'study "empire" as the distribution of sovereignty shaped by forces operating within the Atlantic archipelago'.[27]

## The Act of Union and State Power

If the Act of Union was an attempt to integrate Ireland into its political union, how successful was this process? The failure to incorporate

*Historical Geography to Ireland*, eds. B. J. Graham and L. J. Proudfoot (London: Academic Press, 1993), 152.

[25] Whelan, 'Revisionist Debate', 188; Brendan Bradshaw, 'Nationalism and Historical Scholarship in Modern Ireland', IHS 26, no. 104 (November 1989): 329–51.

[26] The historiography on this topic is too vast to cover in one footnote. For starters, readers should consult Keith Jeffery, ed., *'An Irish Empire'? Aspects of Ireland and the British Empire* (Manchester: Manchester University Press, 1997); Kevin Kenny, ed., *Ireland and the British Empire* (Oxford: Oxford University Press, 2005); Jill C. Bender, 'Ireland and Empire', in *The Princeton History of Modern Ireland*, eds. Richard Bourke and Ian McBride (Princeton: Princeton University Press, 2016), 343–60; Timothy McMahon, Michael de Nie, and Paul Townsend, eds., *Ireland in an Imperial World: Citizenship, Opportunism, and Subversion* (London: Palgrave Macmillan, 2017); Stephen Howe, *Ireland and Empire: Colonial Legacies in Irish History and Culture* (Oxford: Oxford University Press, 2000).

[27] J. G. A. Pocock, 'The Union in British History', *Transactions of the Royal Historical Society*, Sixth Series, 10 (2000): 196.

Catholics, as originally conceived by William Pitt, meant that the
political union 'from the start, was riven with ambiguity and disappointed expectations'.[28] Many contemporaries, including some
nationalists, viewed the Union as either incomplete or a complete
failure. For British policymakers, the political rationale and strategy
of the Union needed constant care, which necessitated wholesale
changes in governing practice.[29] It is a curious fact that Ireland has
received relatively little attention from historians examining the pivotal
'decade of reform', roughly between the passage of Catholic
Emancipation in 1829 and the fall of Melbourne's second Whig ministry in 1841. Rather than its occupying a tertiary role in the minds of
British policymakers, however, this book suggests that Ireland was
central to the shaping of British political culture. This proved true for
at least two reasons. First, the hope that Catholic Emancipation would
operate as a panacea for Ireland's ills, a way to fulfil the implicit
promises of Pitt and Castlereagh from a generation earlier, and provide
legitimacy to the Union by allowing the majority of Ireland's population to have political representation from their own tribe, proved
illusory.[30] It did not help matters that the British government diluted
the power of Irish Catholics by disenfranchising them as part of the
political price of achieving Emancipation.[31] Instead, Emancipation
merely emboldened Daniel O'Connell to seek the repeal of the
Union, opening new difficulties under the umbrella phrase: 'the Irish
question'.[32] However, the erasure of religious disabilities was not simply an Irish matter – it was a fundamental, irrevocable rewriting of
Britishness, the end of the *ancien régime* of 'old society' that had been
defined by its three characteristics, 'Anglican ... aristocratic ... [and]
monarchical', and thus it destabilised the political system and threw

[28] Alvin Jackson, *The Two Unions: Ireland, Scotland, and the Survival of the United Kingdom, 1707–2007* (Oxford: Oxford University Press, 2011), 187. Jackson offers a stimulating comparative narrative of the two unions that ponders the enduring success of the Union between Great Britain and Ireland and challenges the teleologic tendencies of some Irish historiography, which focuses heavily on the revolutionary period.

[29] Hoppen, *Governing Hibernia*.

[30] On the implicit promises of Pitt at the time of the Union, see Thomas Bartlett, *The Fall and Rise of the Irish Nation: The Catholic Question, 1690–1830* (Savage, MD: Barnes & Noble, 1992), ch. 12. On Catholic Emancipation, see Wendy Hinde, *Catholic Emancipation: A Shake to Men's Minds* (Oxford: Blackwell, 1992); Brian Jenkins, *Era of Emancipation: British Government of Ireland, 1812–1830* (Kingston: McGill-Queens University Press, 1988).

[31] Fergus O'Ferrall, *Catholic Emancipation: Daniel O'Connell and the Birth of Irish Democracy 1820–30* (Dublin: Gill and MacMillan, 1985), 249–55.

[32] Oliver MacDonagh, *The Emancipist: Daniel O'Connell 1830–47* (New York: St. Martin's Press, 1989), ch. 4; Angus Macintyre, *The Liberator: Daniel O'Connell and the Irish Party, 1830–1847* (London: Hamish Hamilton, 1965), ch. 4.

everything into turmoil.[33] Catholic Emancipation, therefore, was not the final arbiter addressing perceived Irish injustices, nor did it (in the words of Lord Melbourne) 'spread general sunshine' across Ireland and solve the country's incongruity within the Union.[34]

As a result of the dark clouds that Emancipation failed to chase away, Ireland remained a problem to be solved. Simultaneously, those politicians in power during the 1830s adopted new strategies with which to address governing problems, which often included a more interventionist approach. Rather than existing in a third tier of importance, Ireland became a prominent arena where a group of younger, aristocratic, and interventionist Whigs applied their vision of governance, based in part on religious conviction and in part on an Enlightenment notion of 'justice', and wrested control from an older and more conservative leadership. This reading owes much to Peter Mandler's *Aristocratic Government in the Age of Reform*, which upended the then-dominant thesis that the Whig Party had a smooth transition from an aristocratic political ethos to one based on liberalism and which emphasised government restraint and individualism. Mandler highlighted the intra-party tensions that developed over the 1830s and 1840s between 'Foxite' Whigs that shared an aristocratic background, were tutored in the Holland House clique, and saw government as a positive tool with which to intervene on behalf of the people, versus an older generation that was much more conservative and wary of novel approaches in governing.[35]

Building on Mandler's interpretation, this book shows how the Irish government triumvirate of Lord John Russell as home secretary, Lord Mulgrave[36] as lord lieutenant, and Lord Morpeth as chief secretary enacted a governing policy of reform based on their party's mantra of 'justice to Ireland'. In their endeavours, Daniel O'Connell, and Irish MPs under his sway, lent vital parliamentary and popular support to the Whigs' reforming cause by ending O'Connell's campaign of Repeal, and also appealing for 'justice'. Thus, 'justice' served as a keyword of

---

[33] Clark, *English Society*, 7, 408–20; on the argument that Ireland reflected other European *ancien régimes* see S. J. Connolly, *Religion, Law, and Power: The Making of Protestant Ireland 1660–1760* (Oxford: Oxford University Press, 1992), 2–4.

[34] Lloyd C. Sanders, ed., *Lord Melbourne's Papers*, 2nd edition (London: Longmans, Green, 1890), 100.

[35] Peter Mandler, *Aristocratic Government in the Age of Reform: Whigs and Liberals, 1830–1852* (Oxford: Oxford University Press, 1990), chaps. 1, 3, and 4. Mandler's thesis is challenged by Ian Newbould, *Whiggery and Reform, 1830–1841: The Politics of Government* (Stanford, CA: Stanford University Press, 1990); Richard Brent, *Liberal Anglican Politics: Whiggery, Religion, and Reform: 1830–1841* (Oxford: Clarendon Press, 1987). Brent draws slightly different conclusions than Mandler, but largely agrees that a group of Whigs were set apart from the remainder of the party based on particular characteristics.

[36] Mulgrave's title changed in 1839 when he was made Marquess of Normanby. For clarity, I refer to him throughout the book as Mulgrave, save for direct quotations.

Irish policy under the direction of those with power in Irish administration, who were turning away from what they considered the outdated mode of governing Ireland through coercion.[37] And, vitally, this reforming ethos based on the concept of justice was an attempt by both British and Irish elites to remake Ireland as a society receptive to the project of an incorporating union, although it had hitherto been 'allowed – indeed even at times encouraged – to float further and further out into the Atlantic . . . away from the contemporary glories of British norms, British values and British self-congratulation'.[38]

Attempts to remake Irish society based on an activist and interventionist approach suffered from internal contradictions. On the one hand there was a perception that Ireland needed attention and measures that demonstrated equality with Great Britain within the framework of the Union – in short, that the logics that undergirded governing ideologies should be shared across both islands.[39] Thus, in debating how to deal with Irish poverty, the government utilised a framework that aligned 'welfare entitlement and social citizenship', which according to Peter Gray should be read 'as the product of negotiation between reformist British ministers and significant sections of Irish public opinion'.[40] While government officials sought solutions worthy of dispatching to Ireland for its uplift, many also willingly acknowledged that Irish society suffered from fundamental weaknesses in the relationship between landlord and tenant that undermined their ability to apply ready-made British solutions. Thus, these interventionist Whigs believed in the innate power of government to improve Irish society and they tended to centralise the executive government at the expense of local magistrates. Occasionally, this has led historians to suggest that Ireland operated as a laboratory for British policies; however, as Richard Butler has recently demonstrated in relation to the development of prison inspections, the flow of knowledge went two ways.[41]

---

[37] I borrow the idea of the 'keyword' here from Raymond Williams. See Raymond Williams, *Keywords: A Vocabulary of Culture and Society* (New York: Oxford University Press, 1985). On the legacy of coercion in Irish policy, see Virginia Crossman, 'Emergency Legislation and Agrarian Disorder in Ireland, 1821–41', IHS 27, no. 108 (1991): 309–23; A. D. Kriegel, 'The Irish Policy of Lord Grey's Government', EHR 86, no. 338 (January 1971): 22–45.

[38] K. T. Hoppen, 'An Incorporating Union? British Politicians and Ireland 1800–1830', EHR 123, no. 501 (April 1, 2008): 350.

[39] Hoppen, *Governing Hibernia*, 85.

[40] Peter Gray, *The Making of the Irish Poor Law, 1815–43* (Manchester: Manchester University Press, 2009), 8; John-Paul McGauran, 'George Cornewall Lewis, Irish Character and the Irish Poor Law Debate, 1833–1836', *Journal of Historical Geography* 57 (July 2017): 28–39.

[41] Richard J. Butler, 'Rethinking the Origins of the British Prisons Act of 1835: Ireland and the Development of Central-Government Prison Inspection, 1820–1835', *The Historical Journal* 59, no. 3 (September 2016): 727; Joanna Innes, 'What Would a "Four Nations"

The centralisation of state control proved critical in the reformation of the Irish constabulary in 1836, discussed in greater depth in Chapter 3. Here, however, it is worth noting that the creation of the Royal Irish Constabulary, centrally administered by Dublin Castle, offers an exemplar case of the zero-sum game at work in Irish society that imbued power in the Irish executive government at the expense of Ireland's local notables, mostly made up of the Protestant minority.[42] Rather than trust local magistrates with the task of appointing constables and fulfilling the local functions of law and order, the state entrusted itself to be the arbiter of impartiality. At the same time, this centralisation tended to contribute to the 'technostate', whereby 'around the mid-century bureaucracy in Britain became the object of conscious deliberation and organisation, and in this broad sense "technical"'.[43] The constable became an agent not just of surveillance or coercive power, but also of information gathering. In this capacity, the constabulary were entreated with the task of gathering information about criminal activity, but the government concerned itself with other points of information, too.[44] The government sent circulars with some regularity to constables to ascertain the state of the harvest – especially potatoes – when rumours swirled about potential shortages. Constables proved instrumental in their collection of data concerning inland road use, which the Railway Commission cartographically rendered into beautiful maps.[45] In times of political crisis, for example during the Repeal agitation, government used constables to gather knowledge about its relative support in the countryside and the role played by the Catholic clergy.[46]

Above all else, however, the Irish constabulary was used to ascertain the level of violence in Irish society and to attempt to subdue it. In particular, the Irish government feared particular types of crime, which by the early nineteenth century came to be known as 'outrages'. While both the Irish

Approach to the Study of Eighteenth-Century British Social Policy Entail', in *Kingdoms United? Great Britain and Ireland since 1500: Integration and Diversity*, ed. Sean J. Connolly (Dublin: Four Courts Press, 1999), 181–99.

[42] Butler discusses the centralising reforms carried out on Grand Juries in Ireland, as well as the administrative units of counties. See Richard Butler, *Building the Irish Courthouse and Prison: A Political History, 1750–1850* (Cork: Cork University Press, 2020), ch. 3.

[43] Patrick Joyce, *The State of Freedom: A Social History of the British State since 1800* (Cambridge: Cambridge University Press, 2013), 34.

[44] This has been amply demonstrated in relation to inquiries into Ireland's poor. See Niall Ó Ciosáin, *Ireland in Official Print Culture, 1800–1850: A New Reading of the Poor Inquiry* (Oxford: Oxford University Press, 2014), especially chaps. 1, 7.

[45] [Francis B. Head], 'Railways in Ireland', *Quarterly Review* 63 (January 1839): 45; 'Second Report of the Commissioners appointed to consider and recommend a General System of Railways for Ireland' (hereafter 'Second Railway Report'), P. P. (1837–38, vol. 35, no. 145).

[46] 'Repeal Movement', NAI, Chief Secretary's Office Registered Papers (hereafter CSORP) 1843, A6980 (box 3/617/18).

poor and social elites recognised the legitimacy of 'riots' and 'disturbances' that occurred across the British Isles because they were based on 'the unwritten rules of paternalism and deference', by the mid-nineteenth century, outrages were marked outside these social norms and appeared in an almost exclusively Irish context.[47] This was especially true with the creation of the standardised police reports – known as 'Reports of Outrage' – that the reformed Irish constabulary began to use after 1837 (discussed later in this chapter). Social and political power holders used the term 'outrages' in an overwhelmingly Irish context to rhetorically separate Ireland from Great Britain. The danger of Irish violence, and what warranted its labelling as 'outrages', was a subversive blend of Roman Catholic solidarity, an aversion to the Protestant British state, and radical economic levelling that threatened to undermine the social and political structures of Irish society. Thus, from the perspective of the minority Anglo-Irish ruling class in Ireland, and the wider British state whose response was conditioned by the 'peculiar vulnerabilities of Ascendancy Ireland', the outrages of the Irish rural poor were the manifestation of an unwritten code, 'rooted in culture', that directly challenged the sovereignty of the state to regulate social, economic, political and religious relations.[48] Thus, 'outrages' were more than simply some sort of quasi-Thompsonian moral economy 'defining traditional rights or customs … [and] supported by the wider consensus of the community';[49] instead, they represented a countervailing and contested sovereignty attempting to supplant the functions of the state. As a result, the violent action (or indifference) of a sizeable proportion of the Irish population was interpreted as disloyalty to the British crown, as political insurrection, or as a threat of war.[50]

[47] Stanley H. Palmer, *Police and Protest in England and Ireland, 1780–1850* (Cambridge: Cambridge University Press, 1988), 52. For Palmer's reflections on the similarities and differences between English and Irish crime and protest, see pp. 45–56. On social unrest in England during this same period, see John E. Archer, *Social Unrest and Popular Protest in England, 1780–1840* (Cambridge: Cambridge University Press, 2000), especially ch. 7; on the relationship between crime and an evolving law regime, see Peter King, *Crime and Law in England, 1750–1840: Remaking Justice from the Margins* (Cambridge: Cambridge University Press, 2006).

[48] Ian McBride, *Eighteenth-Century Ireland: The Isle of Slaves*, vol. 4, New Gill History of Ireland (Dublin: Gill & MacMillan, Limited, 2009), 338; Donald E. Jordan, 'The Irish National League and the "Unwritten Law": Rural Protest and Nation-Building in Ireland 1882–1890', *P & P*, no. 158 (February 1998): 146–71, at 148. Although Jordan's article is specifically about the tension between the local and national leadership of the Irish National Land League, Jordan situates this struggle within the context of the earlier modes of agrarian violence, such as the Whiteboy movement.

[49] E. P. Thompson, 'The Moral Economy of the English Crowd in the Eighteenth Century', *P & P* 50 (1971): 76–136, at 78.

[50] This is not to say that British crime did not trouble the state – of course it did. However, this book attempts to demonstrate how Irish 'outrages' were perceived in qualitatively different ways than similar events in England, Scotland, or Wales.

Notwithstanding the rhetorical weight that politicians and newspapers connoted when applying outrage nearly exclusively in an Irish context, the term also became codified, and its reporting standardised in 1837. The newly minted inspector general of the Irish constabulary, Colonel James Shaw Kennedy, created two official documents (forms 38 and 39), dubbed Reports of Outrage, that were used to systematically compile information about every act of agrarian violence across the countryside, categorise the violence into discrete classifications, and track it with acute precision.[51] No counterpart existed in England, Wales, or Scotland. Edwin Chadwick, the model utilitarian bureaucracy builder, was attempting to reform the collection of criminal data in London during this same period, but tellingly he described criminal activity as 'delinquency' and 'depredations' rather than 'outrages' and English magistrates were wary of his centralising tendencies, which they believed might undermine the liberty of the 'Freeborn Englishman'.[52] Thus, these Reports of Outrage provide a crucial insight into understanding what British and Irish power holders meant when they used the term 'outrage' to describe Irish violence. Reifying the concept of outrage into a standardised report, which only included particular types of criminal activity, underscores the preoccupation on the part of British officials with understanding and disciplining the perceived Irish disloyalty that was undermining the two countries' political union. The rigid instructions passed between Dublin Castle and individual constables that demanded 'precision and uniformity' when constables completed their reports, as 'inaccuracies and omissions … embarrass the public business, and cannot be submitted to', demonstrate the importance of standardisation in creating an almost-scientific view of Irish society.[53] Outrage Reports, therefore, were a means 'to map society through the mechanical collection of statistical data' and part of the larger trend underway in the 1830s noted by David Eastwood whereby 'central government exchanged a partnership with the localities for a partnership with experts'.[54]

This book argues that Irish agrarian violence – 'outrages' – served as one barometer for politicians and social elites to measure the relative success or failure of the Union. It was a topic to which Parliament

---

[51] 'Chief Inspectors Circulars', 23 December 1837, TNA, HO 184/111/3.
[52] 'To the Chairman of the Committee appointed by the House of Commons to enquire into the present state of the Police of the Metropolis', UCL, Chadwick MSS. 2, ff. 121–2; David Philips, 'A Weak State? The English State, the Magistracy and the Reform of Policing in the 1830s', EHR 119, no. 483 (2004): 873–91, at 876–7.
[53] 'Abstract of Regulations', TNA, HO 184/111, 8.
[54] David Eastwood, '"Amplifying the Province of the Legislature": The Flow of Information and the English State in the Early Nineteenth Century', Historical Research 62, no. 149 (October 1989): 276–94, at 289, 293.

perennially returned with the establishment of numerous select committees, rancorous debate among both deliberative bodies, and the passage of coercive legislation meant to target it.[55] For Whigs in the latter 1830s, the topic of agrarian violence became a means by which they could attempt to demonstrate that their party's approach to governing Ireland through 'justice' had been successful, and the rise of government statistics and their interpretation became an important part of political debate in this period.

The role that statistical evidence of diminishing Irish outrages played in justifying Whig government opens other avenues to explore the importance of Irish agrarian violence in British political culture, especially within Conservative ranks. In 1841, Sir Robert Peel's Conservative Party won its largest parliamentary majority until 1886.[56] While much has been made of Peel's Tamworth manifesto in the making of the Conservative Party and its approach to party politics,[57] far less has been said concerning the influence of the right wing of Peel's party – ultra-Tories still reeling from the passage of Catholic Emancipation by their hero the Duke of Wellington, aided by Peel. However, by putting Irish issues into the frame it quickly becomes apparent that a significant factor in Peel's victory in 1841 was a vocal campaign by ultra-Tories that capitalised on the Whigs' dependence on Daniel O'Connell. Fuelled in part by the religious zeal unleashed in a 'second reformation', evangelical ultra-Tories stoked anti-Catholic sentiments by remobilising institutions, such as the Protestant Association, as well as a torrent of newspapers and pamphlets, to highlight the unique threat the Whig government posed to Protestant Britons.[58] The Tories' primary piece of evidence was the outrages of Ireland's countryside.

[55] Jay R. Roszman, 'The Curious History of Irish "Outrages": Irish Agrarian Violence and Collective Insecurity, 1761–1852', *Historical Research* 91, no. 253 (August 2018): 481–504. On the record of the state's investigation of the state, see Niall Ó Ciosáin's brilliant article, '"114 Commissions and 60 Committees": Phantom Figures from a Surveillance State', *Proceedings of the Royal Irish Academy, Section C* 109 (2009): 367–85.

[56] On yet another Irish question.

[57] Newbould lays out the prominence of Tamworth in historians' perception of the Conservative Party in the opening pages of his article. Ian Newbould, 'Sir Robert Peel and the Conservative Party, 1832–1841: A Study in Failure?', HER 98, no. 388 (1983): 529–57; See also Norman Gash, 'Peel and the Party System 1830–50', *Transactions of the Royal Historical Society* 1 (December 1951): 47–69.

[58] Irene Whelan, *The Bible War in Ireland: The 'Second Reformation' and the Polarization of Protestant-Catholic Relations, 1800–1840* (Madison: University of Wisconsin Press, 2005); Stewart J. Brown, *Providence and Empire: Religion, Politics and Society in the United Kingdom, 1815–1914* (Harlow: Pearson Longman, 2008), chaps. 1–2; John Wolffe, *The Protestant Crusade in Great Britain, 1829–1860* (Oxford: Clarendon Press, 1991); Gilbert A. Cahill, 'Irish Catholicism and English Toryism', *The Review of Politics* 19, no. 1 (January 1957): 62–76.

Attacks on Protestant tenants focused attention on the existential threat posed to the Established Church in Ireland, and the increasing power of Dublin Castle at the expense of local Anglo-Irish magistrates was packaged into stark religious rhetoric. However, after 1841, with a large majority in the House of Commons, Peel could afford to keep the ultras at arm's length and propose legislation on matters of education, church policy, poor laws, and the state's relationship with the Catholic hierarchy, all of which greatly dispirited the evangelicals that had helped bring him to power.[59]

## Ireland and the Legacy of Violence

Historians of Ireland have been nearly as keen to explore Irish agrarian violence as contemporaries of the phenomena were to exploit it. Two views dominated in nineteenth-century narratives of pre-Famine land relationships and rural society. The first – the orthodox nationalist narrative – attempted to portray rural unrest, embodied in violent agrarian movements like the Whiteboys of the eighteenth century or the Rockites of the nineteenth century, as a proto-nationalist incarnation of a homogeneous Gaelic and Catholic peasantry fighting the oppression of a largely absentee English landlord system, predicated on the illegal dispossession of native Gaels of their hereditary land. For example, in 1868 Irish radical John Mitchel argued that the 'era of "Whiteboy" organisation' was a response to the British having 'despoiled ... [the Irish] of those very lands which the plundered race were now glad to cultivate as rackrented tenants'. 'Resistance to legal oppression by illegal combination among the oppressed', he argued, was simply 'inevitable and far from blameable under the circumstances of the country ... [where] the proscribed race saw only mortal enemies on the bench, enemies in the jury-box, enemies everywhere all around, and were continually made to feel that law and justice were not for them'.[60]

---

[59] On Peel's developing relationship with the Catholic hierarchy in Ireland and its relationship to politics see Donal A. Kerr, *Peel, Priests and Politics: Sir Robert Peel's Administration and the Roman Catholic Church in Ireland, 1841–1846* (Oxford: Oxford University Press, 1982). On the distinct thinking of Irish Tories in this period, see Joseph Spence, 'The Philosophy of Irish Toryism, 1833–52: A Study of Reactions to Liberal Reformism in Ireland in the Generation between the First Reform Act and the Famine, with Especial Reference to Expressions of National Feeling among the Protestant Ascendancy' (PhD dissertation, Birkbeck College, University of London, 1990); on the dynamic between ultra-Tories, Irish outrages, and politics, see Chapters 4 and 5 below.

[60] John Mitchel, *The History of Ireland: From the Treaty of Limerick to the Present Time*, vol. 1, 2nd ed. (Dublin: James Duffy, 1869), 141.

Emblematic of the second approach to understanding and confronting agrarian violence was *On Local Disturbance,* written in 1836 by George Cornewall Lewis, the influential Poor Law administrator and future Liberal home secretary, and later chancellor of the exchequer.[61] In the introduction, Lewis cited the 'political fatalism' directed to the problem of Irish outrages as the single largest problem facing British policy in Ireland, and offered his book as a remedy: 'There are persons who altogether despair of establishing permanent tranquillity in Ireland ... Such reasoners sometimes even push their political fatalism so far as to conceive there is an innate and indelible tendency in the Irish to disturbance and outrage; that Ireland has been cut off by nature from the rest of the civilised world.'[62] Rather than dwell on the prejudices against Irish national character, Lewis directed his attention to an examination of the causes of disturbance and what hitherto untried remedies the government had to offer. Critical of the early interpretations of Irish violence as 'construing the scattered outrages of a suffering peasantry into a political and religious insurrection, supported by French influence', Lewis pointed to 'local troubles arising from the misery of the peasantry' that still plagued the country.[63] Although Lewis did not subscribe to the view held by many alarmists (like the ultra-Tories discussed in Chapter 4) that Irish agrarian violence was a 'political' (read 'nationalist') cause, he did describe motives that attempted to undermine the power of the state. Lewis differentiated between the motives of crimes committed by secret societies – what he called 'the Whiteboy system' – and the effect which these crimes intended to produce. In both instances Lewis noted how the system mimicked that of the state's legal apparatus:

In both cases, it will be observed, the offenders undertake to carry into effect their wishes ... to give to their opinion the weight of the law of the state, by arming it with sanctions as painful as those employed by the criminal law ... The outrages in question are committed by the offenders as administrators of a law of opinion, generally prevalent among the class to which they belong. In this character they look, not merely to particular, but also to general results; not merely to the present, but also to the future; not merely to themselves, but also to those with whom they are leagued, and with whom they have identity of interests. The criminal, who acts with these views, is as it were an executioner, who carries into effect the verdict of an uncertain and non-apparent tribunal.[64]

[61] D. A. Smith, 'Lewis, Sir George Cornewall, Second Baronet (1806–63)', in *Oxford Dictionary of National Biography* (Oxford: Oxford University Press, 2004), www.oxforddnb.com/view/article/16585.
[62] Sir George Cornewall Lewis, *On Local Disturbances in Ireland: And on the Irish Church Question* (London: B. Fellowes, 1836), 1–2.
[63] Lewis, *On Local Disturbances,* 14, 40.   [64] Lewis, *On Local Disturbances,* 94–5.

According to Lewis it is here that we are confronted with the problem of Irish outrages. It was not simply that agrarian violence managed to upset the sensibilities of 'civilised' British administrators, though it did that too. Rather, the problem lay in how peasants pursued a system that had social and political meaning which rivalled the order and coherence of the state, and most problematically of all, sought to supplant it. Outrages, in other words, were not simply ordinary crimes. While ordinary criminals sought personal material gain, the Whiteboy sought no personal reward but rather to punish individuals and 'enforce a law', making their crime an example for all in the community.[65] Worse still, Whiteboy outrages were not confined to a subset of the population, or a small minority of the country. Rather, at least in Lewis's view, the Whiteboy system left its mark on all of Irish society: 'This system pervades the whole society ... not the banding together of a few outcasts ... but the deliberate association of the peasantry, seeking by cruel outrage to insure themselves against the risk of utter destitution and abandonment'.[66] The end goal was not merely the protection of peasants from economic deprivation but rather the establishment of a shadow state that vied for the hearts and minds of Ireland's population as it worked to undermine the social, political, and economic relationships enshrined in British law:

So far as it is successful, it is an abrogation of the existing law, and an abolition of the existing government; for which it substitutes a dominion, beneficial apparently in its immediate consequences to the peasantry, but arbitrary, capricious, violent, unprincipled, and sanguinary, oppressive of the upper, and corruptive of the lower classes, and in the long run most pernicious to the entire society.[67]

Broadly speaking, these two contemporary views have shaped Irish historiography and popular perceptions. Historians have tended to gravitate to aspects of Cornewall Lewis's analysis, while views inspired by Mitchel's polemic were entrenched in popular conceptions. Nevertheless, the historiography surrounding agrarian violence has developed over the past fifty years to become one of the most substantial in all of nineteenth-century Irish history. Of course, this should not come as a surprise. As an agricultural and predominantly rural society with unresolved colonial legacies of expropriation, anxiety over access to the land pressed against Irish men and women as a constant existential reality, especially in times of economic distress or agricultural scarcity. The violence that ushered the Irish Free State into existence, with its concomitant fratricide, also operated as a sort of fountainhead for scholarship that cast its historical eyes back through the nineteenth century to trace violent

[65] Lewis, *On Local Disturbances*, 235.     [66] Lewis, *On Local Disturbances*, 306.
[67] Lewis, *On Local Disturbances*, 306–7.

antecedents, revolutionary traditions, and their relationship to mass politicisation.[68] Furthermore, broad trends in the historical profession, with their own modish theories and questions, shaped the scholarship in a myriad of ways. While the body of work created by historians moved away from facile conceptions of agrarian violence as proto-nationalist, the enduring legacy of violence in Irish society has continued to shape how we think about the nineteenth century, even if no consensus has emerged regarding the meaning or frequency of that violence.[69]

The re-examination of agrarian unrest began in earnest in the early 1970s as social and 'bottom-up' history percolated through seminar rooms and scholarly journals. The scholarship offered a wholesale revision of the dominant nationalist narrative. James S. Donnelly, Jr. wrote a series of articles in the 1970s and early 1980s that offered new interpretations of agrarian violence in eighteenth- and early nineteenth-century Ireland, plotting a path for subsequent historians to follow, critique, and build upon. Among other observations, Donnelly challenged the notion that violence was strictly directed against (in the words of Mitchel) the peasants' 'mortal enemies', and instead suggested that violence was also directed against Catholic priests for demanding too much money to perform a number of sacraments integral to Irish life. Donnelly also attempted to apply theories of collective action and modernisation to his analysis and utilised a number of previously unexamined sources, including regional newspapers.[70]

Several assumptions regarding the motivations and repertoire of actions, and who carried them out, have been revised by the work of subsequent historians. First, many have noted the macroeconomic factors that affected who participated in agrarian violence and the motives for their action.[71] After the Napoleonic wars, the transition from tillage agriculture to a more capitalist system of pasturage entailed the transfer of farms into larger holdings, thereby cutting off labourers and cottiers from their means of subsistence and forcing them to seek extra-legal

---

[68] R. F. Foster, 'Introduction', in *Nationalism and Popular Protest in Ireland*, ed. C. H. E. Philpin (Cambridge: University of Cambridge, 1987), 1–15.

[69] Kyle Hughes and Donald MacRaild, eds., 'Introduction', in *Crime, Violence and the Irish in the Nineteenth Century* (Liverpool: Liverpool University Press, 2018), 1–4.

[70] James S. Donnelly, 'The Whiteboy Movement, 1761–5', *Irish Historical Studies* 21, no. 81 (1978): 20–54; James S. Donnelly, 'The Rightboy Movement, 1785–8', *Studia Hibernica*, no. 17–18 (August 1977/78): 120–202; James S. Donnelly, 'Hearts of Oak, Hearts of Steel', *Studia Hibernica* 21 (1981): 7–73; See also Maureen Wall, 'The Whiteboys', in *Secret Societies in Ireland*, ed. T. Desmond Williams (London: Gill and MacMillan, 1973).

[71] Indeed, Donnelly makes this case in his study of the Rockite Rebellion. See, James S. Donnelly, *Captain Rock: The Irish Agrarian Rebellion of 1821–1824* (Madison: Wisconsin University Press, 2009), 14–15.

remedies.[72] Joe Lee first highlighted the economic rather than political motives for agrarian violence, arguing that violence served as a 'partial index to the market orientation of Irish agriculture', and stressing that the less integrated West had lower rates of violence than much of Leinster.[73] Michael Beames, in an examination of assassinations in County Tipperary between 1837 and 1847, noted that peasants predominantly targeted landlords, their agents, or large farmers for assassination, based on economic motives related to the occupation of land and the increasing rates of rents.[74] This process of enclosure also spurred agrarian violence in the eighteenth century.[75]

Notions of a homogeneous Irish Catholic experience have been deconstructed, and not surprisingly, class emerged as a lens through which to explore agrarian violence and its meaning in Irish society. The class dynamics of pre-Famine Ireland are especially difficult to untangle, as the landholding system produced a variegated pattern of agricultural arrangements. On the surface, a 'tripartite' system of landlord, tenant farmers, and labourers seems clear.[76] However, the variable size of farms and the payment of many labourers through access to land (conacre) rather than simple wages meant that pre-Famine Irish society was built on an unstable and overly complex system. The tendency to subdivide large farms into smaller ones served the interests of farmers' sons eager to have their own family farm, as well as landlords (or their agents), who used the low threshold of 40 s to gain access to voting rolls as a tool for political power. Contemporaries referring to 'peasants', therefore, often meant the labouring poor who were either landless (and therefore especially destitute) or participated in the conacre system, which gave them the bare minimum of land required for subsistence.

Who counted as a peasant? In exploring agrarian violence, historians have noted that class antagonism was mutable in periods of profound distress, or where self-interest aligned. Thus, Maurice Bric has charted

---

[72] On economic transitions in this period, see Cormac Ó Gráda, *Ireland: A New Economic History 1780–1939* (Oxford: Oxford University Press, 1995); or more recently, Andy Bielenberg, 'The Irish Economy, 1815–1880: Agricultural Transition, the Communications Revolution and the Limits of Industrialisation', in *The Cambridge History of Ireland*, ed. James Kelly (Cambridge: Cambridge University Press, 2018), 3: 179–203.

[73] Joseph Lee, 'The Ribbonmen', in *Secret Societies in Ireland*, ed. T. D. Williams (London: Gill and MacMillan, 1973), 26–35.

[74] Michael Beames, 'Rural Conflict in Pre-Famine Ireland: Peasant Assassinations in Tipperary, 1837–1847', in *Nationalism and Popular Protest in Ireland*, ed. C. H. E. Philpin (Cambridge: Cambridge University Press, 1987), 264–83.

[75] McBride, *Eighteenth-Century Ireland*, ch. 9.

[76] Peter M. Solar, 'Occupation, Poverty and Social Class in Pre-Famine Ireland, 1740–1850', in *The Cambridge Social History of Modern Ireland*, eds. Eugenio F. Biagini and Mary E. Daly (Cambridge: Cambridge University Press, 2017), 29.

the ways the middling classes played a decisive role in the Rightboy movements of Co. Cork and its environs in the 1780s, which counted 'estated
Gentlemen' among their ranks and violently campaigned for the reduction
of tithe payments. Seizing on the legitimising language of governance,
a vital component of Irish agrarian violence embodying the will of the
people, the Rightboys called 'nocturnal parliaments' to select their targets,
and 'showed a certain order and discrimination' not often attributed to
popular movements.[77] Critical of the simple dichotomy between
Protestant landlords and Catholic tenants, Samuel Clark argued that
Irish society was instead divided between the large landowning and landholding classes, which included both Protestant and Catholic middle farmers who subleased portions of their land, and the rural poor, consisting of
small farmers and labourers.[78] Class antagonism often structured agrarian
conflict, such as the violence witnessed in the early nineteenth century
between the lower-class Caravats and middle-class Shanavests, but periods
of severe economic distress also had a tendency to broaden the base of
those participating in the 'collective action' of agrarian violence.[79]
Donnelly has demonstrated how this certainly widened participation in
the Rockite disturbances of the early 1820s, and cycles of economic depres-
sion also had an important role to play in agitation after the Famine.[80]

Arguments seeing agrarian violence as reflecting solidarities within or
between classes or along political lines have been challenged most forcefully
by David Fitzpatrick. Fitzpatrick suggested that much of the agrarian violence of Irish society can be explained as faction fighting or kin-based
rivalries – thus highlighting personal rivalry and motivation over any broader
political, social, or religious tension.[81] Fitzpatrick explores this theme of

[77] Maurice J. Bric, 'Priests, Parsons and Politics: The Rightboy Protest in County Cork
1785–1788', *P & P*, no. 100 (August 1983): 100–23; on the branding of peasant violence
as primitive, see E. J. Hobsbawm, *Primitive Rebels: Studies in Archaic Forms of Social
Movement in the 19th and 20th Centuries* (New York: W. W. Norton, 1965).

[78] Samuel Clark, 'The Importance of Agrarian Class: Agrarian Class Structure and
Collective Action in Nineteenth-Century Ireland', *The British Journal of Sociology* 29,
no. 1 (March 1978): 22–40.

[79] Paul E. W. Roberts, 'Caravats and Shanavests: Whiteboyism and Faction Fighting in
East Munster, 1802–1811', in *Irish Peasants: Violence and Political Unrest 1780–1914*, eds.
Samuel Clark and James S. Donnelly (Madison: University of Wisconsin Press, 1983);
Samuel Clark, *Social Origins of the Irish Land War* (Princeton, NJ: Princeton University
Press, 1979); Charles Tilly, *Contentious Performances* (Cambridge: Cambridge University
Press, 2008).

[80] Donnelly, *Captain Rock*, ch. 5; Kerron Ó Luain, '"Craven Subserviency Had Vanished.
Bitter Hostility Had Arrived": Agrarian Violence and the Tenant League on the Ulster
Borderlands, 1849–52', *IHS* xliii, no. 163 (May 2019): 27–54.

[81] David Fitzpatrick, 'Class, Family and Rural Unrest in Nineteenth-Century Ireland', in
*Ireland: Land, Politics and People*, ed. P. J. Drudy (Cambridge: Cambridge University
Press, 1981), 4:37–75.

long-standing internecine feuding through the examination of one parish, Cloone, Co. Leitrim, where 'lofty appeals to common justice and communal solidarity merely masked the ambition of one faction to elbow out another', causing the reader to reflect on the more personal – and, in Lewis's conception, 'ordinary' – motives wrapped up in violence.[82] Fitzpatrick's arguments were further reinforced by W. E. Vaughan, who reflecting on agrarian outrages after the Famine suggested they were generally caused by 'family dispute or a row', that the majority of homicides 'were wild, impromptu affairs', and that we should consider the term outrages a 'catch-all in the taxonomy of total crime'.[83] The research presented here suggests these readings significantly minimise the importance of structural forces in shaping agrarian action, or the gravity with which violence was interpreted by the government; nevertheless, both underscore the reality that the Irish poor directed the preponderance of agrarian violence at their co-religionists.

Sectarian dimensions of agrarian violence have also come under the suspicious eyes of historians in recent years, who have suggested that intra-religious violence was as common a feature of society as the more familiar inter-religious variety, and that occasionally these groups could work in solidarity of common cause. Eoin Magennis, in an article re-examining the Hearts of Oak in Ulster, suggests that Presbyterians played an important role in the leadership of the movement, while more recently, Allan Blackstock has found instances in pre-Famine Ulster where traditional sectarian divides broke down in favour of banding together to defend common economic interests.[84] Notwithstanding Blackstock's suggestion of a fleeting flexibility in traditional sectarian divides, examination of religious and political ideologies has offered important insight into agrarian violence without collapsing into nationalist stereotypes. Religious identity often overlapped with other social and cultural identities in eighteenth- and nineteenth-century Ireland, and also could signify other characteristics – for example, whether one belonged to the polity, or one's economic position based on decades of legal systematic discrimination. Thus, economic tensions mapped onto religious antipathies, for

---

[82] Fitzpatrick, 'Class, Family, and Rural Unrest', 46; on the personal motives shaping agrarian violence, see also Breandán Mac Suibhne, *The End of Outrage: Post-Famine Adjustment in Rural Ireland* (Oxford: Oxford University Press, 2017).

[83] W. E. Vaughan, *Landlords and Tenants in Mid-Victorian Ireland* (Oxford: Oxford University Press, 1994), 143–4.

[84] Eoin Magennis, 'A "Presbyterian Insurrection"? Reconsidering the Hearts of Oak Disturbances of July 1763', IHS 31, no. 122 (1998): 165–87; Allan Blackstock, 'Tommy Downshire's Boys: Popular Protest, Social Change and Political Manipulation in Mid-Ulster 1829–1847', P & P 196 (2007): 125–71.

example in the 'troubles' in County Armagh between Protestant 'Peep o' Day Boys' and Catholic 'Defenders'.[85] Millennialism, especially 'Pastorini's Prophecies' heralding the destruction of Protestantism in the 1820s, also played an important role in shaping the agenda of those participating in Rockite activity.[86] Political ideology, whether nationalist or radical, also inspired collective action, especially among Defenders who joined United Irishmen in rising in 1798.[87] The influence of politicisation has also featured in assessing the legacy of violent nationalism in the creation of the Irish state, and thus historians have long debated the ways politicisation shaped Ribbonism.[88] Kyle Hughes and Donald MacRaild's recent contribution draws a distinction between 'real' and 'general' forms of Ribbonism, in that general flare-ups of agrarian violence often were labelled as 'Ribbonism' by contemporaries and feared as political outpourings á la 1798.[89] But the lines between agrarian violence and popular politics often blurred in the early nineteenth century, which lends weight to the argument that political questions did suffuse throughout Irish society.[90]

---

[85] David W. Miller, 'The Armagh Troubles, 1784–95', in *Irish Peasants: Violence and Political Unrest 1780–1914*, eds. Samuel Clark and James Donnelly (Madison: Wisconsin University Press, 1983), 155–91; David W. Miller, *Peep O'Day Boys and Defenders: Selected Documents of the County Armagh Disturbances 1784–1796* (Belfast: Public Records Office of Northern Ireland, 1990).

[86] Donnelly, *Captain Rock*, ch. 4. The millenarian context is also hugely important for Protestants trying to interpret Catholicism's apparent ascendancy, though its connection to any agrarian violence is much less clear. On Protestant forms see D. H. Akenson's recent biography of John Nelson Darby, Donald H. Akenson, *Discovering the End of Time: Irish Evangelicals in the Age of O'Connell* (Montreal: McGill-Queen's University Press, 2016); and also Crawford Gribben and Andrew R. Holmes, eds., *Protestant Millennialism, Evangelicalism and Irish Society, 1790–2005* (Houndmills: Palgrave Macmillan, 2006).

[87] Jim Smyth, *The Men of No Property: Irish Radicals and Popular Politics in the Late Eighteenth Century* (Houndmills: Macmillan, 1992); Jim Smyth, 'Introduction: The 1798 Rebellion in Its Eighteenth-Century Contexts', in *Revolution, Counter-Revolution and Union: Ireland in the 1790s*, ed. Jim Smyth (Cambridge: Cambridge University Press, 2000), 1–20; Thomas Bartlett, 'Defenders and Defenderism in 1795', IHS 24, no. 95 (1985): 373–81; L. M. Cullen, 'The Political Structures of the Defenders', in *Ireland and the French Revolution*, ed. Hugh Gough and David Dickson (Dublin: Irish Academic Press, 1990), 117–38.

[88] Tom Garvin, 'Defenders, Ribbonmen and Others: Underground Political Networks in Pre-Famine Ireland', in *Nationalism and Popular Protest in Ireland*, ed. C. H. E. Philpin (Cambridge: Cambridge University Press, 1987), 219–44; Beames, 'Rural Conflict in Pre-Famine Ireland'.

[89] Kyle Hughes and Donald M. MacRaild, *Ribbon Societies in Nineteenth-Century Ireland and Its Diaspora: The Persistence of Tradition* (Liverpool: Liverpool University Press, 2018), 22–5; on an infamous case of reported Ribbonism, see Terence A. M. Dooley, *The Murders at Wildgoose Lodge: Agrarian Crime and Punishment in Pre-Famine Ireland* (Dublin: Four Courts Press, 2008).

[90] Maura Cronin, 'Popular Politics, 1815–1845', in *The Cambridge History of Ireland*, ed. Thomas Bartlett, vol. 3 ed. James Kelly (Cambridge: Cambridge University Press,

One feature of the historiography is that much of it focuses on periods of profound unrest, when movements operated across large swathes of the Irish countryside, precipitating extreme reactions by the state in response. The rationale behind this approach is clear and logical; as historians we try to understand the extraordinary or unusual, assessing change over time and putting that change into its proper context. One unintended consequence, however, is that such an approach diverts attention away from periods of continuity, and what they mean for our understanding of pre-Famine society. This book tries to rectify this by offering the reader with a picture of 'everyday' agrarian violence and how it was interpreted by Irish peasants, the upper strata of the social hierarchy, and the British state. I do this by examining a hitherto underused source – the Reports of Outrage – sent daily from the inspector general of the Irish constabulary in Dublin Castle to home secretary Lord John Russell in Whitehall.[91] These daily reports communicated every outrage that took place across the country, offering a macro-level picture of the types of violence across Ireland, the apparent motives for particular crimes, and what steps the police took to deal with them. I have supplemented these reports by including the more often-used Outrage Reports, originally filed at Dublin Castle, which presented a much longer and more detailed description of the crimes and which occasionally included additional notes from the undersecretary, inspector general, or law officials at the castle.[92] What emerges from such an approach is a picture of a pre-Famine society internally divided between the sovereignty of British law, including its legal apparatus and its emphasis on private property rights, and an adherence to communal understandings of justice enforced by members of the community who combined in secret societies or other informal clandestine groups.

Given that this book attempts to uncover the culture operating among Irish peasants in pre-Famine Ireland to better comprehend the motive and meaning behind Irish outrages, it is deeply indebted to the scholarship of E. P. Thompson and his 'history from below'. Thompson's article on English crowds' actions during food riots reimagined their collective action not simply as 'rebellions of the belly' but instead as a breakdown in the 'traditional view of social norms and obligations' resulting in 'an outrage to these moral assumptions' that produced

---

2017), 3: 128–49; Gary Owens, '"A Moral Insurrection": Faction Fighters, Public Demonstrations and the O'Connellite Campaign, 1828', IHS 30 (1997): 513–41.

[91] These Reports of Outrages are interspersed among the Irish Office papers at the National Archives at Kew, see TNA HO 100.

[92] Outrage Reports are found at the Irish National Archives, in Dublin, and are arranged chronologically and by county.

confrontation.[93] At the time, Thompson's analysis was refreshing for its ability to offer expression to the historically inarticulate by uncovering the role popular custom played in informing the motives, rationale, and repertoire of actions the lower classes possessed, as well as the recognised paternal obligations of social elites.[94] Thompson's methods and his commitment to 'rescue . . . the lost causes, and the losers . . . from the enormous condescension of posterity'[95] inspired subsequent generations of historians to look to popular culture as one way to unearth the development of social change as seen from the vantage point of those that were losing their way of life to a changing world around them.

Historians of Ireland have had a somewhat mixed reaction to Thompson's notion of a moral economy, wrestling with its applicability in an Irish context. Some historians have opted to apply Thompson's model in strictly analogous contexts – for example, urban crowd actions and food riots.[96] However, Ireland at this time was one of the least urbanised countries in Europe, with over 90 per cent of its population living in the countryside immediately before the Famine, which meant historians had very few contexts within which to consider Thompson's argument.[97] James Kelly has revised that view in a study tracing the trajectory of food riots and 'plundering provisions' across the eighteenth and nineteenth century, suggesting that a moral economy operated in a limited, and diminishing fashion in Ireland, especially as agrarian violence began to appropriate some of the methods of the food riot.[98] Others have noted how, by the end of the eighteenth century, the measured restraint that had constrained agitation to accepted forms of protest, and limited violence, had convincingly come to an end.[99] More

[93] Thompson, 'The Moral Economy of the English Crowd', 77, 79.

[94] E. P. Thompson, *Customs in Common* (New York: New Press, distributed by W. W. Norton, 1993).

[95] E. P. Thompson, *The Making of the English Working Class* (New York: Pantheon Books, 1964), 12.

[96] Patrick McNally, 'Rural Protest and "Moral Economy": The Rightboy Disturbances and Parliament', in *Politics and Popular Culture in Britain and Ireland 1750–1850: Essays in Tribute to Peter Jupp*, eds. Allan Blackstock and Eoin Magennis (Belfast: Ulster Historical Foundation, 2007), 262–82; Eoin Magennis, 'In Search of "Moral Economy": Food Scarcity in 1756–57 and the Crowd', in *Crowds in Ireland, c. 1820–1920*, eds. Peter Jupp and Eoin Magennis (New York: St. Martin's Press, 2000), 189–211; John Cunningham, 'Popular Protest and a "Moral Economy" in Provincial Ireland in the Early Nineteenth Century', in *Essays in Irish Labour History; A Festschrift for Elizabeth and John W. Boyle*, eds. Francis Devine, Fintan Lane, and Niamh Puirséil (Dublin: Irish Academic Press, 2008), 26–48.

[97] Solar, 'Occupation, Poverty and Social Class'.

[98] James Kelly, *Food Rioting in Ireland in the Eighteenth and Nineteenth Centuries: The 'Moral Economy' and the Irish Crowd* (Dublin: Four Courts Press, 2017), ch. 5.

[99] Thomas Bartlett, 'An End to Moral Economy: The Irish Militia Disturbances of 1793', *P & P*, no. 99 (May 1983): 41–64; on the violence unleashed prior to the 1798 rebellion, see Guy Beiner, *Forgetful Remembrance: Social Forgetting and Vernacular Historiography of a Rebellion in Ulster* (Oxford: Oxford University Press, 2018), ch. 1.

recently, in an examination of social relations in Co. Roscommon, Michael Huggins has argued that moral economy applies to peasant actions in pre-Famine Ireland, but should be reinterpreted not as a conservative desire to go back to a bygone era but rather an attempt to appropriate 'ancient rights in order to establish new precedents'.[100] By emphasising the legitimisation of collective action among peasants, Huggins downplays Thompson's emphasis on reciprocal understandings of obligations between the upper and lower classes. Vitally important for Huggins, and other proponents of moral economy, is the notion that peasants shared cultural assumptions about 'what was right', which informed their collective action and gave their violence legitimacy in the eyes of the wider community.[101]

This book builds on Huggins's argument by suggesting that agrarian violence was animated by a contested understanding of justice and by competing regimes of sovereignty, a point anxiously acknowledged by government officials and the upper classes. In this book, I use 'justice' to describe the moral gravity felt by many in Irish society, as a standard by which they legitimised their actions to the wider community, and a concept contested by those within pre-Famine society, as well as by the British state. Unlike 'outrages', a term whose meaning was largely agreed upon in Britain and Ireland, justice was disputed by politicians of all persuasions; it was a term where, in the words of Raymond Williams, 'actual alternatives in which problems of contemporary belief and affilia-tion [were] contested'.[102] Daniel O'Connell and the Whigs used 'justice' to describe their political programme of reform and the redress of long-standing grievances on the part of the majority of the Irish population, while Tories referred to 'justice and firmness' or deridingly referenced the 'wild justice of revenge'.[103] The idea of justice was part of the political milieu thanks in large part to the French Revolution and politicians' varied reactions to it. I use 'sovereignty' to underscore the political nature of agrarian violence – the purpose of which was control over social, economic, and religious relationships in Irish society – which undermined

---

[100] Michael Huggins, *Social Conflict in Pre-Famine Ireland: The Case of Roscommon* (Dublin: Four Courts Press, 2007), 188.

[101] Martyn J. Powell, 'Ireland's Urban Houghers: Moral Economy and Popular Protest in the Late Eighteenth Century', in *The Laws and Other Legalities of Ireland, 1689–1850*, ed. Michael Brown and Seán Patrick Donlan (Farnham: Ashgate, 2011), 231–53; John William Knott, 'Land, Kinship, and Identity: The Cultural Roots of Agrarian Agitation in Eighteenth and Nineteenth-Century Ireland', *Journal of Peasant Studies* 12, no. 1 (October 1984): 93–108. For a later period, see Jordan, 'The Irish National League'; Heather Laird, *Subversive Law in Ireland, 1879–1920: From 'Unwritten Law' to the Dáil Courts* (Dublin: Four Courts Press, 2005).

[102] Williams, *Keywords*, 22.

[103] Hansard, vol. 21, 3rd ser., cols. 352–60, 14 February 1834; vol. 47, cols. 174–8, 17 April 1839.

the state's legitimacy, thus threatening its existence and causing the insecurity that perpetuated a raft of policies by state administrators. It is my hope that thinking in these terms can help one see how agrarian violence was understood by many perpetrating the violence as a political expression based in communal notions of 'what was right', while also highlighting the subversive nature of the violence from the state's perspective.[104]

## Conclusion: The Road Ahead

A picture emerges when one combines the political mechanisations of politicians, gentry members, and the press with a focus on Irish outrages – one that suggests an obscured facet of the decade of reform. Ireland, in terms of both its problems and their potential solutions, played a crucial role in shaping British political culture and governing policy in the United Kingdom and wider British Empire. The book consists of five chapters that develop this argument. Chapter 1 establishes the main contours of the book's narrative by demonstrating the role Ireland played in shaping British political culture during the pivotal decade of reform. It does this by tracing the consensus established by Whig and Tory politicians concerning the government's Irish policy between 1800 and 1830, and the ways this consensus began to break down after the seismic political ruptures of Catholic Emancipation and reform. Chapter 2 is concerned with Irish agrarian violence and its influence on how contemporaries understood Ireland's problems. While historians of Ireland have long focused their analysis on periods of profound unrest in order to draw important conclusions about the nature, methods, and outcomes of violence, much less attention has been paid to analysing 'normal' violence when no organised movement – such as the Rockite Rebellion of 1821–4 – was afoot. The chapter sets out to answer two questions. First, it explores how Irish agrarian violence was branded as 'outrages' to encapsulate the political, social, economic, and religious meanings inscribed in its perpetration by Irish and British officials. The second part of the chapter examines what normal violence was like in pre-Famine society by using the daily correspondence between the inspector general of the Irish constabulary and the home secretary in 1838, which documented every outrage across Ireland. This analysis demonstrates how many peasants, as well as the British state, understood Irish outrages in 1838 as a counter-sovereignty vying for the hearts and minds of Ireland's peasantry.

---

[104] I also think this helps move past the question of whether agrarian violence was 'nationalist' without jettisoning the important political connotations of its perpetration.

Chapters 3, 4, and 5 shift to an examination of how Irish outrage shaped politics in the latter half of the 1830s and into the new decade leading up to the Famine. Chapter 3 traces the emergence of the paternalist and intervention wing of the Whig Party, who came to prominence in Melbourne's second Whig government of 1835–41. In particular, it explores the triumvirate in charge of Irish affairs – Lord John Russell (home secretary), Lord Mulgrave (lord lieutenant), and Lord Morpeth (chief secretary of Ireland) – and how they approached governing Ireland in new ways, based on a policy they called 'justice to Ireland'. Building on the claim advanced in Chapter 2, that Irish peasant violence was understood as a form of counter-sovereignty, this chapter demonstrates how the Whigs attempted to extend British sovereignty through increased patronage to Roman Catholics, the extension of a centrally controlled constabulary, and legislative attempts at reforming Ireland in line with other British institutions.

While historians have spent considerable time demonstrating the ways in which the period c.1829–41 was 'the decade of reform', much less has been done in terms of discussing how Conservatives rallied to defend the status quo or roll back Whig efforts. Chapter 4 argues that this is because Ireland has largely been left out of the analysis of the 1830s. The chapter focuses attention on how Tories used Irish outrages as a way to attack the Whig government. In particular, the chapter highlights how so-called 'ultra' Tories effectively linked Irish agrarian violence with colonial violence in Canada, the West Indies, and India as a means to resist the Whigs' new governing strategies. They promoted theories that conceptualised Ireland, especially Irish violence, as a malignant tumour which, if left untreated, had the capacity to unravel the wider empire. The chapter also shows how Tories persuasively linked the increasing influence of Roman Catholic's in Ireland with British anti-Catholicism, and fears of 'popery' destroying the Protestant nature of Britain and its empire. It does so by discussing the creation of the Protestant Association, a reformed Gordon-Riots-era organisation that worked in the late 1830s against the Whig government by publishing anti-Catholic tracts, including many discussing Irish outrages, and which included many 'ultra' Tory as its patrons.

Chapter 5 continues to advance one of the central arguments of the book – that making sense of the decade of reform requires incorporating Ireland into one's analysis. The chapter does this by arguing that the increasing influence of the 'ultra' Tories, who had mobilised anti-Irish sentiment to achieve political success in 1841, led to the fracturing of Peel's Tory government in 1845 over the question of government support of the Catholic seminary college at Maynooth. The internal tension was already apparent in 1841 with the appointment of government ministers, like lord lieutenant Thomas De Grey, who had long-standing Orange connections and were intent on reversing the Whigs' governing legacy in favour of the time-honoured policy of coercion. Concerns about Irish outrages continued to be a mainstay of discourse, as the Protestant Association and other anti-Catholic organisations used the spectre of Irish violence for political ends. The chapter concludes by discussing the outbreak of the Famine and its relationship to a decrease in agrarian violence.

# 1    Governing Ireland in the Age of Reform

Writing in the aftermath of the Great Reform Act's passage and assent, the Whig home secretary Lord Melbourne wrote to the Lord Lieutenant of Ireland, Lord Anglesey, offering his reflections on the current state of both countries: 'I have seen, during my life, the Country twice mad – in a paroxysm of madness … once with Anti-Jacobinism, and now with something very like Jacobinism.' He trusted that the Whigs were navigating the difficult waters of 'Jacobinism' admirably with the passage of reform and offered his advice to Anglesey on Ireland that 'our best chance … is to adopt in time the necessary reformations both in the Church and State', before adding the caution, 'But we must not trust to conciliation alone. Nations cannot be governed solely by force, neither can they be managed entirely by concession. There must be a mixture of both.'[1] Tory politicians also puzzled over the proper mixture, though they generally believed that the proper alchemy for all Irish problems began with 'stronger measures', 'severe discipline', or 'laws of coercion'.[2] Nevertheless, Melbourne's Goldilocks approach to governing Ireland – a little stick, a little carrot – was a half-hearted departure from the belief that Ireland's 'idiosyncratic peculiarities deserved nothing but the stick', a belief which dominated British policy for the first thirty years of the Union.[3] But, the question remained, what was the proper mixture?

For British administrators looking across the Irish Sea, there appeared to be no shortage of problems in Ireland: poverty, economic underdevelopment, long-standing sectarian fractures in society, a deficiency of men of property to exert their rightful influence. However, all these problems were symptoms of a deeper fundamental malady – the majority of

---

[1] Melbourne to Anglesey, 12 September 1832, PRONI, Anglesey Papers, D619/29C/69. He admits in a later letter that these observations are probably nothing more than truisms but wryly notes 'I have not the power of offering you observations which are at once novel and just.'
[2] Wellington to Peel, 25 July 1829 in Peel, *Sir Robert Peel: From His Private Papers*, ed. Charles Stuart Parker (London: John Murray, 1899), 2:119; Peel to Wellington, 27 July 1829, ibid., 120.
[3] Hoppen, *Governing Hibernia*, 63.

Ireland's population did not respect British law and order and saw it as a foreigner's weapon for Irish oppression rather than a domestic tool for peace and tranquillity. 'Before any material change can be effected', J. C. Curwen wrote in his *Observations on the State of Ireland*, 'the lower classes of the people must be taught really and in truth to reverence and respect their superiors ... to believe, that from a due obedience to the laws, they would obtain more satisfactory redress than by the indulgence of their private revenge in their personal quarrels.'[4] Changes in the built environment of Ireland in the early nineteenth century, especially the construction of elaborate courthouses and gaols, reflected the need to instil awe and demand social respect. As Richard Butler has recently noted, grand juries went on a building spree, erecting buildings to 'signify the authority and power of the national and imperial government in the traditional areas of justice and punishment', while also highlighting 'the visible presence of the political, economic, and cultural authority of key local elites'.[5] Robert Peel agreed with these sentiments. Writing to Ireland's chief secretary, Lord Francis Leveson Gower, about the state of Irish society, its endemic unrest, and potential solutions in the aftermath of Catholic Emancipation, Peel wrote:

The great object that we must aim at is to establish some permanent protection of life and property, something that shall outlive one or two Sessions of Parliament, and lay the foundation for a better state of society hereafter. We shall do nothing effectual until that period shall arrive when the law – the ordinary established law – shall be regularly and peremptorily carried into execution, and we must be very careful, therefore, that if temporary remedies must be devised, they have no tendency to postpone that period ... by widening the differences and increasing the alienation and distrust that at present exist between the higher and lower classes of society.[6]

This chapter traces how successive British governments approached Irish problems, especially the question of Irish law and order, from the time of the Act of Union into the decade of reform. It does so by focussing on the concept of 'justice' – a politically disputed term used by politicians across the spectrum as a bulwark to their vision for a remade Irish society. Thus, in the words of Raymond Williams, justice in the early nineteenth century was a term encompassing the space in which 'problems of contemporary belief and affiliation [were] contested', or a rhetorical concept that provided intellectual support for the differing governing philosophies of the Tories, Whigs, and O'Connellites, especially as it concerned

---

[4] John Christian Curwen, *Observations on the State of Ireland ... Written on a Tour through That Country*, vol. 1 (London: Baldwin, Cradock, and Joy, 1818), 300–1.

[5] Butler, *Building the Irish Courthouse and Prison*, xxx.

[6] Peel to Leveson Gower, 19 November 1829, in Peel, *Sir Robert Peel*, ed. Parker, 2:133.

Ireland.[7] Justice was part of the political milieu, thanks in large part to the French Revolution and politicians' varied reactions to it. While all parties opposed the tyrannical elements of the later stages of the revolution, the Whigs and O'Connell embraced much of the reforming impetus that had inspired it, while Tories seized on criticisms of the revolution made famous by the Irishman Edmund Burke.[8]

What follows, therefore, is an examination of how Tories, Whigs, and Irish MPs understood the concept of justice and used it when debating a variety of different policies contemplated or enacted by the British government towards Ireland. It is broken into three thematic sections. First, the chapter argues that Tories understood justice in strict terms of law and order, as 'decisive measures, and the exercise, if necessary, of extreme authority which the Law commits to the Executive Government'.[9] Operating with this conception of justice, Ireland's problems would be best addressed by adopting policies meant to suppress Irish agrarian violence through more policing and restricting constitutional freedoms until the Irish population developed a pliant attitude that respected the norms of British law and authority. Successive Tory governments attempted this approach between 1800 and 1830 by creating a special police force in Ireland, the Peace Preservation Force (PPF), as well as their reliance on special legislation that restricted Irish constitutional guarantees like trial by jury or freedom of assembly.

The second section turns attention to Whig conceptions of 'justice' and demonstrates how these ideas influenced their approach to Irish policy, which by the early 1830s was internally dissonant and fractious.[10] On the one hand, many in the Whig Party saw conciliation on key Irish grievances – like Catholic Emancipation – as a way to hush the waves of Irish society and bring tranquillity. On the other hand, many members of Lord Grey's cabinet tended to see Irish society in a similar light to that in which Tories saw it, believing that it needed to be disciplined into an acknowledgement of the sacrosanctity of the law. The debate over Melbourne's Goldilocks approach, mentioned at the start of the chapter, raged not just in relation to Irish agrarian violence but also in how to address the thorny issues of tithe payments to the Church of Ireland, the role of the state in educating Irish society,

---

[7] Raymond Williams, *Keywords: A Vocabulary of Culture and Society*, revised edition (New York: Oxford University Press, 1983), 22.
[8] For an excellent, nuanced exploration of Burke's complicated legacy on modern conservativism, see Emily Jones, *Edmund Burke and the Invention of Modern Conservatism, 1830–1914: An Intellectual History* (Oxford: Oxford University Press, 2017).
[9] Peel to Duke of Northumberland, 11 July 1829, BL, Peel Papers, MS Add 40,327, f. 30.
[10] Mandler, *Aristocratic Government*, 123.

the enactment of an Irish poor law, and the structure of local government (to name but a few). This conflict was resolved, albeit only temporarily, when prominent members of the conservative wing of the Whig Party resigned, most prominent among them Lord Stanley, and when the older leadership of the party retired from politics. This political vacuum in the Whig Party had vital consequences for Ireland, as a group of young, politically aspirant, interventionist Whigs took the reins of the party and shaped its Irish policy between 1835 and 1841, as discussed in Chapter 3.

The final section deals with the integral role Daniel O'Connell played in shaping British politics in this period. It asserts that O'Connell's understanding of justice overlapped with that of many Whigs, which enabled the two political camps to work towards common interests in Ireland and Britain. The Whigs needed O'Connell's votes to pass their reform bill in 1832, and he exerted pressure on the anti-slavery campaigns of the early 1830s, contesting his parliamentary seat on a platform of 'parliamentary reform and the abolition of slavery'.[11] This section also contributes to a reinterpretation of this period in O'Connell's political career as a genuine attempt to rectify Irish grievances exclusively through the parliamentary process rather than simply as a lull between his campaigns for a repeal of the Act of Union.[12] In other words, it takes his campaign of 'justice to Ireland', which he began advocating in 1835, seriously and demonstrates that the vital link between O'Connell and the Whig Party was based on a common motivation towards remedial legislation from London and impartiality from Dublin Castle.

### Tories

Throughout the majority of the early nineteenth century, Conservative governments dominated ministerial benches at Westminster. In the aftermath of the French Revolution and in the context of the changing economic landscape of a newly industrialising Britain and postwar economic slump, Conservatives found themselves bound together by a fear of political radicalism, or even of more moderate reforming political forces. Led by Lord Liverpool, the government 'was profoundly attentive to the voices of local *political* establishments' to forcibly put down popular

---

[11] Nini Rodgers, *Ireland, Slavery and Anti-Slavery: 1612–1865* (London: Palgrave Macmillan, 2007), 269.

[12] For a full articulation of this reinterpretation see K. Theodore Hoppen, 'Riding a Tiger: Daniel O'Connell, Reform, and Popular Politics in Ireland, 1800–1847', in *Reform in Great Britain and Germany, 1750–1850*, eds. Timothy Charles William Blanning and Peter Wende, Proceedings of the British Academy, vol. 100 (Oxford: Oxford University Press, 1999), 121–43.

attempts to force parliamentary reform – attempts which included the
Peterloo Massacre – and passed national legislation limiting the meeting
of political clubs and suspending habeas corpus.[13] Forced later in the
century to introduce more economically liberal elements into his cabinet,
such as George Canning and William Huskisson, Liverpool still maintained an aversion to popular reform efforts and the bugbear of
'democracy'.[14]

Two questions throughout the 1810s and 1820s encapsulated the attitude
of Conservative governments towards Ireland: the Catholic question and
how the government would respond to Irish agrarian unrest. On the first, the
government's stated position was that ministers could form their own opinions regarding Catholic Emancipation. This meant that a number of
attempts to pass Emancipation would clear the House of Commons, only
for the Lords to rebuff them, supported by a hostile monarch, George IV.
Conservative opinion ranged widely on this issue, which explains the broad
coalition that Lord Liverpool commanded while prime minister from 1812
to 1827, as well as the disbelief and ire among ultra-Tories when Wellington
ultimately passed Catholic Emancipation in 1829.[15] Indicative of the mud-
dled, contradictory policy of government was a cabinet reshuffle in 1821 that
included the introduction of a pro-Emancipation lord lieutenant of Ireland
(Lord Wellesley), a strongly anti-Emancipation Irish chief secretary (Henry
Goulburn), a pro-Emancipation attorney general (Lord Plunkett), and
finally an anti-Emancipation home secretary (Robert Peel).[16]

On the issue of agrarian unrest, however, the party found unity in an
insistence on coercive legislation in Ireland. Concepts of justice were
applied in a rather strict sense among Conservatives focussed on the
proper administration of the law courts, an unwavering commitment to
suppress popular agitation, the defence of private property, and adherence to Protestant privilege. This commitment to a concentration of
executive power, embodied in coercive legislation, naturally fit
a political party whose heritage included the defence of royal prerogative
and power, even if the political context and convictions of ministers in the

[13] Malcolm Chase, *1820: Disorder and Stability in the United Kingdom* (Manchester: Manchester University Press, 2013), 21.
[14] Joanna Innes, Mark Philp, and Robert Saunders, 'The Rise of Democratic Discourse in the Reform Era: Britain in the 1830s and 1840s', in Joanna Innes and Mark Philp, eds., *Re-imagining Democracy in the Age of Revolutions: America, France, Britain, Ireland 1750–1850* (Oxford: Oxford University Press, 2013), 114–15; Michael J. Turner, 'Political Leadership and Political Parties, 1800–1846', in Chris Williams, ed., *A Companion to Nineteenth-Century Britain* (Oxford: Blackwell, 2004), 129–31.
[15] Wolffe, *Protestant Crusade*, 20–8.
[16] Boyd Hilton, *A Mad, Bad, and Dangerous People? England 1783–1846* (Oxford: Oxford University Press, 2006), 288–9.

nineteenth century no longer matched those of the mid-seventeenth century.

Robert Peel dominated Irish administration and agenda setting throughout this period of Tory government, first as chief secretary of Ireland (1812–18), and later as home secretary (1822–7; 1828–30). As such, his thinking is a natural starting point for a broader appreciation of Conservative applications of justice. As Norman Gash observed, 'Since the Union there had in fact been no Home Secretary with Peel's experience of Irish matters; none so well informed; and none so prepared to take an active part in the direction of Irish policy', a point borne out in the wealth of Irish material found among Peel's correspondence.[17]

Conservatives understood justice, most aptly exemplified as the 'sword of justice' within the context of law and order. This policy, broadly, included three principles: the creation and continual reformation of an armed police force in Ireland, fortified, when necessary, by the military; preserving when possible the administration of justice on a local level, reinforcing its decidedly Protestant character; and the use of coercive legislation to target groups hostile to the state, such as Daniel O'Connell's Catholic Association. If the government could effectively administer law and order and instil respect within the population of Ireland, Conservatives held some hope Ireland could attract capital investment and flourish under the Union. In the meantime, according to Robert Peel, 'an honest despotic Government would be by far the fittest Government for Ireland'.[18]

### Police Force and Insurrection Acts

Peel's most lasting reform within Ireland was the creation of the PPF, which was inaugurated in 1814. Government hoped the force could bring Ireland's disaffected peasantry under greater control, and its passage acknowledged the failure of Irish magistrates to impartially enforce Ireland's laws, as well as the inadequacy of military policing. The Irish system of law and order was largely based on the English model, which relied heavily on the exertions of an active magistrate whose social standing garnered the deference of the locality. In England, the magistrate's tasks ranged from sentencing criminals at the quarter sessions to directing the military in policing matters, while also personally intervening when

---

[17] Norman Gash, *Mr Secretary Peel – The Life of Sir Robert Peel* (New York: Longmans, Green and Co., 1961), 369–70.
[18] Peel to Gregory, 15 March 1816 in *Sir Robert Peel*, ed. Parker, 1:215.

needed to quell disturbances before troops became necessary. The creation of the PPF acknowledged that Ireland's magistrates were derelict in their duties – many had simply stopped performing any of their proscribed duties – and some did not command the respect of their community. The bill, passed in 1814, created a paramilitary police force that during periods of profound unrest could be called into a disturbed district when 'proclaimed' by the lord lieutenant after the request of several magistrates. Rather than rely on local magistrates to command the force, however, the bill mandated that a paid stipendiary magistrate do so, as well as any resident magistrates in the area. To incentivise the vigorous enforcement of regular law and order by locals on the ground in the first place, the bill also required that proclaimed districts foot the bill for the deployment of the PPF whenever circumstances necessitated.[19]

While Peel intended the PPF to inspire Ireland's magistracy to greater activity, apparent rising levels of violence across the Irish countryside required immediate attention. Economic rivalries among the lower and lower-middling classes of agriculturalists produced by the Napoleonic wartime boom led to widespread violence across large swathes of Munster, culminating in coordinated fighting between two 'factions', the Caravats and Shanavests.[20] Other than the extremely violent confrontations that occasionally resulted in murders, Dublin Castle received anxious reports of nightly assemblages of armed men, arms raids, unlawful oath ceremonies, community-prescribed 'laws respecting the payment of rents and tithes', and acts of intimidation in Tipperary, Waterford, Kilkenny, and Limerick. In an official statement written in 1816 to the home secretary, Lord Sidmouth, the lord lieutenant of Ireland, Lord Whitworth, wrote a history of the preceding few years detailing the 'open and daring manner' in which attacks were made, often during daylight, and the unwillingness of any victim to give information in court. Whitworth reminded Sidmouth of the challenge posed to the state without the adequate operation of the law courts:

I stated, that it was impossible however, that such combinations, although they might not have any plan well digested and arranged … could be considered otherwise than highly dangerous; that they afforded a proof of a very general disposition among the lower orders in those districts where they prevailed, to attempt by force and intimidation the redress of what they considered to be their local grievances; they excited the utmost alarm among the peaceable and well-disposed for the safety of their persons and property, and if suffered to gain

[19] Galen Broeker, 'Robert Peel and the Peace Preservation Force', *The Journal of Modern History* 33, no. 4 (December 1961): 363–73.
[20] Roberts, 'Caravats and Shanavests', 66–77.

strength and consistency, they would become instruments which the designing and disaffected might readily employ in the furtherance of their political views, should some better opportunity occur for the prosecution of them.[21]

In Whitworth's estimation, Irish violence operated as a multipronged threat: first, to the state's legitimacy by substituting the rule of law for local score settling; second, to the exercise of private property, the cornerstone of the developing capitalist vision for Irish society; and third, through the potential that a political demagogue might use these disciplined violent bands of Irishmen for political ends.

In the previous few years, Dublin Castle had received a steady stream of reports from the countryside that supplied the raw material of Whitworth's analysis. The Bishop of Clonfert relayed a story in early January 1814 from Lusmagh, King's County, where magistrates had relied on British soldiers to repress a group of the town's population attacking a group of process servers delivering writs from the court, which ended in the death of four, and the injury of sixteen others. Nevertheless, the local inhabitants refused to point out any person who had been involved with the violence, which led the Bishop to complain to Peel, 'Now, my good sir ... if neither the court out which such a process issued, nor the plaintiff in the case, nor the beaten officer, nor anyone whatever, will take cognisance of such an outrage, or of the predators of it, can we be surprised at the want of general currency of the law in this land?'[22] Peel acknowledged his displeasure to members of cabinet about the strategy of using the military for policing duties, in part because of the potential for fatalities, but stressed the severe limitations of many Irish magistrates, who 'in the event of a commotion and a general disposition to acts of outrage, can scarcely expect from [Irish magistrates] ... that degree of activity and vigilance which is necessary for their suppression'. In June, Peel wrote to the undersecretary, William Gregory, that what Ireland needed was a 'very strong law'[23] that combined the powers of the Insurrection Act with the creation of a permanent police force independent of the county magistrates. This police force, according to Peel's vision, was 'not meant to meet any temporary emergency, but was rendered necessary by the past state of Ireland for the last fifty years and by the probable state of it for the next five hundred', a fact in Peel's estimation that justified coercive legislation in an Irish context. Peel thanked Gregory for the accounts of the 'state of the disturbed districts', as he was

---

[21] 'Statement of Nature and Extent of Disturbances in Ireland and Measures Adopted by Government', P. P. (1816, vol. 9, no. 479, at p. 3).
[22] Peel, *Sir Robert Peel*, ed. Parker, 1:131–2.
[23] Peel to Gregory, 11 June 1814; *Sir Robert Peel*, ed. Parker, 1:143.

sure the vivid descriptions would cajole many unwilling parliamentarians into supporting the PPF but lamented that they also would dissuade English country gentlemen from 'settl[ing]' with their families in Ireland', thus perpetuating Ireland's problem of an uninspiring or absentee gentry class.[24] Parliament acceded to Peel's designs for a permanent police force and also renewed the Insurrection Act; Peel believed it would do the government 'no harm to have the power' it provided.[25]

The PPF and Insurrection Act embodied the Tory approach of dealing with Irish agrarian violence by combining the restrictions of constitutional privileges with coercive measures as a way to smother violence rather than deal with root causes. Some Irish MPs challenged the government's claim that the Irish countryside warranted such serious measures, noting the extraordinary power the bill gave to the government, the immense financial cost, and the questionable efficacy of the force's ability to deliver justice.[26] Tensions emerged with each proclamation, as some magistrates bristled at the fact that the police operated outside of their control, local ratepayers shouldered the significant financial burden of paying for the police force, and both questioned its efficacy in deterring outrage.[27] What is more, the costs proved significant; in 1817, the government proclaimed a number of baronies in counties Tipperary, Kildare, Cavan, Clare, Donegal, Louth, and King's County to the tune of £35,940, which included a £700 annual salary for each chief magistrate, payment for lodging, salaries for constables, forage, and other sundry expenses.[28] By the middle of 1824, the cost of policing and the Insurrection Act amounted to well over £656,000, borne unequally between counties.[29]

Regardless of the cost, Peel remained committed to the police as one way to enforce 'the ordinary established law', a task which he saw as the greatest problem facing Irish society. Writing to Lord Francis Gower in 1829, Peel laid out his vision for how the police operated as an integral piece of establishing a culture of law and order in Ireland. Quoting at

---

[24] Peel to Gregory, 24 June 1814, *Sir Robert Peel*, ed. Parker, 1:145.

[25] *Sir Robert Peel*, ed. Parker, 1:145.

[26] Hansard, 1st ser., vol. 36, cols. 835–42, 23 May 1817; 'Irish Insurrection Continuance Bill', *Dublin Evening Post*, 29 May 1817.

[27] The application of and problems with the police force are discussed in great depth elsewhere. See Palmer, *Police and Protest*, 198–217; Galen Broeker, *Rural Disorder and Police Reform in Ireland, 1812–36* (London: Routledge and Kegan Paul, 1970), 55–93.

[28] 'Account of Proclamations Issued in Disturbed Counties in Ireland, 1817', P. P. (1818, vol. 16, no. 75).

[29] 'Accounts of Sums Paid by Grand Jury Presentments in Ireland under Peace Preservation, Constables and Insurrection Acts, 1817–23', P. P. (1824, vol. 22, no. 351). Some counties (especially in Ulster) remained unscathed – Antrim, Down, Londonderry, and Tyrone returned costs of £0 for the period.

length a historian of ancient England, John Lingard, who had written of how the Saxons had begun to act like the Danes in wanton violence and a contempt for '"peace and justice"', Peel noted: 'this sounds very much like the modern history of Tipperary'. He continued, 'It is not impossible that those measures which were found useful a thousand years since in repressing violence, and "in gradually composing the minds of men to industry and justice", may still have their effect'.[30] In Peel's eyes the outrages of Ireland were not a result of the poverty experienced by the peasantry, high rents paid to absentee landlords, tithes paid to a church the majority of the population did not belong to, or the view among some that the law was an oppressor rather than a guardian – though those were all problems, to be sure. Instead, agrarian violence stemmed from a lack of vigour in enforcing the law, trying criminals in courts, and exacting convictions. 'I postpone the consideration of extensive schemes for the employment, and education, and improvement of the condition of the people', he wrote Francis Gower in late July 1829, 'and address myself to the discussion of two measures which must be preliminary, and are indispensable to the success of all such schemes – the constitution of a thoroughly efficient police force, and the punishment of crime at the immediate instance and through the intervention of government.'[31]

If ordinary law could not condition the Irish into happy submission, then the Insurrection Act might compel compliance. Originally passed during the parliamentary session of 1807, the act empowered the lord lieutenant to proclaim districts, or whole counties, in a state of disturbance. Once proclaimed, the government imposed a curfew for local residents and convened special sessions of the court that bypassed the need for prerequisite grand jury indictments or a trial by jury and instead appointed a judge to adjudicate. The act also prohibited a number of different activities, including the assembly of groups, swearing unlawful oaths, or possessing firearms, all of which often carried stiff penalties such as forced transportation. It was an extraordinary law that modified many of the honoured traditions of the British legal system, and this necessitated the law's frequent renewal.[32] Nevertheless, once Parliament had passed the Insurrection Act it became an oft-used tool to confront Irish

---

[30] Peel to Lord Francis Gower, 19 November 1829, in Peel, *Sir Robert Peel*, ed. Parker, 2:136.

[31] Peel to Lord Francis Gower, 30 July 1829, in Peel, *Sir Robert Peel*, ed. Parker, 2:122–3.

[32] '(Ireland). A Bill to Provide for the Preserving and Restoring of Peace, in Such Parts of Ireland As May at Any Time Be Disturbed by Seditious Persons, or by Persons Entering into Unlawful Combinations or Conspiracies', P. P. (1813–14, vol. 2, no. 301). Indeed, the initial 1807 law lapsed in 1810, which necessitated a renewal in 1814.

agrarian violence, deploying martial tactics that the British public would never tolerate in England or Scotland.

The government relied on coercive legislation during times of distress in Ireland because Conservatives saw government's primary role as administering law and order. A strong arm was necessary to protect private property rights, induce residency among Ireland's gentry, and begin to civilise Ireland.[33] Many in Ireland agreed, like the young Lord Jocelyn (the future 3rd Earl of Roden), who complained that 'the efforts of the Common Law to repress the disturbances in Ireland were quite insufficient' and requested the Insurrection Act's application.[34] Others questioned this propensity to rely on the extraordinary to deal with the mundane. During Peel's time as home secretary in 1829, the lord lieutenant, the Duke of Northumberland, complained to Peel about observers reading rebellion into simple drunken brawls at a fair, or political agitation into every arson. He suggested that according to such people, 'Martial Law, the Insurrection Act, and a Garrison in every hamlet, ... [were] the only remedies by which even hope can be revived.'[35] Magistrates often requested the application of the Insurrection Act as a way to sidestep some of the financial costs associated with policing, because it allowed for the deployment of military detachments, avoided the need for a garrison of police, and also brought a more martial atmosphere to the locality.

In addition to a paramilitary police force, the Tory government regularly sanctioned the use of regular troops in Ireland to assist with civil affairs, suppress disturbance, or enforce orders of the courts. At the conclusion of the Napoleonic Wars, in February 1816, debate ensued over the proper number of troops throughout the United Kingdom. In Ireland, the stationing of troops, along with funds to pay for the Irish militia totalled £2,045,244 in 1815, which accounted for roughly 40 per cent of the total expenditures not applied to pay down the national debt.[36] Concerned about cost, with the threat of French invasion via Ireland diminished, members were anxious to reduce the tax burden on people suffering a postwar economic slump. Whigs such as Sir Robert Heron rose to challenge the government's position regarding the number of troops necessary in Ireland, feeling the large numbers proposed would

---

[33] Jenkins, *Era of Emancipation*, 302.

[34] 'Irish Insurrection Continuance Bill', *Dublin Evening Post*, 29 May 1817.

[35] Northumberland to Peel, 15 September 1829, BL, Peel Papers, Add MS 40327, f. 70.

[36] 'Finance Accounts of Ireland, for the Year Ended the Fifth of January 1815', P. P. (1814–15, vol. 8, no. 184), at 76–7. By 1817 the total expenditure on the military was down to £1,398,681, of which the stationing of regular troops accounted for slightly more than £1,000,000. See 'Finance Accounts of Ireland, for the Year Ended the Fifth of January 1817', P. P. (1817, vol. 12, no. 99), 181.

'endanger the constitution and liberties of the people' stressing flatly 'that the country could not afford to pay the taxes'. Peel, then chief secretary, stressed the need to maintain 25,000 troops in Ireland on the grounds that 'the civil power of that country was perfectly inadequate to maintain public order and tranquility, and that a force of at least twenty-five thousand men was absolutely necessary for that purpose'. Though Peel much preferred an 'army of police' to deal with Ireland's problems, and though the government did not rubber-stamp magistrates' requests for military assistance, Peel stressed Ireland's peculiar lawlessness, as well as the existing precedent for using regular troops in Ireland:

The system prevailed in Ireland at least as far back as 1779 . . . [and] he must say, it was better justice should be executed by a military force than not executed at all. Surely it would not be denied, that the midnight murderer and the incendiary should be apprehended, and stopped in their dreadful career.

Peel set out three roles the military played within Ireland. First, they were stationed for regular military duty; second, towards 'the aid and assistance which it was necessary to give the civil power, in order to preserve the public peace'; and third, for the suppression of illegal distilling, 'that grievous bane to Ireland'. Throughout his speech Peel emphasised that 'Ireland was not England . . . that system of internal policy which would apply to England could not apply to Ireland. It was absolutely impossible', and that while in England a standing army of 20,000 would never be tolerated, in Ireland its necessity was proven by the 'morals and habits of the lower classes'.[37]

The military became a regular feature of the mechanics of law and order in Ireland between 1800 and 1830 and a source of pride for some Conservative ministers. Henry Hardinge, then chief secretary of Ireland and future commander-in-chief, wrote a long letter to Peel in 1830 enumerating the number of guns and troops and amount of ammunition at the government's disposal should a crisis break out in the country. Although the latter was largely about the near-mutiny of Catholic troops of the 87th Regiment of Connaught Rangers, Hardinge noted how 'at an hour's notice we can house 20 pieces of field artillery at any point', stressing that the various arms depots in the north of Ireland could supply troops; another supply source might be 'the Protestants in whom their Landlords place confidence'. Most important, however, 'if ordinary means at the disposal of the Government are inadequate to the emergency, the Lord Lieutenant will I am sure from his resolute character not hesitate to resort to such means as will best enable us to meet the necessity' – in other words, a willingness to proclaim districts under the

---

[37] Hansard, 1st ser., vol. 32, cols. 922–30, 27 February 1816.

Insurrection Act and call the troops to suppress unrest.[38] Cabinet members praised Hardinge's martial air. Lord Ellenborough recounted of Hardinge's letter how he 'is quite himself on horseback' and that he 'dilates with delight upon his military preparations and plans for defence, and seemingly will be disappointed if he cannot put them into execution'.[39] Similarly, in an 1829 letter Peel stressed to Northumberland to 'let a sufficient number of the Military be detached to assist the Civil Powers' if the police were not sufficient. Peel reminded Northumberland that Irish outrage 'must be resisted by decisive measures, and the exercise, if necessary, of extreme authority which the Law commits to the Executive Government'. Northumberland responded that he would not 'flinch ... and shall not hesitate to avail myself for whatever power, Civil or Military ... [that] may most decidedly secure the general tranquility'.[40]

The Chief Secretary Office's Registered Papers at the National Archive in Dublin are replete with landlords' pleas to the government to send troops, fearing nocturnal visits of Captain Rock or Ribbonmen, the groups of Irish peasants using violence to challenge local landlords and magistrates' authority. Charles Smith, a magistrate from Buncrana in Co. Donegal, pleaded with the government to send troops as the place had become 'dangerous', with residents unable to pay their rents and tithes and growing restless; 'their patience & hopes of better times have long since expired'.[41] In June 1825, a magistrate's report from Cushendall, Co. Antrim, outlined the strength of Ribbon societies in the area and stressed the need for troops to confront the challenge.[42] One anonymous letter worried about preparations among the population 'for very bad work', stressing that no place 'can be worse' than Clonmel. The only remedy was more troops.[43] Reporting to Peel in January 1835, Hardinge stressed that 'Requisitions for troops from the Sheriffs have been made in most instances, and the aid required instantly afforded', which he believed quelled unrest.[44] Magistrates also threatened the deployment

---

[38] Hardinge to Peel, 12 October 1830, BL, Peel Papers, Add MS 40313, f. 51–2.

[39] Edward Law, Earl of Ellenborough, *A Political Diary, 1828–1830*, ed. Lord Colchester (London: R. Bentley & Son, 1881), 2:391–2, 399. Ellenborough also wrote in his diary regarding Hardinge on horseback that 'The only fear is that he should be too lively. Peel seems to think he is; but it is a great comfort to have him there instead of Lord Francis Leveson, who was always wrong.'

[40] Peel to Northumberland, 11 July 1829, BL, Peel Papers, Add MS 40327, f. 30; Northumberland to Peel, 14 July 1829, ibid., f. 34.

[41] Charles M. Smith to Charles Grant, 23 November 1821, NAI, CSO/RP/SC/1821/1354.

[42] 'Memorandum on an Affray at the Fair of Cushendall', 16 May 1825, NAI, CSO/RP/SC/1825/31.

[43] 1 January 1825, NAI, CSO/RP/SC/1825/5.

[44] Hardinge to Peel, 12 January 1835, BL, Peel Papers, Add MS 40314, f. 7.

of troops as a tactic to scare inhabitants into better behaviour, appealing both to the martial atmosphere troops would bring to the district and to the serious financial burdens lodging them would carry.

The enthusiasm for sending troops to do the routine duties of the civil authorities, especially the magistracy's, was not met with universal approbation. Instead, the magistracy's dereliction of duty proved a major problem for Conservative governments who on the one hand committed themselves to the localism and volunteerism of nineteenth-century law and order, while on the other hand remaining keenly aware that the system in Ireland was broken. 'I wish to God it was possible to revise the magistracy, for half our disorders and disturbances arise from the negligence of some and corruption and party spirit of others. But what local authorities can you trust?' wrote Peel to the ultra-Protestant Attorney General William Saurin in April 1816.[45] Officers sent to aid local magistrates voiced similar sentiments, stressing that magistrates acted either too zealously or with utter ineptitude.[46] The government complained of the unnecessary appeals to the military by magistrates who made more hay of unrest than the circumstances required, and lacked the vigour necessary to pursue offenders.[47] In such cases the government assigned stipendiary magistrates to particularly disturbed districts, often with mixed results. While the stipendiary magistrates attempted to resolve unrest by working more actively to quell agrarian violence, their presence had the result of reinforcing the laxity of resident magistrates. Hardinge complained to Peel in 1830 about local gentry applying for a stipendiary magistrate despite enough wealth existing in the county for them to bear the financial burden. 'The mischief attending the system of Stipendiary Magistrates is that practically it works so much better than the local Magistracy that a temporary measure of relief becomes a confirmed habit, rendering the resident gentry more weak than they were before.' This situation was exactly what Peel feared most about meddling with the voluntary system of law and order in Ireland and passing reforms that would dilute the already tenuous ties between the gentry and the people.[48]

Notwithstanding the deficiencies of the magistracy in Ireland, Conservative governments committed themselves to the maintenance of

---

[45] Peel to Saurin, 8 April 1816, in Parker, *Sir Robert Peel*, 1:221.
[46] Virginia Crossman, *Politics, Law and Order in Nineteenth-Century Ireland* (Dublin: Gill & Macmillan, 1996), 17.
[47] Northumberland to Peel, 15 September 1830, BL, Peel Papers, Add MS 40327, f. 70. Northumberland made similar complaints to Peel earlier in 1829 regarding magistrates' laziness and the necessity of sending stipendiary magistrates to quell unrest. See Northumberland to Peel, 14 July 1829, ibid., f. 34.
[48] Hardinge to Peel, 23 September 1830, BL, Peel Papers, Add MS 40313, f. 34.

a decidedly Protestant magistracy. Whigs in both Houses of Parliament noted this for the purposes of political point-scoring. Lord Lansdowne in 1822 complained about the lack of social standing among many in the magistracy 'who had no respectability in society, and ... did not even possess the means of subsistence'. More problematic in Lansdowne's eyes, however, was the passing over of men perfectly qualified for the magistracy who had the unfortunate distinction of being Catholic. 'By not being so admitted, a suspicion could not fail to be infused into the minds of the lower classes, that impartial justice was not dealt out to them – a suspicion ... [than] which nothing could be more fatal to contentment and tranquility'.[49] In 1822, the government organised a new commission appointing magistrates in Ireland, which left off a number of Catholics who previously held a commission and reinforced the Protestant flavour of law and order on a local level.[50] Though aware of the religious imbalance in the commission's make-up, Peel stated: 'I think the present system on which the Government of Ireland is conducted is the best', and that, in all affairs, he wanted England to see the Protestant cause in Ireland as 'in the right'. A moderate response to Catholic agitation, however, was crucial, as was the demonstration on the part of magistrates that they were keenly attending their duty in the administration of justice. 'Their [Irish Protestants] real strength in the hour of danger will be a conviction on the part of England that their cause is a just one, and that the hostility which threatens them is the result of sheer religious bigotry ... not the offspring of insulted and irritated feelings'.[51]

## Whigs

Catholic Emancipation and the Reform Act were two seismic events that shifted the tectonic plates of the British political system – whether one or the other acted as a precipitating tremor, or an aftershock, or whether they were equally powerful jolts is an important question, but tangential to our purposes. However, both the effect of Catholic Emancipation and the process by which it was enacted contributed to the Wellington administration's collapse in 1831. It was replaced by a Whig-led government, the first in fifty years. Lord Grey's ministry committed itself to a policy of 'reform', eventually embodied in the Reform Act of 1832 but which also

---

[49] Hansard, 2nd ser., vol. 7, cols. 1051–3, 14 June 1822. For an example in the House of Commons, see Thomas Spring Rice's speech on the Insurrection Act, vol. 12, cols. 675–6, 25 February 1825.

[50] Crossman, *Politics, Law and Order*, 34–5.

[51] Peel to Gregory, 2 April 1815, in *Sir Robert Peel*, ed. Parker, 1:220; Peel to Gregory, 5 April 1823, *Sir Robert Peel*, ed. Parker, 1:341.

included institutional reforms of the Poor Law, prisons, police, education, and the church. Not surprisingly, historians have written extensively about this period examining politicians' motives as well as the nature of reform and its relative success or failure. Whether the Reform Act itself was a product of popular pressure from outside Parliament, an integral plank in a platform of Whig governance, a conservative effort to stave off more cataclysmic episodes, or the result of international events is an issue that has been argued elsewhere.[52] Historians interested in the relationship between ideology, party politics, and the expression of political power have noted how this period lacked clear party coherence, and that this produced dynamic realignments.[53] Thus, when discussing the government of the 1830s one must be aware of subtle differences in social, political, and religious ideology which shaped policy outcomes throughout the decade. One advantage of reflecting on the inherent instability in these political identities has been to 'put some ideas back into nineteenth-century whiggism and, in doing so, to distinguish the whig mind from the liberal mind'.[54]

Reform, though, did not work as a centripetal force for Grey's ministry and ultimately fractured its broad coalition, which included full-blooded Whigs, liberal Tories, and other moderates. Unhappiness and disagreement over the government's Irish policy played a large role in this division. As the decade progressed, an important shift occurred among those vested with power over Irish policy, as older (Lord Anglesey) or more conservative members (Lord Stanley) were forced out by a new group of ministers who reinterpreted justice, disentangling it from former notions

[52] John A. Phillips and Charles Wetherell, 'The Great Reform Act of 1832 and the Political Modernization of England', *The American Historical Review* 100, no. 2 (1995): 411–36; Roland Quinault, 'The French Revolution of 1830 and Parliamentary Reform', *History* 79, no. 257 (October 1994): 377–93; Matthew Cragoe, 'The Great Reform Act and Modernization of British Politics: The Impact of Conservative Associations, 1835-1841', *Journal of British Studies* 47, no. 3 (July 2008): 581–603; Thomas Ertman, 'The Great Reform Act of 1832 and British Democratization', *Comparative Political Studies* 43, no. 8–9 (1 August 2010): 1000–22; Robert Saunders, 'God and the Great Reform Act: Preaching against Reform, 1831–32', *Journal of British Studies* 53, no. 2 (April 2014): 378–99.
[53] Hence an interest in the development of the Liberal Party, or the relationship between Conservatives and Whigs. Brent and Mandler are discussed in detail below, but for other examples, see David Close, 'The Formation of a Two-Party Alignment in the House of Commons between 1832 and 1841', *The English Historical Review* 84, no. 331 (1 April 1969): 257–77; Ian Newbould, 'Whiggery and the Growth of Party 1830–1841: Organization and the Challenge of Reform', *Parliamentary History* 4, no. 1 (December 1985): 137–56; Joseph Coohill, *Ideas of the Liberal Party: Perceptions, Agendas and Liberal Politics in the House of Commons, 1832–52* (Chichester: Wiley-Blackwell for The Parliamentary History Yearbook Trust, 2011), 6.
[54] Boyd Hilton, 'Whiggery, Religion and Social Reform: The Case of Lord Morpeth', *Historical Journal* 37, no. 4 (December 1994): 829–59, quote at 830.

of law and order and instead seeing it as an incorporation of Ireland into an equal partnership with Britain – what Hoppen has helpfully labelled an 'assimilationist' approach.[55]

Though their conclusions may be somewhat in tension, the works of Richard Brent and Peter Mandler are important to uncovering this shift away from a justice understood merely in a retributive sense towards one based on notions of equality, inclusion, and rights-based language. Brent has argued that a number of politicians, including Lord John Russell (home secretary), Lord Morpeth (chief secretary of Ireland), and Lord Mulgrave (lord lieutenant) espoused a 'liberal Anglican' religious conviction that de-emphasised differences in religious dogma and instead sought to instil an inclusive Christian morality which, critically, included Roman Catholics within the nation's polity. It was this Christian morality that, in the eyes of liberal Anglicans, bound the country together and was the basis for the reforms Whig officials wished to enact, especially regarding issues of Church and state.[56] While Mandler's emphasis is less on religious conviction, he nevertheless identifies Russell, Morpeth, and Mulgrave within a political tradition of 'Foxite Whigs' which opposed the novel philosophy of political economy and rise of market-based understandings of the individual and social order, in favour of an established tradition of paternalist social and economic policies. According to Mandler, Foxite Whigs understood their task as a highly interventionist one; that of addressing the social problems of the 1830s through political solutions, especially institutional reform.[57] The question remains: how did these liberal Anglicans or Foxite Whigs affect Irish policy during the decade of reform? The period between 1800 and 1835 reveals a deep contradiction in rhetoric and policy among Whigs concerning Ireland. Once the Whigs came to power in 1831, these contradictions rose to the surface, ultimately culminating in the exodus of the conservative 'high church' faction from the party, and the ascension of young more liberal ministers in place of the old guard. This change in party leadership would open the door for a new approach to governing Ireland, which will be discussed later, in Chapter 3.

## Catholic Emancipation and Whiggery

While Catholic Emancipation proved a thorny and divisive issue among Conservatives, most Whigs considered it rather straightforward. Catholic

[55] Hoppen, *Governing Hibernia*, 67, though he works out this idea throughout ch. 3.
[56] Brent, *Liberal Anglican*, ch. 1, especially 51–8.
[57] Mandler, *Aristocratic Government*, 33–43. See also Arthur Burns and Joanna Innes, eds., *Rethinking the Age of Reform: Britain 1780–1850* (Cambridge: Cambridge University Press), 48.

Emancipation, as well as the repeal of the Corporation and Test Acts, provided Whigs with a political issue that allowed them to advance their political ideology of freeing the nation from tyranny and oppression: in this instance, in the guise of the state imposing its religious restrictions and getting in the way of individuals' right to the liberty of their own convictions.[58] In the debate surrounding the repeal of the Test and Corporation Act in 1828, Lord John Russell – arguably the archetype of both Mandler's 'Foxite Whig' and Brent's 'liberal Anglican' – stated:

> I now come to the great principle involved . . . that every man ought to be allowed to form his religious opinions by the impressions of his own mind, and that, when so formed, he should be at liberty to worship God according to the dictates of his conscience, without being subjected to any penalty or disqualification whatever; that every restraint and restriction imposed on any man on account of his religious creed is in the nature of persecution, and is at once an offence to God, and an injury to man.[59]

Schooling the House of Commons on the history of the Test and Corporation Acts, Russell argued they had long outlived their original intention and that the threat to the Established Church and the crown they aimed to address had died long ago; few, if any, feared the King to be a closeted Catholic or Presbyterian, and in Russell's estimation both of those communities had proved their loyalty to the crown over the preceding century. Numerous speakers in favour of the motion to repeal referred to the 'spirit of the age' and 'Enlightenment' as rationales for Repeal, but also to justice. More importantly, many believed that repealing the Test and Corporation Acts opened the door further for Catholic Emancipation. John Smith, MP for Buckinghamshire, acknowledged as 'the representative of Buckinghamshire Dissent',[60] seconded Russell's motion and called for the Commons to see that 'the motion of that night called upon them to do an act of justice to three-eighths of the population of Great Britain', while hoping for the same future for the 7 million Irish Catholics who were being kept 'in a state of degradation and ignorance ... [which] was not only dreadful to themselves, but dangerous to common weal'. George Wilbraham, MP for Stockbridge, noted that 'every step we make this night will be in favour of Ireland – every advance we make for the relief of the Dissenters will be

---

[58] These two acts, passed in 1661 and 1673, excluded both Roman Catholics and Dissenting Protestants from civil, military, or municipal offices.

[59] Hansard, 2nd ser., vol. 18, cols. 678–9, 26 February 1828.

[60] 'Smith, Hon. Robert John (1796–1868). History of Parliament Online', www.historyofparliamentonline.org/volume/1820-1832/member/smith-hon-robert-1796-1868.

so much gained in the great cause of Catholic emancipation. Break but once through the line of bigotry and prejudice, and the victory is our own.'[61] Though Peel attempted to oppose the measure, arguing that in practice the state did not exclude Dissenters from service, the measure passed by forty-four votes (237–193), and pressed forward the claims of Whigs for Catholic Emancipation.

With the repeal of the Test and Corporation Acts, Whigs rallied around the push for Emancipation, guided by the rhetoric of justice. The *Edinburgh Review*, as one of the most influential Whig periodicals, led the charge.[62] In an article entitled 'The Last of the Catholic Question', published before the passage of the Catholic Relief Act in April 1829, the journal hyperbolically praised Emancipation: 'that future, which we durst not look upon, is rising bright and glorious – and on its forehead is the morning star'; it happily reported that 'the earth seems once more firm under our feet'. More importantly, and emblematically, the author advanced the central claim made by Whigs in favour of Catholic Emancipation: 'The best way to disarm your enemy, is to disarm his mind. You want no security against him when, *by doing him justice*, you have made him your devoted friend.'[63]

The fifty-four-page article advanced a number of important justifications for Catholic Emancipation, all centring on the contradictions embodied in Tory opposition to religious freedom, as well as presenting a revisionist historical agenda. First, the article noted the irony in the Orange Order's yearly parading in celebration of William of Orange's Protestantism, since he had ascended the English throne with the 'most earnest wish to realise the apprehensions of the bigots by making it [England] "an Amsterdam of all religions"'. Second, it pointed out that the darling hero of Conservatives, William Pitt, had secured the Union between Great Britain and Ireland ('that necessary evil') with the sincere desire of securing Catholic Emancipation. His legacy had been sold out; 'his great political achievement has been thus corrupted into a monster,

---

[61] Hansard, 2nd ser., vol. 18, cols. 701, 708, 26 February 1828; also quoted in Hilton, *Mad, Bad, and Dangerous?*, 382–3, fn. 42.

[62] While it would be incorrect to label the *Edinburgh Review* as a party organ, its editors associated closely with the Whigs and its existence depended on the patronage of Lord Holland. Once the Whigs occupied ministerial seats, the journal proved more critical, but nevertheless identified with many of the same intellectual presuppositions as those in power. Finally, it should be noted that political enemies identified the *Edinburgh Review* as a Whig voice piece, acknowledged its successes, and formed their own journal as rivals, most prominently the Tory *Quarterly Review* and the Radical *Westminster Review*. See Biancamaria Fontana, 'Founders of the Edinburgh Review (*act. 1802–1829*)', *Oxford Dictionary of National Biography*, https://doi.org/10.1093/ref:odnb/95409.

[63] [William Empson], 'The Last of the Catholic Question', *Edinburgh Review* 49, no. 47 (March 1829), 218, emphasis added.

half slave, half free – a centaur, not a man'; and now his name was misappropriated in the creation of so-called 'Pitt Clubs', where 'it is clear, beyond all dispute, that Mr. Pitt would not dine at his own dinner'. Finally, and most importantly for the Whigs' agenda, societies across history had advanced when minorities advocated for change. 'This is the very picture of society in progress – as at the Reformation, the Revolution, and on this very question. There have been certain subjects wherein nobody, for a long time, ever dreamt of consulting humanity or justice. A Catholic was as much born to be excluded, as a negro to be sold.' The author argued that, thankfully, that age had passed away and in its place 'a spirit of perfect toleration is among the most brilliant innovations of very recent days'.[64] Thus, the *Edinburgh Review* constructed Catholic Emancipation not as a matter of party politics, but rather elevated it to a question of humanity, progress, and justice. Whiggery believed religious tolerance correlated with a progressive society and served as the means by which transformative social improvement could be achieved.

With characteristic short-sightedness, or self-delusion, some Whig members interpreted the passage of Catholic Emancipation as a panacea for Irish ills. In March 1829, John Newport, the Irish Whig MP for Waterford, believed that placing everyone in the empire on an equal footing would 'secure the prosperity and happiness' of Ireland and 'every reasonable Catholic ought to be satisfied with it'.[65] The political diarist Charles Greville wrote in 1828 that those concerned with Ireland realised 'that complete emancipation is the only remedy for the evils that exist', while Lord Melbourne believed that 'the granting of such a boon, the deliverance from such a badge of inferiority, would spread a general sunshine' across Ireland without the concomitant potential of social instability.[66] The idea that granting Catholic Emancipation would herald a new era of Irish tranquillity, replete with economic development, proved hopelessly naïve. Instead of acting as a panacea, the campaign unearthed numerous grievances felt within Catholic Ireland, and thus politicised the country and created a greater appetite for concession. Some highlighted how emancipation had been too little, too late, as it did not end the manifest inequalities in the administration of Ireland or the economic realities of Protestant privilege. As discussed later, in Chapter 4, the successful inclusion of Catholics into positions of civil

---

[64] [Empson], 'Catholic Question', 224–7.

[65] Hansard, 2nd. ser., vol. 20, cols. 862–3, 6 March 1829.

[66] Charles Greville, *The Greville Memoirs: A Journal of the Reigns of King George IV and King William IV*, ed. Henry Reeve (New York: D. Appleton and Company, 1886), 1:118; Sanders, *Lord Melbourne's Papers*, 100.

and political power only reinforced Protestant fears concerning their security and place in Irish society, which led to a backlash of anti-Catholic sentiment and political unrest.[67] Rather than solving Irish grievances, answering the 'Catholic question' only brought with it an expanded query – 'the Irish question'.[68]

## Whig Government, Ireland, and Justice: Coercion or Conciliation?

The inauguration of Whig government, led by Lord Grey as prime minister, in the late autumn of 1830 happened rather abruptly. After Wellington's government had weathered the storm of conceding Catholic Emancipation in 1829, the leaders of both parties assumed that he would continue in his role as prime minister. However, pressure for electoral reform continued to mount in Britain as continental matters deteriorated with the ascension of Louis Philippe in France, and unrest broke out across England in the form of Captain Swing.[69] In the context of revolutionary political change abroad and domestic agrarian unrest at home, Wellington refused to concede measures of parliamentary reform for which the country clamoured.[70] The Whigs that took over government came from a variety of wings within the party's tent, yet they shared a desire to pass some measure of parliamentary reform, in part to address issues of 'old corruption', which many Radical voices throughout the country railed against.[71]

While the aim of parliamentary reform brought a level of cohesion to Whig policy, the challenges present in Ireland caused a great deal of internal discord among the cabinet. Catholic Emancipation had let down many in Ireland, especially the large number of forty-shilling freeholders disenfranchised in the bargain for emancipation. Daniel O'Connell had fervently begun his appeals for the repeal of the Act of Union, buoyed by general dissatisfaction with the British political system. Additionally, economic challenges focussed the attention of the lower orders on a general resentment regarding the high rate of rents and the odious payment of tithes to the Church of Ireland by a Catholic

---

[67] Cronin, 'Popular Politics, 1815–1845', 142.

[68] Bartlett, *Fall and Rise of the Irish Nation*, ch. 16.

[69] On the concerning link between Louis Phillippe's ascension and the advance of English radicalism, see James Grande, *William Cobbett, the Press and Rural England: Radicalism and the Fourth Estate, 1792–1835* (Basingstoke: Palgrave Macmillan, 2014), ch. 7.

[70] Newbould, *Whiggery and Reform*, ch. 3; Jonathan Parry, *The Rise and Fall of Liberal Government in Victorian Britain* (New Haven, CT: Yale University Press, 1993), 65–71.

[71] Philip Harling, 'Parliament, the State, and "Old Corruption": Conceptualizing Reform, c. 1790–1832', in *Rethinking the Age of Reform*, eds. Burns and Innes, 98–113.

population that had its own clergy to support.[72] In the face of these challenges, those charged with spearheading Irish affairs – Lord Melbourne (home secretary), the Marquess of Anglesey (lord lieutenant), and Lord Stanley (chief secretary) – vacillated between policies of conciliation and coercion, coupled with a good deal of handwringing. While it is reductionist to suggest that the Whigs charged with Irish affairs sought to be Bonapartes for the good of the country or desired the 'unlimited powers of a benevolent despot', a preponderance of Whigs in cabinet still saw coercion as a necessary tool in Irish administration.[73]

Shortly after the Whigs had taken office, significant rural unrest across Co. Clare led to calls for stiff enforcement, and the proclamation of 'martial law' if necessary.[74] The local circumstances illuminate the interwoven layers that often contributed to unrest. The general economic backdrop in Clare had been one of acute poverty in the previous two years, as land prices soared across the 1820s, but successive bad harvests in 1829 and 1830 had left the lowest rung of Irish rural society destitute. A shift from tillage farming to pasture left many without access to potato land and therefore without the means to survive. O'Connell's famous election to Parliament in 1828 spurred intense political organisation, and antagonism, between tenants and their landlords, which developed into a protracted electoral fight in 1831 and often took on a sectarian hue. Roughly 2,900 cases of agrarian violence enveloped Clare in the first five months of 1831, carried out by secret societies grouped under the name of the 'Terry Alts'; their activities included assaulting labourers, levelling fences, turning up pastureland, and intimidating farmers into letting potato plots, as well as murders.[75]

In an attempt to understand events on the ground, and to bring a semblance of order, Lord Anglesey toured through disturbed districts in Clare in early April 1831. He wrote to Stanley in London about the contradictions he witnessed between the perceived state of unrest among inhabitants and the benevolence shown to him by every class of person he met, the stern reprimand he issued to the local gentry and magistrates to do their duty, and the general fitness and well-being of the labourers and small farmers he encountered.[76] Stanley remained sceptical of any practical benefit in Anglesey's visit and pressed ahead with preparing a revised

---

[72] Patrick O'Donoghue, 'Causes of the Opposition to Tithes, 1830–1838', *Studia Hibernia* 5 (1965): 21–8.
[73] Kriegel, 'The Irish Policy of Lord Grey's Government', 41.
[74] Melbourne to Anglesey, 30 March 1831, PRONI, Anglesey Papers, D619/29C/33.
[75] James S. Donnelly, 'The Terry Alt Movement', *History Ireland* 2, no. 4 (1994): 34. One is forced to ponder whether that level of violence is an accurate reflection of what occurred.
[76] Anglesey to Stanley, 7 April 1831, PRONI, Anglesey Papers, D619/31T/29.

Insurrection Act and another bill restricting the number allowed to gather in public to fifty, forbidding those from outside the community to participate in such gatherings, and punishing offenders with the threat of transportation for seven years.[77] Melbourne also pressed for the implementation of more powerful measures to quell violence, admitting that the current situation was taxing his limited capacity to make sense of the state of Irish society: 'I do not know how the law stands, or what means may be taken to carry it into effect, but I own, that men should assemble in such numbers, and commit such outrages, and that there should exist no power effectual either for prevention or punishment, appears to me to be the height and summit of human absurdity.'[78] In February 1831, the lord lieutenant had held onto hope that non-legislative means would prove successful in suppressing disturbances, including dispatching 'moveable columns' of infantry and cavalry to unruly areas, where they would stay 'for days if necessary until All is quiet'.[79] Demands from magistrates that he step in by implementing the Insurrection Act, along with pressure in London, forced Anglesey to grudgingly reconsider, though he still requested that some of the 'offensive clauses' in the Insurrection Act should be removed.[80] Ultimately, after his visit failed to turn the tide, Anglesey acquiesced to the pressure from London for 'more powerful means of restoring subordination', notwithstanding his objection 'upon principle, to all laws which are not of a strictly constitutional nature, and to every species of coercive measure ... not imperatively call[ed] for'.[81]

The process by which government decided its policy in Clare illuminates the internal division that characterised the Anglesey–Stanley–Melbourne relationship, and wider Whig division on its Irish policy. Although it does not appear the personal relationship between Anglesey and Stanley was hostile, both men occupied opposing corners in policy fights, making for a disharmonious Irish executive.[82] During Wellington's administration Anglesey had proven himself to be unreservedly outspoken, no friend to the ultra-Tories, and decidedly in favour of Catholic

---

[77] Stanley to Anglesey, 12 April 1831, ibid., D619/31S/34.

[78] Melbourne to Anglesey, 5 April 1831, ibid., D619/29C/34.

[79] Anglesey to Stanley, 19 February 1831, ibid., D619/31T/7

[80] Anglesey to Melbourne, 25 February 1831, ibid., D619/29B/25; Gosset to Stanley, 25 February 1831, LPL, Derby Papers, 920 DER(14)/121/1/30; magistrates were not unanimous in requesting the Insurrection Act: see 'Important Meeting – Disturbances in Limerick', *Mayo Constitution*, 2 May 1831.

[81] Anglesey to Melbourne, 18 April 1831, ibid, D619/29B/32. The government issued proclamations roughly a month later: 'The Insurrection Act in Clare', *Cork Constitution*, 14 May 1831.

[82] Angus Hawkins, *Forgotten Prime Minister: The 14th Earl of Derby: Volume I: Ascent, 1799–1851* (Oxford: Oxford University Press, 2009), 82; Hoppen, *Governing Hibernia*, 67–71.

Emancipation and of opening the public purse to solve Irish problems – all factors that led to his recall in 1829.[83] Anglesey retained his vocal opinions and advocated for a stronger government role in alleviating poverty to be the first priority, while coercion should only be used when generosity failed. Thus, he pressed the government to provide funds for public works schemes to employ the able-bodied poor and suggested the necessity of some sort of poor law to assist the old and invalid. 'If any thing can save it [Ireland]', Anglesey wrote shortly after his appointment, 'it will be an ample and immediate grant for the employment of the people in draining bogs, making roads, etc. If you cannot do that, you cannot hold Ireland under an Imperial Parliament and therefore, ultimately, not at all.'[84]

These pleas largely fell on deaf ears in London, which only further frustrated Anglesey by demonstrating his lack of power in setting Irish policy. 'Ireland cannot be governed from London', he penned in a missive to Stanley, underlining that 'the projects I sent in must be adopted ... or this country cannot go on'. Brooding over his inability to convince London to see things his way, Anglesey complained about the willingness of the government to give money to the Kildare Place Society – a Protestant organisation that educated the poor, but which also proselytised and enflamed Catholic opinion – while maintaining their principled stinginess in matters that would benefit the Irish population: 'That d[amne]d Kildare Place! There is always an excuse for entrusting them with money. As usual, You say They have anticipated the Grant! More of this when I return'.[85] Stanley and Melbourne reassured him that every other consideration was taking a back seat to the adoption of parliamentary reform. And, while Anglesey certainly sympathised with the amount of political oxygen reform consumed, he was under no illusion that Irish problems would wait.

You write discouragingly upon the subject of Poor Laws for the Aged & Infirm & of the Scheme for the employment of the population, nor do I think that your change in the mode of disposing of the Education Grant, goes far enough. I feel more strongly every hour the absolute necessity of an early & satisfactory arrangement of these matters & as Ireland can have no repose untill [sic] They are settled, you shall have non untill you have accomplished Them.[86]

Whereas Lord Anglesey saw correcting Irish ills as a matter of justice, both Melbourne and Stanley believed that Ireland's outrages set it apart

---

[83] Karina Holton, 'A Turbulent Year: Lord Anglesey's First Viceroyalty and the Politics of Catholic Emancipation, 1828', *Studia Hibernia* 43 (September 2017): 53–93.
[84] Anglesey to Melbourne, 21 December 1830, PRONI, Anglesey Papers, D619/29B/2.
[85] Anglesey to Stanley, 9 July 1831, ibid., D619/31T/48.
[86] Anglesey to Stanley, 15 July 1831, ibid., D619/31T/50.

from Great Britain and justified coercive legislation as the primary vehicle to achieve tranquillity in the country. Holding onto this view left little daylight between them and their Tory predecessors. Melbourne, in the words of his most recent biographer, 'showed little or no sympathy with the poor or those who rioted … if they persisted in being tiresome, troops would be sent against them'. He seemed blind to the real grievances of the poor outside acknowledging their poverty, preferring to lay the blame for any ills on 'the stupidity endemic among Tories' and their policies.[87] Of the Irish, Melbourne wrote to Anglesey in 1832 that they were 'the most conspiring people on the face of the earth' who 'collect and combine all their strength for the purpose of carrying one single object'. He continued, 'You have a very violent and a very fiery people to deal with, but not a very courageous people', and the only solution to governing was 'a re-establishment of the authority of the law, which is at present despised and trampled under foot'.[88] In another letter at the height of the campaign against the payment of tithes and O'Connell's Repeal agitation, Melbourne openly pondered whether Ireland was even worth the trouble, considering the dubious future security of the Union. Comparing Ireland to a country estate, he argued:

If you had an estate, the title of which was disputed with you, and of which it appeared very doubtful whether … you would retain possession of it, you would not be inclined to expend much money in improving it, while the lawsuit was yet pending. Is not that something of the case of England with regard to Ireland.[89]

Lord Stanley, thirty-one at the time of his appointment as chief secretary, shared sentiments similar to Melbourne in hardened form. Detested among Whig partisans, it is unclear the exact reasons why Stanley was chosen for the post, though he possessed extensive estates in Co. Tipperary. A member of the 'high church' faction, Stanley adamantly opposed appropriating funds from the collection of tithes for anything other than the maintenance of the Established Church of Ireland, and would later resign over the issue and defect to the Tories. Reform could not precede the Irish population's acceptance of British legal norms, especially an acknowledgement of its civil authority over popular protest or moral suasion; in other words, the means to alter contracts (like rents), or the sanctity of the Established Church's property (like tithes) could only find solutions through legal means. Thus, his tenure as chief secretary 'stripped his beliefs down to their prescriptive essentials. Ireland

---

[87] L. G. Mitchell, *Lord Melbourne, 1779–1848* (Oxford: Oxford University Press, 1997), at 124, 129.

[88] Melbourne to Anglesey, 30 June 1832, PRONI, Anglesey Papers, D619/29C/53.

[89] Melbourne to Anglesey, 24 March 1832, ibid., D619/29C/49.

became the anvil on which his commitment to fundamental rule of law and property rights hardened under the hammer blows of populist outcry and rural violence.'[90]

Political circumstances in London further complicated Irish policy-making. Much parliamentary discussion in 1831 and 1832 revolved around deliberations among the cabinet as to whether to introduce coercion. The column of deficits included concern that coercion would not garner enough support in the Commons, as the Tories wanted to block any legislation attempted by the Whigs as a way to weaken the chances of reform. Further, the Whigs relied too much on Irish Repealers like O'Connell and on English radicals for their support, both of which groups detested coercive legislation.[91] The correspondence between Anglesey, Melbourne, and Stanley oscillated between demanding additional powers and waiting for things to improve, as Anglesey noted the situation on the ground in Ireland 'is as changeable as the weather'.[92] The passage of the reform bill, along with a newly elected reformed Parliament with a large Whig majority, transformed the political landscape and gave Stanley and Melbourne the freedom to clamp down more forcefully on Irish outrages. Events in Ireland further justified their actions.

### Whigs and the Problem of Irish Tithes

Nothing brought into conflict the viewpoints found within the Whig cabinet and Irish society more forcefully than the problem of payments of tithes to the Established Church of Ireland. It exposed long-standing sectarian divisions, where religious affiliation was a proxy for divergences in economic prosperity, property rights, and political power. It revealed the inherent problems with the system of Irish land tenure and the challenges of securing a tax for a church the vast majority of inhabitants did not belong to. The relationship between popular protest – maybe even explicit violence – and the granting of concessions also weighed heavily on ministers' minds. But the question also underscored challenges within the cabinet regarding questions of the sanctity of property rights, the remit of the government in regulating the church and its finance, and the thorny issue of church reform. Before exploring the competing attitudes shaping government response, it is worth detailing the complicated mechanics of tithe payments and the organised campaign of opposition to them that took place in 1830.

---

[90] Hawkins, *Forgotten Prime Minister*, 76.
[91] Crossman, 'Emergency Legislation', 321–2.
[92] Anglesey to Melbourne, 22 February 1831, PRONI, Anglesey Papers, D619/29B/22.

Across the eighteenth and early nineteenth centuries Ireland's rural population – both the rural poor and the better-off farmers – expressed their odium against the tithe system. Most of their complaints originated not in sectarian concerns but rather through economic grievances, which split rural interest along various fault lines. In 1735, for example, the Irish Parliament passed legislation that exempted dry cattle or dairy produce from tithe payments, exposing rural tension between tillage and pasture farmers.[93] To make matters worse for the rural poor, agricultural produce – especially potatoes – was later incorporated into that tax across much of Munster and parts of Leinster, leading to violent campaigns of protest. Parsons, looking to maintain a steady income without the encumbrance of collecting tithes, sold their interests to so-called 'tithe farmers' who had an economic incentive to make a profit, and therefore demonstrated a greater willingness to enforce their claims on defaulters than their predecessors had done, thus exacerbating tensions. What is more, significant problems arose with how tithes – generally paid in kind until the later eighteenth-century – reached their valuation. Tithe proctors, employed by parsons to value land and collect tithe payments, often overvalued farms' production, which also varied seasonally.[94] In the wake of the Rockite violence that spread across Munster, and into parts of Leinster, where Captain Rock frequently vocalised his desire to abolish the tithe system through the medium of threatening notices and burning down houses, the government attempted to combat abuses with the introduction of the Tithe Composition Act in 1823 – 'arguably the first significant social reform conferred on Ireland by the British parliament since 1800'.[95] The Act, however, was riddled with half-measures and produced unintended consequences (such as subjecting graziers to tithe payments), which created further resentment of the practice. Furthermore, by 1832 only about 60 per cent of parishes in Ireland had accepted composition (a reduced tithe burden), which led the government to pass legislation that forced conversion of the remaining parishes in 1834.[96]

Although Irish people regularly resisted tithe payments, a concerted effort began during an economic downturn in the late 1820s and in the

---

[93] Maurice J. Bric, 'The Tithe System in Eighteenth-Century Ireland', *Proceedings of the Royal Irish Academy. Section C: Archaeology, Celtic Studies, History, Linguistics, Literature* 86C (1986): 275.

[94] For an insightful economic overview of the Tithe War, including the financial implications of various modes of collection, see Daniel J. Shaw, 'An Economic Perspective on the Irish Tithe War of 1831–1838', *The Journal of European Economic History* 44, no. 3 (2015): 91–140.

[95] Donnelly, *Captain Rock*, 209. In chapter 6, Donnelly deals with the relationship between the Rockite movement and tithes quite comprehensively.

[96] Shaw, 'An Economic Perspective', 104–5.

wake of the campaign for Catholic Emancipation, which had politicised more Irish people further down the socio-economic ladder. The resistance to tithes led to violent confrontations between the people and various government bodies, both civil (e.g., tithe proctors) and military (e.g., police, military, yeomanry). In the eyes of the rural poor, tithe composition had not done enough to alleviate economic stress, especially because payment of the tithe always preceded rent payments – thus making a tenant liable to potential ejectment – and because the assessment of the composition had been based on the higher cereal prices of the Napoleonic era. Graziers' interests coalesced with those of the rural poor when the beef market declined in 1829, which led to their involvement in opposition efforts.[97] This cross-class alliance was not an enduring one, and as opposition to tithes spread across Ireland it became more generally 'a spontaneous protest against agrarian conditions', which the government feared might extend to the refusal to pay other rates, or rents.[98]

The campaign came as a financial shock to the Church of Ireland. Between 1829 and November 1832, Irish people amassed £485,301 in arrears, roughly half of the overall income of the Church annually, which was estimated in 1835 at £815,333.[99] The Archbishop of Armagh, John Beresford, controlled a relief fund to alleviate the financial burdens of dioceses, or even individual clergymen. 'It is with much reluctance my Lord I apply to your fund for this temporary relief', Rev. Robert B. Greene wrote Beresford in late February 1833, enumerating the economic peril he faced: 'twelve months my income has been withheld by the people which has obliged me to borrow'. This had left him no choice but to issue writs on four substantial farmers, to meet the demands of creditors. This decision, Greene feared, may have been a fatal error, as he attached a threatening notice he received to his correspondence with Beresford:

You did me a good turn once, no matter when or how, but for that I would not like to see harm come on you without giving you a warning, so mind what I say and leave this country before the first of March or prepare to follow Ferguson and Whitly, Your days after that are numbered but no man will lay a finger on you to then.[100]

Beresford wrote Stanley pleading with government for more funds for dioceses in the southern parts of Ireland, where 'unlawful combinations'

---

[97] David Patrick Reid, '"The Tithe War" in Ireland, 1830–1838' (PhD diss., Trinity College Dublin, 2013), 30–3, www.tara.tcd.ie/handle/2262/79326.
[98] Macintyre, *Liberator*, ch. 5, quote at 177.
[99] Arrears calculated from 'Return of Arrears of Tithe due in Ireland in Dioceses, 1829–33' (P.P. 1833, vol. 27, no. 509); 'Return of Incomes of Archbishops, Bishops, and Parochial Clergy of Ireland, under Church Temporalities Act', P.P. (1835, vol. 47, no. 461).
[100] Rev. Robert B Green to Beresford, 28 February 1833, RCBL, Beresford Papers, MS 183, Folder 1/9.

had left clergy in 'destitute condition'.[101] Newspapers across the United Kingdom reported on a London meeting in March 1833, chaired by the Bishop of London, that had raised funds, supplementing their reportage with details of local noteworthy contributions.[102] Although these funds paled in comparison to the shortfall of revenue, which Angus Macintyre calculates as £818,518 by 1833, Beresford commanded a sizeable amount of funds, which he doled out throughout the mid-1830s.[103]

In the face of concerted opposition, which included leadership from Bishop Doyle and Daniel O'Connell, the government found itself forced to choose how to respond – through reform or force?[104] So-called 'Hurlers' – men who organised hurling matches as a way to coordinate neighbourhoods against upcoming tithe sales, including by intimidating parsons and their bailiffs – had appeared in counties Wexford, Kilkenny, and Carlow in the winter of 1830–1.[105] In response, the government authorised the use of the police as a means to prevent riots when bailiffs distrained cattle or during the tithe sale itself; these forces were occasionally supplemented with regular military. In the parish of Graigue, on the Kilkenny–Carlow border, farmers coordinated to move their livestock into locked and latched spaces utilising a provision of the Tithe Composition Act that expressly forbid proctors from breaking locks or doors, and the stand-off ended peacefully, notwithstanding an empty-handed parson.[106]

Other events took a more tragic course. In Newtownbarry, Co. Wexford, the Protestant yeomanry fired on a group of tithe resisters, killing fifteen and wounding two dozen more. The government had decided reviving the yeomanry was necessary to help maintain the peace earlier in 1831, with Anglesey writing to Melbourne about how the force might tend to break up nascent allegiances between Catholics and Protestants 'upon the subject of Rent and Tithe'. Stanley justified the move as 'Ireland was in such a condition that it required the most vigilant

[101] Beresford to Stanley, 12 January 1833, LPL, Derby Papers, 920 DER(14)/128/11/1/9.
[102] For example, 'Distress of the Clergy in Ireland', *Leeds Intelligencer*, 23 March 1833, which noted that £201 2s. was raised in the district; or £625 14s. raised in Cheltenham, 'Subscriptions for the Temporary Relief of the Distressed Clergy in Ireland', *Cheltenham Chronicle*, 28 March 1833.
[103] Macintyre, *The Liberator*, 182; Beresford Papers, RCBL, MS 183.
[104] On Bishop James Doyle's intervention, see James Warren Doyle, Letter to Thomas Spring Rice, Esq. M.P. &c: On the Establishment of a Legal Provision for the Irish Poor, and on the Nature and Destination of Church Property (Dublin: R. Coyne, 1831); Macintyre, *Liberator*, 184–8.
[105] Bishop of Ferns [Thomas Elrington] to Gregory, 25 December 1830, NAI, CSORP/1830/334; File on 'Hurlers', CSORP/1830/494; William Cox to Gregory, 6 January 1831, NAI, CSORP/1831/193.
[106] Reid, '"The Tithe War"', 37–49, 61–2.

superintendence' and stated that he trusted 'the zeal and discretion of the Yeomanry'.[107] While Stanley lamented the loss of life, he also deflected any responsibility on the part of the government – the magistrates had called out the yeomanry, the courts were actively considering whether prosecutions were necessary, and he did not want to influence 'the administration of justice'.[108] Anglesey showed more contempt for the way the whole event had been handled, writing to Stanley that the magistrates had called out the yeomanry illegally, and in their failure to read the Riot Act they did not give the people a chance to disperse, nor did they provide themselves with legal cover to use violent force. From a political perspective, the fact that Newtownbarry was the first appearance of the yeomanry since their rearmament 'must produce a very bad effect', causing a further chasm between the people and the administrators of law and order.[109] Anglesey continued:

I own that I dislike it [the yeomanry] more than any other, yet who will say that in the State in which I found this Country, with agitation very clearly bordering upon open Rebellion, & with a very inadequate regular force, I was not bound to arm every Man whose loyalty could be depended upon, even at the hazard of exciting party & religious violence by it. It was a choice of Evils. *I thought I chose the least, but upon my word, the least is a very great One.*[110]

Rectors and tithe owners hoped government would step in with more decisive measures, and possibly that the police could serve as proctors to 'driv[e] from the people a notion … that the Government are on their side' and prevent 'the law from becoming a dead letter'.[111]

Reading the correspondence between Stanley and Anglesey is a study in the divided personality of British thinking on Ireland, its remedies, and the meaning of 'justice'. Stanley emphasises the necessity of showing Irish people the government's power – power to enforce the law, to exert the rights of private property, and to enforce the claims of the legally Established Church; Anglesey stresses the need for reform and an improvement in material conditions in Ireland before enforcing the

---

[107] Anglesey to Melbourne, 24 December 1830, PRONI, Anglesey Papers, D619/29/B/5; Hansard, 3rd ser., vol. 2, cols. 814, 816, 21 February 1831.
[108] Hansard, 3rd ser., vol. 4, cols. 558–61, 30 June 1831.
[109] The yeomanry was an exclusively Protestant force associated with violent sectarian reprisals during the Rebellion of 1798. See Allan Blackstock, *An Ascendancy Army: The Irish Yeomanry 1796–1834* (Dublin: Four Courts Press, 1998).
[110] Anglesey to Stanley, 23 June 1831, PRONI, Anglesey Papers, D619/31T/38, emphasis added.
[111] Rev. Robert Butler to Stanley, 16 July 1831, 'Select Committee of House of Lords on Collection and Payment of Tithes in Ireland, Second Report, Minutes of Evidence, Appendix, Index [hereafter Lords Committee on Tithes]', P. P. (1831–32, vol. 22, no. 663, at 203–4).

absolute rights of tithe holders. 'Something must absolutely be done, unless we intend the Clergy to starve in some districts', Stanley wrote to Anglesey on Christmas Day 1831 before providing what appears to be his dictum on Irish solutions: 'Besides, the Law, *which it is the Law*, should not be suffered to be a dead letter.'[112] A couple months later, after suggesting Anglesey request more troops from Britain, Stanley advocated for a more active role for government forces in the collection of tithes: 'That of enabling the Crown to collect the Clergy's dues, will, I am sure have a good effect, as showing that we *really mean* to put down disturbance'.[113] By June the government had come up with a plan that gave Anglesey money to mete out to clergy and allowed the government to collect their arrears due in 1831. When Anglesey expressed concerns about the serious violence that would result from the government attempting to collect arrears from the people, Stanley remained unperturbed: 'Of course you will recollect that the amount of money collected is a very secondary consideration, and that the main object is to show the determination of the Government to uphold the law.'[114] And, while Stanley identified the necessity for church reform, the solutions he envisioned never questioned the nature of church property, which he thought 'to be just as much, and as irrevocably devoted to that Church, as the property of any Corporation'.[115]

Anglesey's vision for Irish solutions – especially in relation to tithes – came from the opposite direction. Rather than more troops, or stiffer coercive measures, Anglesey wanted to cut the bloat of the Established Church and save it from itself. Replying to one of Stanley's early missives about more troops, Anglesey stressed that 'an addition of 20,000 Men cannot secure the tranquillity of Ireland', and instead promoted the need for 'healing measures': 'If the Poor be provided for as proposed, & if the various other projects for the improvement of this Country be vigorously pushed forward, there will be no need of much coercion'.[116] In fact, Anglesey believed that coercion simply would not work. Stanley and Melbourne hoped that if the Irish government could apprehend some of the respectable big farmers, or Catholic clergy, refusing to pay tithes and put them in jail, it would eventually break the will and organisation of those who persisted in non-payment. Anglesey poured contempt on any notions, writing to Stanley: 'I am certain that when the new plan is attempted to be enforced . . . there will be general understanding that every One shall go to Prison & we shd. have to fill 20 Jails in each

[112] Stanley to Anglesey, 25 December 1831, PRONI, Anglesey Papers, D619/31S/73.
[113] Stanley to Anglesey, 7 February 1832, ibid., D619/31S/80.
[114] Stanley to Anglesey, 12 July 1832, ibid., D619/31S/93.
[115] Stanley to Grey, [June 1831], LPL, Derby Papers, 920 DER(14)/16/5.
[116] Anglesey to Stanley, 6 February 1832, PRONI, Anglesey Papers, D619/31V/5.

County, were they as large as your Penitentiary'.[117] Instead of coercion Anglesey pressed for benefices to be reduced in order to protect the longevity of the church, lest it 'destroy itself soon' from 'its own stubborn follies'. More consequential, however, was Anglesey's conviction that the government should control church funds: 'I wd vest All superfluities in the State, in trust for the Church, & to meet & provide for hereafter, the extension of protestantism, (if that creed should increase), but in the interim I would make it available for the exigencies of the State.'[118] Anglesey's idea of church appropriation would fall on deaf ears until later in the decade, as would his advocacy of other immediate reforms. In a matter-of-fact tone of exasperation, Anglesey summed up his frustrations with the differing views between Dublin and London:

Of the Tythe Bills I need say nothing. I have recorded my opinions over & over again of the whole measures that ought to have been adopted & of the desperate dilemma in which we shall be placed by only adopting them partially & by beginning as I conceive *at the wrong end*. ... Arms Bill – however desirable I do not expect you will be able to pass any further measure for ... Ireland this year ... still you must suffer me to reiterate my deep regret that the *whole* Tythe Scheme was not at once adopted as a Government measure upon which it should stand or fall .... To wind up this lengthy Epistle ... let me say prophetically that if all these measures were carried [coercive ones], we have still heavy labours to look to & that whether you will or not, Poor laws & labour Rate will force themselves upon you – they are inevitable.[119]

Without the reformation of ills in Ireland, violence simply continued. Farmers and landless labourers, in many cases allegedly led by their priests, organised to petition against tithes and high rents. While the government allowed, even protected, the rights of people to petition the government, when petitions turned into rallies planning tactics to avoid the payment of rents, and when violence grew, both voices in London and the Irish gentry clamoured for a renewal of coercive measures. Thousands attended meetings like the one organised in New Kildimo, Co. Limerick in July 1832 advocating the abolition of tithes; funds were collected at the event to support those the government prosecuted. Prosecutions included charges of 'conspiracy against the payment of tithes, and publishing an inflammatory notice exacting others to do likewise', which in the case of William Godfrey Twiss, one among thousands prosecuted, resulted in four months' imprisonment for his first offence.[120] All the

---

[117] Anglesey to Stanley, 4 June 1832, ibid., D619/31V/23.
[118] Anglesey to Stanley, 21 March 1832, ibid., D619/31V/13.
[119] Anglesey to Stanley, 15 July 1832, ibid., D619/31V/28, emphasis added to 'at the wrong end'; italic emphasis of 'whole' is in the original.
[120] 'Anti-tithe Meeting at New Kildimo', FJ, 7 July 1832; 'Anti-tithe Meetings', FJ, 6 November 1832.

agitation against the payment of tithes resulted in a marked increase in
Irish outrages. Reports reached the government of a string of attacks
against tithe collectors in Co. Cork during the latter half of 1832, which
troubled magistrates because of the people's 'consciousness of strength',
as well as the influence of priests in resisting the payment of tithes.[121]
Intimidatory violence – like the dragging of a process server by a mob of
300 into a potato field, where they forced the man to eat several of the
tithe papers and dug a grave for him – led to actual murders, as in the case
of Michael Drohan, who was killed after attempting to distrain cattle in
Wooden Grange, Co. Kilkenny.[122]

By 1834 the new lord lieutenant, Lord Wellesley, emphatically pressed
for the application of the Insurrection Act as a way to quell disturbances
and temporarily outlaw assemblages of people intent to plot against
paying their tithes. In his mind the connection between political agitation
and violent outrages was akin to simple cause and effect, and it was the
government's job to use coercion as an instrument to undermine the
cause of agitation. 'I cannot employ words of sufficient strength to express
my solicitude that His Majesty's Government should fix the deepest
attention on the intimate relation ... between the system of agitation,
and its inevitable consequence, the system of combination, leading to
violence & outrage: they are, inseparably, cause & effect', Wellesley wrote
in his official report on the state of Ireland to Melbourne in April 1834.[123]
This observation by Wellesley embodied the intractability of many Irish
problems. Either the government needed to restrict the freedoms guaranteed to its subjects by the constitution, or take the risk that Irish
political agitation would ultimately devolve into violence outrages. The
decision to restrict personal liberty and apply coercive force to Ireland
proved much easier for the other members in charge of the Irish government, Lord Melbourne and Lord Stanley, then it had been for Anglesey,
who by 1833 had resigned as lord lieutenant.

## The Die Cast: Embracing Coercion

With the passage of the Reform Bill and the overwhelming Whig majority
from the resulting elections the government no longer relied on support
from Irish Repealers or radicals, thus freeing Stanley to endorse more
forceful legislation in Ireland. Anglesey had already worked under
a modified Whiteboy Act that allowed government to transport

---

[121] 'Timeline of Outrages in Cork from June 1832 to February 1833', TNA, HO 100/
244/84.
[122] 'Lords Committee on Tithes', 196–7.
[123] Wellesley to Melbourne, 15 April 1834, TNA, HO 100/245/165.

individuals convicted of sending threatening letters or administering illegal oath, equipped the lord lieutenant with the power to proclaim districts, and increased the discretion of local magistrates or military officers to act.[124] Stanley removed all restraints in the bill introduced in 1833, which included provisions for the use of court martial, and pushed to centralise power in the office of the lord lieutenant. The bill was prompted, at least in part, by Melbourne's uncertainty as to the efficacy of the Insurrection Act of old, as he pondered the 'more effectual and decision measure of martial law'.[125] In his speeches in the Commons in 1833, Stanley used the violence of Irish outrages to highlight the peasantry's 'extraordinary evil', and stressed the need for the government to meet such evils with 'extraordinary powers'. 'They asked for powers most undoubtedly without limitation', Stanley argued, 'because, while disgraceful outrages were committed, while murder, and violence, and marauding prevailed ... it was impossible to say "here is a limit beyond which you do not require powers, beyond which you shall not pass"'.[126]

Though Stanley had rather hoped for carte blanche, the final bill imposed some modest restrictions, including the requirement of a supermajority (seven of nine officers) to convict a suspect in court-martial proceedings and limiting the applicability of a court martial to agrarian violence and political disturbances until after the bill had been passed.[127] 'I am afraid that some of the alterations which have been made will impair its efficiency and the facility of its working', Melbourne confessed to Stanley after the amended bill cleared the Lords, but felt buoyed by the fact that 'the two great points are obtained – the putting down [of] illegal seditious bodies, and the making it actually unlawful to be out by night in a proclaimed district'.[128] Considering the great lengths to achieve the passage of this modified Insurrection Act, it is somewhat ironic that its use remained rather limited. Anglesey, the man responsible for proclaiming districts, continued to show great restraint in its application, and instead praised the effect the fear of proclamations seemed to have on troubled districts.[129] Nevertheless, in many ways the die had been cast; the Whigs who entered government critical of coercive legislation now saw its effectiveness in dealing with many of the problems they saw as peculiarly Irish.

---

[124] Hansard, 3rd ser., vol. 7, 487–8, 22 September 1831; Anglesey to Melbourne, 23 February 1831, PRONI, Anglesey Papers, D619/29B/23.

[125] Sanders, *Lord Melbourne's Papers*, 189.

[126] Hansard, 3rd ser., vol. 15, cols. 1252, 1254, 27 February 1833.

[127] 'Bill for More Effectual Suppression of Local Disturbances and Dangerous Associations in Ireland (as Amended by Committee)', P. P. (1833, vol. 2, no. 93).

[128] Melbourne to Stanley, 2 April 1833, in Sanders, *Lord Melbourne's Papers*, 194.

[129] Anglesey to Melbourne, 15 March 1833, PRONI, Anglesey Papers, D619/29B/77.

The *Edinburgh Review*, certainly speaking for some within the Whig camp, found itself defending the policy of coercion while also underscoring all the legislation that had been attempted by the Whigs to offer Ireland remedial justice. Dispelling the sophism popularly espoused by the Tory press that Catholic Emancipation actually brought Ireland further into the grips of violence, the article stressed that 'the principles of justice' on which emancipation were based 'are eternal ... [while] these sources of evil are but transitory and evanescent'. Rather than focussing on the necessity for coercive legislation, the author directed attention to the historical commitment of the Whigs to Ireland, and the consistency between Whig rhetoric during their time in the minority and on government benches. 'Even with regard to Ireland, where their difficulties were the greatest, a series of measures has been submitted to the Legislature ... [that] would have sufficed to ensure the strength and popularity of any Irish Government'. Listing seven areas of Irish reform, what the author described as 'the more gratifying duties of legislation', the article admitted that while the government had advocated for, and passed, coercive legislation, it now could focus on meaningful reforms to correct Irish ills.[130] Crucially, however, the article also implicitly admitted the fallacy of the belief of many in government that emancipation and reform would end Irish violence. 'It may be asked, if wisdom and benevolence have thus characterised the acts of the Legislature and of the Government, have those acts been successful? We cannot answer this question in the affirmative.' The author, in concluding, stressed the necessity for the government to push forward in ending 'all real abuses' now that coercive legislation had passed both Houses, and place 'immediate attention to the wants and necessities of Ireland'.[131]

But, the immediate attention to Ireland's wants referred to in the *Edinburgh Review* proved too difficult for Lord Grey's government. Suffering internal divisions on a number of issues, including church appropriation, led to the government folding after Stanley resigned, taking roughly sixty MPs with him. In the end, the resignations helped to consolidate the Whigs along more activist, aristocratic, and liberal lines. These new ministers – including Lord John Russell, Lord Mulgrave, and Lord Morpeth, adopted a programme of 'justice to Ireland' more analogous to Anglesey's advocacy for liberal spending, which they believed was paramount to ensuring Ireland's prosperity and

---

[130] The seven areas included landlord–tenant relations, the necessity for capital investment, repeal of taxes, reform of the Grand Jury system, tithes and church establishment, Orange and Ribbon processions, and the inclusion of Catholics into offices of government.

[131] 'Ireland', *Edinburgh Review* 57, no. 115 (Jan.–July 1833): 251, 259, 275, 276–7.

the security of the wider empire. Picking up the mantle of remedial legislation, the reconstituted Whig government pursued policies conceived during the first half of the decade. They did so aided in part by a rather unlikely collaboration with Daniel O'Connell, who gave up his Repeal banner to focus on 'justice for Ireland'.

## Daniel O'Connell and 'Justice'

Arguably, no man divided both public and private opinion in the United Kingdom more than Daniel O'Connell did during the twenty-five years prior to his death in 1847. Known to Irish Catholics as the 'Liberator' or 'Emancipator', and respected by American abolitionists like Frederick Douglass for his principled stand against slavery, in the House of Commons O'Connell's presence was marked with either 'the fiercest hatred or the most unbounded love', but in either case he was readily identified as the 'Agitator'.[132] The necessities of dealing with O'Connell's understanding of justice are all but self-apparent, as his was the dominant voice (though certainly not the only one) of Irish politics between 1825 and 1845. However, for all the importance his voice carried, his legacy has remained complicated by the seemingly endless paradoxes he embodied: one with the people, yet quasi-aristocratic; willing to appeal to the spectre of violence, yet wedded to peaceful constitutionalism; an advocate for religious equality, yet one who saw Irish identity as intimately tied to Roman Catholicism. O'Connell could easily be identified as an idealist, a demagogue, and a pragmatist, a fact that endeared him to few within Parliament, especially those who privileged 'political principles' while failing to recognise that O'Connell possessed his own.

O'Connell's philosophical inspiration came from the works of Jeremy Bentham and William Godwin, as O'Connell identified as a lifelong utilitarian. Godwin's *Political Justice* had the greatest influence on O'Connell's political outlook, especially the author's belief that unearned privilege ultimately led to corruption, which immediately recalled the Protestant Ascendancy to the forefront of O'Connell's mind.[133] O'Connell confided in his journal in 1796: 'I have finished Godwin. His work cannot be too highly praised. All mankind are indebted to the author. The cause of despotism never met a more formidable

---

[132] Tom Chaffin, *Giant's Causeway: Frederick Douglass's Irish Odyssey and the Making of an American Visionary* (Charlottesville, VA: University of Virginia Press, 2014), ch. 7; *The Assembled Commons; or, Parliamentary Biographer, with an Abstract of the Law of Election, by a Member of the Middle Temple* (London: Scott, Webster, and Geary, 1838), 187.

[133] Sean McGraw and Kevin Whelan, 'Daniel O'Connell in Comparative Perspective, 1800–50', *Éire-Ireland* 40, no. 1 (2005): 62.

adversary'.[134] Indeed, Godwin's belief that reason trumped force, and that the latter could seldom be justified, also likely anchored O'Connell's commitment to constitutionalism, 'If . . . the cause we plead be the cause of truth, there is no doubt that by reasonings, if sufficiently zealous and constant, the same purpose may be effected in a mild and liberal way.'[135] Although O'Connell would hold tight to a commitment to truth and reason, the impediment blocking the advancement of his political agenda was the contested nature of politics, and the 'cause of truth'. Thus, O'Connell adapted to the political climate in which he was immersed, appealing to broadly universalist principles of liberty and freedom of conscience during the fight for Catholic Emancipation in the 1820s, only to later shift to a more narrowly focussed campaign for the redress of Irish grievances in the 1830s, often couched in language that appealed to engagement with the wider public, both priest and peasant.[136]

There is perhaps no better example of the apparent paradox of O'Connell's political vision than his oscillation between a campaign for 'simple Repeal' of the Act of Union, and the pressure he exerted for popular reforms, embodied in his mantra of 'Justice for Ireland'. Nevertheless, after the paradigmatic victory O'Connell secured in Catholic Emancipation, this dizzying swing between Repeal and reform provided him with a stable foundation to advance a political agenda that rectified grievances held by the majority of Catholics in Ireland since well before the Union. In effect, Repeal served as an 'opening bid' or 'attempt to open up negotiation', which challenged the British government to provide a counter-offer that would carry with it material benefits to the vast majority of Irish people.[137]

## Catholic Emancipation and the 'Spirit of the Age'

Catholic Emancipation, though one of the most intractable issues of the early nineteenth century, especially for Conservative governments between the Act of Union and O'Connell's election as MP for Co. Clare in 1828, evolved into a debate that ultimately yielded under the 'Spirit of the Age' – a steady erosion year after year of the intellectual framework justifying the exclusion of any man from political office based

---

[134] Daniel O'Connell, *Daniel O'Connell: His Early Life, and Journal, 1795 to 1802*, ed. Arthur Houston (London: Sir I. Pitman, & Sons, 1906), 118.

[135] William Godwin, *An Enquiry Concerning Political Justice: And Its Influence on General Virtue and Happiness* (London: G. G. J. and J. Robinson, 1793), 195–6.

[136] Hoppen, "'Riding a Tiger'", 133–6.

[137] Oliver MacDonagh, 'O'Connell's Ideology', in *A Union of Multiple Identities: The British Isles, c. 1750–c.1850*, eds. Laurence Brockliss and David Eastwood (Manchester: Manchester University Press, 1997), 155.

on religious belief. None other than Robert Peel, in advancing Emancipation before the Commons, admitted this point: 'They [Parliament] must advance, or they must recede. . . . They must remove the barriers that obstruct the continued flow of relaxation and indulgence, or they must roll back to its source the mighty current which has been let in on us, year after year, by the gradual withdrawal of restraint.'[138]

O'Connell and the Catholic Association advocated Catholic Emancipation based on understandings of justice that reached the quasi-spiritual and which often appealed to notions of morality, truth, and reason. One tactic involved organising extravagant public dinners to attract the support of prominent liberals. At one such dinner in Dublin in February 1826, a number of Irish gentry attended to pledge their support of Catholic Emancipation, using the language of equity and justice. Lord Portarlington stressed his commitment to emancipation 'because, in the first place, it was but a bare act of justice', while Sir Marcus Somerville, MP for Co. Meath, stressed that the laws disbarring Catholics from Parliament 'should be repealed without delay' as 'the spirit of the age required'.[139] Those that could not attend the meeting used similar sentiments privately in their correspondence with O'Connell. Edward O'Brien, MP for Co. Clare, wrote declining the invitation to attend but stressed his thirty-year record advocating for Catholics and underscored that 'to place all the Majesty's loyal subjects on the same footing would be no less an act of policy than of justice'. Samuel War, a prominent Dublin attorney, offered similar sentiments, writing to O'Connell to praise him for having preached the 'unerring truth' that would open the possibly for Emancipation, 'founded as it is in justice, humanity and political expedience', to pass without delay.[140] When Emancipation failed to pass in 1827, Bishop Doyle wrote O'Connell to offer consolation by way of theological explanation, urging him to read the fifth and sixth chapters of Exodus and remember the plight and deliverance of Israelites from Egyptian slavery, 'before you complain that our arguments are left unanswered, that our prayers are slighted, that our sufferings are unpitied [sic] and that our efforts to extricate ourselves only serve to rivet faster our chains'. Instead, the

---

[138] Robert Peel's speech in the House of Commons, 5 March 1829, quoted in Boyd Hilton, 'The Ripening of Robert Peel', in *Public and Private Doctrine: Essays in British History Presented to Maurice Cowling*, ed. Michael Bentley (Cambridge: Cambridge University Press, 1993), 72–3.

[139] 'Catholic Dinner', *Morning Chronicle*, 9 February 1826.

[140] Daniel O'Connell, *The Correspondence of Daniel O'Connell*, ed. Maurice O'Connell (Dublin: Irish Manuscripts Commission, 1972–80), 3: 225, 233.

Bishop urged O'Connell to remember, 'our cause is in the hand of God and God is just'.[141]

The assurance that Catholic Emancipation was in the hands of God, or soon to be brought about through the will of public opinion, did not preclude O'Connell from action. 'We *never, never, never* got anything by conciliation', O'Connell wrote to the Knight of Kerry, Maurice Fitzgerald in December 1826, before continuing, 'we must call things by their proper names – speak out boldly, let it be called intemperately, and rouse in Ireland a spirit of *action*'.[142] What followed were the dizzying activities of petition drives, a renewed publicly subscribed Catholic rent, and public meetings in favour of Emancipation. Most worrying for the government, those public meetings saw local factions, hitherto locked in cycles of retributive violence, lay down their arms and unite under O'Connell's banner – thus suggesting O'Connell's ability to control the people and their capacity to violent political action.[143]

O'Connell's dependence on the action of the people brought sustained accusations from opponents that he stood at the head of a violent, even murderous, mob. O'Connell vehemently denied these charges and was intimately involved in directing his regional lieutenants to exclude miscreants from the movement. After reports surfaced in Co. Tipperary that an accused murderer named Kirby had attended a reconciliation meeting of various factions in open defiance of the warrants for his arrest, O'Connell was incensed.[144] O'Connell wrote to Rev. Michael Slattery, the priest of Cashel:

I beg you will at your earliest convenience write to me to enable me to contradict what I presume to be a calumny on the good people of Tipperary. It is said that at one of those public meetings to make peace . . . which we all so much approve, the noted Kirby, who is charged with the horrid crime of murder . . . had the audacity to appear in the midst of the honest and worthy men to whom I am so deeply indebted for taking my advice. Our cause is too sacred and too holy to allow it to be tarnished by the society of men who are stained with crime. The great Catholic cause of Ireland is the cause of virtue and honesty. The great God of heaven will not allow it to prosper if we associate with murderers or criminals of any kind.[145]

The theme of respectability runs through this letter, and others, as O'Connell felt keenly aware that obtaining Emancipation required

---

[141] Bishop Doyle to O'Connell, March 1827, ibid., 296.
[142] O'Connell to the Knight of Kerry, 31 December 1826, ibid., 283.
[143] Owens, 'A Moral Insurrection', 513–41.
[144] 'Irish Intelligence', *The Times*, 3 September 1828; 'Ireland', *Morning Chronicle*, 10 September 1828.
[145] O'Connell to Rev. Michael Slattery, 2 September 1828, in O'Connell, *Correspondence*, 3: 402. Emphasis in the original.

gaining the esteem of public opinion. Those engaged in collecting the Catholic rent must be '*good, honest, religious men*' who could be described as '*sober, industrious, attentive to their religious and moral duties*'. In short, O'Connell desired 'steady men who are good sons, good brothers, good husbands'.[146] Later in 1829, as magistrates in Tipperary clamoured for an application of the Insurrection Act, O'Connell stressed that the way for people to defeat their enemies was to 'observe the law, to avoid all riots and outrages and not strengthen the hands of their enemies by committing crimes. Crimes must and will be punished.'[147] O'Connell reiterated his ardent adherence to agitation within the bounds of the law in his correspondence with Thomas Attwood, the founder of the Birmingham Political Union (BPU), then beginning their campaign for parliamentary reform. 'There are two principle means of attaining our constitutional objects which will never be lost sight of', O'Connell wrote in February 1830. 'The first is the perpetual determination to avoid anything like physical force or violence and by keeping in all respects within the letter as well as the spirit of the law', which would enable the movement 'to continue peaceable, rational, but energetic measures so as to combine the wise and the good of all classes'.[148]

Guided by these principles of lawful agitation and respectability, O'Connell's campaign for Catholic Emancipation was politically transformative and monumentally successful.[149] Yet, O'Connell and others within his orbit used justice as a way to appeal to larger universal principles embedded in Enlightenment thinking. Capitalising on increasingly positive public opinion, O'Connell cast Protestant defenders of the *ancien régime* as bigots and oppressors, while anti-Catholic-petition signings were met in many of the newly industrialising cities of England with disdain, counterdemonstrations, and occasional violence.[150] These ideals could also be used as a weapon, as O'Connell believe that appeals to justice and humanity in the face of 'sophistry and bigotry' would 'debase the English character in the eyes of the civilized world', and shame the British government to action.[151] As O'Connell shifted attention from

---

[146] Ibid.

[147] O'Connell to Nicolas Maher, 13 September 1829, in O'Connell, *Correspondence*, 4: 98.

[148] O'Connell to Attwood, 16 February 1830, ibid., 4:128–9.

[149] McGraw and Whelan, 'Daniel O'Connell in Comparative Perspective', 66–70; Patrick Geoghegan, 'The Impact of O'Connell, 1815–1850', in *The Cambridge History of Ireland*, ed. James Kelly (Cambridge: Cambridge University Press, 2018), 3:110–12. Historians have posited a degree of coordination between O'Connell and clandestine organisations, such as the Ribbonmen; see Hughes and MacRaild, *Ribbon Societies*, ch. 3.

[150] Hinde, *Catholic Emancipation*, 138–42.

[151] O'Connell to Edward Dwyer, 5 April 1826, in O'Connell, *Correspondence*, 3: 303–4.

Emancipation to Repeal, however, this strategy of appealing to universally agreed upon ideas of justice and humanity would lose their traction to an increasingly narrow political question.[152] In turn, rhetorical uses of justice re-entered a contested political space as O'Connell attempted to articulate the case for 'simple Repeal' while also exacting reform from the British government in its administration of Ireland.

## Repeal and Reform

Catholic Emancipation did not solve all of Ireland's problems, a fact that O'Connell recognised on his entrance into Parliament. O'Connell spent the intervening years between Emancipation and his eventual political compact with the Whigs in 1835 both advocating for a repeal of the Act of Union and attempting to wrest measures of reform from the Whig government. O'Connell's success in orchestrating the passage of Catholic Emancipation had made him a political force no government could afford to ignore, and his campaign for Repeal during the early years of the 1830s frustrated Whigs in power, especially Stanley, who pushed for the government to prosecute O'Connell in 1831. O'Connell's relationship with the government oscillated between organising support for Repeal, sparring with Stanley and other government ministers over their Irish policy, and hoping to get the best possible outcome for his efforts. His political programme was a complex mixture of pragmatism, rhetorical flair, and advocacy for his political idea of 'simple Repeal'.

In September 1833, O'Connell wrote from his estate at Derrynane to his political lieutenant P. V. FitzPatrick regarding the shake-up in the British cabinet, and rumours that ministers were attempting to invite O'Connell into office. Lord Anglesey had been pushed out as lord lieutenant, and hopes were entertained that the attorney general Francis Blackburne might be sacked; in O'Connell's eyes all for the sake of clearing away those he refused to work with. Surely this was the moment O'Connell had waited all his life for – an opportunity to be invited into government and affect change for Ireland from within the bastion of power. Apparently not:

If I went into office I should be *their servant*, that is, their slave. By staying out of office I am, to a considerable extent, their master. ... Without taking office I will be able to get, first, a number of bad magistrates removed; second, the yeomanry disarmed, third, the tithes abolished; fourth, the establishment of the Protestant church reduced in every parish ... fifth, to have offices filled with Liberals to the exclusion of Orangeists. These are great things and instead of soliciting some of

[152] Macintyre, *The Liberator*, 13.

them, as I *should* do were I in office, I will command them when out of office. ....
Then lastly, but first in order of magnitude, there is the Repeal of the Union.[153]

O'Connell went on to ask, rhetorically, 'But may not Repeal be dispensed with if we get beneficial measures without it?' answering that ultimately the only guarantee of Ireland's permanent prosperity was a domestic legislature.

This letter offers insight into the complexities of O'Connell's political programme, one that encompassed Repeal as an ultimate goal in the far-off distance coupled with the realities of potential reform in the immediate future. From outside government, but inside Parliament, O'Connell could achieve tangible concessions of injustices long suffered. And in this letter the three characteristics of idealist, pragmatist, and agitator find ample expression. Thus, the period between 1830 and 1835 upsets the neat periodisation that attempts to create a dichotomy between Daniel O'Connell the Repealer and Daniel O'Connell the Reformer. Rather, O'Connell's programme embodied both Repeal and reform in varying degrees of concentration, which was reflected in the varied contexts where justice was rhetorically deployed.

Fundamentally, O'Connell believed that the remedies to Ireland's problems were to be found in 'simple Repeal', a phrase that lacked precision and therefore abounded in space for political manoeuvring, but, if taken literally as a turning back of the clock to 1799, was simply nonsensical.[154] While the meaning of Repeal took a variety of forms, one constant was the return of a domestic legislative body. O'Connell believed that a return of such a body would ensure that members who legislated on Ireland's behalf actually had a stake in the outcome of legislation. It would anchor members of Ireland's gentry in Ireland, thus rectifying the problem of absenteeism, while also ensuring that Ireland's economic interests were settled by Irishmen rather than through the constraints of an imperial parliament that favoured British interests.[155]

Above all, O'Connell believed that a domestic legislature would end the impulse to deal with Irish agrarian distress simply by coercive legislation. While the Whigs debated whether to pass coercive legislation for Ireland, O'Connell mused to FitzPatrick how they were doing the work of Repeal for him: 'Believe me that it was not possible to give so strong an impulse to Repeal by any other means in this country as by those coercive

---

[153] O'Connell to FitzPatrick, 17 September 1833, in O'Connell, *Correspondence*, 5: 71.
[154] MacDonagh, *Emancipist*, 80–1.
[155] As such, it sounded remarkably similar to Isaac Butt's federalist approach a generation later. See Colin W. Reid, '"An Experiment in Constructive Unionism": Isaac Butt, Home Rule and Federalist Political Thought during the 1870s', EHR 129, no. 537 (April 2014): 332–61.

measures.' Most gratefully, the debate convinced those 'in the House and out of the House' that 'they do not see any chance of justice for Ireland without a resident legislature'.[156] Five days later, hours before the bill's second reading, O'Connell steamed, 'But, take it in any shape, it is a measure of atrocious tyranny and demonstrates that no Parliament but a local one can do justice to Ireland.'[157]

O'Connell bellowed such sentiment within Parliament, too. In the final debates on the coercion bill, he forcefully argued that such legislation undermined the very fundamentals of the Act of Union and demonstrated clearly the unequal relationship between both countries. Alluding to a mythical day when Protestant and Catholic MPs would unite together bound by their 'deeper interest in their native land than in that of party', O'Connell argued they would speak with one voice 'that it was not generosity and kindness which they wanted [from Britain], but equality and justice'. He continued:

They would say to the Ministers of England, 'Govern your own beautiful country as you please – legislate for Britain wisely and well – but we Irishmen, bearing allegiance to a common King, and living under a common Constitution, will legislate for ourselves.' Government might depend upon it, that they were not putting down but strengthening the cry for the Repeal of the Union by these coercive measures; that they were not retarding but accelerating the progress of Ireland to that great act of justice of which he was the humble advocate.[158]

These sentiments were echoed in newspapers as the coercion bill worked through Parliament. In April, the *Freeman's Journal* published an article essentially regurgitating O'Connell's speech regarding the patriotic benefits of Repeal, while noting that coercion in Ireland only further undermined the logic of a united imperial parliament, one recently reformed and supposedly liberal. 'If in the discussion of the most atrocious and revolting measure that was ever submitted to the consideration of any Parliament, composed of high-born and educated gentlemen', the *Freeman's Journal* opined, 'we would have been perhaps disposed to make large allowances for the ignorance and prejudices of foreign legislators.' But they were talking about Great Britain, home of Magna Carta, 'freeborn Englishmen', and defenders of men's liberty, freedom, and conscience. Can any Irish gentlemen, whether Catholic or Protestant, 'place any hope or confidence in the justice, virtue or magnanimity of such a House of Commons?' The editor thought not, as 'not only was every privilege of free debate violated … every appeal to facts

---

[156] O'Connell to FitzPatrick, 6 March 1833, in O'Connell, *Correspondence*, 5: 14.
[157] O'Connell to FitzPatrick, 11 March 1833, ibid., 5:16.
[158] Hansard, 3rd ser., vol. 16, cols. 1277, 29 March 1833.

disregarded . . . every decency outraged, but the voices of honest, devoted Irishmen shouted down with yells that would disgrace a circle of squatting Indians', causing the editor to say 'adieu for ever to all chance of justice from a British parliament'.[159]

O'Connell's overestimation that 'the Protestants [would] forget ascendancy and consent to endure equality with cordial good temper' fatally undermined the efficacy of Repeal's passage.[160] But, ever the pragmatist, O'Connell recognised the variety of uses Repeal offered and started 'using Repeal as a political instrument rather than pursuing it as a goal'.[161] In a letter to Bishop John MacHale – later Archbishop of Tuam – O'Connell confidently wrote: '"The Repeal of the Union" is good for everything. It is good as the means of terrifying the enemies of the people into every concession practicable under the present system.'[162] Ten days before the passage of the Great Reform Act, O'Connell again stressed the variated applications of Repeal: 'Repeal will be our cry; it will serve every purpose', which included its ability to 'compel a better Reform Bill for Ireland'.[163] And, when the Irish-born Chartist Fergus O'Connor argued for advancing a motion for Repeal during the parliamentary session of 1833, O'Connell came down on him like a ton of bricks. To FitzPatrick he fumed, 'Heaven help them! If any one anti-Unionist save myself COULD get what I could . . . how little do men in Dublin know of the precarious state of public affairs'.[164] Two days later he responded to a letter from FitzPatrick ridiculing O'Connor's clique for thinking they could advance Repeal while the government was in a state of flux, adding 'I have a much better opportunity of knowing how the land lies and what are the circumstances which could render any discussion available for any useful purpose whatsoever'.[165] In short, Repeal acted as the crook in

---

[159] 'Repeal of the Union', FJ, 3 April 1833.

[160] O'Connell to FitzPatrick, 27 May 1833, in O'Connell, *Correspondence*, 5:33. As irrational as O'Connell's sentiment on Protestant goodwill sounds in retrospect, he did try to appeal to Protestants' self-interest and patriotism in his continual references to the Volunteers of 1782, as well as in his attempts to find common ground with Tories. The idea of finding common ground with Irish Tories was suggested by Dr Boyton, who foreseeing the potential for dissolution of the Conservative Society due to the passage of the Coercion Act, wondered openly whether Tory and Repealer could find common ground. See O'Connell, *Correspondence*, 5:11–12.

[161] MacDonagh, *Emancipist*, 80.

[162] O'Connell to Bishop MacHale, 3 December 1830, in O'Connell, *Correspondence*, 4: 241–2.

[163] O'Connell to John Dwyer, 17 May 1832, ibid., 4:417.

[164] O'Connell to FitzPatrick, 17 June 1833, ibid., 5:45. Suffice to say, O'Connor and O'Connell did not get along, but their projects shared interesting overlaps. See Matthew Roberts, 'Daniel O'Connell, Repeal, and Chartism in the Age of Atlantic Revolutions', *The Journal of Modern History*, 90, no. 1 (March 2018): 1–39.

[165] O'Connell to FitzPatrick, 20 June 1833, *Correspondence*, 5: 46–7.

a shepherd's staff, pushing or pulling the government to exact concessions that it otherwise would simply pass over. And O'Connell, ever the good shepherd, willingly used his tool to 'get *what I can* and use Repeal *in terrorem*' to bring Ireland to the promised land.[166]

If the mantra of Repeal served this function, then what benefits did O'Connell expect from the government of Ireland? In his own words, he demanded 'full justice'. In late May 1834, writing to the Archbishop of Cashel, Michael Slattery, O'Connell related that the government was attempting to consolidate its strength by gaining the support of popular men in the House of Commons. This necessitated a more liberal shift in proposed policy, as many of those the Whigs courted attached themselves to measures with wide popular support. 'As to myself I am perhaps not worth *purchasing* but if they think I am, they can *buy* me only by doing justice, full justice to Catholic Ireland.'[167] Full justice for Catholic Ireland included many of the important reforms that the Whig government attempted to instate between 1835 and 1841, including addressing the want of capital investment in Ireland, a settlement on the Irish Church, and a permanent solution to the tithe question. O'Connell in 1830 listed no fewer than twelve reforms he wished to see for Ireland, whereas in 1834 he referred to 'common sense measures for Ireland'.[168]

Justice naturally concerned large economic, religious, and social questions, but in O'Connell's eyes it also included the minutiae of local administration. Thus, O'Connell could write Lord Duncannon – the de facto ambassador between the Whigs and O'Connell – confessing his 'despair of the present Administration for doing anything for Ireland', but writing because 'the death of Judge Jebb gives the Minister an opportunity to prove itself', as it would 'be vain to ask the popular party to tolerate you if you throw away this lucky chance'. O'Connell proceeded to propose a series of appointment recommendations (eight in total), including moving attorney general Francis Blackburne ('the prime patron' of Orangeism) to the judgeship and replacing him with someone suitable to the creed of a Whig government. Rather than writing a humdrum letter about patronage, O'Connell writes to Duncannon as one of Ireland's best legal minds, highlighting the chasm between Whig rhetoric and reality:

You are going on with Orangeists at the Castle, at the Bar, in the Shrievalties [appointment of sheriffs], in the magistracies – in all places and officers, especially

---

[166] O'Connell to FitzPatrick, 7 May 1834, ibid., 5:129.

[167] O'Connell to Slattery, 29 May 1834, ibid., 5:137.

[168] O'Connell to Richard Newton Bennett, 7 December 1830, in O'Connell, *Correspondence*, 4: 244–5; O'Connell to FitzPatrick, 19 May 1834, 5:134.

the police and then you blame the Irish people, sore from centuries of Orange oppressions, because they refuse to believe in the good intentions of a Ministry who appoint . . . the people's enemies in all stations of honour and emolument. . . . You should be spared the trouble of reading . . . if I was not convinced of the patriotism and purity of your disposition to serve Ireland.[169]

A letter with similar sentiments passed from O'Connell to Duncannon a month later, at the beginning of October, complaining of Orangemen running Dublin Castle and pondering whether much would change 'if Peel and Goulburn were still in management of this country'.[170]

### Conclusion: Hope for the Future

That Grey's government fell to Wellington and Peel within weeks did not come as a surprise to O'Connell, and he received it with some hope at future prospects.[171] The failure of Repeal, along with the fall of the Whigs, brought with it the hope of an eventually more liberal government – one that went 'from half Whig, half Tory Government to one half Radical, half Whig' – a government that would pledge full justice to Ireland.[172] And the Lichfield House Compact in 1835 between Whig, Radical, and O'Connellites, which pledged to end the cry of Repeal in return for concessions in Ireland, was the eventual result. While much of this book aims to disentangle the overlap between O'Connell's vision and the Whigs' understanding of 'justice for Ireland', it is worth noting that both swam in the same ideological waters. Yes, it was true that O'Connell consistently stated that his ultimate goal was Repeal of the Union, a destination to reach in the not-too-distant future; but, in the meantime, O'Connell gave up Repeal in 1835 for what appeared to be the more useful tool of cooperation.

Moreover, on the face of things, in 1836 there seemed to be much reason to rejoice in the success of the tacit partnership. Reflecting on the re-establishment of Whig rule under Lord Melbourne, with Mulgrave, Morpeth, and Thomas Drummond at the helm of Irish affairs, the newly established O'Connellite journal *The Dublin Review* praised the new administration, which based itself 'in every work of peace and justice'. The journal applauded Mulgrave for having the moral courage to dump Attorney General Blackburne where others had faltered, but reserved its highest praise for the new undersecretary at Dublin Castle, Thomas Drummond. The article commended his commitment, his labour to reform in 1832, his reputation as a man of business and action, and his

---

[169] O'Connell to Lord Duncannon, 2 September 1834, 5:172.
[170] O'Connell to Duncannon, 2 October 1834, ibid., 5:189.
[171] O'Connell to Mary O'Connell, 18 November 1834, ibid., 5:202–3.
[172] Macintyre, *Liberator*, 134.

commitment to '*Principle*, pure and decided'. Above all, however, it praised the government for its record in office, as 'the Irish people had often been deluded by professions; but here were acts, so decisive, that they could not be understood or interpreted, in any other sense, than as the earnest and pledged of substantial justice'.[173]

[173] 'Earl Mulgrave in Ireland', *The Dublin Review* 1, no. 1 (May 1836): 30–1, 34.

## 2   'Outrage' in Ireland
### Agrarian Violence and Irish Claims
### to Counter-Sovereignty

On either 31 December 1838 or 1 January 1839, unknown assailants shot Lord Norbury while he walked part of his estate with his steward in Durrow, King's County. Newspaper accounts did not know what to make of the event. Norbury held a fairly good reputation in the surrounding area, and as the conservative *Mail* noted, he was a 'resident landlord [who] dispensed the rites of hospitality with a munificent hand', and 'exercised towards his tenants and the poor all kindliness and benevolence which their relative positions could demand'. While certainly less grandiloquent, even the nationalist *Dublin Pilot* conceded that Norbury's tenants had little motive to attack him, as they had 'always heard of him as an excellent landlord'. The *Pilot*, however, did note that peasants often targeted their landlords on account of what the newspaper called 'the landlord[s'] exterminating war', which pushed tenants off the land they occupied, inducing them to respond through modes of resistance that included assassination. Whig government officials feared the effects Norbury's murder would have on Irish society and how it might embolden their Tory opponents to draw negative conclusions about the state of Ireland[1].

While newspapers struggled to form a coherent narrative that adequately explained the event, the magistrates of King's County met to condemn the murder and plan a course of action. At proceedings organised by the county's lord lieutenant, Lord Oxmantown, the forty-six assembled magistrates passed resolutions condemning the murder, offering large financial inducements to the public for their cooperation in identifying and convicting those responsible, and reproving Lord Mulgrave's Irish government for encouraging disaffection by its lax administration of law and order. Oxmantown asserted that the world knew none as morally depraved as the Irish peasantry:

What can have caused this diabolical outrage? The answer is this – it is part of an extensive conspiracy or combination to effect that by assassination which they

---

[1] *The Mail*, 3 January 1839; *The Pilot*, 4 January 1839; Russell to Normanby [formerly Mulgrave], 14 January 1839, MC, Mulgrave MSS, M/926.

78

dare not attempt by open rebellion. . . . I ask you, gentlemen, to look for a parallel for this amongst the nations of the world? I do not mean to confine your researches to the civilised world; take any quarter of the globe. Does the Turk set at nought his solemn pledge upon the Koran? Does he foster his cowardly assassin? In the Hindoo, do we find a similar picture of depravity? Why, there is not a greater contrast between virtue and vice, then between the poor unchristian Hindoo, and the depraved Irish peasant of the present day. What then can have caused this diabolical outrage? – What could have prompted the cowardly assassin to assail a man who had never given just cause of offence to anyone? . . . Unfortunately confiding in the attachment of a people, now the most treacherous, and in the virtue of a peasantry calling themselves Christian, but disgracing the name by crimes which even the heathen would not commit.[2]

While Oxmantown certainly framed his speech in polemical language, aware of the wider audience who would read his statement, his speech from the chair of the King's County courthouse nevertheless relied on characterisations of the Irish peasant rather common in nineteenth-century British discourse. To many, Ireland constituted the most debased, uncivilised population the world had ever known, and needed the positive redemptive influence of British culture, British religion, and British law and order. Unworthy of the title of Christian, more treacherous than that of the 'heathen', Irish society was falling into 'a state of the most fearful demoralisation' as the peasantry had become transformed from a kind, warm-hearted, faithful, and deferential people to one that ranked below any in the known world. Somewhere, according to Oxmantown, the political union had gone astray and Norbury's murder was a clarion call to correct course.

In spite of Oxmantown's criticism of the morality of the Irish peasantry, he reiterated one fact throughout his speech: that Norbury's murder was part of a wider 'combination' by the Irish peasantry for some particular objective. Oxmantown lamented that, regardless of how many actively took part in wanton outrages, 'common reason' indicated that 'no set of persons, however numerous, could carry on such a system . . . were it not that they were supported by the mass of the peasantry, and *by them screened from justice*'.[3] Most alarming to landlords, politicians, and magistrates therefore was not that murders or assassinations occurred in Irish society, but rather that they happened for particular purposes akin to rebellion and with the sanction of the wider community.

Norbury's murder was sensational, and it elicited debate within Parliament along with plenty of discussion in the press. In many ways, the murder of a member of the landlord and gentry class was atypical,

---

[2] 'Meeting of the Magistrates of the King's County', FJ, 12 January 1839.
[3] Ibid., emphasis added.

which explains the volume of discourse his death generated. Nevertheless, Norbury's murder was not part of some larger regional disturbance or campaign of agrarian unrest of the type witnessed often in Ireland, such as the Rockite campaign of 1821–4, the Rightboys protests of 1785–8, or the coordinated fighting among the rival Caravat and Shanavest factions that occurred off and on between 1802 and 1811. On the contrary, the murder occurred during a period of relative tranquillity in comparison to those former periods of profound unrest. In this respect, Norbury's murder, while extraordinary in terms of his social station, was one instance of everyday violence in the Irish countryside. However, if one is to put any stock in Lord Oxmantown's assertion that the murder was part of a greater combination that a wide section of Irish society implicitly sanctioned with their silence, what should one make of the so-called outrages that were a commonplace part of pre-Famine Irish society even in periods of relative calm?

This chapter focusses on interrogating the acts of 'everyday' agrarian violence that the British labelled outrages and explores the motives that spurred the actions of many Irish men and women. It argues that segments of the Irish poor used collective action such as burning homes, targeting crown witnesses, or stealing weapons as ways to resist the imposition of British sovereignty and to assert their own local conceptions of justice. These notions of justice often cut across religious, political, and social boundaries. As a result, the chapter demonstrates how the complexity of motives and actions challenge some historians' interpretations of violence during periods of profound unrest across the eighteenth and nineteenth centuries that have stressed solidarities of class and religion, or proto-nationalism. The chapter also argues that the British perceived Irish outrages as particularly dangerous because these crimes carried with them the imposition of a countervailing sovereignty that threatened Ireland's political stability within the Union. This fear of particular criminal activity justified the man-hours of meticulous record-keeping and constant correspondence between Dublin and London that this chapter uses as part of its evidentiary basis. In the eyes of the British state, outrages were not ordinary criminal activity but instead posed an existential threat to that state's legitimacy which warranted their constant surveillance and special attention.

While popular notions of justice often informed agrarian violence and shaped peasants' actions, this reaction among peasants was by no means universal or complete. On the contrary, the Whig government put forward their own version of justice by offering Ireland remedial legislation intended to address Irish grievances. The reformation of the administration of law and order, especially the creation of the centrally administered Irish Constabulary, was on one level an attempt to rectify a long held Irish objection of partiality.[4] On another level, however, it was the Whig government's endeavour to more fully integrate Ireland into its political union and extend its sovereignty over the Irish countryside. Whether the wider community would accede to British sovereignty or to an Irish-articulated sovereignty was contested on the ground, as people were forced to choose between cooperating with the constabulary, magistrates, and other government officials or remaining silent in solidarity with the actors who perpetrated agrarian violence. Using sworn testimony, local newspapers, and government correspondence, this chapter explores how Irish people negotiated these two competing notions of justice that operated on the ground in pre-Famine society.

### Reports of Outrage

How does one study pre-Famine agrarian violence? Most historians in the past have opted for one of two sources – the correspondence that flooded the chief secretary's office; or, after 1836, so-called Outrage Papers (OP), both housed at the National Archives of Ireland (NAI). Supplementing these sources, historians have relied on newspapers, parliamentary reports, and estate papers. However, this study relies on a different source – the succinct 'Reports of Outrage', made up of the daily correspondence between Dublin Castle and Whitehall outlining every act of outrage across the Irish countryside, which were prepared by the inspector general of the Irish Constabulary for the home secretary. Although these are terse reports, they allow us to see violence in Irish society in aggregate form, whereby we can explore the variety of outrages perpetrated across the country. This study focussed on 1838 because it was the only year from which all 365 reports survived. From these reports I created a database listing every outrage committed across Ireland, which included the location of each outrage, and any notes or plan of action that the constable included in the report. The database comprises over 5,400 unique entries of outrages for the calendar year of 1838. Historians studying Irish agrarian violence have largely overlooked this source base, possibly because of the short period it covers (1836–40), which does not correspond to any time of profound unrest. Furthermore, historians keen to gain insight from more discursive sources wisely passed over these laconic reports for the more verbose Outrage Papers, especially if they were interested in information from one county or barony.[5]

---

[4] Constabulary (Ireland) Act, 1836, 6 & 7 Will. IV, c.13.
[5] A good example of this is Michael Beames, 'Rural Conflict'. Additionally, the Reports of Outrage are unorganised and are scattered across a number of references at Kew. In short, they are unwieldy.

Nevertheless, the Reports of Outrage are a value source for this study because they provide detailed information about every outrage that occurred in Ireland during a period of relative tranquillity, thus offering a view into dynamics of pre-Famine Irish life that have hitherto been unexplored.

To acquire more detailed descriptions of agrarian violence, and to better understand the variety of responses pursued by Dublin Castle to combat Irish outrages, I supplemented the Reports of Outrage database with the Outrage Papers of a four-county sample, in which I read each filed report. This four-county sample of Armagh, Cork, Longford, and Sligo was chosen for its diversity in economic, religious, political, and environmental make-up. Table 2.1 shows the variety in population, geographic area, population density, and religious demographics of the four-county sample.

County Armagh, with a population of 232,393 according to the Irish census of 1841, was comprised of roughly equal portions of Protestant (29 per cent Anglican, 20 per cent Presbyterian) and Roman Catholics (51 per cent). In comparison, both counties Longford and Sligo had overwhelmingly large Catholic populations, 91 and 89 per cent respectively; whereas, County Cork had a sizeable Anglican population which totalled over 55,000, but only accounted for 7 per cent of the county's overall population, which included nearly 800,000 Catholics. Population size also varied considerably between these counties, with Co. Cork having Ireland's largest population at over 850,000, while Co. Longford's population was roughly a seventh of Cork's, at just under 115,500.

Additionally, each county had different economic characteristics which affected the experience of rural life in these counties. David W. Miller has

Table 2.1  *Geographic and demographic information for four-county sample*

|  | Geographic area (km$^2$) | Population | Population per km$^2$ | Roman Catholics (%) | Protestants (%) |
|---|---|---|---|---|---|
| Armagh | 1,354 | 232,393 | 185 | 51 | 49 |
| Cork | 7,457 | 854,116 | 115 | 93 | 7 |
| Longford | 1,091 | 115,491 | 106 | 91 | 9 |
| Sligo | 1,836 | 180,885 | 98 | 89 | 11 |

Source: W. E. Vaughan and A. J. Fitzpatrick, eds., *Irish Historical Statistics: Population, 1831–1971* (Dublin: Royal Irish Academy, 1978) and data collected by David W. Miller from 'First Report of the Commissioners of Public Instruction, Ireland', P. P. (1835, vol. 33, nos. 45–7)

noted the importance linen manufacturing played in Co. Armagh's economy, along with its effect on subsequent landholding patterns and the county's history of sectarian violence.[6] County Cork, on the other hand, exported large quantities of butter, roughly £1,000,000 worth in 1835, which required vast quantities of grazing rather than tillage farms. As a result, James Donnelly has argued that roughly 45 per cent of all cultivated land in the early 1840s was dedicated to grassland and meadows for dairy cattle.[7] In County Sligo the small number of large farmers grazed cattle to fatten for Dublin markets, while the majority of the farms in the county were small and focussed on the tillage of potatoes and oats.[8] Unlike the diverse landscape of Sligo that included mountains, ample coastlands, and a number of rivers, the surveyor Samuel Lewis wrote of Co. Longford, 'The general outline of the county presents little to attract the eye or excite the imagination.' The economic output of the county chiefly consisted of small farmers producing potatoes and oats for market, along with large landholders grazing sheep, and the fattening of pigs for sale in Britain.[9] Thus, these four counties embodied a wide diversity of economic, religious, and social characteristics that reflected the diversity of Ireland as a whole.

If the Reports of Outrage were based on the daily correspondence between Dublin Castle and Whitehall, then the Outrage Papers were the raw data that informed this correspondence. After the reorganisation of the Irish Constabulary in 1836, the new Inspector General Col. James Shaw Kennedy introduced the standardised reporting form, form 38, which was called an Outrage Report (see Figure 2.1). The inspector general required constables reporting an outrage to fill out the form, which included a number of particular points of discrete information for government. The top left of the form required the constable to include the barony, parish, and townland where the outrage took place, along with the distance to the nearest police station and the last date or time at which the police had patrolled the area prior to the outrage's occurrence. On the upper right-hand corner of the form the constable indicated whether he thought money should be offered for private or public information, an action that often needed the approval of officials at Dublin Castle. The constable made his statement on the left-hand side of the form.

[6] Miller, 'The Armagh Troubles, 1784–95', 155–91.
[7] James S. Donnelly, *The Land and the People of Nineteenth-Century Cork: The Rural Economy and the Land Question* (London: Routledge & Kegan Paul, 1975), 40–1.
[8] Samuel Lewis, *A Topographical Dictionary of Ireland: Comprising the Several Counties, Cities, Boroughs, Corporate, Market, and Post Towns, Parishes, and Villages, with Historical and Statistical Descriptions*, vol. 2 (Baltimore, MD: Genealogical Pub. Co, n.d.),564–5.
[9] Ibid., 2:307–8.

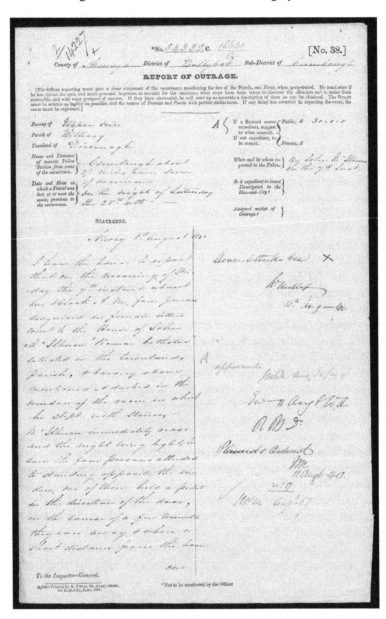

Figure 2.1  Outrage Report, form 38

Instructions at the bottom of the form demanded the officer 'give a clear statement of the occurrence, mentioning the day of the Month, and Hour, when perpetrated'; indicate whether he had visited the scene of the outrage and made personal enquiries, along with detailing 'what steps [had] been taken to discover the perpetrators and to make them amenable'; or providing the suspects' physical description if they had absconded. The report also demanded that the constable write 'as legibly as possible, and the names of Persons and Places with perfect distinctness'.[10] On the right-hand side of the form, officials at Dublin Castle would make notes about the report, and convey any plan for action or admonishments to the officers that had filed the form. Thus, the strength of the source lies in both the descriptive statements made by constables that often alluded to potential motives and the correspondence among government officials including members of the law offices, such as the attorney general, landlords and magistrates offering their analysis, as well as depositions that could run to several pages in length.

## Historians and Irish Agrarian Violence

Over the past four decades the historiography surrounding agrarian unrest has flourished. Generally, this scholarship has focussed on periods of profound unrest across the eighteenth and nineteenth centuries, producing three archetypical models to explain such unrest: (1) purely economic motives; (2) inter-class solidarity against capitalist modernisation being carried out by landlords and their agents; or (3) intra-class conflict within a given social strata, including among families.[11]

Writing in the 1973 collection of essays entitled *Secret Societies in Ireland,* Joseph Lee argued that outbreaks of agrarian violence can be understood as the result of economic factors. While acknowledging that agrarian violence was an endemic feature of pre-Famine Irish society, Lee argued that major outbreaks in violence 'can be traced directly to economic causes'. Tension between cottiers and landless labourers and the larger farmers from whom they rented their small plots of land for subsistence tillage produced economic grievances that led to violence. In this way, Lee suggested that agrarian violence acted as a gauge by which historians could measure the market orientation of various parts of

---

[10] 'Report of Outrage', 29 October 1838, NAI, OP, 1838/26/83.
[11] For a more thorough examination of the historiography of agrarian outrage, see the book's Introduction.

Ireland based on outbreaks of agrarian violence and the relative distinctions between different classes.[12]

Whereas Lee's model emphasised the conflict between farmers and cottiers, Michael Beames stressed a different class conflict – one between small landholders and landlords. Drawing on evidence from assassinations in County Tipperary between 1837 and 1847, Beames demonstrated that peasants targeted landlords and their agents more than any other group. By using newspaper articles (though, curiously, not Outrage Reports), Beames contended that the attempts of so-called 'improving landlords' to consolidate and rationalise their estates led to assassination attempts and other forms of peasant agitation. Identifying these improving landlords as '"oppressors of the poor"', the lower sections of society bound together 'to risk their lives "for the good of the people, and die in the cause"'.[13] Beames's emphasis on the predatory characteristics of the landlord class in Ireland and on conflict between landlord and tenant reinforced old nationalist interpretations that Lee and other historians attempted to critique and revise.

The third approach, posited by David Fitzpatrick in his 1981 essay 'Class, Family and Rural Unrest in Nineteenth-Century Ireland', posited that conflict existed between members of the same social class rather than between different classes. Fitzpatrick came to his conclusions by analysing the Outrage Reports of one parish, Cloone in Co. Leitrim, between 1835 and 1852, which led him to conclude that neither Lee's nor Beames's assertions of class conflict made sense of pre-Famine society. Instead, Fitzpatrick highlighted the apparent intra-familial conflict inherent in the ever-increasing subdivision of land, whereby a peasant's holdings operated as their lifeline. In this context, rival families, or rival groups within a family, would fight to defend 'their share in the inegalitarian distribution of landholdings', and 'many outrages were directed against rival claimants to coveted farms, houses or jobs, signifying competition within peer groups for benefits in short supply'.[14]

In recent years these models have been revised by other historians, in particular in the work of James Donnelly. In Donnelly's 2009 book on Captain Rock, he advanced a more nuanced argument on agrarian violence that stressed the relationship between national or regional fluctuations affecting which social classes participated in unrest. Donnelly

---

[12] Lee, 'The Ribbonmen', 27–8. Lee's article suffers from a conflation of terminology, in which he refers to Ribbonmen but by that term means Whiteboys. For a discussion on Ribbonism see Tom Garvin, 'Defenders, Ribbonmen and Others', 219–44.

[13] Beames, 'Rural Conflict', 281.

[14] Fitzpatrick, 'Class, Family and Rural Unrest', 41, 44. Of course, inter-familial conflict does not preclude other forms of violence described by other historians.

asserted that in periods of relative prosperity, those that participated in agrarian violence were restricted to the lowest strata of Ireland's population, whereas, during periods of economic distress more affluent actors joined with cottiers and labourers.[15] Additionally, Donnelly's scholarship has highlighted the importance of the millenarian tinge in the agrarian disturbances of the Rockites during the period 1821–4 as well as the interchange between the largely urban phenomenon of the Ribbon movement and the rural Rockite movement.[16] Michael Huggins has also been critical of the three predominant interpretations, and instead has not only highlighted the importance of the parochial solidarity of peasants acting collectively within inherited traditions, but also the fact that in doing so they were being influenced by the egalitarianism of the French Revolution.[17]

Most work by historians has focussed on periods of profound unrest in Ireland across the eighteenth and nineteenth centuries. Donnelly has defended this approach by arguing that 'waves of unrest accounted for by far the greater portion of the collective violence that took place in early nineteenth-century Ireland'.[18] This point is debatable, and even if one concedes that the majority of violence in pre-Famine Ireland was perpetrated during periods of profound unrest the argument also obscures the motives, character, and frequency of violence experienced by the population during 'normal' times – that is, during periods outside those dominated by well-organised regional or national movements.[19] Therefore, there is merit to exploring everyday violence because it gives historians a more accurate picture of how agrarian outrages shaped the experience of those living in pre-Famine society.[20]

[15] Donnelly, *Captain Rock*, 15.

[16] James S. Donnelly, 'Pastorini and Captain Rock: Millenarianism and Sectarianism in the Rockite Movement of 1821–4', in *Irish Peasants: Violence and Political Unrest 1780–1914*, ed. Clark and Donnelly, 102–36; Donnelly, *Captain Rock*, 100–4.

[17] Huggins, *Social Conflict*, 128.   [18] Donnelly, *Captain Rock*, 14.

[19] Huggins makes a similar point in his discussion of Donnelly's scholarship, offering his own study of Co. Roscommon as an alternative approach. Michael Huggins, 'Whiteboys and Ribbonmen: What's in a Name?', in *Crime, Violence and the Irish in the Nineteenth Century*, ed. Kyle Hughes and Donald M. MacRaild (Liverpool: Liverpool University Press, 2018), 32–3.

[20] Other studies worth mentioning in this same vein that have focussed on periods of normalcy or have explored agrarian violence more generally include, Blackstock, 'Tommy Downshire's Boys', 125–71; John Cunningham, 'Popular Protest and a "Moral Economy"', 26–48; Huggins, *Social Conflict*; Knott, 'Land, Kinship, and Identity', 93–108; Desmond McCabe, 'Social Order and the Ghost of Moral Economy in Pre-Famine Mayo', in *A Various County: Essays in Mayo History, 1500–1900*, ed. Raymond Gillespie and Gerard P. Moran (Westport: Foilseacháin Náisiúnta Teoranta, 1987), 91–112; Desmond Mooney, 'The Origins of Agrarian Violence in Meath, 1790–1828', *Records of Meath Archaeological and Historical Society* 8, no. 1 (1987): 45–67; A. C. Murray, 'Agrarian Violence and Nationalism in Nineteenth-Century Ireland:

### Irish Agrarian Violence and the Production of Knowledge

The passage of the 1836 Irish Constabulary Act brought with it
a revolution in the production of state knowledge regarding Irish crime
and outrage. The creation of standardised reporting of what constituted
an 'outrage' was a process akin to those James Scott has described as the
'rationalizing and standardizing of what was a social hieroglyph into
a legible and administratively more convenient format ... [which] greatly
enhanced state capacity'.[21] It provided the government with the tools to
'know' the Irish countryside in both qualitative and quantitative ways that
allowed for statistical representation, which previously had been limited
by the uneven (and unreliable) knowledge networks build on landlords
and resident magistrates writing to Dublin Castle. Soon after the act
received royal assent, the newly deputised inspector general of the Irish
Constabulary began sending daily summations of all the outrages across
Ireland to the Home Secretary, Lord John Russell. Russell requested
copies of the police reports after the Whigs lost their tithe bill in
August 1836, as he was concerned about the 'consequences on the state
of the Country' after the government's inability to pass such an important
legislative reform.[22] The inspector general took the Reports of Outrage
that constables sent to Dublin Castle and compiled them on a daily
basis.[23] Rather than decide at Dublin Castle whether a criminal act was
an outrage or not, the inspector general entrusted his constables to make
this determination locally, a decision which later proved politically
controversial.[24]

Each report of outrage began with a cover sheet listing every outrage
committed in each county of Ireland for that given day, as shown in
Figure 2.2. The constable organised his report alphabetically by county
and listed the type of outrage, such as 'threatening notice' or 'firing into
a dwelling', and the number of particular outrages committed in each
county. Thus, in Figure 2.2, the constable listed sixteen separate outrages
in twelve different counties including two threatening notices in Co.

---

The Myth of Ribbonism', *Irish Economic and Social History* 13 (1986): 56–73;
David Ryan, '"Ribbonism" and Agrarian Violence in County Galway, 1819–1820',
*Journal of the Galway Archaeological and Historical Society* 52 (2000): 120–34.

[21] James C. Scott, *Seeing Like a State: How Certain Schemes to Improve the Human Condition Have Failed* (New Haven, CT: Yale University Press, 1999), 3.

[22] Russell to Mulgrave, 5 August 1836, MC, Mulgrave MSS, M/835.

[23] Chief Inspector Circular, 23 December 1837 TNA, HO 184/111/3.

[24] Because the 1836 Act empowered the lord lieutenant to appoint constables, opponents of Lord Mulgrave and his political project in Ireland argued that constables were instructed to keep figures of Irish outrages artificially low in order to bolster the Whig government's claims of increasing Irish tranquillity. More on this in Chapter 3. For one example (among many), 'Lord Mulgrave and His Special Reporters', DUM 11 (63) 1838: 257.

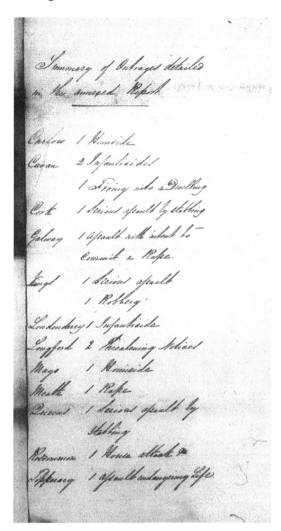

Figure 2.2  Report of outrages, 1838, p. 1

Longford, one firing into a dwelling in Co. Cavan, and a homicide in Co.
Mayo. On the following page, Figure 2.3, the constable noted the date
that the outrage was reported to the constabulary office in Dublin Castle,
in this case on 13 September 1838. Figure 2.3 also shows how the
inspector general described an outrage: 'On the morning of the 11 inst.
Henry Pollard was attacked at Tankardstown, parish of Tullow, by 3 Men

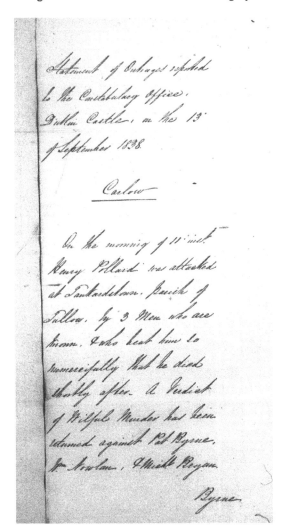

Figure 2.3  Report of outrages, 1838, p. 2

who are known, & who beat him so unmercifully that he died shortly
after.' The report goes on to note that a jury indicted three men, Pat
Byrne, William Nowlan, and Michael Bryan for 'willful murder' and that
Byrne was in police custody.[25] Reports were usually between six and ten

---

[25] 'Reports of Outrage', 13 September 1838 TNA, HO 100/255/78–9.

sheets of paper in length, concluded with the signature of the inspector general or one of his deputies, and were addressed to Russell at the Home Office in London.

Russell used these daily reports, along with his correspondence with the lord lieutenant, to inform himself – both in his capacity as home secretary and as leader of the House of Commons – about the state of Ireland and the direction of subsequent government policy. For example, after receiving the daily Reports of Outrage in September 1836, along with correspondence from Mulgrave concerning affairs in Donegal, Russell seemed optimistic about the state of the country, as 'the reports of outrages give at present scarcely any existence of disturbance & none of homicide arising from tithes'.[26] By October 1837, however, Russell had written Mulgrave, deeply concerned about the increase in outrages that carried with them a 'darker character', which suggested to him that 'experience has shown that individual cases of outrage have in Ireland an unfortunate tendency to produce habitual & sometimes general disorder'.[27] These reports, therefore, proved a vital asset in deciphering the state of affairs across the Irish countryside.

### The Significance of Reports of Outrage

Reports of Outrages are a valuable source of information concerning violence in pre-Famine Irish society. In particular, by documenting every single incident of outrage across an entire calendar year when there was no organised campaign of violence, the reports offer insight into levels of violence and its lived experience before the Famine. The calendar year of 1838 produced over 5,400 outrages that the inspector general reported to Russell. Among the major developments implemented by the inspector general after the passage of the Constabulary Act was the introduction of four major categories of outrages: 'Offences against the Person, 'Offences against Property', 'Offences Affecting the Public Peace', and 'Other Offences'. These four broad categories were then subdivided into a number of different individual criminal acts that the inspector general required all constables to specify when reporting an outrage, which is displayed in Table 2.2. Practically, this meant that constables on the spot were obliged to assign some sort of motive to every incident that they reported back to Dublin Castle.

---

[26] Russell to Mulgrave, 19 September 1836, MC, Mulgrave MSS, M/841.
[27] Russell to Mulgrave, 17 November 1837, Russell to Mulgrave, MC, Mulgrave MSS M/885.

Table 2.2 *Outrages by aggregate designation*

| Offences against the Person | Offences against Property | Offences Affecting the Public Peace | Other Offences |
|---|---|---|---|
| Homicide | Incendiary fire | Demand or robbery of arms | Combination |
| Firing at the person | Burglary | Appearing armed | Coining |
| Conspiracy to murder | Highway robbery | Faction fights | Prison breaking |
| Assault with intent to murder | Robbery | Riots | Forgery |
| Administering poison | Taking and holding forcible possession | Administering unlawful oaths | Concealing birth |
| Rape | Cattle stealing | Threatening notice or letter | Obstructing of clergymen |
| Assault with intent to rape | Illegal shearing of sheep | Pound breach | |
| Infanticide | Killing, cutting, or maiming cattle | Turning up land | |
| Abduction | Plundering wrecks | Attacking houses | |
| Assault on police | Sacrilege | Rescuing prisoners | |
| Aggravated assault | Larcenies | Resistance to legal process | |
| Assault endangering life | | Illegal meetings or processions | |
| Assault with intent to rob | | Leveling | |
| Assault on a bailiff or process server | | Injury of property | |
| Cutting or maiming the person | | Firing into dwelling | |
| Desertion of child | | Injury to places of worship | |
| Serious assault on stipendiary magistrate | | Rescue of property under seizure | |
| Assault | | Display of party emblems | |
| Assault on excise officer | | Playing party tunes | |

Source: Chief Inspector Circulars (TNA, HO 184/111/13)

The Irish Constabulary reported a total of 5,417 outrages across Ireland in 1838. Figure 2.4 is a graph displaying how the constabulary classified these outrages using the four broad designations. It shows that the three major categories accounted for roughly equal portions of outrages. 'Offences Affecting the Public Peace' occurred with the greatest frequency in 1838 with 34 per cent of total outrages (1,848), followed by 'Offences against

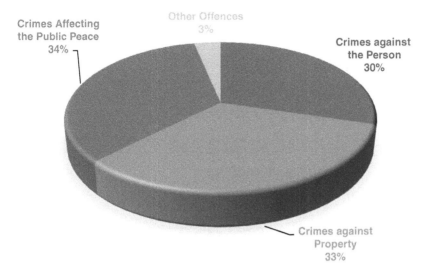

Figure 2.4 Outrages categorised by designation, 1838

Property' at 33 per cent (1786), 'Offences against the Person' at 30 per cent (1,606), and 'Other Offences' at 3 per cent (177).

Figure 2.5 displays the two types of outrage in each category that occurred with the greatest frequency in 1838. Aggravated assaults occurred most frequently of all outrages in 1838, occurring 661 times, followed by 442 incidents of incendiary fire, and 423 threatening notices reported during the year.

Finally, Figure 2.6 shows the monthly frequency of outrages committed by the Irish population. This chart shows that, excluding the month of February, outrages occurred at a fairly steady rate throughout the year, ranging between 355 as a lower limit in the month of June and 522 as the higher limit in May, where February was an anomaly due to a change in reporting practices.[28] Some of the same types of crimes –such as larcenies, common assaults, injury to property, riots, and cattle stealing – were included in both the 'General Consolidated Return' and the 'Reports of Outrage' and oftentimes in far greater numbers. For example, in

---

[28] The constabulary included 107 larcenies and 81 assaults in its Outrage Reports for February, which was an anomaly in reporting as these two types of outrages never occurred more than ten times in any other month during 1838. This suggests that the constables miscategorised these crimes as outrages rather than including them in the 'General Consolidated Return' of ordinary criminal activity. The government's opponents charged that this changing reporting practice demonstrated the government's active role in trying to manipulate the numbers. See 'Lord Mulgrave's Defence', DUM 11, no. 62: 157.

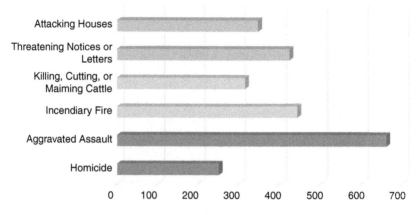

Figure 2.5  Highest frequency of outrages by designation, 1838

August 1838 the 'General Consolidated Return' included 3,664 common
assaults, 827 larcenies, and 100 different incidents of injury to property. In
comparison, the Outrage Reports for August 1838 included no common
assaults, three larcenies, and thirty-two incidents of injury to property. Thus,
the 5,400 outrages take on much greater significance because they indicate,
at least in the eyes of the Irish government, that the particular crimes the
constables reported as outrages had some larger purpose or signified something particularly dangerous to social order or the state's stability.

How representative was 1838 in terms of the violence perpetrated across
the Irish countryside? This question is somewhat complicated by the data
available to the historian and the evolving practices of record-keeping
engaged in by officials. In June 1839, the Undersecretary Thomas
Drummond argued before a House of Lords Select Committee that outrages were diminishing in Ireland and that both committals and convictions
were increasing, and that this indicated the efficacy of the constabulary and
an increasing willingness to cooperate with the courts. His testimony, discussed in detail in Chapter 5, formed the basis for the Whig government's
claims about the success of their 'justice to Ireland' policy. Drummond
highlighted how accounting practices in use before the inauguration of the
new system 'were not made out with that accuracy which would admit of
a safe deduction being made for a comparison of past and present times'.[29]

---

[29] 'Report from the Select Committee of the House of Lords, appointed to enquire into the
state of Ireland in respect of crime, and to report thereon to the House; with the minutes
of evidence taken before the committee, and an appendix and index' [hereafter 'Select
Committee on State of Ireland'], P. P. (1839, vol. 11, no. 486, 1077).

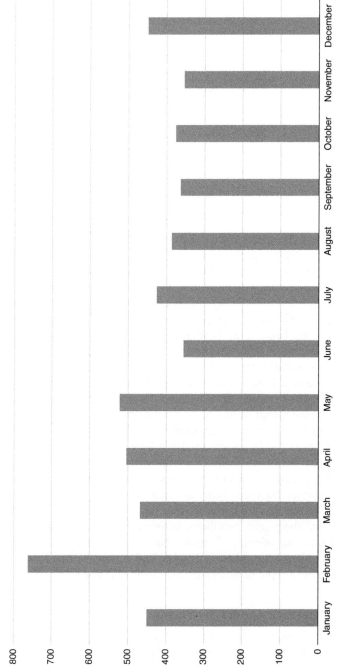

Figure 2.6 Frequency of outrages by month, 1838

Table 2.3 *Return of outrages reported to the constabulary office, July 1836 – 30 April 1839*

| Reporting Period | Outrages |
| --- | --- |
| 1 July 1836 – 31 Dec. 1836 | 4,257 |
| 1 Jan. – 30 June 1837 | 4,005 |
| 1 July. – 31 Dec. 1837 | 3,473 |
| 1 Jan. – 30 June 1838 | 2,622 |
| 1 July. – 31 Dec. 1838 | 2,356 |
| 1 Jan. – 30 April 1839 | 1,811 |

Source: 'Select Committee on State of Ireland', p. 1082

In addition to the questionable reliability of reporting prior to 1836, many of the changes discussed above about which crimes to include and how to categorise them further complicate meaningful comparison. Drummond offered the committee documents that communicated the total number of outrages reported to the constabulary office for six-month cycles, beginning with 1 July 1836 and ending with 30 April 1839, and these figures are presented in Table 2.3. The table suggests that outrages were on a downward trajectory in the period, though the meaning of these statistics was open to varied interpretation based on one's political perspective.

I have organised the discussion that follows by examining each category of outrages in 1838 as a way to understand the variety of motives that informed agrarian violence in Ireland, and to demonstrate that much of the collective action pursued by Ireland's population was based on popularly conceived notions of justice. The discussion that follows also suggests that many 'outrages' were probably motivated by nothing more than local feuds, banal acts of revenge, or greed. However, the Reports of Outrage demonstrate that the British government consciously decided to label many of these events as outrages because of the prejudice that informed their opinion of the Irish population, their past rebellious activity, and their politically aspirant Roman Catholic identity. I argue that it is therefore unsurprising that everyday violence embodied a complex, and at times contradictory, character that defies simple dichotomies and neatly packaged theoretical models.

### Offences against the Person

'Offences against the Person' encompassed a wide variety of outrages and included some of the more mundane acts of violence, or at least events that most likely did not affect the public peace in any way. On the one hand, homicides, firing at the person, conspiracy to murder, assaults on police, and assaults on bailiff or process servers were included within this designation; these were all activities that, depending on the circumstances, could easily be understood in a larger context of economic, religious, or political motives. On the other hand, the category also included assaults (a very broadly defined category in itself), rape, abduction, and infanticide. It is difficult to understand why some of these events were included in the Outrage Reports, and many seem to conform to Fitzpatrick's model of inter-familial violence.

One compelling reason why crimes like infanticide and rape may have been included within the Reports of Outrage was the way these crimes transgressed contemporary sexual ethics, and therefore, required particular attention so that they could be rooted out of Irish society.[30] If convicted of infanticide a woman could face capital punishment, which testifies to the seriousness of the crime in Irish society, although James Kelly and Elaine Farrell have demonstrated that Irish courts were generally sympathetic to Irish women, often identifying that the women were vulnerable and had been seduced (and were therefore less culpable), or had been motivated by economic despair, and therefore had had no alternative.[31]

Information garnered on infanticide from the Reports of Outrage and Outrage Papers seems to confirm that many cases were unresolved as the perpetrator had not been identified, or ended in the suspect's being jailed without any capital conviction. Most often, little if anything was known about the infant that could have pointed towards a perpetrator. On the Shankill Road in Belfast, an infant was found dead in late January 1838. At the inquest the doctor concluded that the baby had died from exposure but said 'it had been born alive', thus confirming the baby was murdered rather than stillborn.[32] No information, however, was known about the perpetrator. Similarly, in Templemore, Co. Tipperary, a baby was found dead, and at the inquest a verdict was returned that 'persons unknown' had murdered the infant.[33] Many similar cases occurred throughout 1838

---

[30] James Kelly, 'Infanticide in Eighteenth-Century Ireland', *Irish Economic and Social History* 19 (January 1992): 5.

[31] James Kelly has linked the rise of infanticide cases to the closure of foundling hospitals in the early nineteenth century. See, James Kelly, '"An Unnatural Crime": Infanticide in Early Nineteenth-Century Ireland', *rish Economic and Social History* 46, no. 1 (1 December 2019): 66–110; Elaine Farrell, '"Infanticide of the Ordinary Character": An Overview of the Crime in Ireland, 1850–1900', *Irish Economic and Social History* 39 (2012): 69–70. See also Elaine Farrell, *'A Most Diabolical Deed': Infanticide and Irish Society, 1850–1900* (Manchester: Manchester University Press, 2015), ch. 1.

[32] 'Report of Outrage', 1 February 1838, TNA, HO 100/253/175.

[33] Ibid., 9 February 1838 TNA, HO 100/253/197.

in which little to nothing was known about the dead infant, and where the constabulary made little further inquiry into finding those responsible. In cases where the mother was known, she was jailed (unless she had absconded), but it is unclear whether the crown intended to charge many of these women for capital offences.[34] Only one case I found mentioned a capital charge. In the city of Cork, Mary Anne Lane delivered a baby in her home in mid-August. According to the constable, immediately after the child's birth, Mary Anne and her mother Joanna left the house with the baby but returned without the infant, claiming they had 'dropped the child'. The constable made inquiries into where the baby had been left, but on returning without finding it he arrested both women for the 'capital charge', informing Dublin Castle they would be tried at the next assizes.[35] No newspaper carried the story or mentioned the case when reporting Cork's following assizes. The few newspaper accounts that do mention cases of infanticide tried at assizes highlighted the accused's 'handsome and interesting' demeanour, the accused's relative poverty, or noted that the accused had been acquitted of murder, with the court opting for the significantly lighter sentence of wilful concealment.[36]

Cases of rape and abduction, though likely not originating in matters that could be read as political, could be imbued with significant meaning in representations of Irish brutality. Kiera Lindsey has demonstrated how British newspapers reported on the 'sexual spectacle of these vulnerable and often violated women to trigger anxieties about the nature of civilisation in Ireland ... preoccupied with drawing unfavourable contrasts between Irish and British masculinity'.[37] Lindsey traces the number of British newspapers publishing accounts of abductions, which in the decade 1800–9 stands at '2' but by the 1830s totals '401', and highlights how newspapers employed 'narrative conventions' that amplified the 'shocking brutality of Irishmen', noting that the men who rescued abducted women were often 'aligned with the imperial state.'[38]

Cases of rape, although brutal, rarely elicited much attention from constables or Dublin Castle. Most were reported as crimes of passion without the inclusion of information as to how the assailant knew the

---

[34] Ibid., 28 March 1838, TNA, HO. 100/253/152; 20 January 1838, TNA, HO 100/253/433; 10 August 1838, NAI, OP, 1838/6/164.

[35] 22 August 1838, NAI, OP 1838/6/162.

[36] FJ, 1 April 1839; BNL, 6 March 1840; FJ, 28 July 1841. For more on juries opting for lighter sentences, see Farrell, '"Infanticide of the Ordinary Character"',70.

[37] Kiera Lindsey, '"The Absolute Distress of Females": Irish Abductions and the British Newspapers, 1800 to 1850', *The Journal of Imperial and Commonwealth History* 42, no. 4 (2014): 626–7.

[38] Lindsey, '"The Absolute Distress of Females"', 636. Parliamentarians also highlighted these narratives, for example in the passage of the 1833 Coercion Acts.

victim or whether the rape was a crime of opportunity or premeditation. Not surprisingly, constables often questioned the veracity of the changes, depending on the character of the victim, and logged the crime as 'alleged rape'. In Sligo, Bridget Handly reported that Patrick Molany raped her in February 1838, but the constable who took her testimony believed the case to be 'altogether doubtful', and the case went no further.[39] In Cork city, a case involving a publican's maid was also considered questionable until the constable examined the victim, Mary Brien, and concluded that 'she tells her story well [and] appears young and innocent and has been a very good character'.[40] In spite of the rather lax concern for cases of rape, the Whig government brought cases of rape to trial more frequently than their predecessors had done, and demanded that credible cases should be prosecuted. Testifying before the House of Lords committee concerning Irish outrage in 1839, Edward Hickman, the crown solicitor for Connacht, stated that under the Tory Attorney General William Saurin, 'we did not order Rapes to be prosecuted unless they were attended with very aggravated Circumstance', whereas since Mulgrave's Irish government had come into power, 'Where the Woman swears to her Person being violated contrary to her Wish ... we generally prosecute'.[41] Rapes were personal, brutal, and clearly a part of pre-Famine Irish life, but still fit oddly into the designation of outrages, and further fail to fit into any overarching narrative regarding motive or purpose.

Abductions, however, more clearly involved larger issues around marriage, land ownership, and wealth that certainly fit David Fitzpatrick's theory that agrarian violence primarily existing amongst intra-class factions in pre-Famine Ireland. While rapes were occasionally reported as cases that involved two lovers caught in the act of sexual intercourse against the wishes of their family, and therefore (probably at the behest of the woman's father) prosecuted as a rape to protect the virtue of the woman,[42] abductions often revolved around one family's attempt to force a marriage either against the wishes of another family or against the wishes of the father. Men targeted women that stood to inherit land or money. Some reports tended to make this process sound relatively benign in that a group of men, some armed, would visit a home where the woman lived and carry her off, occasionally meting out violence to the other inhabitants of the home. Retreating to another location, say a house of remote area, they would then forcibly marry her to one of the men in the group.[43] Maria Luddy, however, has demonstrated how violent abductions such

---

[39] 19 February 1838 NAI, OP 1838/26/30.     [40] 25 October 1838, NAI, OP 1838/6/202.
[41] 'Select Committee on State of Ireland', 650.
[42] For example, see 7 January 1839 NAI, OP 1838/26/231.
[43] 19 February 1838, NAI, OP 1838/26/32; 12 October 1838, OP 1838/26/177.

could be; the woman was often subjected to repeated sexual violence, as well as the long-term psychological trauma of the event.[44]

Prearranged 'sham' or consensual abductions were common enough throughout Ireland to warrant notice by the Scottish traveller Henry Inglis while observing the assizes at Ennis, Co. Clare.[45] Although details from Reports of Outrage are sparse, some include titbits of information that implicitly confirm the occurrence of prearranged abductions, such as notes remarking that an abduction had been carried out 'but no violence' had been done to the victim, that the victim had refused to prosecute, or simply that the party had carried the girl or woman away without any indication of a struggle.[46] Michael Durey has suggested that this practice occurred in the late eighteenth century as a way of premarital negotiation – a way of forcing an unwilling father to allow a marriage because after the abduction his daughter's reputation 'had been irrevocably ruined'.[47] Inglis also witnessed a case of abduction – 'originating, as indeed they always do, in love of money'– that proved detrimental to the peace of the surrounding area; as he noted, 'many subsequent fights invariably result from these outrages'.[48]

Reports of Outrage confirm Inglis's observation about genuine cases originating in feuds about the suitability of marriages or the desire to inherit money. For example, in February, an armed party visited the home of the Widow O'Shaughnessy in Garrane, Co. Limerick, to carry off Miss Mary-Anne Burke. According to the constable, five of the offenders were known to Burke and Widow O'Shaughnessy (two of them were arrested) and had attempted to carry Burke off on account of 'her fortune, which is a large one'.[49] A group of twenty men outside Easky, Co. Sligo visited the home of Thomas Burns in late February. Having apparently refused to allow his daughter to marry Tobias Burke, the party had returned to forcibly take her, while also violently assaulting Burns and his wife. The constable reporting the outrage noted that Burke had been arrested, and three others from his raiding party were known to the police, who issued warrants for their arrest.[50]

---

[44] Maria Luddy, 'Abductions in Nineteenth-Century Ireland', *New Hibernia Review/Iris Éireannach Nua* 17, no. 2 (2013): 30–3.

[45] Henry D. Inglis, *A Journey Throughout Ireland, During the Spring … of 1834* (London: Whittaker & C., 1834), 118, 289–90. Inglis also noted cases of sham rape charges meant to force marriages between unwilling parties.

[46] Report of Outrage, 15 October 1838 TNA, HO 100/256/83; ibid., 16 February 1838 TNA, HO 100/253/266; ibid., 15 February 1838 TNA, HO 100/253/261. Also, see 'Select Committee on State of Ireland', 1044.

[47] Michael Durey, 'Abduction and Rape in Ireland in the Year of the 1798 Rebellion', *Eighteenth-Century Ireland* 21 (2006): 33–4.

[48] Inglis, *A Journey Throughout Ireland, During the Spring … of 1834*, 190.

[49] Report of Outrage, 21 February 1838 TNA, HO 100/253/230.

[50] Ibid., 22 February 1838 TNA, HO 100/253/237; 25 February 1838, NAI, OP 1838/ 26/32.

While cases of rape, abduction, and infanticide were serious enough to include in the Reports of Outrage, they do not appear to offer much insight into how particular Irish criminal activity was deemed an 'outrage' versus ordinary crime. While abductions could be motivated by rivalry between families concerning land or the inheritance of fortunes, existing records do not reveal much about these motives other than a passing sentence or phrase that allows us to infer a meaning. The rapes that women faced in pre-Famine Ireland, along with the desperation that led some to commit infanticide, appear to arise from very personal circumstances, and the only argument in favour of including them in the Reports of Outrage is the seriousness of the punishment they incurred, and potentially a prejudice that treated Irish rape and infanticide as somehow different from rape and infanticide in England.

Whereas rapes, infanticides, and abductions were rather rare occurrences included in the Crimes Against the Person Designation, various types of assaults and homicides comprised the bulk of outrages in this category. They elicited more attention from the constables, newspapers, and politicians reporting and observing Irish affairs because of the motivations attributed to them. Before exploring the meaning and motives behind many of these crimes it is worth pausing to acknowledge that many of the assaults and murders that were perpetrated seem, again, to be attributable to the petty commonplace violence of any society – drunken fights after a fair, robberies gone wrong, simple quarrels. For instance, in March 1838, a domestic dispute arose between Mary Kilmartin and her husband Michael in the parish of Ahamlish, Co. Sligo. Though the constable did not note the cause of the quarrel, it was significant enough to warrant intervention from Mary's sister Anne Feeny, along with other people in the household. As Anne stepped in to defend her sister from Michael's assaults, he retaliated and hit Anne 'with a severe blow on the Head with a Spade'.[51] The constable noted that Michael Kilmartin was 'proving difficult to arrest' and he lodged the crime as a 'serious assault'.[52] No one at Dublin Castle made any further inquiry in the case, and Kilmartin's name does not appear in the newspaper records for trial at the quarter sessions or assizes, which indicates that either he was never tried, or the case was of so little importance that newspaper editors chose not to mention it in their reporting of Sligo's trials. Numerous such assaults took place throughout 1838 whereby the constable had little information to share with the inspector general in his Outrage Report, and often included the phrase 'no motive can be given',

---

[51] Report of Outrage, 3 March 1838, TNA, HO 100/253/17.
[52] 2 March 1838, NAI, OP 1838/26/37.

or simply stated when the assailants had been arrested. Such examples lead one to infer that although little significance could be drawn from this kind of event, constables would often include these assaults in their reports, as 'we are expected to report all these sorts of things'.[53]

Even some cases of murder roused little suspicion concerning rebellious motives or worry about the so-called 'state of the country'. On the Saturday before Christmas, Daniel Bourke, an engine-man employed at the mill of Mr Kidd near Keady, Co. Armagh, had been drinking whiskey with his friend and fellow labourer Hugh Liggatt. Liggatt and Bourke parted ways late in the evening, and Bourke was 'hearty' on their departure. Bourke decided to walk to the mill and attempted to steal some linen from the green when the watchman, Archibald Allen, spotted Bourke and demanded him to stop. Bourke began to run and Allen fired a shot that killed him. Allen was arrested, charged with murder, and the report was lodged as a homicide. At the Spring Assizes of 1839, Allen's trial was rather straightforward. He received character witnesses from the Rev. Samuel Malcolmson as well as his employer Mr Kidd, and although he was charged with murder, he was instead convicted of manslaughter and sentenced by Justice Burton 'to be imprisoned for one week from the commencement of the Assizes'.[54]

While these examples demonstrate the fluidity of what was included in the Reports of Outrage, which often included the commonplace, domestic and tawdry, 'Crimes against the Person' were by no means devoid of larger political, social, economic, or religious motives that reinforced local codes of conduct. Assaults of all variety were carried out both against individuals as well as those participating in state-sponsored employment, such as police, tithe servers, and estate agents. Irish people reserved special disdain for tithe servers. In the parish of Clongesh, Co. Longford, a group of six or seven men visited the home of Michael Lynch, a man employed in driving cattle distrained for tithe to the pound for the Rev. Dr Craw and a Roman Catholic farmer, Mr Gregory. Two of the party entered Lynch's home, beat him with sticks, and told him their visit was intended to 'teach him not to go out again for tithes'. The constable writing to Dublin Castle noted that this was the second time Lynch had been visited by a party of men, although the first time they had merely dragged him out of bed into the cold night as a way to intimidate him.[55] Accompanying this assault on Lynch was a threatening notice left for Mr Gregory, accusing him of not acting like

[53] 1 December 1838, NAI, OP 1838/26/206.
[54] 'County of Armagh Assizes', BNL, 26 March 1839; 25 December 1838, NAI, OP 1838/2/94; Reports of Outrage, 27 December 1838, TNA, HO 100/256/535.
[55] 19 January 1838, NAI, OP 1838/19/13.

a true Catholic for his role in collecting Rev. Craw's tithes, and warning him 'before the God that Created me if you dont decline your driving we will use you in the most murderous manner that ever a man was used or killed'. More interestingly, the notice alluded to the fact that their group had desired to act against Gregory in times past, but had delayed any action on account of 'the interference of People' who had testified to his work in electing a liberal candidate for Co. Longford. These people no longer defended Gregory's actions, however, and the anonymous letter writer reminded Gregory: 'I can command the County in a Moments warning.'[56] Similarly, in March in the townland of Coolagh, Co. Cork, ten or twelve men approached Michael Kearney, a man employed to drive cattle to the Pound of Newcastle, severely beat him, tore the legal documents authorising the cattle's seizure, and drove off the cattle.[57] Men mistaken for tithe servers were similarly harassed before being allowed to go on their way. Two men outside Glanworth, Co. Cork were attacked and stripped naked before the crowd of twenty or thirty men realised that their captives, Thomas Hinchon and John Fitzgerald, were prosecuting persons for unlicensed game dogs and not serving tithe notices, and 'allowed them to depart without any further injury'.[58]

Constables reported attacks on tithe servers from much larger crowds, totalling in the hundreds, that often included throwing stones and destroying all writs the tithe servers carried.[59] In County Cork, on 25 March a group of mounted soldiers and 16 infantrymen were called out to suppress a crowd of over 100, after 10 bailiffs were attacked for 'serving processes For Tithes', 4 of whom lay seriously injured in the county hospital. On approaching the general area where the men had been issuing legal processes, the magistrate noted 'all the Male inhabitants fled – the Houses shut up, horses tackled to ploughs in various directions without drivers', which indicated that the entire neighbourhood joined in the action against the men.[60] The payment of the tithe, which went to the maintenance of the established Protestant Church of Ireland, was the single most loathed institution among Irish peasants. By the 1830s, the Catholic middle class had joined in the opposition, in part because of a new political consciousness as a result of Catholic Emancipation, as well as changes to the composition of tithes that actually increased their financial burden.[61] The Reports of Outrage demonstrate

[56] Ibid.    [57] 3 March 1838, NAI, OP 1838/3/39.
[58] 13 March 1838, NAI, OP 1838/3/59.
[59] For a few examples among many, see Reports of Outrage, 3 January 1838 TNA, HO 100/253/334; 23 January 1838, HO 100/253/432–3; 25 January 1838, HO 100/253/445.
[60] 25 March 1838, NAI, OP 1838/3/62.
[61] O'Donoghue, 'Causes of the Opposition to Tithes', 26–8.

that a wide community supported opposition to tithes, aversion to those employed in their collection, and equally importantly a disregard for the legality of the claims embodied in the issued writs, which mobs often sought to destroy.

Land disputes also prompted violent assaults. In March, a group of seven men visited and 'cruelly beat' John and Patrick Rorke on their farm in the townland of Corbay, outside Edgeworthstown, Co. Longford.[62] Although the Rorkes held the farm 'by the mutual consent of the Landlord & the former occupant', the seven men warned them that if they continued to hold it, 'even worse treatment' awaited them. Both men remained silent about their attack, and the constable excused his late report as resulting from the Rorkes' hesitancy to report the outrage on account of their 'fear of a repetition of this wanton cruelty', while alluding to his certainty that the Rorkes knew their attackers but could not be induced to testify against them. At Dublin Castle, Undersecretary Thomas Drummond approved offering a reward of £40 for publicly sworn information, and 'whatever he [the constable] thinks necessary for private information'.[63] In the parish of Creggan, Co. Armagh, on 17 March, a group of men lured James McNulty out of his house and 'beat him violently + cut him', before making him kneel and swear that he would not offer more than £1 per acre for land; they then fired a shot into his house and rode off. On making his report, the constable noted that McNulty's father had recently died, leaving him with money to lease newly available land. If McNulty was willing to pay higher rents for the land, some in the neighbourhood feared it would set a precedent for other landholders to charge increased rents. The rationale of the assault seemed clear to the constable: 'This example may deter others on the property from offering an increased Rent for their farms while the present proprietor purposes increasing some a third and others less in proportion to the quality of their holdings.'[64]

If one beating did not deter farmers, sustained attacks by throngs of people and threatening notices could prove more persuasive. In County Louth, notices were posted at the Catholic chapels of Knockbridge and Kilkerly 'threatening death to any person [who] would pay more than six pounds an acre for their Land'. The constable reported that farmers generally let land for potato crops at £8 per acre and that farmers were disturbed by the coordination among 'their Labourers' to seek £6 per acre. A recent fair that coincided with a holy day served as a perfect

---

[62] Report of Outrage, 7 March 1838, TNA, HO 100/253/86.
[63] 17 March 1838, NAI, OP 1838/19/52.
[64] 11 March 1838, NAI, OP 1838/2/19; Report of Outrage, 14 March 1838, TNA, HO 100/253/63.

pretext for violence, as peasants pretended to be amusing themselves while actually 'Attacking the Farmers and compelling them to let out more of their land ... for Potatoes'.[65] Mobs had visited several Catholic farmers later in the month of April and attacked them, and the posting of notices at the Catholic chapels demonstrated that the regulation of economic practices by labourers proved stronger than any religious solidarity shared among Ireland's Catholic population.[66]

Most alarming to politicians, newspapers, magistrates, and Dublin Castle was the perpetration of murders or attempted assassinations. Although murders garnered the most attention, by no means were the majority of them politically, economically, or religiously motivated.[67] As already mentioned above, the Reports of Outrage demonstrate that a number of murders arose from personal disputes, domestic arguments, or passionate outbursts of violence, contrary to Beames's argument that the majority of murders related in some way to landlords or their agents.[68] County Cork in 1838 is illustrative: of the twenty-two murders recorded in the Outrage Papers in the county, no fewer than sixteen arose from domestic or personal disputes, two from fights between rival 'factions' (which often were simply rival extended families), and two more where no cause was given. Only two cases, both involving the seizure of cattle for rent, could be considered political or economic in motivation, but in neither case was the homicide premeditated.[69] Even if the majority of murders arose from personal or domestic disputes, government officials focussed their efforts, attention, and resources on the murders they deemed important, which most often meant murders that arose in consequence of larger political, economic, or religious aspirations. What might raise the ire of peasants motivating them to murder, and how did the wider community respond?

Premeditated attacks often resulted when someone with political, economic, or social power acted against the interests of those within the larger community – euphemistically referred to as 'becoming obnoxious'. For example, Rev. Edward Synge, an Anglican minister holding a sinecure in Co. Galway,[70] was nearly assassinated outside Corofin, Co. Clare in January 1831. Synge was returning with his servant from visiting a sick woman when assassins fired at him and his servant, Patrick

---

[65] Plunkett to Gossett, 26 March 1835, NAI, CSORP Box 43, 13/35/20.

[66] Ibid.; Report of Outrages, 25 April 1835, ibid., Box 43, 21/35/20.

[67] Richard McMahon, *Homicide in Pre-Famine and Famine Ireland* (Liverpool: Liverpool University Press, 2013), 32–3.

[68] Beames, 'Rural Conflict in Pre-Famine Ireland', 267.

[69] Outrage Papers, County Cork, NAI, OP 1838/6/1–252.

[70] 'First Report of the Commissioners of Public Instruction, Ireland', P. P. (1835, 45, 46, 47) XXXIII.1, 829, XXXIV.1.

Donellan.[71] Three bullets hit Synge, including one that allegedly struck a Bible in his breast pocket: 'One of the balls struck it, and only for this interruption his heart would have been perforated.'[72] Synge made it safely back to his home on his horse, but Donellan was shot in the attack, knocked from his horse, and left lying in the road while a crowd of tenants gathered around him but refused to help him back to Synge's home.[73] Donellan died of his wounds in February, and word of the attempted assassination quickly travelled back to Dublin Castle where the Undersecretary, Col. Gosset, directed the inspector of the Connacht Constabulary George Warburton to carry out a special investigation.[74] Although initially Warburton believed that one of the arrested men would give information, in late February the Resident Magistrate J. P. Vokes complained of how the neighbourhood boasted that: 'Millions could not get one of that Parish to become an informer'.[75] Government feared the worst in Clare after the failed assassination attempt on Synge, numerous nightly outrages, and the successful killing of magistrate William Blood a few weeks earlier. These events prompted the Lord Lieutenant, Lord Anglesey, to tour Clare exhorting the magistracy not to shrink from their duty, while examining the state of the peasantry and debating the necessity of proclaiming the district under the Insurrection Act.[76]

Synge had long been the target of disapprobation for his proselytising activities throughout the district. Income from his sinecure, along with income from the murdered Rev. Blood, had funded the Anglican parochial school in Corifin.[77] Synge was notorious throughout the area for his proselytising efforts where, 'he was in many respects a most charitable amenable Gentleman, but entire <u>concurrence</u> was necessary for everyone expecting kindness from him and of everyone refusing this <u>entire concurrence</u>, he instantly became the most heartless persecutor'.[78] In a debate in Parliament, Daniel O'Connell claimed that that the disturbances in Clare had been spurred by Synge's efforts to force Roman Catholic children in the parish to attend his school against the wishes of their parents, and, of

[71] 'State of the County of Clare', FJ, 19 January 1831.

[72] 'Attempt to Assassinate Edward Synge, Esq.', BNL, 22 February 1831.    [73] Ibid.

[74] Warburton to Col. Gosset, 19 February 1831, TNA, HO 100/236/221.

[75] J. P. Vokes to Col. Gosset, 24 February 1831, TNA, HO 100/236/266–7.

[76] For a selection of correspondence relating to County Clare and the Synge shooting, see Anglesey to Stanley, 22 February 1831, PRONI, Anglesey Papers, D619/31/T/9; 12 March 1831, D619/31/T/12; 6 April 1831, D619/31/T/28; 7 April 1831, D619/31/T/29; Melbourne to Anglesey, 30 March 1831 (D619/29/C/33).

[77] Samuel Lewis, *A Topographical Dictionary of Ireland: Comprising the Several Counties, Cities, Boroughs, Corporate, Market, and Post Towns, Parishes, and Villages, with Historical and Statistical Descriptions*, vol. 1 (Baltimore, MD: Genealogical Pub. Co., 1984), 444–5.

[78] James O'Shaughnessy to W. H. Bourne, Esq., 17 February 1831, TNA, HO 100/236/297–8 (emphasis in the original).

course, their priests. James Grattan, the Liberal Protestant Irish MP and son of the famous Irish patriot Henry Grattan, brought forward accounts of Synge dismissing labourers who did not send their children to his school: 'The outrage committed on him was caused by the great unpopularity of these proceedings.'[79] Though Synge did not exert the same influence as some Evangelical landlords who moved Catholic tenants off their land in favour of Protestants or exerted pressure to convert their tenantry, his behaviour did conform to the larger influence of the Evangelical proselytising of the 'second reformation' in the early nineteenth century.[80] The religious persecution of the Roman Catholic majority of the population around Corofin, including the restriction of their access to work and land, ultimately prompted members of the peasantry to act together to end Synge's behaviour while the remainder of the community kept silent.[81]

While proselytising angered Catholics, access to land was the single most important issue facing many who engaged in agrarian violence. Nothing was more sacrosanct in pre-Famine Ireland than land, and a number of unwritten rules governed peasants' behaviour in the event of rent hikes, land consolidations, and evictions. Although many of these rules were enforced through intimidatory tactics such as threatening notices, incendiarism, and levelling homes, breaking these rules also prompted assassinations, sometimes multiple attacks across a number of years. When peasants could not enact revenge on their landlord, they often attacked new inhabitants or landlords' agents.

The example of the townland of Ballinamuck in Co. Longford, one of the estates of the Evangelical Protestant landlord, Lord Lorton, demonstrates the ways in which peasants used collective action to resist landlord attempts to clear tenants off the land, consolidate their holdings, and introduce new 'industrious' (read: Protestant) tenants onto their estates. Over time, the Ballinamuck estate had been subdivided among the existing tenantry into smaller and smaller holdings. Either through genuine concern for the people, or at the behest of his land agent looking to make the estate profitable, Lorton offered the majority of his tenants a payout to emigrate to North America, which a number of tenants agreed to accept.[82] In

---

[79] Hansard, HC, 3rd ser., vol. 4, cols. 1320, 1323, 15 July 1831.

[80] David W. Miller, 'Soup and Providence: Varieties of Protestantism and the Great Famine', in *Ireland's Great Famine and Popular Politics*, eds. Enda Delany and Breandán MacSuibhne (New York: Routledge, 2017), 59–80; Whelan, *The Bible War in Ireland*, 152–91.

[81] 'Religious Persecution', FJ, 23 June 1831; Testimony of Mathew Barrington, Esq., 'Report from the Select Committee on the State of Ireland; with the Minutes of Evidence, Appendix and Index', P.P. (1831–2, 677) XVI.1, pp. 13–14.

[82] Courtenay to Drummond, 14 March 1836, NAI, OP 1836/19/24.

May 1835, John Brock was introduced to the estate. Brock was a Protestant from Co. Down who planned to grow and spin flax for Lorton. On 24 June, two men attacked Brock in the early evening and 'murdered [him] in a most brutal manner with stones', inflicting 'nineteen wounds on his head & back', before retreating away from Brock's body and towards the town of Ballinamuck.[83] Lord Lorton, along with the magistrates and landholders of the county, offered a £1,200 reward for information leading to the conviction of those responsible, while alluding to the silence of the community, which 'tend[ed] to prove a deep and organised system of intimidation'.[84] Although Mrs Brock pointed out the killer at trial in the spring of 1836, the jury acquitted him of the murder charge, allegedly influenced by threats of violence they had received.

Lord Lorton continued his efforts to consolidate his estates, and brought in another Protestant tenant to cultivate the land leased to John Brock. The assassinations continued. James Diamond arrived on the estate in early 1836 and within a month was beaten so badly that he remained permanently disabled. A Protestant named Cole, brought in March 1836 to graze cattle on one of Lorton's adjoining parcels, the townland of Shanmulla, was attacked within a month by an armed party and nearly killed while on his way to the fair to purchase stock. All of these attacks shared similar characteristics – that each new tenant had been brought in as a replacement for those who had been forcibly removed; that each new tenant was Protestant while the previous tenants had been Catholics; and that no one in the community was willing to speak to the authorities about the crime, despite large rewards being offered.[85]

In 1838, matters deteriorated further with a number of extremely brutal murders on Lorton's estate. On February 9, 1838 Arthur Cathcart, Lord Lorton's bailiff, was returning from visiting the Tory MP Mr Lefroy and riding 'in company with a man named Davis'. Not wishing to take the main highway because they had escaped assassination attempts there in the past, the pair chose to travel on rural roads. On approaching a boreen[86] they had decided it best to walk their horses over the rough terrain; when doing this, 'two men jumped out from behind the hedges, and fired at Cathcart, who immediately fell ... the wretched man was found weltering in his blood with a gun-shot wound through his back,

---

[83] 'Statement of Facts as to the Ballinamuck Estate, in the Co. of Longford, the Property of the Right Honorable Lord Viscount Lorton', O'Hara Papers, NLI, MS 36,406/4; Robert Singleton, Esq. to [unknown], 26 June 1835, NAI, CSORP Private Index 1836/51.

[84] Ibid.

[85] Ibid.; Chief Constable John Forde to Sub Inspector Simpson, 20 April 1836, NAI, OP 1836/19/24.

[86] Irish term for a narrow, rough, rural road.

the top of his skull blown off, and his own pistol thrust into his mouth'.[87] Hatred of Cathcart ran so deep in the community that when the authorities brought a cart to collect his body, it was found that persons unknown had rendered it unusable by removing the pole that connected the cart to the horses.[88] The inspector's report noted that the assailants had taken Cathcart's pistol; he suspected Davis, as well as a tenant farmer of Lord Lorton's named Peter Prunty.[89]

Prunty had gained a level of notoriety in liberal and O'Connellite circles a year earlier. In a hotly contested election in January 1837, Prunty and his family swore that Cathcart and William Morrison, another agent of Lord Lorton, had detained him and threatened that if he did not cast his vote in favour of the neighbouring landlord's candidate, the conservative Michael Fox, he would be evicted. Evidence suggests that Prunty came from a middle-class background since he possessed the right to vote; this may indicate that a broad section of local society participated in the outrages occurring in Longford in 1838. In the end, Prunty voted against the Tory candidate (who was also supported by Lorton), and subsequently fell out of grace with Lord Lorton while becoming a hero in liberal circles as an exemplar of an 'honest farmer' standing up to Tory intimidation tactics.[90]

Within nine months of Cathcart's murder, another bailiff of Lord Lorton's was murdered. In October 1838, '6 or 7 men Armed' went to the house of Margaret Crawford in Drumlish, Co. Longford. Lying asleep on a bed they found William Morrison, 'bailiff to Lord Lorton', intoxicated. 'They snapped a gun at him, and then beat out his brains, so that he expired in a few minutes.' Constables arrested five men on suspicion while the government waited for the results of an inquest from the Grand Jury.[91]

Morrison's death caused a noticeable stir in both Irish and British newspapers. The *Freeman's Journal* reprinted an excerpt from the Tory *Evening Mail* which noted how Morrison's assailants 'actually beat his brains out with the ends of their muskets, one of which was broke, as appeared by the piece of it found', the incident providing the *Evening Mail*'s readers with 'some idea of the ferocity of those savages, who were ... prepared for the destruction of their victim'.[92] The *Freeman's*

[87] 'Murder', FJ, February 16, 1838.
[88] Douglas to Drummond, 13 February 1838, NAI, CSORP 1841/C7067.
[89] Report of Outrage TNA, HO 100/253, 254.
[90] 'A LeFroy Tenant and the Freedom of Election! Or the Case of Peter Prunty', FJ, January 2, 1837; 'The Victory in Longford – Extent of Tory Intimidation', ibid.
[91] Report of Outrage, TNA, HO 100/256/113.
[92] 'Horrible Murder', FJ, 20 October 1838.

*Journal* responded by publishing a letter to the editor calling into question the character of the *Evening Mail's* correspondent, and challenging his assertion that Morrison 'had long been pointed out from the altar' by the county's Catholic clergy.[93] Commenting after these two murders to the 1839 House of Lords' committee on Irish crime and outrage, the stipendiary magistrate appointed to deal with the disturbed state of Longford, John Barnes, made his opinion known regarding the motives for the murders of both of Lord Lorton's bailiffs:

Q: As far as you have been able to form an Opinion, will you have the goodness to state what you conceive to have been Causes of those Murders?

A: From everything which has come to my Knowledge ... I am inclined to think, nay, I am certain, those murders have occurred in consequence of Persons having been turned out of their lands, and those Lands having been granted to Persons of an opposite Religion and Character.[94]

Barnes also noted that Cathcart had 'rendered himself obnoxious' to the tenants because he worked closely with Lorton's agent, Courtenay, to implement the new division of land. When Morrison was appointed after Cathcart's death, Barnes told the committee, 'it was notorious to Every person that he would be killed'.[95]

Examples like these could be found all over pre-Famine Ireland. While these incidents arose from particular local issues, peasants all over the country acted to defend their access to land, protect their religious solidarity, or punish those that dared to collude with the state, landlords, or the Church of Ireland's clergy. These acts of violent assault or assassination often shocked politicians and newspaper editors, as word of the heinousness of the crimes reached the reading British and Irish public. In a long column highlighting the alarming state of Tipperary and Longford, *The Times* claimed Ireland was 'the execration of the civilised world', and that 'within three years upwards of 1,000 human beings have been sacrificed to advance the designs of Popery'.[96] Week after week, newspapers printed headlines that proclaimed 'Outrages in Ireland' and gave so-called first-hand accounts of Ireland's base state. Underneath this rhetoric, however, was an understanding on the part of politicians and government officials that some of the violence witnessed in Ireland did not emanate from Irish peasants' moral depravity but rather from

[93] 'To the Editor of the Freeman', FJ, 3 November 1838, 2.
[94] 'Select Committee on State of Ireland', 920.    [95] Ibid., 921–2.
[96] 'Alarming State of the County of Longford', *The Times*, 29 October 1838.

a concerted effort among the rural poor to impose their own laws, rules, or order, contrary to the established law of the government. This is one reason, I would argue, why government officials at Dublin Castle willingly grouped banal, domestic, or ordinary criminal acts of assault, manslaughter, rape, or infanticide with the acts that clearly defied the state's role as the sole arbiter of justice.

## Offences against Property

The practice of reporting nearly every incident that might carry more sinister political, economic, or sectarian connotations continued in the variety of outrages that Col. Shaw Kennedy included under the designation of 'Offences against Property'. Even more so than 'Offences against the Person', many of the different individual crimes within this designation likely arose from personal or domestic motives. Burglaries, larcenies, and robberies seldom originated in larger political, economic, or sectarian struggles, especially considering that a separate category existed for stealing firearms. Burglars carried off clothing, furniture, plate, foodstuffs, or cash, often without the victims' presence. Robberies, often perpetrated on the highway, seemed to happen as a result of opportunism rather than specific targeting. In any event, constables rarely had much information to share about these offences other than to state whether the offenders were known and to estimate the prospects of their arrest. For example, in Antrim Town, Co. Antrim, the roof of John Hitchcock was stripped of its lead in February 1838 and taken by Patrick Carrigan, who was 'committed to gaol for the offence'. The Outrage Report (form 38) filed for this offence, instead of including the usual amount of detail, merely added that Carrigan was Catholic while Hitchcock was Protestant, furnishing no other details about the motives of the crime or why it warranted special reporting.[97]

Less straightforward are crimes related to the stealing, shearing, or maiming of livestock (a practice also known as houghing). As Sean Connolly has amply shown, the tradition of maiming cattle and killing sheep had a long tradition in Ireland, predating the agrarian violence of oath-bound societies in the latter half of the eighteenth century. 'The Houghers', as they were known, acted in 1711–12 to protest the expansion of large-scale pasture farming in the west of Ireland, specifically in Co. Galway and parts of Co. Mayo, which had put economic pressure on small landholders when access to land decreased and rents

---

[97] Report of Outrage, 15 February 1838, TNA, HO 100/253/258; 10 February 1838 NAI, OP 1838/1/21.

increased.[98] The practice of cattle maiming continued throughout the eighteenth century as one tactic in the Houghers' campaigns for economic, social, or political redress.[99] What is striking in the evidence reported in 1838, however, is the volume of crime related to houghing or stealing livestock. Cattle houghing, stealing livestock, and the illegal shearing of sheep accounted for 38 per cent of all 'Offences against Property', and roughly 12.5 per cent of all outrages committed in 1838. Whereas secret societies of the nineteenth century used houghing as a form of retribution for economic or political grievances, how should we understand the level of crime when there was no overarching social movement? Did these practices operate in similar fashion?

The Reports of Outrage official categories conflated the killing of horse, cattle, or sheep in their statistics, but the Outrage Papers for individual counties often explore the differences in motives between maiming sheep, cattle, or horses. In Cork, the killing and stealing of sheep occurred on a frequent basis, as did the illegal shearing of sheep (although this was a separate outrage). Many of these acts may have been motivated by simple economic incentives – sheep killed in the night found their way to the butcher's block in the morning, and the perpetrator lined their pockets with whatever the butcher would pay for fresh meat or for sheep fat.[100] Other incidents may have been motivated by economic or political animus, but constables often did not include much detail in their reports of the theft and killing of sheep, rendering definite conclusions impossible. Nevertheless, it is worth noting that a number of cases of sheep stealing, fleecing, or killing were perpetrated against individuals that would be classified as socially respectable, and potentially economically well off. For example, in April, two sheep were stolen from the demesne of Michael Roberts, a local JP in the parish of Carrigaline, south-east of Cork. Although the constable gave no motive, Roberts was the proprietor of two large mills that exported local grains from Cork to England, which in times of dearth likely led to his being ostracised by the local population. Roberts also served on the Cork City Grand Jury, which could have exposed him to harassment from the friends or family of those he helped convict, or those passed over for jobs determined by the Grand Jury.[101]

---

[98] S. J. Connolly, 'The Houghers: Agrarian Protest in Early Eighteenth-Century Connacht', in *Nationalism and Popular Protest in Ireland*, ed. C. H. E. Philpin (New York: Cambridge University Press, 1987), 132–3.

[99] Powell, 'Ireland's Urban Houghers', 247–8.

[100] 25 December 1838, NAI, OP 1838/3/241; 24 December 1838, NAI, OP 1838/3/243.

[101] Lewis, *A Topographical Dictionary of Ireland*, 1:278; 13 April 1838, NAI, OP 1838/3/76; FJ, 'Cork City Grand Jury', 16 March 1838. There are numerous examples in the Reports of Outrage of the stealing, fleecing, or killing of sheep that belonged to those

Those Outrage Reports that offered any real details about individual acts of sheep stealing, killing, or fleecing were largely related to issues around the occupation of land. In Longford, constables noted that a sheep that was the property of Robert Miller was killed in the parish of Kilglass. The report speculated as to the reason behind the act, and who was suspected: 'A man named Patrick Coffey, occupied the land, & was ejected previous to Miller's taking possession & the general feeling is that it is on account of this circumstance, that Miller's property has been injured.'[102] Similarly, in Co. Sligo, George Brett's sheep were killed when he took possession of a farm that previously had been held in common by the surrounding neighbours.[103] These examples, while illustrative of the potential motives behind some crimes, were the exception rather than the rule: the majority of cases revolving around the maiming, stealing, or fleecing of sheep, as measured by the four-county sample of Outrage Reports, received little attention from constables or Dublin Castle, and therefore probably had little to do with the motives that caused alarm among governing officials.

The maiming of cattle and horses gave rise to greater scrutiny among government officials than that of sheep. In part, this could have been due to the fact that cattle houghing had a long tradition in Ireland associated with secret societies; or, from the sheer fact that these livestock were of greater value than sheep. Bailiffs captured cattle or horses for non-payment of rent or tithes, impounded them, and sold them at auction. If peasants could not recapture their livestock from the pound (a separate outrage altogether), then one form of retribution available to them was to maim the livestock of those responsible for their dispossession or that of those who purchased the livestock at auction. Similarly, peasants dispossessed from their land retaliated against landlords and their agents by houghing cattle.[104] Victims with the means to offer rewards often did so, but with little effect. For example, after Thomas Powell allowed his horse to graze on land where a number of tenants had recently been ejected, in Cloghfin, Co. Sligo, his horse's leg was cut with a hatchet, and it later died from its wounds. Mr Cooper, MP for Co. Sligo and owner of the land, promised the various tracts of land to Powell after dispossessing the existing 150 tenants for non-payment of rent, or, according to the nationalist *Sligo Champion*, because of his hatred of Catholics and desire to 'colonise the whole of his property with rampant Orangemen'.

of higher social rank, who were denoted in the reports by the courtesy title of 'Esq.' See Reports of Outrage, TNA, HO 100/253/1–472.

[102] 15 February 1838, NAI, OP 1838/19/30.

[103] 17 January 1838, NAI, OP 1838/26/12.

[104] 4 July 1838, NAI, OP 1838/26/124; 20 June 1838, NAI, OP 1838/26/108.

Considering the circumstances surrounding the outrage, the constable thought offering a reward, however great, was pointless as the entire neighbourhood was determined to act together in opposing Mr Cooper.[105] Similar cooperation among neighbours intending to intimidate those attempting to extend their land claims existed on one of Lord Palmerston's Sligo estates. When a new tenant, 'a wealthy shopkeeper' from Grange, Co. Sligo named Mr Gallagher, attempted to enlarge his holdings, six of his cattle were houghed, resulting in four of them dying; this had been 'no doubt Committed by some ... to intimidate Gallagher from taking [land]'. Palmerston's agent, James Walker, offered £50 as a reward for private information (no small sum, especially for cattle houghing), but it produced no results, even though Gallagher was 'himself a Catholic & very unoffending man & well liked'.[106] Nothing was more sacrosanct in pre-Famine Irish society than land occupation, and it did not matter whether you were Catholic or Protestant: if you violated the unwritten code of conduct, a violent retribution would invariably follow.

A classic form of collective action used by peasants in pre-Famine Ireland was arson, known officially as incendiary fire. This was used to enforce communal norms and local understandings of justice. Historians of both Britain and Ireland have noted the use of arson to intimidate, punish, and terrorise; as Gemma Clark has recently argued, arson was 'the symbolic purging of the enemy' who had 'committed some (perceived) social, economic, or political misdemeanour'.[107] In Britain, Hobsbawm and Rudé's 1968 study offered the first systematic exploration of Captain Swing's violence, carried out across southern England in 1830, and suggested that labourers' actions (e.g. breaking threshing machines and widespread arson) were motivated by the loss of their customary rights and a serious downturn in the English economy. More recently, Daniel Jones has suggested that whereas Swing the 'rioter' was the expression of the movement's public will and acted as the negotiator with English elites, 'Swing the arsonist, on the other hand, was a mysterious and malign face ... he was the movement's enforcer'. Arson operated as the tool by which Captain Swing enacted his pronouncements, as authorities noted examples of farmers pre-emptively breaking their own threshing machines to avoid becoming the "'objects

---

[105] 3 June 1838, NAI, OP 1838/26/91; 'The Extermination System – Mr. Cooper, M. P.', FJ, 22 May 1838.
[106] James Walker to Lord Palmerston, 10 April 1839, USSC, Broadlands Papers, BR 146/1/4/1.
[107] Gemma Clark, 'Arson in Modern Ireland: Fire and Protest before the Famine', in *Crime, Violence and the Irish in the Nineteenth Century*, ed. Kyle Hughes and Donald M. MacRaild (Liverpool: Liverpool University Press, 2018), 223.

of incendiaries'".[108] In the case of Ireland, historians have noted the prominent role arson played in the Anglo-Irish War (1919–21) and Irish Civil War (1921–2) to punish former large landowners, or as a form of everyday violence used against those deemed outside of the dominant community.[109] And, of course, it featured in many of the agrarian disturbances of the eighteenth and nineteenth centuries, especially that of the Rockites of 1821–4 who, according to Donnelly, were the first to use it systematically in their repertoire of collective action: 'Among Irish Whiteboys, the Rockites were the incendiaries par excellence.'[110]

The descriptions of incendiary fires in contemporary reports offer a clear picture into how law officials, victims, politicians, and newspapers understood the motives of actors in pre-Famine Ireland; their evidence suggests that in many cases incendiary fires were interpreted as a local expression of justice that countered the existing law concerning employment and land ownership. The most common explanation cited by the constabulary for an incendiary fire was punishment for the eviction of former tenants or to prevent their land being leased to another family. For example, in Knocknanagh, Co. Cork, a small house and stable belonging to Denis O'Callaghan, Esq., were set on fire and burned in May 1838. The constable reporting the outrage to Dublin Castle noted how O'Callaghan's tenant Timothy Galvin had been ejected after a legal battle that included a recent judgement against him at the Mallow Quarter Sessions. As a result, the constable stated, 'It is supposed that they [Galvin's family] burned the House to prevent Mr OCallaghan [*sic*] from obtaining a Tenant for the land.'[111] A similar fire occurred in Ardgivna, Co. Sligo when an unoccupied house, the property of William Moston, was burned. 'I have visited the scene of the Outrage', reported the constable, 'by which I find that Mr Moston dispossessed a tenant of the House and a small farm, about three months ago, for nonpayment of rent, and that another tenant was about getting possession of it, which leads me to believe the house was maliciously burned to prevent him from occupying the farm'.[112] It is instructive to note the

---

[108] E. J. Hobsbawm and George F. E Rudé, *Captain Swing* (New York: Pantheon Books, 1968), 15–16; Peter Daniel Jones, 'Captain Swing and Rural Popular Consciousness: Nineteenth-Century Southern English Social History in Context' (PhD dissertation, University of Southampton, 2002), 17; C. J. Griffin, 'The Violent Captain Swing?', P & P, 209, no. 1 (15 November 2010): 166.

[109] Gemma Clark, *Everyday Violence in the Irish Civil War* (Cambridge: Cambridge University Press, 2014), ch. 3; Andy Bielenberg, 'Exodus: The Emigration of Southern Irish Protestants during the Irish War of Independence and the Civil War', P & P, 218 (2013), 204.

[110] Donnelly, *Captain Rock*, 267.     [111] 8 May 1838, NAI, OP 1838/6/97.

[112] 4 March 1838, NAI, OP 1838/26/39.

constable's honesty in making an educated guess as to the perpetrator of the arson; this suggests the dominant paradigm of government thinking – that arson was one tactic used by the community to prevent landlords from exercising their legal rights to evict tenants for non-payment of rents or to not renew rents on their expiration, or to offer land to new tenants regardless of the community's approbation.

Constables often noted wider community involvement in the enforcement of these norms, and a willingness to conceal the perpetrators from law officers. Lewis Johnston, a Protestant and caretaker working for Mr Roe in Armagh, had both his turf and house burned down, valued at £4 and £10 respectively. When the constable made his visit to the location and began talking to Johnston's neighbours, he noted their unwillingness to speak to him. 'There is not the least wish amongst the people in that neighbourhood to give the Constabulary the slightest information with regard to outrage[s] of any description', wrote the constable to the inspector general, 'although I explain to them that the inhabitants of the townland must pay for the damage done in every case.'[113] Similar experiences occurred across Ireland, as constables complained that they 'could not obtain the slightest information from those residing in the neighbourhood' and lamented the fruitlessness of offering rewards to entice Ireland's peasantry to open their mouths.[114] Constables also highlighted passive support of outrages from communities, for example in instances where neighbours did nothing to help put out fires lit under thatched roofs.[115]

Many cases related to the occupation of land proved costly. In County Longford, the land agent of Capt. Shirley Ball, a Mr McCally, witnessed the complete destruction of his outhouses and offices – damages valued at £137. Recently, McCally had cleared a number of tenants for Ball and taken a farm, 'although he heard that the tenants had threatened any one who might take the farm'. At the Presentment Sessions in Granard, where the magistrates proposed tax rates for their baronies, the inhabitants came to the conclusion that the fire was purely accidental, saving cess (tax) payers the liability of paying for the damages, despite the fact that McCally's nephew found burning turf under the roof, and the government thought it necessary to offer £50 for sworn information, plus whatever could be raised for private information. McCally was convinced that the fire was 'the dastardly act of assassins', and rhetorically asked in

---

[113] 4 December 1838, NAI, OP 1838/2/93. A few weeks later another man 'much disliked in the neighbourhood' had his turf burned, and the constable noted the futility of offering any reward, as the people were unwilling to help the government.
[114] 30 April 1838, NAI, OP 1838/6/94.
[115] 24 January 1838, NAI, OP 1838/1/11; 'Reports of Outrage', TNA, HO 100/253–6.

a letter to Capt. Ball, 'when, or if ever, we are to be emancipated from this tyranny'.[116] In another extraordinarily expensive case (over £300 in damages), paper mills in Ballingohig, Co. Cork, the property of Thomas Cleary, were completely destroyed, 'the dwelling house burned to the ground – the Mill broke and destroyed – [and] the Machinery torn down and taken away'. Cleary, after years of legal wrangling, secured writs of ejectment against the Meade family, who were suspected of the crime. Most intriguing, the constable noted that Meade's neighbours had formed 'a number of Persons, Horses and Cars' to remove Meade's possessions from the home and assist in destroying the mill and burning the home.[117]

Retribution for transgressing the agrarian code was not limited to responding to land occupation or evictions – incendiarism was also utilised to regulate wages and the amount of money paid for rents, and against those paying tithes and testifying at assizes, as well as in cases related to employment. The constable that reporting the burning of a house in Co. Cork in May 1838, which nearly killed the owner Richard Madden and his entire family, was due to Madden's 'having a few days before pointed out to some Bailiffs the stock of Tithe Defaulters in that neighbourhood ... [this] is certainly the cause'.[118] James Leahy of Schull, Co. Cork suffered the loss of his turf to fire in the middle of winter for paying the tithes he owed when the rest of the community refused to pay.[119] Like those who took the farm of an evicted tenant, those who entered into employment when another had been discharged were subject to punishment. After Patrick Howley had discharged a man named O'Horce from his employment, the cabin where O'Horce had formerly lived was burned to the ground, which the constable believed was the result of O'Horce's discharge. The constable, much to his chagrin, 'did not believe anyone [would] come to justice from the disinclination of people in general to give any information in causes of this nature', which thus suggests the wider approval of the punishment in the community.[120]

While many of the crimes against property could very well have been motivated by personal greed, opportunism, or rivalry, Dublin Castle and the Irish Constabulary assumed the worst and asked questions later. At a deeper level, however, some crimes against property struck at one of the two cores that terrified Tory and Whig politicians alike – the fear that

[116] 18 April 1838, NAI, OP 1838/19/74; BNL, 'Incendiarism in Longford', 24 April 1838; FJ, 'Longford – The Late Alleged Malicious Burning', 16 May 1838.
[117] 10 July 1838, NAI, OP 1838/6/135; BNL, 'Malicious Burning', 20 July 1838.
[118] 24 May 1838, NAI, OP 1838/6/106.     [119] 8 January 1838, NAI, OP 1838/6/7.
[120] 4 June 1838, NAI, OP 1838/26/92.

a battle between property and poverty was on the verge of breaking out, and that this might tear Ireland apart. Writing to Robert Peel in October 1830, Chief Secretary Hardinge alluded to this fear: 'The outrages continue or rather are on the increase, almost invariably originating in ejectments of tenant – they become intent to vengeance follow[ing] injury – & if the Police did not vigilantly do its duty, by apprehending the offenders, we should soon have a midnight warfare of Poverty against Property.'[121] And, in the face of rising concern about the state of County Tipperary in 1829 and the rumours of imminent political insurrection and rebellion (the other core fear, which will be discussed in the next section), the Duke of Northumberland summed up his conviction regarding the motivation behind the outrages in Tipperary:

I believe that neither religion nor politics have any direct influence on the disturbances ... but I am convinced that System is there of full vigour, & alive in many parts of Ireland for interfering by force with the demise and disposition of Property – for resisting all Process of Law by evidence – and for preventing the Exercise of Civil rights by menace and by destruction of Life + Goods.[122]

This concern about the insecurity of property was echoed in 1839 when the Tories referenced 'that spirit of confederation and combination in the commission of crime against the rights of property', which warranted the creation of a Select Committee on Irish outrage, which was proposed by Lord Roden.[123] The challenge exerted by Irish peasants on the established property rights and their apparent attempts to enforce local understandings of justice necessitated the inclusion of crimes against property in the Reports of Outrage sent between Dublin and London. This motivation of attempting to establish a popular countervailing rule of law, dictated by the mandates of the Irish peasantry, was also abundantly evident in the final designation created by Inspector General Shaw Kennedy.

### Offences Affecting the Public Peace

Whereas many of the outrages in the previous two designations often arose from matters of private concern, which led to confusion about the

---

[121] Hardinge to Peel, 15 October 1830, BL, Peel Papers, Add. MSS 40313, f. 89. Though never explicitly mentioned, the French Revolution cannot have been far from the minds of government officials concerned about a general war of poverty versus property – indeed, references to the Continent, events in Belgium, and the eventual ascension of the July Monarchy peppered the correspondence between government officials concerned with how developments might motivate both Daniel O'Connell and the Irish peasantry.

[122] Duke of Northumberland to Peel, 15 September 1829, BL, Peel Papers, Add. MSS 40327, f. 70.

[123] Hansard, 3rd ser., vol. 46, cols. 38, 7 March 1839.

seriousness of the 'State of the Country', for both contemporaries and historians, almost all of the outrages included in 'Offences Affecting the Public Peace' appear more straightforwardly ominous to those concerned about maintaining a tranquil countryside. Some crimes could be perceived as quasi-political, even insurrectionary, while others clearly had roots in other social, economic, or religious motivations. And, I would argue, it is in examining many of the crimes under this designation committed in 1838 where a countervailing notion of justice emerges most clearly from the sources, one that a subset of Ireland's population attempted to exercise and extend.

Among the variety of outrages included under 'Offences Affecting the Public Peace' was that of sending or posting threatening notices. Unlike a majority of the Outrage Reports, those concerning threatening letters afford one the opportunity to hear Irish people speak on their own terms. Stephen Gibbons has put these threatening notices front and centre in his brilliant *Captain Rock, Night Errant* showcasing, 525 anonymous notices sent or posted between 1801 and 1840. Gibbons outlines the variety of demands expressed in these notices and points to important motives that often propelled people to write them, and to commit many of the acts they threatened. Gibbons rightly underscores the articulation of a popular justice that many of the notices bear witness to – a 'code of laws, quite separate from that represented by government, magistrates or police, and applied by the Irish countryman to his own kind and to anyone interfering with age-old custom'.[124] The limitations of *Captain Rock, Night Errant*, however, is that Gibbons's sources are drawn from a preponderance of material from periods of profound unrest, which Gibbons notes map nicely onto Lee's three 'major eruptions of agrarian disturbance' between the Act of Union and the Famine; these occurred in 1814–16, 1821–3, and 1831–4.[125] Furthermore, Gibbons underplays the hazards that Captain Rock's popular justice conveyed to the British state due to his overemphasis on debunking 'the myth of Ribbonism', by which he means the preoccupation of Irish historians with correcting the Irish nationalist thesis that agrarian violence was proto-nationalist in its origin and purpose.[126] In discounting the notion of widespread integrated proto-nationalist secret societies across the country, Gibbon undermines the importance of Dublin Castle's perceptions, and of the fact that British officials received Rock's anonymous missives with appropriate concern because they bore witness to this

---

[124] Stephen Randolph Gibbons, *Captain Rock, Night Errant: The Threatening Letters of Pre-Famine Ireland, 1801–1845* (Dublin: Four Courts Press, 2004), 22–3.
[125] Ibid., 43.    [126] Ibid., 11–13.

countervailing justice (a 'combination'), which undermined British sovereignty, law, and order in Ireland.

While the Reports of Outrage between Dublin Castle and Whitehall referenced the posting of threatening notices or letters, these reports never mentioned what the actual notice said but simply what threat was made. For example, a report was made concerning a letter received by Thomas McCann, of Newport, Co. Mayo, which made a threat against his life if he continued to serve tithe decrees for the Rev. Mr Stoney.[127] No mention is made of the actual language used by the anonymous writer, nor any context surrounding the letter. Thus, while the Reports of Outrage give an excellent picture of the number of threatening notices posted throughout Ireland in 1838 as well as some insight into the motives of their writers, we do not hear the 'voice' of Captain Rock. In contrast, the Outrage Papers for each county often included verbatim copies of the threatening notices. In the four sample counties no fewer than forty-nine notices were reported in 1838, and the majority of these reports included copies of the threatening notice.

Although it is clear from the language of these anonymous notices that many developed from personal or local grievances, they were often couched in terms appealing to larger legitimising rationales (e.g., 'Captain Rock's law', 'holy punishment'). Numerous threats condemned local actors for evicting tenants, paying low wages, or 'land jobbing' and bolstered their threats with reference to Captain Rock's men, claiming that they numbered in the hundreds or thousands. A letter to a 'Respectable R. Catholic Farmer name Gregory' condemned him for participating in the distraining of cattle for the Rev. Dr Craw's tithes. The notice mentioned a previous warning issued by Captain Rock, as well as the mercy extended to Gregory on account of the 'interference of People saying that you exerted Yourself very well at the time of Elections', but made its threat quite explicit:

Before the God that Created me if you dont decline your driving we will use you in the most murderous manner that ever a man was used or Killed[.] dont think we will give you as easy a death as the Police Man got[,] and I send four of my Men to that What must the case be if I send one Thousand Men to you ... But again Swear by the contents of this paper and mortal God we will take revenge of you in open daylight for remember I can command the County in a Moments warning [sic] or if I chose the three forths [sic] of Ireland.[128]

In Co. Sligo, the writer of a December notice attempted to widen the scope of a local dispute between two neighbours concerning the division

---

[127] Reports of Outrage, 6 March 1838, TNA, HO 100/256/20. Examples like this are legion in the Reports of Outrage for 1838, totalling in the hundreds.
[128] 19 January 1838, NAI, OP 1838/19/13.

of a farm so that it also included the wider community; he did so by signing the letter 'Captain Rock's Men' and sought to legitimise his demands by sentencing the victim 'according to Captain Rocks Laws [sic]'.[129]

In fact, much of the language peasants used to offer threats employed the legitimising discourse of the courtroom. Like a judge on his quarterly circuit listening to cases at the various assizes, Captain Rock seemingly travelled across Ireland to adjudicate as well. Here is a notice delivered to Thomas Burns, a farmer from Co. Armagh, who was directed to give up the land that he lived on with his wife and that his father had acquired years earlier when the former tenant failed to pay their rent:

Notice of Death or Glory [Picture of a coffin with T. B. in the middle]
   Thomas Burns I give ten days notice for you to give up the 3 acres and ½ up from the lake and I am in my journey to Carnteel those days I will visit you at my returning. It is 3 years since I called with you[.] Now by the Great God if you make me go Back again I will Flay the hind of your Backside and Belly [and] Kill you[.] [You] may pray for your Soul those Ten days[, and] remember the Wild Goose Lodge; your end will be seventeen times worse.
   Now I h[e]ard the case and [it] has been tried before me and I give you timely notice.
   Gun under my hand
   Captain Rock.
   You may prepare for there never was more Poswer [powder] and Ball just in the County Armagh Be Fore [sic].[130]

This notice is remarkable for a number of reasons. First, it is written as if it were a pronouncement from the bench at trial and includes a time frame for the judgement to be carried out, presumably in an effort to offer Burns a form of clemency before enforcing the sentence. The author draws precedent for his sentence of death by referring to past warnings that Burns did not heed, and indeed the constable investigating the outrage noted in his report that a number of men had attacked Burns three years before, and that he lived in fear of another attack. It is fascinating that the notice mentions travelling to neighbouring Co. Tyrone (Carnteel), suggesting both a uniformity in Captain Rock's personhood, and therefore, his actions. This lends to his legitimacy as an adjudicator and is supported by an allusion to the circuit that judges and barristers travelled. Furthermore, as if in an effort to draw on the popular corpus defining Captain Rock's code, the author refers to the gruesome murder by burning of Edward Lynch and his family at Wildgoose Lodge in October 1816 in neighbouring Co. Louth. Lynch, a Catholic, was apparently killed for

[129] 4 December 1838, NAI, OP 1838/26/209.    [130] 8 March 1838, NAI, OP 1838/2/17.

his cooperation in testifying against men who earlier in the year had raided his home for firearms. Burns, the constables, and Dublin Castle would have immediately understood the reference to Wildgoose due to Burns's proximity to its occurrence, its prominence in local folklore, and the fact that it was further publicised in William Carleton's 1833 short story 'Wildgoose Lodge'.[131]

References to other violent cases that held local significance and meaning also appear in many of these notices. In Co. Longford, a number of threatening notices written in 1838 mention the murders of John Brock, Arthur Cathcart, and Hugh Moorehead on Lord Lorton's Ballinamuck estate in County Longford. A notice was posted on the house of Robert Cooke who, according to the constable, planned on taking land adjoining his farm once the agent of the Earl of Belmore evicted the current tenant, Widow Sheerehan. 'I am going to give you Notice or a forewarning that if you have anything to do with that Ground that you will get the same usage that Brock, Cathcart & Moorehead got. Captain Rock will come from Mullingar [Co. Westmeath] upon that business he won't think the journey far, do not think it is what I jest or Mark it is from his Majesty Captain Rock.'[132] As Cathcart, Moorehead, and Brock were attacked for taking land from evicted tenants, it is not surprising that the anonymous letter writer chose these examples to warn Cooke, who was apparently considering the same transgression. Perhaps equally interesting is the author's reference to Captain Rock as 'his Majesty', highlighting an allegiance to a rival authority to Queen Victoria. Similarly, Morrison (another of Lord Lorton's tenants who was attacked) is referenced in another County Longford notice in which the language of a law court is also used: 'Henry Duffey take notice that we are the prosecutors of land jobbing. ... We will take him [Mr Ball, a land agent] down as Morrison for a Man Hung is as well as a man Shot.'[133]

In all these notices the anonymous letter writers attempt to appropriate the legitimacy of the law. At the local level, constables found this countervailing law both authoritative in silencing the community and able to frustrate any attempt to bring perpetrators of outrage to justice in Irish courts. In Foygh, Co. Longford, a party of men, headed by James Jordan (known to some as 'the boy that could rule Foygh'), attacked the public house of Timothy Sesnan, a man who had given information on a number of previous outrages, and since then had been marked for punishment. Even though James Jordan was known to be the perpetrator by the

---

[131] Dooley, *The Murders at Wildgoose Lodge*; William Carleton, *Traits and Stories of the Irish Peasantry* (London: Routledge, 1877), 170–84.
[132] 17 May 1838, NAI, OP 1838/19/91.    [133] 11 December 1838, NAI, OP 1838/19/256.

authorities, Sesnan refused to prosecute. This left the constable asking the community to cooperate, without success. 'I could not have any thing, which might be of service in procuring the punishment of the delinquents, so determined are the people not to become instruments of conviction', complained the constable; 'some from fear, & others from illegal connection I really believe, & *a disinclination to support any laws but their own*'.[134]

Although issues concerning land occupancy formed the majority of threatening notices, other threats involved cases of employment, including wages, and who should or should not be employed. When 'Christopher Rectifyer' learned about the low wages of men employed by John Brady to build a road outside Corrinagh, Co. Longford, he threatened 'the ruin and mortification of the disobeyers ... [like] Speculators at the death [of] Samson my vengenance [*sic*] shall pour on you and bury you and your effect under its ruin'. Comparing himself to God, however, Rectifyer promised, 'as the Almighty gives the sinner a long day My tenderness allows me to give you another day'.[135] Captain Rock also could frame his threats as both a warning to those with power and a notice of his solidarity with those he thought exploited. In Sligo, Mr John Taaffe, Esq. decided in March to let 5,000 acres of mountainous wasteland to the Irish Waste Land Company at the yearly rent of half a crown per acre.[136] In the eyes of some, employees of the Irish Waste Land Company worked for wages that were too low. To add insult to injury, before letting the land to the company, Taaffe had also evicted a number of 'pauper-tenants'. Captain Rock offered this warning:

Notice to Labourers:
    As many as may arrogate to themselves the power of trespassing on the mandates of Captain Rock or work for the agriculture company Mount Taaffe under the Subsistency of man such I say will be punished to the highest severity therefore good people take advice from this insertion that you may not incur the misfortune of becoming our victim for we the system of Cap Rock have unanimously concured [*sic*] to suppress the Disposition of the Children of disobedience ... Be it also noticed to the tenants of Castlerock that I will put an end to their Baseability [*sic*] and trespass on one another.
                                                        Thurophilos Capt Rock

In addition to the continual reference to Captain Rock's laws ('trespassing on the mandates', 'the system of Cap Rock', 'Children of disobedience'), the author of the notice appears most upset by the company's employment of men under subsistence wages.[137]

---

[134] Ibid., 11 November 1838, NAI, OP 1838/19/230, emphasis added.
[135] 12 September 1838, NAI, OP 1838/19/172.
[136] 'Irish Waste Lands', FJ, 2 March 1838.    [137] 4 July 1838, NAI, OP 1838/26/119.

A number of threatening notices made special mention of Captain Rock's hatred of 'approvers' (informers), as well as those that participated in legal proceedings. One notice from Co. Sligo warned: 'Take notice, that if Thos. Haran or Brian Renalds gets James Burke fined or confined that they may have their coffins made before that day week, and that they will become examples in the County. Captain Thunderbolt.'[138] In the parish of Killoe, Co. Longford, constables reported finding Rockite notices 'signed Captn. Rock' threatening a man named Kernan, 'who was stated in the Notice to be an informer'.[139] An 'Omnipotent C____ R____' wrote to Thomas Sheeran about his 'telling [his] inferanal [*sic*] lies to Mr Greg and accusing your neighbours of larceny', and went on: 'if I understand you relatives you beware of what you are doing you informer'. Although the omnipotence of Captain Rock did not prevent his party from accidentally visiting the wrong house, the writer assured Sheeran that if he did not change his ways, 'we [would] then put our laws in force with great severity'.[140] Stories circulated of priests denouncing informers from their pulpits, and offering an unofficial sanction to the community to exact revenge.[141] Whether these stories were true is unknown, but the evidence from threatening notices as well as from the Reports of Outrage as a whole clearly reveals that the title of 'approver' carried with it a particular odium among many in the community.

Finally, threatening notices also dealt with national issues such as tithes or elections. These notices occasionally diverged from the standard practice of threatening violence and appealing to Captain Rock's statutes as their justification. For example, in Co. Cork notices were posted on the Roman Catholic chapel doors in Coolmoohan that advocated flooding the tithe sale taking place the following day with people. Rather than stressing the need to prepare coffins or to fire shots, instead the notice advocated a different tactic:

Come then pour in your Mountain Boys tomorrow, strong in numbers, bold and determined, But at the same time calm & peaceable. Shew to the World by your conduct that the men of this district are as Sturdy in their opposition as those of any other part of Ireland. May our hatred to Tythes be as lasting as our sense of their injustice.[142]

The notices had been printed rather than handwritten, which suggests a coordinated campaign to oppose tithes led by elements in the Catholic

---

[138] 15 February 1838, NAI, OP 1838/26/27.
[139] 17 September 1838, NAI, OP 1838/19/175.
[140] 31 October 1838, NAI, OP 1838/19/220.
[141] 'Select Committee on State of Ireland', 174, 305.
[142] 3 January 1838, NAI, OP 1838/6/2.

community other than Captain Rock.[143] These notices advocating peaceful opposition to tithes were supplemented by numerous notices threatening violence against those who paid, collected, and profited from tithes.[144]

Threatening notices were one way to challenge the British state's sovereignty in Ireland, but Irish peasants relied on an expansive repertoire designed to undermine British law and order. Whereas threatening notices put forward an explicit claim, demand, or appeal, a number of other outrages under the designation of 'Offences Affecting the Public Peace' symbolically questioned the authority of the state, especially the claim to a monopoly of violence. Demanding or stealing arms from private citizens, attacking homes, appearing armed in the countryside, and administering oaths all challenged British legitimacy while also extending an alternative system demanding peasants' allegiance, what David W. Miller in the context of 1798 has referred to as 'politically salient rituals'. Unlawful oaths, for example, both 'acted as a revolution on a personal level, a *coup d'état* in miniature', and drew on the fears British and Irish politicians and men of property carried from their collective memory of the variety of oath-bound secret societies in Ireland generally, and the damnable consequences of unlawful oaths in relation to the carnage and chaos of 1798 in particular.[145] After the 1823 Unlawful Oaths Act, passed in response to the Rockite crisis, magistrates could summarily adjudicate cases and sentence offenders to three months without bail for the first offence; or, if they opted to bring the case to trial, penalties included transportation for seven years.[146]

Similarly, ownership of a gun in Irish society was imbued with symbolic and political meaning. Restrictive legislation regulated gun ownership in pre-Famine Ireland, especially in the eighteenth century with the codified strictures of the Penal Laws. Whereas, throughout most of the eighteenth century, gun ownership was restricted to Protestants and operated as

---

[143] For example, see FJ, 'Attempted Sale of Cattle for Tithes – Laughable Defeat of the Tithe-Eaters!!', 3 February 1838; ibid., 'County Cork – Tithes', 8 March 1838; ibid., 'Tithes – County Cork', 13 March 1838.

[144] 15 February 1838, NAI, OP 1838/6/30; 28 September 1838, NAI, OP 1838/6/187; 11 August 1838 NAI, OP 1838/7/91.

[145] David W. Miller, 'Radicalism and Ritual in East Ulster', in *1798: A Bicentenary Perspective*, ed. Thomas Bartlett (Dublin: Four Courts Press, 2003), 197; Petri Mirala, 'Law and Unlawful Oaths in Ireland: 1760–1835', in *Politics and Popular Culture in Britain and Ireland 1750–1850: Essays in Tribute to Peter Jupp*, ed. Allan Blackstock and Eoin Magennis (Belfast: Ulster Historical Foundation, 2007), 212, 216–18.

[146] 4 Geo. IV. Sess. 1823. *(Ireland.) A bill [as amended by the committee] to amend and render more effectual the provisions of an act, made in the 50th year of His Late Majesty's reign, for preventing the administering and taking unlawful oaths in Ireland.*, P. P. (1823, vol. 2, no. 385, 1–8).

a demarcation of membership of the Irish polity, by the end of the century the Volunteer movement and the arming of Catholics within the Irish militia during the crisis of the 1790s had destabilised social relations by informally inviting Catholics into that polity. This process was formally completed with the passage of Catholic Emancipation and repeal of the Test and Corporation Acts.[147] The conclusion of Catholic Emancipation, however, did not mean that Ireland's gentry or Dublin Castle were enthusiastic about Catholic gun ownership; rather, Catholic gun ownership, especially when it came about through the midnight robbery of arms, raised the spectre of open rebellion. Speaking in 1839 before the Lords' committee, Inspector General Shaw Kennedy noted that attacks on houses in search of arms were generally conducted by strangers to the locality, and often were coordinated 'by Connexion with local Societies' or 'a certain Combination among themselves'. Furthermore, when the committee asked Shaw Kennedy 'with reference to what you know of the Civilization of the Irish Peasantry', whether he believed Catholics should be given access to weapons, tellingly, he replied: 'I think it is better in regard to Ireland that there should be a Control to the Possession of Arms'.[148] According to Matthew Barrington, the crown solicitor of Munster, every case of arms theft involved Catholics attacking exclusively Protestant homes; Maxwell Hamilton, the crown solicitor for north-east Ulster, also noted the disproportionately high number of Catholics who participated in stealing arms.[149]

The chief concern of government officials regarding the theft of arms, swearing illegal oaths, and appearing armed was the potential connection these activities might have with proto-nationalist groups, such as the infamous Ribbonmen (also referred to by contemporaries as Ribandmen). The historical reality of Ribbonism has been somewhat difficult to pin down. While politicians waxed poetic about the threat of Ribbonism, especially in the 1839 Lords' Committee, the details about the scope of the organisation, its goals, its politics, and its structure remain rather elusive to historians. Was it local or national, a rural phenomenon or primarily urban in scope, distinguished from agrarian outrages, or one and the same? Historians have somewhat neglected these

---

[147] Miller, 'The Armagh Troubles, 1784–95', 186–9; David W. Miller, 'Irish Christianity and Revolution', in *Revolution, Counter-Revolution and Union: Ireland in the 1790s*, ed. Jim Smyth (Cambridge: Cambridge University Press, 2000), 200–1; Bartlett, 'An End to Moral Economy', 41–64; on the specifics surrounding the formation of the Irish Militia see Ivan F. Nelson, *The Irish Militia, 1793–1802: Ireland's Forgotten Army* (Dublin: Four Courts Press, 2007), ch. 2.
[148] 'Select Committee on State of Ireland', 29.    [149] Ibid., 600–1, 694, 698–701.

important questions in an attempt to use the existence of Ribbonism in pre-Famine Ireland to draw a causal link with post-Famine revolutionary or sectarian organisations like Fenianism and the Ancient Order of Hibernians.[150]

Contemporaries offered a variety of opinions about the characteristics and importance of Ribbonism. Dr Patrick Burke, the Roman Catholic Bishop of Elphin, described the organisation as 'a contemptable [*sic*] remnant ... [which] of late years has assumed quite a different character from its original nature and has no <u>defined</u> object'. Rather than a political organisation, according to Burke, Ribbonism was more of a brotherhood of protection and a glorified drinking club, meeting in shebeen houses.[151] Numerous government informants described Ribbonism as fractious and divided, 'without a head', and consisting primarily of the lower classes of labourers.[152] Others argued Ribbonism exerted great influence in their localities, while reports emerged that Ribbonmen had infiltrated the constabulary. Additionally, reports circulated that Ribbonmen were organising the emigration of Irish Catholics for employment in the burgeoning English industrial cities, like Manchester and Liverpool, which served as a way to build solidarity among those abroad.

While the strength of Ribbonism's organisation and its political motives will most likely remain shrouded in considerable uncertainty, the perception of Ribbonism as an ominous threat by the Irish gentry, Dublin Castle, and British politicians is strikingly clear. Some, including Anglo-Irish Tories in Parliament amplified this perception for political gain – scaremongering proved an effective tool with which to undermine the Whig narrative of improving tranquillity in the Irish countryside. Politicians and the Irish gentry heard about masses of Irish peasants collecting at night, often armed with guns, and engaging in raiding neighbourhoods for more weapons, and feared a wider rebellion was looming. The events of 1798 certainly weighed on the minds of government officials, as did continuing unfounded fears of a French-led invasion.[153] Passwords found on alleged Ribbonmen in

---

[150] The best recent account is Hughes and MacRaild, *Ribbon Societies in Nineteenth-Century Ireland*; see also Jess Lumsden Fisher, '"Night Marauders" and "Deluded Wretches": Public Discourses on Ribbonism in Pre-famine Ireland', in *Crime, Violence and the Irish in the Nineteenth Century*, eds. Kyle Hughes and Donald MacRaild (Liverpool University Press, 2018), 53–67; Garvin, 'Defenders, Ribbonmen and Others'; Beames, 'The Ribbon Societies'; for a more sceptical view, see Murray, 'Agrarian Violence and Nationalism'.

[151] F. B. Haly to Drummond, 20 May 1839, TNA, CO 904/7/134–7.

[152] Patrick Hynes to Drummond, 25 July 1839; [?] to Edmond Rourke Esq., 11 November 1839, TNA, CO 904/7/271–2; 376; 'Letter on the Proceedings of the Ribbon Society in Ireland and England', n.d. TNA, CO 904/8/82–9.

[153] One government informant claimed that once Napoleon Bonaparte's body was returned to France from St Helena, then France would lead a revolution that would spread to Ireland and England. 9 November 1840, TNA, CO 904/8/150.

1838 referred to the recent rebellion in Canada as a source of inspiration for Irishmen, and called for freedom 'From British ties and tyranny'.[154] Whether Ribbon societies actively sought to actualise their dreams is certainly a worthwhile historical question, but I simply want to demonstrate here that Ribbonism was another manifestation of an Irish-articulated system of justice vying for the hearts and minds of Ireland's peasantry during the 1830s.

Although landlords wrote government officials with news of outlandish conspiracy theories and accounts that embellished the nefarious actions of their tenants, occasionally peasants put on large displays of power. In March 1838 the police and local gentry witnessed visible quasi-public forms of political theatre meant to intimidate the community around them and display the apparent strength of a secret society. Two subconstables, John Eastwood and James Lyle, returning to their station in Skyhill, Co. Louth, less than a kilometre from the Co. Armagh border, accidentally met a large party of men parading in military formation on a mid-March night. The subconstables estimated there to be between 100 and 130 men in the party and noted that almost all of them were armed with guns. 'On passing the party they observed one man who wore a cloak draw a sword and give the word halt front, the Party immediately formed into rank and file.' Another constable lodging at a publican's house made similar reports, noting the military discipline of the party marching to the tune of Jacobite standards such as 'White Cockade', and the nationalist 'Patrick's Day in the Morning', before firing over 100 shots into the air.[155]

On receiving this report at Dublin Castle, Undersecretary Drummond aired his concern, as it was 'the only case that [had] been reported within the last three years, of an organised body of armed men'. He immediately demanded a detailed report, along with an investigation in the area as to what other activities the armed party was involved with on the night in question. Reports circulated of armed parties breaking off from the main group, attacking homes, and searching for arms. The group was successful at three homes, where they beat the residents and carried off their weapons. 'The objective of the party on the above night appears to have been a search for Arms', wrote Co. Armagh's Deputy Lieutenant, 'and by a display of members to effect intimidation.' It appeared to the constabulary that the armed party's tactics were working: 'unless precautionary measures the most efficient are taken ... [then] outrages still more serious than any as yet reported may be expected[,] as already has this nocturnal

---

[154] 4 May 1838, NAI, OP 1838/20/67.
[155] 16 March 1838, John Eastwood to Drummond, NAI, CSORP, 1838/55/2987, emphasis in the original; 23 March 1838, ibid.

legislation effected its object on the peaceable and well disposed by limiting a report of outrages ... to the Police [with] no individual daring to appeal to the Constituted authorities for redress.'[156]

This event on the Armagh–Louth border certainly was one of the most spectacular displays of the armed resistance among peasants in 1838 that seemingly justified in one fell swoop all the fears, prejudices, and memories of an Irish gentry distressed by the assumed intentions of the population that surrounded them. The disciplined marching, displays of strength, and large-scale arms raiding certainly mark a sort of extreme boundary of action by peasants. However, the Reports of Outrage and Outrage Papers provide other examples of these same activities, simply on a less grandiose scale. Bearing in mind their smaller scale, we should not simply dismiss raiding for arms, attacking homes, and compelling peasants to swear oaths as merely events concerned with local matters of land occupation or inter-familial rivalries. Instead, these outrages demonstrated in many contexts a popularly conceived notion of 'what was right', generally acknowledged by peasants, which challenged British sovereignty in Ireland and contended for the allegiance of Ireland's peasantry.

## Crown Rewards and the Secret Service Fund

The government attempted to win the support of the Irish population and solidify the legitimacy of law and order through the deployment of money, which it used to either influence the population through the newspapers, or to reward law-abiding citizens through crown rewards in return for testimony at trial. At best, this policy paid small dividends towards government interests. Parliamentary pressure questioned the efficacy and ethics of essentially bribing newspapers to adopt a friendly disposition to government in Ireland, while the number of witnesses who claimed rewards was woefully low.

Paying for the support of newspapers in Ireland from the British Treasury began after Parliament passed the Act of Union. The Treasury paid the press roughly £10,000 annually for favourable cover-age: the *Dublin Gazette* received between £3,000 and £3,500 a year to publish proclamations, while the remainder was used to buy support from various newspapers. This amount had substantially diminished by the 1830s, as the Whig government pursued a policy of retrenchment, and questioned the ethics of government support of newspapers.[157]

---

[156] Ibid.; 20 March 1838, NAI, OP 1838/2/26.
[157] Arthur Aspinall, 'The Use of Irish Secret Service Money in Subsidizing the Irish Press', EHR 56, no. 224 (October 1941): 639–46; Arthur Aspinall, 'The Irish "Proclamation" Fund, 1800–1846', EHR 56, no. 222 (April 1941): 265–80.

Retrenchment was not abolition, however, and in 1831 Thomas Spring Rice as secretary to the Treasury moved for Parliament to supply £41,000 for foreign and secret services, which paid Irish rewards and bribes. Pointing out that the fund had been reduced from £260,000 in 1826 to £45,000 in 1829, Spring Rice claimed that the sum had been reduced to £41,000 because of the government's desire to reduce costs. Other members, most prominently Joseph Hume and Daniel O'Connell, openly questioned why so much money was needed during a time of peace, including a payment of £4,300 for Irish secret service money. O'Connell implicitly questioned whether payment of the Irish press should be continued, comparing the practice with that of the United States, where 'embezzlement of a small sum of money was considered in the United States, of sufficient importance for a State prosecution'.[158] However, by the end of the 1830s, newspapers were receiving smaller and smaller sums from the British exchequer, and this reduction forced many to cease publication.[159]

Whereas the practice of subsidising the press slowly faded out of favour, the government used secret service funds for the employment of state-paid stipendiary magistrates, along with the protection or later support of crown witnesses and their widows and children. Annually the vice treasurer of the Exchequer would issue £5,000 to the chief secretary or undersecretary in Ireland, under Act 33 Geo. 3 c. 34, which authorised officials to disperse the funds without account. In addition, either official could request more money from the British Treasury provided they swore it would go towards 'detecting treasonable, or dangerous conspiracies against the State, but for no other purpose'. The passage of the Constabulary Act of 1836, however, shifted the cost of maintaining the stipendiary magistrates to the Consolidated Fund, leaving the Treasury curious about what purpose the secret service fund served. Morpeth, in October 1839, enumerated the £3172. 10s. 11d. of annual costs for that year, which included the pensions of retired stipendiary magistrates, as well as funds for a number of widows and families of former crown witnesses.[160] Some questioned the legality of using the secret service funds for the payment of pensions, including the former Undersecretary William Gregory in 1833, but it seems that the funds continued to be used in this capacity throughout the 1830s.[161]

---

[158] Hansard, 3rd ser., vol. 4, 1436–7, 18 July 1831.
[159] Aspinall, 'The Irish "Proclamation" Fund', 279–80.
[160] 'Yearly Payment of Secret Service in Ireland in 3 Classes', October 1839, TNA, CO 904/7, 348–51.
[161] John F. McEldowney, 'Legal Aspects of the Irish Secret Service Fund, 1793–1833', IHS25, no. 98 (November 1986): 135.

How often did the crown resort to disbursing money from the secret service fund to crown witnesses? The evidence from the Outrage Reports, along with that of parliamentary reports, is somewhat contradictory. On the one hand, evidence from Outrage Reports in 1838 for counties Longford, Cork, Armagh, and Sligo suggests that Dublin Castle officials were quite willing to dole out money for information. For example, of the 278 Outrage Reports in Co. Longford, no less than 52 recorded that Drummond or Morpeth had authorised payment for private or public information (roughly 20 per cent of cases). Dublin Castle issued roughly the same amount of rewards in County Armagh (24 per cent). Though the figure was somewhat lower in Cork and Sligo, Dublin Castle granted funds in about 15 per cent of cases in Co. Cork in 1838, and in 17 per cent of cases in Co. Sligo.[162] Though this is only a partial account of all potential rewards issued throughout Ireland, the diverse characteristics of these four counties bolster the confidence with which preliminary conclusions can be drawn – that Dublin Castle used rewards in a sizeable minority of outrages to leverage information about a sizeable minority of outrages, varying somewhere between 15 and 20 per cent of cases.

On the other hand, a Parliamentary Report for part of 1836 and 1837 suggests that rewards were used far less often than this. In 1836, the report indicates that the lord lieutenant or crown justices issued reward proclamations for 252 separate cases. While we do not know the total number of outrages committed in 1836, as the creation of the constabulary and the system for reporting outrages developed later in 1837, the Parliamentary Report lists a total of 4,257 outrages between July and December 1836. This puts the total number of rewards offered at about 6 per cent, though this number is artificially high because it includes rewards for the entire calendar year, but outrages for July–December. In 1837, for the 7,480 outrages committed that year, only 267 rewards were offered, a rate of about 3.5 per cent.[163]

What accounts for the disparity in figures? There are two possible explanations, which are not mutually exclusive. First, officials at Dublin Castle may have decided to increase the frequency with which it offered rewards for crown prosecutions. As the Tories assailed the Whigs' Irish Policy in March 1839, Lord Morpeth explained that the Whigs had in fact resorted to offering more rewards in part to demonstrate to victims the

---

[162] Outrage Reports, Sligo, Cork, Armagh, and Longford, NAI, OP 1838/26; OP 1838/6; OP 1838/2; OP 1838/19.
[163] 'Outrages (Ireland). Return of rewards offered by proclamation of Lord Lieutenant, &c., and of all crimes and outrages reported by the stipendiary magistrates and officers of police in Ireland', P. P. (1837–8, vol. 46, no. 157), 1–30.

importance of capturing their assailants, but also so that the 'country . . . would receive the impression that the Government was in earnest in its endeavours to suppress crime'.[164] Although Morpeth was comparing previous government policy (specifically, that of the Tories in 1829–30) with that of his own, it does stand to reason that with all the changes in reporting, tracking, and attempting to discourage outrages, the amount of rewards offered would have evolved alongside these.

Second, the Parliamentary Report only mentions instances when the lord lieutenant or chief justice made an official proclamation for a reward, whereas the Outrage Reports detailed rewards for private and public information made at a local level. If the constable deemed it appropriate to offer a reward, Drummond or Morpeth could approve this without issuing an official proclamation, which would have been posted throughout the locality and printed in the newspapers, with the lord lieutenant's name affixed to it. For example, after a group of unknown men attacked Archibald Wilson in Faughts, Co. Sligo, most likely because Wilson had come to Sligo to buy potatoes and then return to Co. Roscommon, Drummond approved the chief constable's issuing a £15 reward for private information – no official proclamation and reward, however, was ever issued.[165] Though other factors could also account for the rise in the number of rewards offered between 1837 and 1838, these two explanations help shed light on the disparity.

Dublin Castle may often have resorted to rewards to entice witnesses to come forward and give evidence, but the Irish public seldom volunteered to claim the money and provide testimony. In the twenty-four months of 1836 and 1837, crown witnesses claimed only 19 of the 519 rewards, a dismal 3.6 per cent. In that same period Dublin Castle offered a total of nearly £25,000 in reward payments, and the average reward was just under £50 – a sizeable amount of money for an Irish labourer or small farmer. Of the nearly £25,000 offered in rewards, the Castle only paid out £970.[166] To offer one imperfect, but apt comparison, at the height of the Swing Riots in England the British Treasury paid out a total of £28,212 across nineteen different English counties.[167]

The imbalance between the sum of £970 rewards claimed and the potential sum of £28,212 is striking and underscores the apparent

---

[164] Hansard, 3rd ser., vol. 46, 62, 7 March 1839.

[165] Sligo, Outrage Report, 23 July 1838, NAI, OP/1838/26/133. Numerous other examples like this appear throughout the reports.

[166] 'Outrages (Ireland). Return of rewards offered by proclamation of Lord Lieutenant, &c.', pp. 2–9.

[167] 'Rewards. Abstract of an account of rewards paid, or ordered to be paid, in 1830, for the discovery of offenders in the disturbed districts', P. P. (1831–2, vol. 33, no. 390), 1–2.

unwillingness of much of the Irish population to cooperate with law enforcement in bringing perpetrators of outrages to justice. Both positive and negative factors certainly contributed to this disinclination to speak to law enforcement. Fear was undoubtedly one major motivation for remaining silent. On 25 July 1838, a party of twelve to fourteen men paid a visit to the home of James Gregg, in Garrowhill, Co. Longford. The men, many of them armed, warned Gregg's daughter, Mary, 'to keep herself quiet in future and let Capt. Rock's Men pass', afterwards breaking thirteen panes of glass and all the earthenware vessels in the home. The constable filing the report noted to the inspector general that this was the second such visit to Gregg's home and suspected that both Gregg and his daughter knew the party, but 'to induce Gregg or his daughter to prosecute [was] quite out of the question' because of the serious intimidation of the gang.[168] A similar case of intimidation in Ardloy, Co. Sligo concerning the low rate of pay for labourers employed in road construction left the chief constable frustrated because 'the fact is they [the peasantry] are afraid even if they know ... the perpetrators', which made the offer of a reward a pointless venture.[169] The implications of potential violence in threatening notices, which often included illustrations of coffins, gallows, and tombstones, secured the silence of many.

The explicit violence directed against government 'approvers' and witnesses made the implicit threats of Captain Rock's men a harsh reality. Men like Edward Goldrick from Co. Sligo faced serious bodily harm for prosecuting persons for offences at quarter sessions or assizes. In April, a party of twenty men visited his home and threatened to make 'four quarters of him ... if ever he went to Sligo again to prosecute', while also swearing to kill Goldrick if he went to church. Goldrick, a Protestant, had witnessed the abduction of Thomas Allen, election agent of the Tory candidate Alexander Perceval during the parliamentary election of 1837; Allen had been travelling to Goldrick's to take him to the hustings.[170] Goldrick's testimony kept a number of men responsible for Allen's later murder confined in jail. Before leaving, the party had taken a number of Protestant books from Goldrick's house, including biblical extracts translated into Irish, as well as copies of the New Testament.[171] Goldrick, as a Tory, and likely an Evangelical proselytiser (considering the Irish-language bibles in his possession), would already have stood apart from the majority of his surrounding community. While these factors may have

---

[168] 25 July 1838, NAI, OP 1838/19/133.
[169] 19 September 1838, NAI, OP 1838/26/159.
[170] 'The Sligo Murder', *The Hull Packet*, 29 September 1837; 'Rev. Mr. Spelman's Case – Murder of Allen', *Sligo Champion*, 7 October 1837.
[171] 12 April 1838, NAI, OP 1838/26/77.

made him a target for disapprobation, his assailants instead justified their actions in terms of his testimony at the assizes. According to Goldrick's sworn testimony to Chief Constable Armstrong, when Goldrick asked why he was beaten, 'They replied that it was in consequence of his having prosecuted the men who were tried for the Murder of Allen at the last assize of Sligo.'[172] A number of individuals who prosecuted in the courts were later targeted for serious assaults, house burnings, and threatening notices; these actions were a way to punish those who spoke, as well as to intimidate others who might be considering offering their testimony.[173]

## Conclusion

This chapter has suggested that much agrarian violence in pre-Famine Ireland, which took the form of so-called 'outrages', operated as an alternative system of justice contesting the expansion of British sovereignty on a local level, and working to defend locally understood conceptions of what was right concerning a number of issues vital to peasant life. While this code was itself subject to negotiation and contest, it was largely recognised by both peasants and the British state. In fact, this chapter has demonstrated that the very system of meticulously reporting agrarian violence was inherently prejudicial in its tendency to assume a political basis for that violence; if constables sensed even a whiff of larger political, social, economic, or sectarian motives they lodged the event as an outrage. This has made the task of sorting out the motives and meaning of everyday violence in pre-Famine Ireland a difficult one for historians, as a number of theories explain some cases excellently while downplaying or neglecting those that do not fit a favourite model. In contrast, this chapter has attempted to untangle the variety of reasons why everyday violence took place, highlighting that a number of the types of crime the inspector general decided to include in his list of outrages may be given more commonplace explanations, such as human avarice, familial rivalry, domestic disputes, or commonplace interpersonal misunderstandings with tragic outcomes. On the other hand, this chapter has attempted to correct a shortcoming in the literature, which, with a few notable exceptions, has focussed on periods of profound agrarian violence. This passing over of everyday violence in pre-Famine Ireland has marginalised the complexities of meaning this violence not only represented to Ireland's

---

[172] Ibid.

[173] The Outrage Reports are replete with examples of reprisals carried out on those who had given testimony. For example, see Armagh, 10 November 1838, NAI, OP 1838/2/86; Antrim, 21 June 1838, NAI, OP 1838/1/81; Longford, 10 November 1838, NAI, OP 1838/19/232.

population, but that outside actors, like politicians, Irish landlords, or the British state imbued in its perpetration.

Ultimately, a large portion of the everyday violence in Ireland involved a contest between two rival systems demanding Irish peoples' commitment. It is easy to romanticise popularly conceived notions of justice, as if the 'Rockite code' represented the wishes of every Irish person and benefitted them equally; or to construct a simplistic dichotomy between native versus alien, Irish versus British, good versus evil. Outrages were violent. Irish people were murdered, intimidated, and often prevented from living peacefully. This chapter suggests that common people had to negotiate and operate in between two systems, neither of which necessarily fully represented their interests. Thus, Dublin Castle did succeed in encouraging a small number of Irishmen to testify against those who engaged in violent acts of retribution. Neighbours put out fires started by arsonists or ran to the nearest police station to request help in the midst of a nocturnal visit. Unfortunately, due to a lack of sources, it is difficult to know exactly how many Irish people assisted the state in combatting outrages and undermining any popularly conceived notions of justice.

One limitation of analysing each category of outrage separately is that it presents an outrage as one discrete event – an incendiary fire, an assault, or an attack on a house. So often, however, the outrages perpetrated and witnessed in pre-Famine Ireland encompassed more than one act. As a way of concluding this chapter and reinforcing its argument concerning an alternative system of justice influencing much of the everyday violence in pre-Famine Irish society, I want to outline the experience of Alexander Sims and the people in the vicinity of Collooney, Co. Sligo. In doing so, I hope to demonstrate that the outrages advancing this form of popular justice worked together in concert and cannot simply be understood as discrete atomised incidents.

Alexander Sims,[174] a Scottish merchant living in Collooney, bought a flour mill in Camp Hill, Co. Sligo from a popular local man named William Kelly. Kelly ran up a debt with the Provincial Bank of Ireland to the tune of £8,000 and the bank planned a public auction in Dublin on 7 June, but then decided to forgo the auction and sell the mill to Sims privately. Almost immediately, the community of Collooney[175] reacted with the posting of a number of illegal notices threatening anyone who sold or carried grain for Sims: 'Any man that sells oats to Sims' the Scotch Man of Colloony prepare his Coffin . . . any Man not complying with this will get a sore Death. The Irishman.' Another notice posted a few days later and signed by 'Lieutenant Spear' warned carmen not to deliver corn,

---

[174] Sometimes recorded as Sim or Simm.    [175] Also spelled Colloony.

threatening death and promising 'I do solemnly swear that I will exhibit on the bridge of Colloony before twelve Months the scul [*sic*] and bones of the old Deceiver Sims.'[176] Within a week, a carman named Cormack Gallagher was seriously assaulted after returning from selling oats to Sims. When Gallagher was summoned before the magistrates for investigation, he confessed that while he knew the men who attacked him, who he named as John Dunleary and John Ormasby, he 'was afraid to lodge information against the parties', and would prefer to go to jail for contempt of court.[177] Collooney's local men of influence – landlords, clergy, merchants and resident magistrates – issued a panicked proclamation condemning the violence and suggested that 'such lawless violence' dissuaded economic investment in Ireland, and specifically 'prevent[ed] wealthy persons from settling amongst us, and employing our poor'.[178] The outrages continued. On 28 June 'some persons unknown' stole a cart of John McNamara's and cut its harness. McNamara, it was noted, had 'sold Oats' to Sims 'against whom Combination exists', and according to McNamara's sworn testimony was told Gallagher's beating was 'for not keeping the rules' concerning Sims. The next day a notice appeared threatening John Rooney 'if he continued to work for Mr Simm'. On the same day, in the neighbouring parish of St. John, '2 Men unknown' paid a visit to another employee of Sims's, John Walker, and 'beat him so unmercifully that his life is in danger'. Not long after, in August, Sims 'was struck on the head with a stick' while walking his grounds. Notices posted throughout the area threatened anyone who attempted to have anything to do with Sims – boycotting tactics that would become famous fifty years later with the Land League and Charles Stewart Parnell – and no fewer than twenty-six separate outrages, ranging from incendiary fires, cattle houghing, and serious assaults to threatening letters, took place between May and the end of October.[179]

Dublin Castle responded by sending a stipendiary magistrate, Bartholomew Warburton, to sort things out and bring the perpetrators to justice. After arriving in early July 1838, Warburton attempted to find out who was responsible for carrying out these outrages against Sims. Drummond directed Warburton 'not to spare Money or Exertion to put [the unrest] down', promising to send artillery horses and wagons if Warburton thought it necessary.[180] Nevertheless, the townspeople

[176] 16 May 1838, NAI, OP 1838/26/109.    [177] 22 May 1838, NAI, OP 1838/26/85.
[178] Ibid.
[179] 'Reports of Outrage', TNA, HO 100/254/182; ibid., HO 100/255/172–3, 176–7, 183; for the relevant outrages connected to Sim see Outrage Reports for County Sligo, NAI, OP 1838/85–175.
[180] 'Select Committee on State of Ireland', 738.

refused to speak. The combination against Sims extended over a twenty-mile perimeter across the county lines of Mayo, Roscommon, and Leitrim. Long after these incidents, witnesses called before the Lords' committee on crime in Ireland would claim this was clearly a case that displayed all the characteristics of a so-called 'Ribbon system'.

After months of violence directed against Sims and anyone that came in contact with him, the violence abruptly ended. Had government succeeded in beating the population into submission and re-establishing law and order? On the contrary, according to one resident magistrate, Malachy Douclan:

Mr Sims gives up Camp Hill to Mr Madden the brother-in-law to Mr Kelly – he (Mr Sims) being repaid the £5000 which he gave to the Bank. . . . Thus endeth the War in this province. The cry is now 'Sims + Kelly for ever'!! . . . It is to be regretted that the Strong Arm of the law could not have been made the Arbiter between these parties – rather than that a bad example should be set of the apparent triumph of illegal combination.

The sub-inspector of Connacht also lamented, 'This compromise will have the effect of restoring tranquillity to that part of the Country, but at the same time it will afford unequivocal evidence of the triumph of combination.'[181] As this chapter has suggested, the violence directed against Sims was not simply that of illegal combination, or lawlessness, but rather was, in the words of one constable, demonstrative of a people 'bent upon a lawless spirit of law giving' – a law that was their own.[182]

[181] Malachy Douclan to [?], 10 October 1838, NAI, OP 1838/26/83; Sub-Inspector Robert Curtis to Inspector General McGregor, 9 October 1838, ibid.
[182] 9 March 1838, NAI, OP 1838/19/53.

## 3  'Justice to Ireland'
### Whigs and Ireland, 1835–1840

In March 1835, Daniel O'Connell wrote to his trusted political lieutenant P. V. FitzPatrick of rumours swirling through London that Peel's Conservative government had surrendered their ministerial positions. 'Blessed be the great God for this prospect!', confessed O'Connell, 'It is joyful to think that the iron rule of Orangeism is so nearly at an end.'[1] Brought in less than a year earlier by King William IV after his unwillingness to submit the House of Commons to the leadership of Lord John Russell, which ended Melbourne's Whig government, Peel's government resigned after consecutive defeats in the House of Commons regarding the election of a Speaker for the House and the thorny issue of the appropriation of surplus funds from the Church of Ireland – what became known as 'church appropriation'. These defeats necessitated a rather awkward invitation by the king to the Whigs to form another government, with the implicit understanding that any Whig government would feel compelled to deal with the issue of church appropriation, revisiting the conflict between crown and Parliament that had precipitated the Whigs' dismissal in 1834.

If it was clear that Peel's government was out, however, it was less clear who would lead the new government, under what form, and guided by what principles. Charles Greville, the posthumously famous diarist and Clerk of the Council in ordinary, wrote concerning the difficulty of securing a unified cabinet, 'I certainly never remember a great victory for which *Te Deum* was chanted with so faint and joyless a voice.'[2] Some in the party hoped for a reunion with the conservative-leaning faction led by Lord Stanley, such as the former PM Lord Grey, who believed Stanley 'a necessary card in the formation of an administration'.[3] Others, like Lord Duncannon, saw an opportunity to co-opt O'Connell and English Radicals, turning their talents towards legislating reform.[4] Thus, while

---

[1] O'Connell to P. V. FitzPatrick, 27 March 1835 in O'Connell, *Correspondence* 5:287.

[2] Greville, *The Greville Memoirs*, 3: 254.

[3] Grey to Melbourne, 1 February 1835, TNA, Russell Papers, PRO 30/22/1E, f. 21.

[4] Lansdowne to Russell, 13 February 1835, ibid., f. 17. On Duncannon's value as an emissary to O'Connell and his knowledge of Irish affairs, see A. H. Graham, 'The

O'Connell praised God for the Whigs' ascension, the leaders themselves questioned the Lords' providence and their own futures.

This was one dominant narrative of the period 1835 to 1841 adopted by some contemporaries as well as subsequent historians: the Whigs had thrown out Peel's government without the means to secure one on their own terms and were forced to accede to a loose coalition with Radicals and O'Connellites. This marriage of necessity with O'Connell led the Whigs to bring the problems of Ireland more centre stage, often leading to significant defeats in the House of Lords on Irish questions. Finally, this strain between balancing Whig principles – a so-called Whig *via media* – and aligning with Radicals and O'Connellites ultimately led to a political fracture and the fall of Melbourne's government in 1841. The fall of Melbourne's administration and an examination of its parliamentary achievements have led some historians to regard the Whigs' time holding a majority as a failure, while others argue it was an inevitable outcome of the Reform Act, which had made the counties decidedly Tory and the reformed towns overwhelmingly Radical.[5]

While much of this historiographical narrative is compelling, it also leaves much to be desired in terms of explaining the commitment to a programme of 'justice to Ireland' that the Whigs adopted after 1835. It runs the risk of underestimating the profound commitment among some ministers to approaching Ireland's problems in fresh ways, or their philosophical desire to more fully integrate Ireland as an equal partner within the political union through reform. Indeed, writing in 1837 reflecting on their Irish policy and the challenges it brought, Russell reminded Melbourne of their commitment:

The attempt to govern on Orange maxims broke down in 1829 – the attempt to govern by a neutrality between different parties broke down in 1834. Neither of these plans can be permanently reestablished. I remember you were the first person in 1829 to whom I heard it said that Ireland would henceforth claim to be treated according to its importance as a branch of the United Kingdom. It has done so, + will do so, + has a right to do so.[6]

A cursory examination of the important questions that government attempted to address through legislative reform in these six years demonstrates the vital part 'the Irish question' played in parliamentary politics,

Lichfield House Compact, 1835', IHS 12, no. 47 (March 1961): 209–25; K. Theodore Hoppen, 'Ponsonby, John William, Fourth Earl of Bessborough (1781–1847)', *ODNB*, https://doi.org/10.1093/ref:odnb/22500.
[5] Newbould, *Whiggery and Reform*, 314–21. On the unstable state of political parties in the period and Peel's assisting Melbourne's government to retain power, see Hilton, *Mad, Bad, and Dangerous*, 513–24; Mitchell, *Lord Melbourne*, 186.
[6] Russell to Melbourne, 9 September 1837, TNA, Russell Papers, PRO 30/22/2F, f. 73.

on matters including tithes, the constabulary, poor laws, church appropriation, and municipality reform.[7] Furthermore, outside of Parliament,
the sources indicate among much of the population of Ireland a genuine
appreciation for the Whigs' commitment to justice, even if many of their
bills did not make it past the House of Lords. Take, for example, the
'Morpeth Roll', an enormous spool of parchment 420 metres in length,
presented to Lord Morpeth at the end of his tenure as chief secretary and
which promised 'the warmest Good Wishes of our Country [that] will
ever Accompany You, in Your Future Progress through Life', complete
with the signatures of roughly 160,000 Irishmen.[8] This testimonial suggests the serious admiration of many in the country for Whig policy,
which is largely missing from or underemphasised in much of the existing
literature.

The 1830s are also important, and too often overlooked, in Irish
historiography. This period in O'Connell's career has largely been characterised as a lull between his successful campaign for Catholic
Emancipation and his infamous 'monster meetings' for Repeal in 1843
at the end of his life, which ended in failure. Rather than seeing
O'Connell's parliamentary support for Whig government as a genuine
alignment of principles, historians have read it as a period in which
O'Connell dithered before gathering his forces for his ultimate
end – Repeal. Tellingly, in the most recent O'Connell biography,
Patrick Geoghegan's chapter on the later 1830s is titled 'Despair and
Decline', whereas his chapter on the early 1840s begins the second part of
the book and is titled 'The Resurrection of O'Connell: The Campaign for
Repeal, 1840–1843'.[9] This view, however, significantly underestimates
O'Connell's commitment to the Whig government, his belief in its good
intentions in terms of offering Ireland a more prosperous and hopeful
future, and its 'reformist interests [which] were perhaps wider than those
of any other leading politician of his day'.[10] Nevertheless, this union
between O'Connell and the Whigs has important implications as
a moment of fusion of the nationalist and parliamentary ways; one
which slowly soured and fissured, and would not be reconciled until
Parnell's attempts to subsume violent nationalism into his parliamentary
way nearly fifty years later.

---

[7] Peter Gray, *Famine, Land and Politics: British Government and Irish Society, 1843–50*
(Dublin: Irish Academic Press, 1999), 28–35.
[8] Christopher Ridgway, ed., *The Morpeth Roll: Ireland Identified in 1841* (Dublin: Four
Courts Press, 2013), chs. 2, 3.
[9] Patrick Geoghegan, *Liberator: The Life and Death of Daniel O'Connell, 1830–1847*
(Dublin: Gill & MacMillan, 2013), chs. 7, 8. Geoghegan also refers to O'Connell as
Moses in his chapter on 1843.
[10] Hoppen, 'Riding a Tiger', 136.

This chapter argues that 1835 marked a distinct break in British governing policy, which saw the increasing importance of the Irish office triumvirate of Lord John Russell, Lord Mulgrave, and Lord Morpeth in shaping a new approach to Irish questions. This new approach was twofold, advocating the need to rectify the distinctively Orange character of Dublin Castle's administration while also attempting larger parliamentary reforms to solve many of Ireland's long-standing challenges. These bold new strategies would have lasting consequences as a result of their uniting the Tory party and propelling it to its electoral victory in 1841, discussed later in Chapter 5. What follows, therefore, is an attempt to uncover what so upset Tory politicians and members of the gentry that it would lead to such an overwhelming backlash.

## Political Realignments

The eighteen months between January 1834 and June 1835 provided significant political turmoil in the British political system, much of it centring on important political differences between the two parties' Irish policies. The result of this tumultuous period was the ascension of a Whig government in April 1835 that departed from the status quo in its Irish policy and adopted a strategy of 'justice to Ireland'. Therefore, the political debates that took place during this year are an important part of the larger story delineating the changes in personalities that charted a new approach to Ireland – what Hoppen has referred to as an assimilationist approach.[11]

Disagreement over Irish policy at the beginning of 1834 created great strain within Grey's Whig government. The issues of church appropriation and the role of coercive legislation in imposing British law and order in the Irish countryside exposed the political fault line between the conservative faction within the cabinet and the more liberal wing of the party. Lord Stanley, a rising star in the party, presumptive future prime minister, and former chief secretary of Ireland, led the conservative grouping of the party. As a 'high churchman' who fully supported the Established Church in Ireland, regardless of the paltry number of Irish people who belonged to the church, Stanley along with his clique, labelled the 'Derby Dilly', were adamantly opposed to the government's appropriating funds from the Established Church for secular purposes such as education or poor relief.[12] He had also enthusiastically promoted coercive

---

[11] Hoppen, *Governing Hibernia*, ch. 4.

[12] 'Memo on Irish Church', June 1831, LPL, Derby Papers, 920 DER 14/16/5. On some Whigs' belief that Stanley was the logical choice as party leader and prime minister, see

legislation to subdue Irish outrages in 1833, supported by other prominent conservative members of the government, like the First Lord of the Admiralty James Graham.[13] Initially, the liberal members of the government, most prominently among them Lord John Russell, had agreed to drop the issue of Irish church appropriation in June 1833 in an effort to hold the party together so it could continue its political programme of reform. But in May 1834 Russell 'upset the coach' by proposing to use Irish church monies for secular purposes, which led Stanley and Graham to resign from Grey's cabinet and jump ship with twenty-four other MPs to join Peel's Tory party.[14] Although this did not end Grey's government, it did have the effect of severely weakening the government's parliamentary majority. More importantly for future Irish policy initiatives between 1835 to 1841, however, the resignation of the high church faction brought with it a 'freer course of action' to the remaining Whigs and greater clarity in their political agenda.[15] Furthermore, Stanley's departure cleared the way for Lord John Russell to assume a more prominent role in the party's leadership, which would have a profound impact on Ireland in the coming years.

With the greater freedom afforded by the departure of the 'Derby Dilly', some members of the Whig government attempted to tackle the serious problem of Irish tithes. Although O'Connell returned to his campaign for the repeal of the Act of Union in 1834, much to the chagrin of the government, the Chief Secretary of Ireland E. J. Littleton was convinced that O'Connell would end his agitation if Parliament addressed the tithe problem with a new bill. Proposing a *quid pro quo* to O'Connell, Littleton promised that the Whig government would soften measures in the upcoming coercion bill to allow O'Connell the right to public meetings and petitioning, along with ending court martial for civilians, provided that O'Connell supported the Whigs' tithe bill. When Lord Grey, who despised O'Connell, refused to agree to this compromise and declared that the coercion bill would remain unaltered, O'Connell cried foul and publicly declared he had been wilfully misled by

John Prest, *Lord John Russell* (Columbia: University of South Carolina Press, 1972), 65–6.

[13] Newbould suggests Stanley's 'brilliant speech' on Irish coercion secured its passage; see Newbould, *Whiggery and Reform*, 13.

[14] Hilton, *Mad, Bad, and Dangerous*, 496; David Close, 'The Formation of a Two-Party Alignment in the House of Commons between 1832 and 1841', EHR 84, no. 331 (April 1969): 261. Thirty-eight members would sign a pledge to Peel at a meeting called by Stanley on 23 February 1835, see LPL, Derby Papers, 920 DER 14/20/1/1.

[15] Baron Edward John Walhouse Littleton Hatherton, *Memoir and Correspondence Relating to Political Occurrences in June and July 1834*, ed. Henry Reeve (London: Longmans, Green and Co., 1872), 8.

Littleton. With a fractured cabinet, Lord Althorp tendered his resignation as leader of the House of Commons in July 1834, which ultimately led to Lord Grey's resignation as prime minister, though this did not end his attempts to influence the Whigs' political agenda.[16] As a result, the king was forced to ask Lord Melbourne to serve as prime minister, a man considered by his contemporaries as someone who lacked political ambition or a desire to govern, and with Parliament out of session Melbourne happily led the government without doing any active governing.[17]

Meanwhile, events in Ireland continued to showcase the popular dissatisfaction over the issue of tithes, which led to reoccurring violent confrontations between the people and government forces and further internal discord among government ministers. Lord Wellesley, the lord lieutenant, sounded alarm bells in an April 1834 letter to Melbourne stressing that the revolutionary aim of the people was not simply to resist the imposition of tithes but to subordinate the authority of the state. The peasants across Co. Galway were using 'secret combination, concealed organisation, intimidation, suppression of all evidence of crime, and the ambition of usurping the government, of ruling society by the authority of the common people, and of superseding the law by the decrees of illegal association'.[18] Between January and March 1834, the government received reports of twelve outrages targeting those serving tithe notices, including a mob of 200 peasants preventing the delivery of notices in Co. Donegal, an incident in which 2 tithe proctors were shot at and nearly killed in Co. Westmeath, and the sudden adjournment of a meeting of magistrates in Rathkeale, Co. Limerick when a mob assembled outside to prevent them from adjudicating on tithe cases.[19] In the spring and summer of 1834 Wellesley declared large portions of counties Kilkenny, King's, Westmeath, and Galway in a state of disturbance, thus triggering the imposition of curfews and summary convictions for acts deemed to be of an insurrectionary nature under the Coercion Act.[20] Tensions continued to simmer but received little to no attention from Melbourne, who was seemingly content to function as a caretaker prime minister.

Although Stanley's defection in 1834 weakened the government's position, the Whigs' fall from power in November came as a shock to many. Greville, capturing the mood around London exclaimed, 'Yesterday

---

[16] Hatherton, *Memoir and Correspondence*, 9, 12–18; Mitchell, *Lord Melbourne*, 143; Macintyre, *Liberator*, 134–40; Hansard, 3rd ser., vol. 24, cols. 1336–42, 9 July 1834.

[17] Mitchell, *Lord Melbourne*, 146–7.

[18] Lord Wellesley to Lord Melbourne, 15 April 1834, 'Papers Relating to the State of Ireland' (P. P.) 1834, vol. 43, no. 459, 3.

[19] 'Papers Relating to the State of Ireland', 99–104.

[20] 'Papers Relating to the State of Ireland', 8–56.

morning the town was electrified by the news that Melbourne's government was at an end. Nobody had the slightest suspicion of such an impending catastrophe.'[21] The shock centred on the king's decision to exercise his royal prerogative and dismiss the government because of his distaste for many of its policies, especially its principled position on the question of Irish church appropriation. When Lord Althorp's father, Lord Spencer, died, it forced Althorp's retirement to the House of Lords and left Melbourne with few options for his replacement. Melbourne's best option, Lord John Russell, was unacceptable to the king, who disdained Russell's political outlook and personality.[22] Nevertheless, the king's dismissal '*á la militaire*' surprised everyone, including a majority of the ministers, who learned of their new political situation by reading about it in the papers the next morning.[23] Conservatives in Ireland reading their newspapers read this as their deliverance. The *Belfast News-Letter* published addresses from inhabitants of many towns and cities across Ulster proclaiming their loyalty to King William IV, their support for his ability to choose his own ministers, and the positive signal his choice of Wellington and Peel to form a government sent to the Protestants of the island. Alluding to the 'glorious Constitution' that the Whigs had placed in danger with their 'injudicious and vacillating measures', 8,450 signatories from Lisburn, Co. Antrim praised the king for his invitation to 'such Ministers as will preserve inviolate those Sacred Institutions for which our forefathers fought and bled, and under which we hitherto enjoyed unparalleled prosperity and happiness'.[24]

For Whigs, Radicals, and O'Connellites, Melbourne's dismissal was profound and influenced the combative nature of politics between November 1834 and the eventual fall of Peel's government in April 1835. In many ways, the king's unorthodox method of dismissal had a silver lining for the Whigs as it galvanised public opinion and united a broad spectrum of personalities within the party. Russell argued that the king had acted out of 'caprice rather than reasonable judgment' by dismissing a ministry still supported by the majority of Parliament.[25] The

[21] Greville, *Greville Memoirs*, 3:292.
[22] Melbourne to Grey, 14 November 1834, Sanders, *Lord Melbourne's Papers*, 225. Dislike of Russell, or at least uncertainty about his ability to lead the House of Commons, extended to many of his colleagues. See Prest, *Lord John Russell*, 76–81.
[23] Wellesley to Grey, 9 December 1834, in *The Wellesley Papers: The Life and Correspondence of Richard Colley Wellesley, Marquess Wellesley, 1760–1842* (London: Herbert Jenkins, 1914), 255; Newbould, *Whiggery and Reform*, 154–160.
[24] 'Belfast Address to His Majesty', BNL, 12 December 1834. Many such addresses appeared in Irish newspapers.
[25] Lord John Russell, *Recollections and Suggestions, 1813–1873* (Boston, MA: Roberts Brothers, 1875), 108.

*Morning Chronicle* noted the effect the king's action had had on the public, stressing that there existed:

The perfect unanimity of all classes and sections of Reformers, against either the threats or bribes of a Tory Government. Radicals, Ultra-radicals, and Whigs, were everywhere to be seen acting together, and wisely casting aside all minor dissentions, in order to oppose a united front to their common enemy.[26]

O'Connell confidently predicted that Melbourne's dismissal would cause a more liberal government to form, suggesting to his wife, Mary, 'you never were so near being the Wife of a Ministry of State as you are', as he worked to 'combine [with] all classes of reformers'.[27]

### Centring Ireland: The Whigs' Irish Policy and the Fall of Peel's Government

While O'Connell exaggerated his prospects as a future government minister, his jocular letters to Mary demonstrate his astute political awareness and the growing sense of his own importance given the unique state of politics in November 1834. Circumstances presented the Whigs with a choice heretofore unknown in British politics because it would involve joining political forces with Irish Catholics. Either they could accept and support Peel's Tory government and try to moderate it, or they could align with English Radicals and O'Connell's Irish MPs, which would force their party to embrace more radical reforms. The resignation of Stanley, the retirement of Lord Grey, and the ascension of Lord Althorp to the House of Lords opened the party's leadership to a number of different members who were decidedly more liberal in their outlook, especially vis-à-vis Ireland. After overcoming initial hesitancy from some of the 'old guard', especially Melbourne and Lord Lansdowne, by February 1835 the liberal contingent of the party had agreed on a strategy that embraced an unspoken partnership with O'Connell and a focus on active opposition to every important action of Peel's government.[28] The decision to work with English Radicals and O'Connell culminated with

---

[26] 'State of Public Opinion and Movements in the Metropolis', *Morning Chronicle*, 19 November 1834.

[27] O'Connell to Mary O'Connell, 18 November 1834; O'Connell to Mary O'Connell, 20 November 1834; O'Connell to Mary O'Connell, 21 November 1834 in O'Connell, *Correspondence*, 5: 201–4.

[28] On the process of convincing the conservative members of the Whig party to adopt a combative strategy to Peel's government, see Duncannon to Melbourne, 18 December 1834, Sanders, *Lord Melbourne's Papers*, 229; Hobhouse Diary, 25 January [1835], BL, Broughton Papers, Add MS 61826, f. 75–7.

the meeting of roughly 180 MPs on 18 February 1835, at the home of Lord Lichfield, in London.

The meeting at St. James's Square, the so-called Lichfield House Compact, has been shrouded in both historical mystery and historiographic controversy. As O'Connell was one of the most disliked figures in British politics, association with him carried with it a potential stain on one's character. The self-interest of politicians like Lord John Russell and Lord Melbourne lay in their ability to assert plausible deniability, and they maintained their ignorance regarding any collaboration with O'Connell, which leaves historians to ponder how deeply involved either were in any alliance with O'Connell or the English Radicals.[29] Nevertheless, the evidence suggests rather convincingly that Russell and Melbourne involved themselves in the deliberations regarding the Whigs' political tactics, which, due to the nature of the various parties, meant either a concert with those on the Whigs' left, or a capitulation with Peel and those on the right. In short, while it is plausible that Melbourne had little to no direct involvement in building any alliance, Russell was fully aware of developments, if not positively directing them through intermediaries like Duncannon, Hobhouse, and Poulett Thomson. Russell's decisive leadership at the first meeting at Lichfield's home on 18 February 1835, regarding the political ground upon which the united opposition would fight, seems to confirm his foreknowledge and approbation, which is corroborated by Hobhouse's diary charting Russell's evolution from initial opposition to leader.[30] At the end of his life, Russell suggested that during this period of political turmoil he conceived of the Whigs as a big-tent party and wanted to carefully select the terrain to collectively lead them forward:

The Liberal Party had a clear majority of the elections, but that majority consisted of every shade, from the most moderate of the Whigs to the most resolute of the Radicals. It seemed to me, as commander-in-chief of an army so variously composed, that they could not be too soon brought into action, and that motions ought to be framed in which the whole party could agree.[31]

Russell knew that the only way to dislodge Peel was to forge a new working relationship with O'Connell and the English Radicals, and although he refused to acknowledge that what happened at Lichfield

---

[29] Thus Russell's letter to Melbourne on 11 February (1835), which included a postscript about 'a question of having a meeting on the 18th, to which Whigs, Radicals, and Repealers should be invited', which Russell felt 'doubtful about', should be regarded with a heavy dose of scepticism. See Russell to Melbourne, 11 February [1835], Sanders, *Lord Melbourne*, 254–5.

[30] Hobhouse Diary, BL, Broughton Papers, Add MS 61826, ff. 25–93.

[31] Russell, *Recollections*, 109.

was a compact, he firmly saw it as 'an alliance on honourable terms of mutual co-operation'.[32] The Lichfield House Compact, 'one of the most decisive events in British political history between 1832 and 1847',[33] secured a decidedly left-leaning tack for the party and heralded the end of Lord Grey's more conservative leadership over it. The ship had sailed on Grey's vision of a Whig Party guided by moderating its reforming tendencies, and it had sailed with his leadership of the party on board. In his place a group of younger men, led by Lord John Russell, asserted control and led a more heterogeneous and progressive group of men onto the government benches.

What was the ground Russell chose on 'which the whole party could agree'?[34] In short, it was on Irish questions. First, Russell put Peel on notice of the Whigs' intention to oppose his governing agenda with the party's decision to contest the election of the Speaker of the House of Commons. With the support of progressive members of his party, like Lord Mulgrave and John Cam Hobhouse whipping votes in the House, the Whigs success-fully elected their candidate James Abercromby over Peel's choice of Thomas Manners Sutton, with their new Irish partners, led by O'Connell, providing the majority.[35] Upon the opening of Parliament in February Lord Morpeth, hitherto a non-entity among the Whig leadership, proposed an amendment to the king's address and stressed the 'keen and irresistible demand for the reformation of all abuses', which included 'abuses in the Church which ... disturb society in Ireland, and lower the character of the establishment in both countries'.[36] After three nights of debate, Morpeth's amendment passed the Commons by seven votes (309–302), highlighting Peel's relative weakness in the House, especially in votes related to matters of the Irish church.

Members of the English Radicals and Irish MPs attempted to embar-rass and undermine Peel by demonstrating the government's reliance on the support of ultra-Protestants in his party, and of the rabidly anti-Catholic Orange Order in Ireland. Joseph Hume, a leading English Radical, worked in tandem with O'Connell to reveal how Peel's govern-ment had accepted a number of so-called 'Loyalty Addresses' from members of the Orange Order in Ireland presented on the floor of the Commons by Tory MPs, which pledged their fidelity to William IV and thanked Peel for restoring Tory government.[37] When government

[32] Ibid., 111.   [33] Macintyre, *The Liberator*, 144.   [34] Russell, *Recollections*, 109
[35] Greville, *Greville Memoirs*, 2:253; on O'Connell and English Radicals' enthusiasm for Russell's course of action, see Hobhouse Diary, 18 February [1835], BL, Broughton Papers, Add MS 61816, 88.
[36] Hansard, 3rd ser., vol. 26, cols. 172–3, 24 February 1835.
[37] 'Addresses to the King', BNL, 3 March 1835.

ministers stated that these addresses were 'most graciously received' by the king, English Radicals and Irish MPs questioned whether such an acknowledgement was appropriate for the government to make, given the rather dubious legality of the Orange Order. In the Commons the Home Secretary Henry Goulburn argued that it was impossible for the government to inquire into the propriety of every address presented to the king, that these had been received on behalf of individuals 'not as addresses coming from societies', and that their acknowledgement was in no way a reflection of the legality of the Orange Order.

These excuses did not fly with O'Connell, who used the opportunity to press for Parliament to uncover the true nature of the Orange Order and disclose whether it was a secret society bound together by an oath to commit sectarian violence. O'Connell quoted at length on the floor of the House of Commons from a portion of an alleged Orange oath: '"Thy foot shall be wet with the blood of thy enemy: the tongue of the dog shall be red with the same"', O'Connell read, suggesting to the House, 'it was high time, then, that the country should know precisely what Orangeism was'. Dominick Ronayne, MP for Clonmel, alleged that Peel's government placed Orangemen in appointments throughout Ireland and Britain, thus giving them sanction and support. Addressing the prime minister, he argued that the appointments seemed intended to reassert Protestant dominance over Catholics, as if Catholic Emancipation had never happened: 'The very appointment of such persons in Ireland, was quite calculated to inspire the people of that country, with the notion that they were again to be handed over to Orangemen, and to be again oppressed by them, as they had been for the last quarter of a century.'[38] The debate achieved its desired effect. The extreme right wing of the Conservative Party, including many Conservative backbenchers, proudly proclaimed themselves as Orangemen and professed the organisation's legality and loyalty. This bit of political theatre painted Peel's position as secured only by the most zealous reactionaries; the *Morning Chronicle* predicted: 'the Orangemen will not serve him without some return ... [one] more troublesome to himself than to his opponents'.[39]

Russell decided that Irish church appropriation offered Whigs the most politically advantageous means to end Peel's government. Not only had it been the issue that 'upset the coach', thus driving Stanley to resign earlier in 1834 and propelling Russell to lead the Whigs, it also unified Whig, Radical, and O'Connellite. Russell would later call appropriation the 'frontier line between Liberal and Tory principles', and as such it won

---

[38] Hansard, 3rd ser., vol 26, 536–54 (col. 547), 4 March 1835.
[39] 'The Morning Chronicle', *Morning Chronicle*, 5 March 1835.

support from the more reluctant member of the Whig Party, like Lord Grey's son Lord Howick, and was 'the basis of an alliance with O'Connell and the Irish members'.[40] Machinations began amid 'rumours of ministers' resignations' on 27 March, when a quasi-shadow cabinet met at Russell's to discuss what measure to adopt concerning appropriation and settled on proposing the formation of a committee to inquire into the monies of the Irish church and their various uses.[41] At a dinner to celebrate Russell for his parliamentary leadership the following day at the Freeman's Lodge chaired by Lord Morpeth, which was attended by some 250 MPs, O'Connell declared the evening '"the most delightful ... he ever passed in his life", [and] publicly acknowledged John Russell as his leader'.[42]

On 30 March, Lord John Russell presented his motion to form a committee to inquire into the Church of Ireland and how most effectively to appropriate any surplus revenue to 'all classes of the community'. The speech went to great lengths to highlight the outrages perpetrated in Ireland, which resulted in the population having more to fear from 'the combination of those who set up against the law, than the ministers who execute the law', thus rendering law and order ineffectual. Importantly, however, Russell's speech set out a new vision for how to deal with Irish problems – problems that began with the Church of Ireland and the collection of tithes. Russell's new vision centred on a policy of justice that he believed would effectively win Irish affection, thus ensuring its people's loyalty, as well as the prosperity of the empire. His speech is worth quoting at length as it demonstrates the Whig belief in the vital connection between Irish prosperity based on legislating justice and the wider security of the British Empire:

Notwithstanding those outrages and acts of violence to which I referred in the commencement of my speech, it is a singular fact, that no traveller ever goes into Ireland who does not declare that he has been received every where, by the poorest peasant ... with the utmost friendly and open-hearted kindness. ... Such being the feeling, and such the conduct of that nation to individuals, the House has now an opportunity of earning that gratitude and making that affection its own, by asserting the principle for which I contend, and by thus doing justice to the people of Ireland. We have now the power of acting free from fear – free from any compulsion ... It is in our power at length to settle and gain the affections of that country, to silence the question of a Repeal of the Union, to gain the tribute of grateful homage from a people so warmhearted, so eminently brave and loyal;

---

[40] Russell, *Recollections*, 110–11; for discussion on Russell's calculation pressing for appropriation in 1834, see Prest, *Lord John Russell*, 65–9.

[41] Hobhouse Journal, 27 March [1835], BL, Broughton Papers, Add MS 61826, 112.

[42] Greville, *Greville Memoirs*, 374.

which we shall, at the same time, have the satisfaction of reflecting, *that in doing justice to Ireland we shall have contributed more . . . to the future prosperity of the empire*, making her unconquerable by her enemies, and an example of religious liberality to the rest of the world.[43]

In reporting on Russell's speech, which ended with 'long pronounced cheering' throughout the House, the *Morning Chronicle* highlighted the importance of equal justice, asking rhetorically: 'When, in the history of the world, was injustice seen to produce order?' They further stressed that the course forward held 'no halting half-way between oppression and equal justice. From the moment we relaxed our treatment of the Catholics, we conceded to them power to force further concessions from us.'[44] In short, any Irish policy under Russell's leadership would be founded on the principles of justice and equality, with the understanding that further institutional reforms were necessary to achieve these goals.

Russell's motion successfully brought down Peel's government with a majority of twenty-seven votes. On 7 April the House of Commons divided on the question of whether to include the principle of church appropriation in any measure passed by the House addressing the problem of Irish tithes. In debate, Russell returned to the theme of justice, condemning the Tories for ignoring whether the laws they passed for Ireland were just, while also tying the question of appropriation to an equitable settlement of the tithe question and to a policy of education for the whole of Ireland's population.[45] Connecting church appropriation, the tithe question, and the general education of Ireland's population was not simply the result of a political calculus meant to dispatch Peel's Conservative government, though it certainly had this effect. While asserting that the Whig Party was run by an entirely new group of politicians sharing a united vision of principles certainly stretches the truth, it is no surprise that Russell chose an Irish issue to bring his disparate party together, and from it a new departure for Whig policy in Ireland. When Melbourne returned as prime minister, he gave Russell 'a suzerainty over Ireland' as home secretary, happily conceding that he allowed his ministers to run 'their own departments as independent kingdoms'.[46] A prospective new day dawned for Ireland, full of possibilities based on a Whig ministry that was committed to act on principles of justice and equity – storm clouds, however, lay just beyond the horizon.

[43] Hansard, 3rd ser., vol. 27, cols. 364, 384, 30 March 1835, my emphasis.
[44] 'The Morning Chronicle', *Morning Chronicle*, 31 March 1835.
[45] Hansard, 3rd. ser., vol. 27, cols. 880–4, 7 April 1835.
[46] Mandler, *Aristocratic Government*, 161–2; Mitchell, *Lord Melbourne*, 156.

## 'Justice to Ireland'

King William IV requested Lord Melbourne assume the role of prime minister six days after Peel resigned, an unusually long time. The king had hoped he could entice Lord Grey to return as prime minister, or that a political marriage between the conservative section of the Whig Party and the liberal section of the Conservative Party might lead to a grand coalition between Peel, Melbourne, and Stanley.[47] When Melbourne and Lord Lansdowne stoutly refused, the king was forced to give Melbourne the freedom to form a government. 'Notwithstanding the good face which the King contrives to put upon the communications with his hated new-old Ministers and master, he is really very miserable', Greville wrote in his diary, while also recounting how the king's sister, the Duchess of Gloucester, told Greville that the king 'was in the most pitiable state of distress, constantly in tears, and saying that "he felt his crown tottering on his head"'.[48] The king feared what the government intended to do with the institutions of Protestantism in Ireland. These fears, though exaggerated, were not entirely unfounded. The Whigs had rallied around Irish questions and promised further reforms, compromises that most conservatives, including the king, would find wholly unacceptable. To make matters worse, the Whigs had chosen an Irish question to defeat Peel as a means to work with O'Connell, who now propped up Whig parliamentary majorities. For members of the Protestant establishment, these were ominous times.

Melbourne and Russell indicated their new direction in Ireland with the appointment of two politically aspirant young men to the key positions that shaped the government's Irish policy – Lord Mulgrave as lord lieutenant of Ireland and Lord Morpeth as chief secretary of Ireland. Mulgrave, thirty-eight at the time of his appointment, served as governor of Jamaica during the turbulent period around emancipation in 1832–3, when he pressed to 'reconstitute the authority of the Home Government' over the colonial assembly, and wrestled with how to deal with fundamental divisions in Jamaican society over questions of sovereignty, race, and labour, which may go towards explaining his appointment over the previous Whig Lord Lieutenant, Lord Wellesley.[49] On Mulgrave's official arrival in Dublin in May 1835, the moderate Tory *Belfast News-Letter* wrote, 'Never did we behold such a mass of human beings; flags and

[47] Hobhouse Journal, 16 April [1835], BL, Broughton Papers, Add MS 61826, 119–20.
[48] Greville, *Greville Memoirs*, 3:386.
[49] Wilbur Devereux Jones, 'Lord Mulgrave's Administration in Jamaica, 1832–1833', *Journal of Negro History* 48, no. 1 (January 1963): 44–56, at 50. Wellesley was incensed at being passed over and eventually resigned the ceremonial role as Lord Chamberlain; in the early 1840s he would pledge his support to Peel, see Wellesley to Peel, 25 May 1841, BL, Peel Papers, Add MS 40429, f. 277–8.

banners waved in every direction, such as "Mulgrave for ever", "Mulgrave and reform", [and] "the triumph of justice"', as tens of thousands came to greet the new lord lieutenant with enthusiasm never before witnessed on such an occasion.[50]

To represent the government's Irish policy in the House of Commons, Russell and Melbourne chose Lord Morpeth, then thirty-three. Coming from an influential family connected by marriage with some of the most powerful Whig houses, Morpeth was sympathetic to demands for Irish reforms. He had been chosen to move the amendment to the king's address and given the honour of chairing the dinner given to Russell that cemented his leadership over Whig, Radical, and Repealer. From this, one can infer that Russell deemed Morpeth a capable speaker and debater, essential skills for a chief secretary required to answer the Commons regarding the government's policy. Morpeth had a winning personality and unimpeachable character that gave further weight to his appointment.[51] Above all, both these men shared fresh perspectives on how to govern Ireland based on a belief in equality, and were the 'Young men ... [of] which there was a dearth in 1830' and that according to Lord Holland offered fresh hope for Whig governance.[52] O'Connell was ebullient with news of the appointments, writing to his trusted lieutenant P. V. FitzPatrick, 'We have an excellent man in Lord Mulgrave, the new Lord-Lieutenant. I tell you there cannot be better. Lord Morpeth, too, is excellent. ... We are, I believe, on the verge of better times. I cannot tell you all my reasons for being satisfied, but I have abundant reasons for hope, nay, certainty.'[53]

The government had grand plans for legislating Irish reforms on 'assimilationist' terms – what was good enough for Great Britain, in the eyes of these new Whigs, should be extended to Ireland. After the Whigs passed municipal reform in England and Wales in September 1835, which established a uniform system of borough governance through

---

[50] 'Arrival of their Excellencies the Earl and Countess of Mulgrave', BNL, 15 May 1835.

[51] Ian Machin, 'Howard, George William Frederick, seventh earl of Carlisle (1802–1864)', *Oxford Dictionary of National Biography*, https://doi.org/10.1093/ref:odnb/13902; Ridgway, *The Morpeth Roll*, 37; James Grant, *Random Recollections of the House of Lords: From the Year 1830 to 1836, Including Personal Sketches of the Leading Members* (London: Smith, Elder, & Co., 1836), 113–14.

[52] Henry Richard Vassall Holland, The Holland House Diaries 1831–1840: The Diary of Henry Richard Vassall Fox, Third Lord Holland, with Extracts from the Diary of Dr John Allen, ed. Abraham D. Kriegel (London: Routledge & Kegan Paul, 1977), 290.

[53] O'Connell to FitzPatrick, 21 April 1835, O'Connell, *Correspondence*, 5: 294. O'Connell's praise garnered much criticism among others within and without the ministry. Both appointments were severely criticised, even ridiculed, and a running joke was made comparing two famous actors, Charles Kemble and John Liston, to Mulgrave and Morpeth. Mulgrave had a flair for theatrics, and Morpeth resembled Liston. See Greville, *Greville Memoirs*, 3:389.

a town council elected by ratepayers, Russell wanted to extend similar reforms to Ireland. Morpeth identified the reform of Irish municipalities as 'the only sure course for a Political regeneration' in Ireland, which meant it was 'the measure most dreaded by the Orange Aristocracy' because municipal governments functioned as one of the last bastions of Protestant Ascendancy.[54] Mulgrave believed Irish municipal reform embodied the party's mantra of 'equal rights or justice' and stressed that those involved with politics in Ireland anticipated passage of the measure as a symbolic 'triumph' over the Orange party.[55] The issue offered several advantages for the Whigs. First, since the passage of the Reform Act in 1832, it had become clear that English boroughs were corrupt institutions and that the country clamoured for their reform. A parliamentary committee had been formed to study the issue and make recommendations, which the Whigs' 1835 bill incorporated. Therefore, looking to bring similar reforms to Ireland was a logical next step and came on the heels of a huge political victory years in the making. The municipal corporations also controlled many of the levers of local law and order, as well as finances, and after Catholic Emancipation the burgeoning Catholic middle class aspired to gain access and control over these bodies that had hitherto remained under Protestant control. Therefore, O'Connell identified the bill as the most important legislative priority for the advancement of his political agenda, which meant the bill had the potential to reinforce the Whig–O'Connell compact.[56]

Russell's desire to resolve the dispute over the payment of Irish tithes also preoccupied the initial legislative agenda of the Whigs in 1835 and 1836. The issue of tithes had been simmering in Ireland since the early 1830s, which ultimately produced violent confrontations across the Irish country-side, especially in 1833 and 1834. During the last month of Peel's adminis-tration a fatal confrontation at Rathcormac, Co. Cork between seventy-two soldiers employed to collect tithes and a group of Irish peasants left nine dead and another nine wounded.[57] Another incident in Kilshannick, Co. Cork brought 300 peasants together, who attempted to kill the Rev. Edmond Lombard and James Hanlon as they intended to auction a horse seized for tithe arrears, which led to the use of eighty British regulars to the protect the rector and assist in his tithe collections.[58] Similar incidents

<hr/>

54 'Irish History Manuscript', n.d., CH, Morpeth Papers, J/19/11/14, 108.
55 Mulgrave to Russell, 15 April [1836], TNA, Russell Papers, PRO 30/22/2B/43-4.
56 MacDonagh, *Emancipist*, 131–2, 150–2.
57 Hansard, 3rd ser., vol. 26, cols. 500–16, 3 March 1835.
58 'Correspondence between Magistrates and Irish Government on Police Force being sent to Glanntane and Kilshannick to protect Persons employed in Collection of Tithes' (P. P.) (1834, vol. 43, no. 109).

occurred in 1834 and early 1835 in Ballybay, Co. Monaghan and Keady, Co. Armagh, with violent confrontations between Irish peasants, police, and British troops, demonstrating that opposition to tithes extended into the religiously diverse province of Ulster. Considering that the Whigs had chosen Irish issues to topple Peel's government – Irish church issues, no less – it was politically impossible to abandon these principles now that the Whigs found themselves in office.

The legislative process, of course, necessitated conciliation with Tory opinion, especially to achieve assent in the House of Lords. In an effort to quell Tory fears and pass effective Irish reforms Russell proposed a moderate reform of Irish tithes that would convert the money owed by peasants into a 70-per-cent rent-charge payable to their landlord. This was coupled with a sliding scale for clergy salaries based on the number of parishioners in their respective parish – at the bottom end of the scale, parsons with fewer than 50 parishioners received a salary of £100 per annum, while at the upper end the 51 parishes with more than 3,000 parishioners received a salary of £500 per annum and a 30-acre glebe. This generous pay scale meant that the church would only have £65,000 in surplus, and Russell proposed that rather than appropriating all of this money (as some more liberal members proposed) the government should use £50,000 to pay into the General Consolidated Fund that paid for the Irish schools created in 1831 and leave the remaining £15,439 for new purposes. This bill passed the Commons in June 1836 (300 to 261), which included the support of O'Connell, who initially offered faint praise for the reform.[59]

Both these measures embodied the new Whig mantra of 'justice to Ireland' and marked a clear break from older Whig and Tory policy on Ireland. What is more, with a parliamentary majority solidified by the support O'Connell provided, legislative victories seemed within reach. However, the cost of such a bold strategy of reform and 'equal justice' in Ireland was an inevitable collision with the upper House of Parliament, whose conservative nature made reforms to the Irish church or Irish municipalities impossible. Tory opposition to the measures passed by the House of Commons, discussed in detail in Chapters 4 and 5, led to bitter arguments among liberals about the viability of the upper house as an institution. The *Edinburgh Review* proclaimed in January 1837, 'If the House of Lords persists to keep itself … in an attitude of hostility to a popularly elected House of Commons, it will soon become utterly impossible for those who are, and wish to continue warm friends of the institution, successfully to defend it.' The author also stressed that as long

---

[59] Prest, *Lord John Russell*, 106–7; MacDonagh, *Emancipist*, 132.

as Lord Lyndhurst remained leader of the upper house it would be the 'enemy of the Irish people – that people whom he has denounced [as] aliens in blood, language, and religion'.[60] Liberal newspapers echoed these sentiments. 'This night the Peers will be called upon to decide – first, whether Ireland is to be governed as an integral portion of the British empire, or as a conquered province; and, secondly, whether their own privileges, nay, their House, is compatible with the common weal', quipped the *Morning Chronicle* in May 1836, before debate commenced on Irish municipal reform.[61] As the House of Lords began to amend legislation, stripping out the clauses that effected Whig justice, the *Morning Chronicle* complained of how the Lords 'mutilated' bills, or how the amended legislation was like 'the cloven-foot', or that the Lords exemplified a 'hatred of popular rights'. For all the buoyant expectation expressed by O'Connell on the Whigs' entry to power, their legislative record in Ireland (as opposed to their legislative principles) left much to be desired.

### Greening Dublin Castle

Although the obstinacy of the House of Lords prevented the successful passage of the Whigs' legislative agenda, the triumvirate of Russell, Morpeth, and Mulgrave identified other ways to achieve 'justice' that did not require acts of Parliament but instead revolved around the executive power of the lord lieutenant, including the power of patronage and government policy regarding policing and military matters. Thus, while 'justice to Ireland' in its highest form meant sweeping legislative reforms, ultimately it was only one branch of a multipronged strategy to rectify long-standing Irish grievances.

Immediately upon entering Dublin Castle, Mulgrave and Morpeth, with the support of Russell in London, set out to rectify the abuses they identified in executive administration. Among the first, and symbolically important, was the forced retirement of Sir William Gosset, undersecretary at Dublin Castle. While the title suggests subordination to the chief secretary, the undersecretary held tremendous power as the person

---

[60] 'The Approaching Session', *The Edinburgh Review* 64, no. 130 (1836–7): 544. The House of Lords was defended by a young Benjamin Disraeli in his *Vindication of the English Constitution*, published in 1835. In it, Disraeli focussed on a sustained critique of the Whig–O'Connell alliance and of O'Connell himself, who according to Disraeli operated as 'the authorised agitator of the administration itself … sent upon a provincial tour of treason … vomiting his infamous insolence in language mean as his own soul'. See Benjamin Disraeli, *Vindication of the English Constitution in a Letter to a Noble and Learned Lord* (London: Saunders and Otley, 1835), 141.

[61] *The Morning Chronicle*, 9 May 1836.

responsible for the routine working of multiple Irish bureaucracies. As the chief secretary spent over half his time in London articulating government policy, the undersecretary was responsible for the daily functioning of the administration. He served as the first point of contact for magistrates, the constabulary, and the local gentry, consulting with the lord lieutenant on matters and replying on his behalf. Thus, while bound to execute the will of the chief secretary and lord lieutenant, the undersecretary had his hands on the minutiae of operations at Dublin Castle, and directly influenced the lord lieutenant and chief secretary, with indirect influence via these ministers on other members of cabinet.[62] O'Connell considered Gosset one of the chief obstacles to the government achieving popularity in Ireland, and argued that his political predilections were distinctively Orange.[63] Other friends of the government argued that Gosset embodied the old system of Irish government that relied on Protestant partiality and excluded Catholics from local and national positions. While he had served under Peel and Melbourne faithfully for the last seven years, he had done so under the old governing philosophy that the Irish needed strong coercive measures to instil loyalty rather than the new philosophy shared by Russell, Mulgrave, and Morpeth, who were eager to use the power of executive appointments to foster loyalty and attachment among Irish Catholics. Melbourne hesitated to accede to replacing Gosset, but the new Attorney General Louis Perrin prevailed on the prime minister that the undersecretary was akin to the government's 'right eye, and if we have to spend our time plucking old beams out of it, your Government will not go straight'.[64] Although the government gave Gosset a new job as sergeant-at-arms, which carried with it greater pay and hardly any responsibility, his displacement from Dublin Castle alarmed the king, and indicated the serious commitment shared by the Whigs to start afresh in their administration of Irish affairs.[65]

Gosset's replacement, Thomas Drummond, has garnered a reputation as one of the most influential appointments in the nineteenth century, aided in part by his tragically early death in 1840, due primarily to his relentless work ethic.[66] Born in Edinburgh in 1797 to an old, landed family with large debts and few means of support, Drummond, blessed

[62] R. B. McDowell, *The Irish Administration, 1801–1914*, Studies in Irish History, Second Series, No. 2 (London: Routledge & Kegan Paul, 1964), 62–3.

[63] O'Connell to E. J. Littleton, 16 August 1833, 5:61; O'Connell to Duncannon, 2 September 1834, 5:170–2.

[64] W. M. Torrens, ed., *Memoirs of William Lamb, Second Viscount Melbourne* (London: Ward, Lock, and Co., 1890), 367–8.

[65] Holland, *Holland House Diaries*, 317.

[66] Thomas Drummond, *Memoir of Thomas Drummond*, ed. John Ferguson McLeannan (Edinburgh: Edmonston and Douglas, 1867), 430–5; M. A. G. Ó Tuathaigh, *Thomas*

with a scientific mind, joined the Royal Engineers and secured a position working on the Ordnance Survey of Ireland in 1824. Drummond built a reputation for long-suffering dedication to his work, which along with his scientific aptitude, placed him in contact with a number of prominent Whigs connected to the Society for the Diffusion of Useful Knowledge, ultimately leading to a job with Lord Althorp in 1834 as the chancellor of the exchequer's private secretary.[67] As private secretary to Althorp, Drummond displayed his talents for organisation and administration, but his appointment as undersecretary likely resulted from the government's desire for an administrator 'untrammelled by the traditions of the place', as well as Drummond's self-confessed 'partiality for Ireland'.[68] Morpeth wrote Drummond enthusiastically in May 1835, demanding 'they must give you to me and Ireland', while Drummond's mother noted that 'the sooner Government can send you there the better, as the place is ill supplied by such a Tory, and must retard public business very much by the present Under Secretary'.[69] By August, just a month after Drummond's arrival in Dublin, Lord Mulgrave celebrated his appointment; as Russell wrote him, he was: 'delighted to hear that you are pleased with Drummond – he will work hard, & is as honest as honesty itself'.[70]

Drummond's appointment signalled a sizeable shift in the way Mulgrave intended to dole out executive appointments, and other bold selections to influential positions followed. O'Connell had admonished the previous Whig administration to place Catholics in prominent legal positions 'if emancipation is not to continue to be a dead letter', but found himself continually disappointed.[71] However, the new ethos adopted by the Whigs in 1835 ensured that many of O'Connell's former suggestions might be reconsidered. O'Connell targeted the Attorney General Francis Blackburne for replacement, a man whom had attempted to prosecute O'Connell in 1831 for defying government proclamations related to O'Connell's nascent Repeal agitation, and whom O'Connell regarded as tainted with Orange bigotry.[72] Lord Stanley lobbied for Blackburne to keep his job, but wrote lamenting that with 'party spirit so high' the

---

*Drummond and the Government of Ireland, 1835–41* (Dublin: National University of Ireland, Dublin, 1978).

[67] Stanley H. Palmer, 'Drummond, Thomas', *ODNB*, https://doi.org/10.1093/ref:odnb/8084.

[68] Richard Barry O'Brien, *Thomas Drummond: Under-Secretary in Ireland, 1835–40; Life and Letters* (London: Kegan Paul, Trench, & Co., 1889), 75.

[69] Morpeth to Drummond, 7 May [1835], E. Drummond to Thomas Drummond, 21 May 1835, ibid., 76–7.

[70] Russell to Mulgrave, 16 August [1835], MC, Mulgrave MSS, M/791.

[71] O'Connell to Duncannon, 2 September 1834, O'Connell, *Correspondence*, 5:172.

[72] Geoghegan, *Liberator*, 32; MacDonagh, *Emancipist*, 21-3.

friends of government had no problem 'hail[ing] with exclamations, any slight put upon you; and would be at no loss for an argument, in your having occupied office under Sir R Peel'.[73] The liberal Protestant Louis Perrin was appointed attorney general, while Catholic Michael O'Loghlen was appointed solicitor general. When a judgeship came up on the King's Bench in August 1835 the government placed Perrin on the bench, moving O'Loghlen to attorney general, and appointing another liberal, John Richards, as solicitor general.

These appointments all fell within one of O'Connell's main objectives for actively supporting the Whigs – the dismemberment of 'the Orange system' that had hitherto reinforced the sectarian character of the administration of law and order, and which predisposed Catholics to distrust the judicial system. While Dublin Castle carried the greatest symbolic significance in the Orange system – the seat of power from which inequality flowed – arguably more impactful for the majority of Ireland's population was the routine functioning of local law and order. In this respect appointments to the position of sheriff, a critical post, was identified by O'Connell as 'one of the great causes of alienation from Government of the Irish people' due to the 'partial administration of justice'. Among other important legal functions, the sheriff selected juries, and in the eyes of O'Connell and other Catholics had the power to extend a double discrimination whereby both judges on the bench and jurors in the box were Protestants with matching political prejudices. 'What must the condition of the people be if the judges, instead of being checked by juries, find that they have sheriffs to aid them by giving juries who, instead of resisting, will favour party spirit, give party verdicts and enable judges to distribute vengeance not to administer justice[?]', O'Connell asked Lord Mulgrave. He also assured the lord lieutenant that 'the People of Ireland are quite prepared to believe that you will do all you possibly can to procure justice and impartiality to them'.[74] Mulgrave invited O'Connell's input on 'subjects of public importance', an invitation that O'Connell mobilised to defend his support for the new administration against his critics. 'I stand exceedingly well with the present Ministry', beamed O'Connell to his political confidant P. V. Fitzpatrick: 'They have but little patronage but that little will be disposed of only to sincere friends of the country.'[75] Within the first six months of Mulgrave's tenure as lord

[73] Stanley to Blackburne, 2 July 1835, LPL, Derby Papers, 920 DER (14)/172/2.
[74] O'Connell to Mulgrave, 4 December 1835, MC, Mulgrave MSS, M/598. On the role of sheriffs see Kathleen S. Murphy, 'Judge, Jury, Magistrate and Soldier: Rethinking Law and Authority in Late Eighteenth-Century Ireland', *The American Journal of Legal History* 44, no. 3 (July 2000): 231–56.
[75] O'Connell to Fitzpatrick, 4 September 1835, O'Connell, *Correspondence*, 5:330.

lieutenant, O'Connell solicited patronage for a number of influential appointments, including for his brother John as high sheriff of Co. Kerry.[76]

These executive appointments came at a significant political cost. Newspapers and periodicals of the growing conservative press lambasted the government for what it saw as political subservience to O'Connell, a theme discussed in greater detail in Chapter 4. However, even stolid periodicals like the *Quarterly Review* noted how 'Russell does what Mr O'Connell desires, as far as Sir Robert Peel will allow him', or that 'O'Connell, a man notoriously in the confidence, as he is professedly the master, of Ministers', was pulling the strings behind the Whigs' legislative agenda.[77] Insinuations about O'Connell's influence over the government found visual representation with a series of cartoons by John Doyle ('HB') beginning in late 1835 and lasting till the end of the ministry.[78] O'Connell's apparent influence distressed the king, too, leading him to question the propriety of nearly any Whig legislative proposal. In the thick of debates about reforming the Church of Ireland, the king's private secretary, Sir Herbert Taylor, warned Russell that 'there may be considerable danger in taking advantage of the influence of Mr O'Connell towards carrying into effect Measures of remedial & conciliatory nature, experience having shown that no Government can rely upon the honesty or feel secure that the Workers with which he is interested may not be turned against His Employer'.[79]

Despite the invective by the conservative press, popular sentiment among a majority of Ireland's population remained avowedly positive. The newly established *Dublin Review* published an article that praised the ministry, especially Mulgrave, for the sincerity of purpose that its appointments demonstrated. 'The Irish people had often been deluded by professions; but here were acts, so decisive, that they could not be understood or interpreted, in any other sense, than as the earnest and pledge of

[76] O'Connell to Mulgrave, 13 August 1835, MC, Mulgrave MSS, M/596; O'Connell to Mulgrave, 19 August 1835, ibid., m/597; O'Connell to Mulgrave, 8 December 1835, ibid., M/599.

[77] [ J. W. Croker ], 'The New Reign: Sermon, by the Rev. Sydney Smith, on the Duties of the Queen', *The Quarterly Review* 59, no. 117 (July 1837): 248; 'Domestic Prospects for the Country under a New Parliament', *The Quarterly Review* 59, no. 118 (December 1837): 553.

[78] A quarter of Doyle's political cartoons featured O'Connell between 1829 and 1847. See Leslie A. Williams and William H. A. Williams, *Daniel O'Connell, the British Press and the Irish Famine: Killing Remarks* (London: Routledge, 2016), 49–50. The National Portrait Gallery and the Wellcome Collection have made hundreds of Doyle's cartoons available digitally.

[79] Taylor to Russell, 23 October 1835, USSC, Broadland Papers, RC/D/10. See also Taylor to Russell, 3 January 1836, ibid., RC/D/14.

substantial justice.'[80] Dozens of addresses sent by parishioners, mayors, sheriffs, chambers of commerce, and corporations to Lord Mulgrave in 1835 and 1836 echoed the sentiments of the *Dublin Review*, praising 'the wise and liberal policy', 'enlightened policy', and the '*equal and impartial administration of just laws*' that Mulgrave's tenure had thus far enacted.[81] The new government had committed to a new policy of equal justice with its appointments of liberals and Catholics in positions of prominence within the state's legal apparatus, such as O'Loghlen and later Stephen Woulfe. For the first time since the Act of Union Catholics could look to Dublin Castle, the symbolic seat of British rule in Ireland, as representing their interests rather than as merely the embodiment of Protestant Ascendancy. Building on this success, and the support it engendered with O'Connell and his MPs, as well as wider popular opinion, the Whigs turned to national issues that necessitated rectification, including the government's policy in tithe collection, as well as the legality of the Orange Order.

## Administration in Ireland

The half-baked approach to the Act of Union in 1800, which did not fully consider the implications or unintended consequences of the political union, left a lord lieutenant with considerable executive powers, especially as it related to law and order.[82] Thus, while Mulgrave, Morpeth, and Russell worked to appointment more Catholics, and furiously drafted legislation for consideration in Parliament, Mulgrave could exercise important influence in reshaping government policy vis-à-vis the use of the military, the reviewing of the commission of magistrates actively involved in the Orange Order, or the commutation of sentences for everyday Irish men and women whom the government determined had been judged too harshly. This approach, though effective in accomplishing a change in political direction, carried significant political risk for the lord lieutenant because those opposed to his designs could target him directly for responsibility.

---

[80] [Arranged by Thomas Drummond?], 'Earl Mulgrave in Ireland', *The Dublin Review* 1, no. 1 (May 1836): 34.

[81] 'County of Town and City of Sligo', 'King's County', in Anon. , *Addresses Presented to His Excellency the Earl of Mulgrave [...] with His Excellency's Answers* (Dublin: William Fredrick Wakeman, 1836), 217, 219.

[82] On the lack of strategic consideration of the Act of Union see Hoppen, *Governing Hibernia*, 19–20; and, on the evolving and contradictory role of the Lord Lieutenant in Ireland see Peter Gray and Olwen Purdue, eds., *The Irish Lord Lieutenancy in Ireland, c. 1541–1922* (Dublin: University College Dublin Press, 2012).

Popular resistance to the payment of tithes to the Church of Ireland had led previous governments to employ the compulsive power of the state to reassert the legitimacy of the imposition. Popular resistance itself oscillated between principled ideological opposition to the maintenance of an alien church establishment and larger macroeconomic factors, such as downturns in agricultural prices that resulted in a lack of money with which peasants could meet their obligations.[83] However, the mass politicisation of Ireland's peasant population during O'Connell's campaign for Catholic Emancipation, and a renewed enthusiasm for proselytisation among Protestant landlords provided the volatile political, economic, and sectarian context out of which the tithe war of the 1830s emerged.[84] Previous governments, especially during Lord Stanley's time as chief secretary, suppressed large meetings organising tithe strikes due to 'the danger which must threaten the whole frame of society if a combination against a legal impost be permitted ultimately to triumph over the provisions of the Law', and this led to the adoption of coercive legislation.[85]

While the government pushed coercive legislation through Parliament in 1833, they also allowed clergy, tithe owners, or their agents to request military detachments to assist in the collection of tithe payments, which led to fatal confrontations. The application for a detachment was a rather simple one. The tithe owner, or his agent, would make a sworn statement before two magistrates concerning the potential for physical force to be used against them in the collection of their tithes, and the magistrates would then inform the police or military of their need to accompany the tithe owner on his rounds to collect payment, or instruct them to seize property in lieu of payment.[86] The system carried with it a number of inherent problems. First, and foremost, oftentimes Church of Ireland clergymen also served the function of magistrate, which either allowed the parson to swear before only one other magistrate, or occasionally simply apply to Dublin Castle directly for permission for troops.[87]

[83] Shunsuke Katsuta, 'The Rockite Movement in County Cork in the Early 1820s', IHS 33i, no. 131 (May 2003): 286–7; Noreen Higgins-McHugh, 'The 1830s Tithe Riots', in Riotous Assemblies: Rebels, Riots and Revolts in Ireland, ed. William Sheehan and Maura Cronin (Cork: Mercier Press, 2011), 82.

[84] O'Donoghue, 'Opposition to Tithes', 11–13. On the 'second reformation' among Irish Protestants and increased proselytisation see Irene Whelan, Bible War, ch. 5.

[85] 'Report of the Select Committee on Tithes', Parliamentary Paper (1831–2, vol. 21, no. 177), p. 4; Anglesey to Cabinet, 'Illegal Confederacies & c.', 7 January 1833, TNA, HO 100/244/394-403.

[86] Henry Hardinge to Rev. C. O'Neill, 30 January 1835, TNA, HO 100/246/80.

[87] In 1835, no fewer than 275 magistrates also served as Church of Ireland or Presbyterian clergymen, while no Roman Catholic priest was a magistrate. This list, of course, does not account for those magistrates who also owned tithe land. See, 'Commissions of the

Thus, these clergy had a vested interest in employing any means necessary in collecting their due and made their magisterial decisions with a clear conflict of interest. Secondly, magistrates joined the military or police dispatch and were in charge of ordering these bodies into action if they deemed it necessary. Thus, situations could arise where the magistrate in charge of the troops or police was also the clergyman attempting to collect his tithes.

The Irish public alleged that the clergy used the armed detachments unlawfully to break into homes or distrain property for a future auction. Even in cases where other magistrates headed the police or troop detachment, a spirit of camaraderie and trust existed between clergy magistrates and their peers, further undermining the impartiality of magistrates. In an 1835 incident in Keady, Co. Armagh, the Rev. James Blacker attended the collection of tithes due to him with twenty-nine armed policemen, which led to a large assembly protesting the police breaking down peasants' doors; this resulted in a confrontation and the death of James Hughes.[88] Similar violence occurred in Co. Monaghan where Samuel Gray, a tithe collector for Rev. Dean Roper, was joined by a number of police in his attempted collection. Gray was known as a 'hot head' and began breaking down peasants' doors with the aid of his men, distraining property rather than accepting payment of tithes in cash, actions Dublin Castle deemed illegal. Although the police did not contribute to these acts of illegality, the magistrate who commanded the police, Mr Mansfield, did nothing to stop Gray. The police's inaction implicitly condoned Gray's zealotry, thus undermining the credibility of the police as impartial arbiters in the eyes of Ireland's peasantry.[89]

Upon taking office, Mulgrave and Russell considered how to rectify the government's position regarding tithe collection. In a cabinet meeting on 26 May 1835, Russell presented a letter from Mulgrave seeking the government's opinion on how best to proceed regarding the tithe case of Mr O'Neill.[90] On the face of things, the cabinet simply clarified its position, agreeing to 'follow as nearly as we can the instructions and system of the late Secretary and the Attorney General', and circulating instructions to officers of the law to preserve the public rather than to act as assistants in the collection of tithes. Additionally, the instruction

---

Peace (clergy), Ireland. A Return of all the clergymen now in the Commission of the Peace in Ireland', P. P. (1835, vol. 47, no. 102).

[88] 'Tithes (Keady). Copy of proceedings relative to transactions in the neighbourhood of Keady, on collecting an arrear of tithe due to the Rev. James Blacker', P. P. (1835, vol. 47, no. 179).

[89] 'Monaghan Tithes. Papers Relating to collection of tithes in the country of Monaghan', P. P. (1834, vol. 43, no. 239), 2–3, 7.

[90] Russell to Mulgrave, 31 May [1835], MC, Mulgrave MSS, M/780.

explicitly clarified that regardless of the magistrate's legal authority over any force, the police and military should never obey any order that would make them party to an illegal act, such as attempting to collect tithes at night, breaking into property, or any other forcible acts.[91] In a subsequent letter to Mulgrave, Russell expanded on the cabinet's deliberations. First, he emphasised to Mulgrave the role of the lord lieutenant in any case regarding the use of troops, stressing that the central government embodied in the lord lieutenant, rather than local magistrates, had authority over the military. Whereas before it had been enough for the tithe owner to swear an affidavit before two magistrates, now 'no Military Force should be granted without making an application to the Castle in every instance. . . . An application having been made to the Castle, and the Lord Lieutenant being satisfied that serious risk of life will be incurred . . . Military assistance may be specially granted.'[92]

At a subtler attitudinal level, however, Russell demonstrated the government's shifted emphasis from supporting the claims of Protestant clergy by any means necessary to merely acknowledging the tithe owner's legal right to his tithes. Although Russell asserted that 'You cannot advise the Tithe owner to forego or suspend his claim', he nevertheless suggested to Mulgrave that there were ways of employing the military and police less frequently. Russell wrote stressing, 'Your own Opinion of the expediency of granting Military aid in preserving the Peace may be affected by the circumstance that the whole matter is under the consideration of the Legislature. You must of course never positively decline assistance in preserving the Authority [of the] Law, but you may with propriety suspend Your decision for a time.'[93] Russell sarcastically noted to Mulgrave that the applications from clergy for military protection would decrease, as it would 'be too serious an impediment to the Lords throwing out out [sic] our bill, if another Rathcormac should take place in the interim', meaning the clergy would rather see the Whigs' legislative reform trashed than risk a fatal confrontation while forcibly collecting tithes that might influence public opinion in favour of reform.[94] By October 1835 the Lords had thrown out the Whigs' tithe bill, prompting Russell to write another letter to Mulgrave assuring him of the inevitability of a renewed

[91] Holland, *Holland House Diaries*, 302.
[92] Russell to Mulgrave, 27 May 1835, TNA, Russell Papers, PRO 30/22/1E, f. 152.
[93] Ibid.
[94] Russell to Mulgrave, 31 May [1835], MC, Mulgrave MSS, M/780. Outside Gortroe, Co. Cork a large confrontation between crown forces (troops and police) collecting tithes and the peasant population left at least twelve peasants dead and forty-two wounded in December 1834. The proctor, Archdean Ryder, also attended as a magistrate and was implicated with encouraging the military to engage the peasantry. See O'Brien, *Thomas Drummond*, 82–7; Hansard, 3rd ser., vol. 26, cols. 500–16, 3 March 1835.

emphasis on military aid, and stressing his confidence in Mulgrave's judgement.[95]

The task of sorting applications for military aid fell to Drummond, and his preference followed Mulgrave, Morpeth, and Russell's of relying on the military only *after* a breach of the public peace had occurred. Meanwhile, opposition to tithes continued to simmer across the countryside. Printed notices appeared across parts of Tipperary in December 1835, and while it did not 'appear there was any tendency to a breach of the peace', the notices were posted while 'the Protestant congregation ... was engaged in divine services at the time [and] was much annoyed by the Shouting at the Chapel which is situated about 200 years from the Church.' The notice stated:

TITHES!! TITHES! TITHES!
We, the Undersigned,
Request a Meeting of the Parishioners of Clonulty, & Rosmore, on Sunday the 12th Dec., for the propose of Making Arangements [*sic*] for defending the *PEOPLE* of those Parishes, against whom, MR ARMSTRONG has expressed his intention of taking **LAW PROCEEDINGS FOR TITHES!!**[96]

Another notice appealed to all classes to join 'heart in heart' and take the advice of 'OConnell and of your Priests' to resist paying 'this dreadful Monster Tithes ... Stalk[ing] through our already miserably oppressed and half starved land'.[97] With the scuttling of the Whigs' tithe bill in Parliament, Russell requested police reports from Drummond to appraise him of the 'frequency & nature' of tithe opposition, as well as 'whether the Tithe War will affect the tranquility of the Country in the future more than it has hitherto done'.[98]

In the face of the Irish government's unwillingness to grant military or police protection to tithe servers, Conservative landlords, magistrates, and clergymen began strategising other means to force the government to aid their collection. In November 1835 a Lay Association was formed in Dublin 'for the protection of the Irish clergy, by enabling them to recover their tithes by legal process in the superior courts'. The benefactor list of the association included many Anglo-Irish ultra-Tories, including Lords Roden, Enniskillen, Bandon, Lorton, and Farnham, who each gave between £200 and £400 towards the fund.[99] Clergy applied to the fund to defray the legal costs associated with pursuing cases against individuals

[95] Russell to Mulgrave, 9 October 1835, TNA, Russell Papers, PRO 30/22/1E, f. 200–1.
[96] [?] to Morpeth, 15 December 1835, NAI, CSORP 1835, Box 44, 29/52; 'Tithes, Tithes, Tithes', ibid.
[97] 'Handwritten appeal posted on School House Door', 15 December 1835, ibid.
[98] Russell to Mulgrave, 5 August 1836, MC, Mulgrave MSS, M/835.
[99] 'Lay Association', BNL, 3 November 1835.

in tithe arrears in the Court of Exchequer. The Lay Association helped file over 600 cases before the court, often for rather trivial amounts, including a few for 1s. 1d. The assumption of Conservative members was that the court would issue a writ of rebellion against any tithe defaulter, which would result in a law officer delivering these notices to debtors and a concurrent attempt to collect arrears. As the court guaranteed the personal safety of all its personnel, it would be obliged to assign military and police aid to protect those serving writs. Between the beginning of 1835 and mid-1836, clergy and other tithe owners brought 1,552 suits against thousands of tithe defaulters across Ireland from every stratum of society including widows, parish priests, and large farmers; and, in the first six months of 1836, the Court of Exchequer issued over 270 writs of rebellion against individuals in arrears.[100] Money also flowed from a relief fund that by March 1836 had paid out £26,165. 10s. 7d. to clergy who applied, citing the precipitous fall in their income and risk of economic ruin.[101]

Nevertheless, conservatives' assumptions that it would be possible to force the government to provide military protection proved erroneous. Drummond refused to grant police or military protection to issue writs of rebellion as consistently as he refused protection of tithe process servers, stressing the responsibility of the government to determine whether the public peace was threatened rather than simply allowing clergy, magistrates, or the courts to usurp this responsibility.[102] Matters came to a head when Major Miller, one of the district inspectors of police, countermanded an order by an officer of the Court of Exchequer for a police detachment to aid in delivering writs of rebellion and collecting tithes. The court summoned Miller for 'not obeying the Commissioners', at which point the government sent both the attorney general and solicitor general to defend Miller. In their defence, the chief law officers asserted an 1825 precedent handed down by Henry Joy, then the law officer of the crown, and now the chief baron (head judge) of the Irish Exchequer, that 'constables cannot legally be employed by the sheriff or his deputy in the execution of civil processes'.[103]

Morpeth flaunted Joy's 1825 recommendation with gusto before the House of Commons, arguing that the matter of jurisdiction over the police had already been decided, not by his government, but by Peel's. Morpeth quoted the former undersecretary William Gosset, writing to

---

[100] 'Return of Number of Suits and Causes instituted in Courts of Law of Ireland for Recovery of Tithe, 1835–36', P. P. (1836, 582, XLI.145).
[101] 'Clerical Fund Account', 4 March 1836, CRBL, Beresford Papers, MS 183, folder 1, f. 40.
[102] O'Brien, *Thomas Drummond*, 228–9.    [103] Ibid., 223.

Co. Meath magistrates uncertain about their authority over the police in 1835. In his letter Gosset wrote that he had asked the lord lieutenant and 'In reply, I am to acquaint you that the law adviser does not think that the police should be employed to execute process[es] of this nature, nor have you any Jurisdiction to direct them to do so.' Morpeth concluded his remarks before the Commons by sarcastically noting that the 'answer was not by the authority of Lord Mulgrave, but Lord Haddington – not from the "O'Mulgrave" – the Radical Lord, but the true Protestant and Conservative Lord-Lieutenant [Haddington]. Into what error or criminality, then, could he [Mulgrave] be led by following the advice of Mr Baron Joy, or the example of Lord Haddington?'[104] 'My Dear Drummond', Morpeth wrote after the debate, 'the Exchequer case was glorious, and the Haddington precedent invaluable: it brought down the House in shrieks, and it was great sport reading Gosset's letter in his presence.'[105]

Nothing encapsulated inequality in Irish life so completely as the Orange Order and its snug relationship with aspects of the legal system. Organised in the 1790s within the context of sectarian animosity and economic competition in Co. Armagh, the Orange Order began as a lower-class secret society pledged to defend the Protestant community from the perceived threat of republicanism and an increasingly assertive Catholic community. Winning the support of a handful of Protestant elites and drawing on an overlapping membership with the exclusively Protestant Yeomanry, the Orange Order expanded its social base during the latter half of the tumultuous 1790s and into the early nineteenth century. The unsavoury aspects of Orangeism – its oath-bound secrecy and the sectarian parading and violence – marked it as an object for suspicion for those outside of Ireland. Within Ireland, however, many Protestants within Ireland's gentry tolerated, if not overtly encouraged, the development of the Orange Order as a means to protect Protestant communities and exert local influence, and a number of Tory MPs openly professed their membership.[106]

---

[104] Hansard, 3rd ser., vol. 31, cols. 605–6, 18 February 1836.
[105] Morpeth to Drummond, February 1836, O'Brien, *Thomas Drummond*, 224.
[106] For a discussion on the context leading to the rise of the Orange Order, especially the results of economic development leading to a breakdown of paternal control over young Protestants, see Miller, 'The Armagh Troubles, 1784–95', 155–91; Sean Farrell, *Rituals and Riots: Sectarian Violence and Political Culture in Ulster, 1784–1886* (Lexington: University of Kentucky Press, 2000), chs. 1–2. The government outlawed secret societies in 1825, which led the Orange Order to reconstitute itself without an oath, see 'Report from the Select Committee appointed to inquire into the nature, character, extent, and tendency of orange lodges, associations or societies in Ireland; with the minutes of evidence, and appendix', P. P. (1835, 377) XV.1), 6.

The accusation that Conservative governments treated Protestants preferentially and received support from Orangeism was an old complaint among Irish nationalists and liberals. As part of their strategy to unseat Peel from ministerial power the Whigs allowed the Radical MP Joseph Hume to press for an inquiry into Orange Lodges in the Great Britain and its colonies, along with a separate committee to investigate lodges in Ireland.[107] The committees produced hundreds of pages of testimony exposing the sectarianism ingrained in the Orange Order and the cosy relationship between the Order and sections of the army, as well its influence in the royal family. William IV's brother, Ernest Augustus, the Duke of Cumberland, served as the Grand Master of the Empire, the highest officer of the Orange Order, and Hume's committee took issue with the royal family having so intimate a connection with an organisation of such 'a decidedly political character' in which 'almost all their proceedings have had some political object in view'.[108] Although Hume represented a political viewpoint that was anathema to the king, His Majesty agreed with Lord John Russell and others regarding the inappropriateness of his brother's connection to the Orange Lodges, especially in his signing blank warrants for the creation of new lodges throughout the Empire.[109] The commander-in-chief of the British army issued instructions in August 1835 banning the participation of officers or soldiers in Orange Lodges, which effectively ended army involvement in the Orange Order throughout the colonies and Ireland. Although Hume and other MPs made further attempts to prevent retired military officers from participating in the Orange Order, Russell and his colleagues felt satisfied by the positive effect banning the Order had on active soldiers and felt this this would protect it from spreading in the future.[110]

Addressing Orange influence in Ireland as a whole proved more difficult than it had in the army. On the one hand, Melbourne actively advised Russell against attempting to deal with the Orange Order without very serious consideration, partly because of the political consequences, but

---

[107] 'Report from the Select Committee appointed to inquire into the origin, nature, extent and tendency of orange institutions in Great Britain and the colonies; with the minutes of evidence, appendix and index', P. P. (1835, 605, XVII.1).

[108] Ibid., viii.

[109] William IV to Lord John Russell, 7 August 1835, USSC, Broadland Papers, RC/B/34.

[110] Hansard, 3rd ser., vol. 31, cols. 146–7, 8 February 1836; ibid., cols. 345–52, 12 February 1836; Russell to Mulgrave, 6 December 1835, TNA, Russell Papers, PRO 30/22/1E/253; William IV to Russell, 13 February 1836, USSC, Broadland Papers, RC/B/46; William IV to Russell, 24 February 1836, ibid, RC/B/50; William IV to Russell, 27 February 1836, ibid., RC/B/52. Hume was not satisfied and wrote to Russell stressing that the Orange Lodges 'with secret sayings & religious ceremonies' deserved to be dealt with as harshly as the government had dealt with trades unions. See, Hume to Russell, 20 October 1835, TNA, Russell Papers, PRO 30/22/1E/229–30.

also because he believed the life of the Order was near its natural end. Comparing the Orange Order to trades unions, Melbourne reminded Russell that had the government drafted a measure effectively dealing with the trades unions 'it would have been prudent & justified', but that 'it was better to leave them to the absurdity & impracticality of their own objects, which has caused them to decline'.[111] On the other hand, Morpeth and Mulgrave both expressed their desire to undermine Orange influence in Ireland, seeing it as an integral part of their 'justice' programme. A handwritten, undated manuscript in the Castle Howard archive entitled *Irish History Manuscript*, although officially anonymous, seems to shed light on Morpeth's attitude to Orangeism's influence in Ireland, and his government's responsibility in its dissolution:

> The Irish Orangeman alone has the infatuated ignorance to be the destroyer of his Country. From his long connexion with those in power, the heads of the dominant Caste of which he is one of the lowest members, he is equally enraged and wonder-struck with the present posture of, the whole engine of misrule dislocated, and thrown from its centre ... The Parson must be made to know that his duty is that of a Pastor ... the Orangeman must be broken from his ranks and made to feel that he is a Citizen and not a Soldier in the Secret service of a faction ... the Government must be the sole centre of Organisation, and must be one represent-ing the Spirit of a liberal public of Britain and of the enlightened and impartial in Ireland, – one from which all can obtain counsel and protection.[112]

This excerpt offers a useful insight into Morpeth's governing mentality, and the project he and his colleagues wanted to pursue – undermining the power of local administrators who had historically demonstrated their propensity to govern for a small minority of the people, and to replace them with a centralised powerful executive government committed to governing for all classes. Rather than leading to further despotism, these Whigs identified the growth of government as an institution promoting civilisation, equity, and justice in Ireland.

While not as forthright in language, Mulgrave certainly agreed with Morpeth's desire to make government the centre of organisation and to eradicate 'Orange police, Orange Magistrates, and Orange local Judges'.[113] Mulgrave complained of 'the disposition to outrage on the part of the Orangemen' throughout the north of Ireland, while the

---

[111] Melbourne to Russell, 6 October 1835, TNA, PRO 30/22/1E/196.
[112] 'Irish History Manuscript', n.d., CH, Morpeth Papers, J19/11/14, 105–6, 108. While it is unclear whether this was written by Morpeth or was simply a copy of a pamphlet, it is in his hand. Though it does not have a date, the contents suggest it was written sometime between 1835 and 1837, most likely late in 1835 or at the beginning of the new parliamentary session in February 1836.
[113] Ibid., 106.

remainder of Ireland was 'otherwise perfectly tranquil'.[114] In response to these outrages, and Mulgrave's disapproval of the conduct of many magistrates, sheriffs, and judges, the lord lieutenant suggested to Russell the possibility of striking off any known Orangemen from the list of magistrates and judges. Russell thought this would cause more harm than good: 'It is one thing to weed out Orangeism from the army & police, organised bodies under the order of Government, & another to deprive Magistrates their Commissions as Justices of the Peace – such a step as this but [sic] would excite great commotion & perhaps strengthen the Orange Lodges.'[115] This did not mean Russell was opposed to dealing with the influence of Orangeism in Ireland; in fact, matters were quite the contrary. Russell proposed rules for Mulgrave's conduct vis-à-vis Orangemen in government service. First, Russell noted the government's ability to dismiss any police officer who was an Orangeman from the service. Second, he stressed the importance of not admitting any Orangeman to a position of trust or authority, and while Russell did not believe Orangemen could be dismissed from 'clerkships, places in the revenue, &c.', he dissuaded Mulgrave from admitting 'any fresh ones'. Finally, Russell asserted that any magistrate 'who shall be found encouraging a violation of the law' could be excluded from the magistracy, along with any young applicants who could be turned away on account of their youth in favour of older and more experienced magistrates.[116] A few days later, Russell communicated that the king approved of their plan requiring any future magistrate to renounce their membership of the Orange Order before being sworn in as a magistrate.[117]

In the end, the scrutiny placed on the Orange Order by Hume's committees, buoyed by the policy of isolating Orangemen in Irish positions of power, brought about the dissolution of the Orange Order. On 23 February 1836, Hume gave a long speech, lasting over three hours, drawing on the testimony of the committee to demonstrate the impunity with which many Orangemen operated in Ireland and their conduct in administering Ireland's laws inequitably.[118] In addition, Hume tried to implicate prominent Tory MPs who were members of the Orange Order in various intrigues related to the succession of the British crown, although these claims were considered by most in the House of

---

[114] Mulgrave to Russell, 17 November 1835, TNA, Russell Papers, PRO 30/22/1E/232.
[115] Russell to Mulgrave, 3 December1835, MC, Mulgrave MSS, M/810. On Russell's conversation with the king related to Orangemen in service of the crown, see Russell to Mulgrave, 6 December 1835, TNA, Russell Papers, PRO 30/22/IE/253-4.
[116] Ibid.    [117] Russell to Mulgrave, 6 December 1835, MC, Mulgrave MSS, M/811.
[118] Hansard, 3rd ser., vol. 31, 791–811, 23 February 1836.

Commons to be nonsense.[119] His speech culminated with a resolution not only outlawing the Orange Order 'and all other political Societies which have secret forms of initiation', but also removing every Orangeman who was a 'functionary employed in the administration of justice, and in maintaining the peace of the country'.[120] Hume sent Russell a copy of his motion earlier in the week emphasising his opinion that the country desired decisive action against the Orange Order, and perhaps equally importantly to Russell, a weapon that 'if passed [will] arm the Irish Executive with the requested powers to administer justice'.[121] Although it would seem that such a motion would have been favoured, at least by Mulgrave, Russell decided for a more moderate, though no less decisive course. In a speech that 'actually drew tears from the Orangemen, enthusiastic appropriation from Stanley, [and] a colder approval from Peel', Russell suggested an amendment that asked the king to take measures for 'the effectual discouragement of Orange Lodges'.[122] Although not nearly as radical as Hume's intervention, Russell's motion still explicitly named the Orange Order as an organisation worthy of condemnation from the crown to which its members professed their unfettered loyalty. While Peel, Stanley, and a number of Orangemen spoke attempting to persuade Russell to consider not naming the Orange Order, he refused on principle 'in a quiet reply amidst great cheering', which concluded in the House giving 'the death blow to Orangeism'.[123]

The resolutions of the Commons, along with the king's approval, did indeed bring the deathblow to Orangeism. The Duke of Cumberland sent orders to dissolve the Loyal Orange Institution while various members of Parliament and government officials published letters resigning their membership and advocating for their brethren to follow their example.[124] Rather than require a vote to pass a motion from the House of Commons, Russell's speech had garnered enough goodwill for the resolution to be adopted by the House without calling a formal vote. In Ireland, Russell encouraged Mulgrave to vigilantly ensure that the dissolution proceed at pace and to graciously encourage those gentry that renounced their affiliation, to 'make the most of it, by receiving them with confidence & praise. It will be a great thing for us all if this

[119] *Hobhouse Journal*, 23 February 1836, BL, Broughton Papers, Add MS 56558, 93; Greville, *Greville Memoirs*, 464.

[120] Hansard, 3rd ser., 23 February 1836, 811.

[121] Hume to Russell, 21 February 1836, TNA, Russell Papers, PRO 30/22/2A/246-7.

[122] Greville, *Greville Memoirs*, 464–5.

[123] *Hobhouse Journal*, 23 February 1836, BL, Broughton Papers, Add MS 56558, 93.

[124] Duke of Cumberland to Russell, 26 February 1836, MC, Mulgrave MSS, M/828a; 'Dissolution of the Orange System', BNL, 4 March 1836.

Confederacy is broken up.'[125] As lord lieutenant, Mulgrave also had the power to offer clemency, which he offered to a number of Orangemen arrested in October 1835 for illegally marching, while stressing that no such clemencies would be extended in the future for those that broke the law forbidding so-called 'party processions'.[126]

The dissolution of the Orange Order began as an initiative in Parliament guided by Hume, but advanced as a matter of Irish policy emanating from a new Irish administration committed to equal justice and that actively excluded Orangemen, and concluded with a resolution of a united Parliament. Even Hume's initial boldness was likely a product of the shift brought about by government ministers approaching Irish questions in new ways. Nevertheless, dismissing all magistrates, judges, or functionaries connected to the Orange Order was politically untenable. Ultimately, the influence of Orangeism could not be curtailed simply by executive policy, and arguably, even Parliament could not end the influence of Orangeism as a political principle, even if it could outlaw it as a political organisation. It also underscored for Russell, Mulgrave, and Morpeth the deeply entrenched relationship between Orangeism and the administration of law and order in Ireland, and the complaints of many Irish peasants about the pernicious influence partiality had among Ireland's magistrates and the police force. Although the Whigs failed in nearly every other legislative effort in 1835 and 1836, their conviction of equal justice and impartial administration of the law provided the inspiration for their longest-lasting reform, which endured until the creation of the Irish Free State – the Irish Constabulary Act of 1836.

### Legislative Success: Whigs and the Irish Constabulary Act of 1836

Between the Whigs' return to ministerial benches in April 1835 and the death of William IV in June 1837, Melbourne's government maintained a slim majority in the House of Commons, thanks in large part to the Lichfield House Compact. However, the legislative agenda of the Whigs, especially their Irish policy, continued to run aground in the House of Lords. Irish municipal reform passed the Commons in 1836, only to fall victim to the ultra-Tory Lord Lyndhurst's opposition as the de facto Conservative leader in the House of Lords. The Lords threw out every Whig tithe bill proposed between 1835 and 1836, in large part due to

---

[125] Russell to Mulgrave, 28 February 1836, MC, Mulgrave MSS, M/829.
[126] 'Copy of Lord Lieutenant's Proclamation', n.d., TNA, Russell Papers, PRO 30/22/ 2A/261–2. On the Party Processions Act and various government attempts to curb illegal marching, see Neil P. Maddox, '"A Melancholy Record": The Story of the Nineteenth-Century Irish Party Processions Acts', *The Irish Jurist* 39 (2004): 243–74.

Tory intransigence regarding the question of Irish church appropriation. In short, the Whigs' legislative record on Ireland was a record of failure.

The Whigs gained one major legislative victory in Ireland with the passage of the Irish Constabulary Act in 1836. If ever the party of law and order might find common ground with the party of justice and equity, one would suppose it would be on the issue of the Irish police. Both Whig and Tory identified the outrages across Ireland as the chief inhibiting factor to the country's prosperity and saw the use of a police force as one way to deal with these problems. The Tories, led by Peel, had created the Peace Preservation Force in 1814, and made amendments to the force in 1822. Further efforts at reform, especially through the centralisation of the police force, were attempted by the Tories in 1830 and later by the Whigs in 1832 but were dropped for a want of effort among politicians, as well as due to concern about Ireland's political climate and doubt that the public would tolerate a centralised police force. It has been argued that the passage of the 1836 Constabulary Act simply took the old ideas of the early 1830s and enacted them, stressing the mutual desire among Tories and Whigs to strengthen Dublin Castle's hand in the administration of law and order, and their agreement regarding an emphasis on hiring Catholics for the constabulary, while downplaying the sectarian nature of that constabulary.[127]

Although there is evidence to support some of these assertions, especially the precedent for reform, a number of important circumstances attest to the unique importance of the Constabulary Act of 1836. First, and foremost, political circumstances had drastically changed. A new group of Whigs had come to power that believed in a policy of justice that was more than hollow rhetoric' which, on the contrary, identified stronger executive government coupled with an end of the patronage of the minority of Ireland's population as the key to making Ireland an integral part of the United Kingdom.[128] Equally important, the genuine overlapping of political principles between O'Connell and the ministers charged with Irish policy opened new opportunities to build trust and goodwill, which led to parliamentary cooperation. This cooperation between O'Connell and the Whigs stands in marked contrast to O'Connell's attitude to former Whig and Tory ministries between 1829 and 1835, as well as the attitude of those ministries to O'Connell.[129] In addition to changing political circumstances, the reality of new

---

[127] Palmer, *Police and Protest*, 342–68.

[128] Hoppen, *Governing Hibernia*, 95–8; on the philosophical commitment to centralising reform, see Mandler, *Aristocratic Government*, ch. 5.

[129] For example, take Mulgrave officially inviting O'Connell to dinner at the Viceregal lodge, which led to a great amount of criticism in the newspaper and privately between

government policy at Dublin Castle, which removed avowedly Orange functionaries, actively promoted Catholics, and took on local Orange magistrates certainly put the confidence of Ireland's politically active population in Mulgrave, Morpeth, and Russell. A *Pilot* article from August 1835 illustrates this public confidence as it reshapes the political struggle on Whig-vs-Tory lines:

> The crisis – life or death – despotism or liberty – peace with improving institutions – or dogged corruption precipitating convulsion– are at this very moment while we are writing struggling for mastery; and the cause of the people, of liberty, peace, and improving institutions must triumph if the people are true to themselves ... The Lords, who represent the spirit of Toryism in one branch of the legislature, have gone so far that there is now no pretence for delusion, and whoever does not join at this juncture heart and hand in the common struggle ... in his heart he is the partisan of corruption, and the foe of practical liberty. ... The ministers must stand firm. We believe them too sincerely hated by Toryism not to be sincere in Reform. If the ministry cannot carry measures now, it is no ground for giving up office. In power *they can govern the appointments in spite of the Lords*, and through them may waste Toryism, by bestowing them, not on doubtful, but on true, and firm, and constant Reformers.[130]

This change in Irish opinion made centralising reforms more palatable – the Irish public (with O'Connell's support) trusted the new Whigs to operate on a principle of justice rather than coercion, whereas they had never trusted the Tories or Whigs of earlier in the decade, who had relied on coercion as a means to subdue Ireland's recalcitrant population.

By 1830, the police force had been split into two separate forces in Ireland. Peel had set up the County Police in 1822, which established a countywide police force supervised by a chief constable appointed by Dublin Castle but controlled locally by the resident magistrates in each county. The county forces organised themselves on provincial lines (Ulster, Munster, Leinster, and Connacht), with an inspector general appointed for each by Dublin Castle who created the rules and regulations of each province's force and oversaw its general operation. Crucially, however, local magistrates retained the power to appoint all constables and were considered equals to any Dublin Castle appointed stipendiary magistrate who might be dispatched during times of profound

---

politicians, including a letter from William IV, who criticised Mulgrave for not excluding O'Connell 'from the society of gentlemen'. See Sir Herbert Taylor to Russell, 23 October 1835, USSC, Broadland Papers, RC/D/1/10; Russell to Taylor, 21 October 1835, TNA, Russell Papers, PRO 30/22/1E/222-3; Russell to Mulgrave, 24 October 1835, MC, Mulgrave MSS, M/802.

[130] 'The Crisis', *The Pilot*, 31 August 1835, emphasis added. On O'Connell's support for Irish Constabulary Bill see 'Mr O'Connell's Speech', *Cobbett's Weekly Political Register*, 5 September 1835.

unrest.[131] The other force, the Peace Preservation Police, colloquially known as the 'Peelers', was a much smaller force controlled by Dublin Castle and deployable to areas in acute need during periods of particular violence. By 1833, the force included roughly 1,200 men and was used on a number of occasions by Lord Stanley during his time as chief secretary of Ireland. Both forces had a complex funding structure that included local support by taxpayers and national monies from the general fund.[132]

The Whig government proposed substantial changes to the Irish constabulary in their 1835 bill. First, they planned to integrate the two existing bodies of county police and 'Peelers' into one force. Rather than having four provincial inspector generals that issued rules on a province-wide basis, the government proposed one inspector general for the entire force, to be appointed by the lord lieutenant. The inspector general would be the head of the force, supported by a deputy inspector and thirty-two sub-inspectors, one for each county. Whereas before magistrates controlled the appointment of constables along with other matters related to the enforcement of law and order, Morpeth's 1835 bill divested the power of patronage from local magistrates and placed it under the jurisdiction of the lord lieutenant. The cost of the force increased from £250,000 per annum to £380,000, and Irish taxpayers would continue to foot half the bill.[133]

Immediately upon the bill's introduction, opposition arose among Conservative Anglo-Irish MPs like Frederick Shaw and Col. Alexander Perceval. Shaw demanded to know on what grounds the government was attempting to degrade the magistrates by depriving them 'of the power of selecting police – a duty for which no men were more competent', while expressing his concern at the absurdity of placing all power in the person of the lord lieutenant, who could 'exercise the capricious authority that was given him as he chose'.[134] Both MPs raised further complaints about the increased cost burden the reform would place on the country as it proposed to increase the number of officers in the force. Notwithstanding these complaints, however, the bill made it through the House of Commons and proceeded to the Lords for a second reading two weeks later. In the upper house, the ultra-Tories, led by Roden, proceeded to pour scorn on the bill that they had proposed just a few years earlier. Lord Londonderry objected to the bill because by giving power of appointments to the lord lieutenant, it gave all control to O'Connell, 'the hand of

---

[131] Broeker, *Rural Disorder*, 147–9.    [132] Palmer, *Police and Protest*, 328–31.
[133] '6 Will. IV.–Sess. 1835. (Ireland.) A bill to amend an act of the third year of the reign of His Late Majesty King George the Fourth, for the appointment of constables in Ireland', P. P. (1835, 493, I.487).
[134] Hansard, 3rd ser., vol. 30, col. 655, 18 August 1835.

the individual to whom the noble Viscount and his friends were so much indebted for being in Government'.[135] The Earl of Winchilsea, another prominent ultra-Tory, alleged that the Constabulary Bill was simply a ransom, 'one of three instalments which were to be paid to the hon. and learned Member of Dublin [O'Connell] for his support of the present administration'.[136] The Lords rejected the bill by a vote of 51/39, defeating it under the presumption that the bill would strengthen O'Connell's hand and that the magistrates in Ireland did not deserve to have the power of patronage stripped from them. Russell wrote to Mulgrave in early September 1835 frustrated by the whole situation in the House of Lords, writing 'Irish bills stand no chance with the Lords. It is but to say "O'Connell" & reason goes for nothing.'[137]

The Whigs bided their time between the end of the parliamentary session in 1835 and the new session in 1836. The obstinacy of Lyndhurst and his ultra-compatriots created an intra-party rift, with Peel's moderate branch of Conservatives upset by Lyndhurst's actions.[138] Furthermore, the Lords' opposition to all Irish reforms created concern among many about a coming 'collision' between the two houses. In the meantime, Russell, Morpeth, and Mulgrave planned to reintroduce a Constabulary Bill at the beginning of the new session. Russell consulted the king about a new bill in December, at which point His Majesty suggesting keeping four provincial inspectors under the command of one inspector general, most likely to reduce the potential cost of reform. Morpeth brought the new bill before the House of Commons on 18 February and justified the necessity of the bill by arguing that the peculiar circumstances of Ireland, by which he meant Irish outrages coupled with historic Orange partiality, necessitated a uniform system of policing controlled by central government:

This was, perhaps, the most material alteration to the Bill, transferring as it did the power of the local Magistracy to the Lord-Lieutenant. It was a material alteration, but he humbly submitted that it was a most important and judicious one. ... This would supersede all the cumbrous machinery which it now became necessary to resort to whenever a district was to be proclaimed; and would enable the Lord Lieutenant to diminish the amount of the police force with corresponding rapidity.[139]

Morpeth acknowledged the transfer of responsibility in appointing all members of the constabulary from the magistracy to government. He

---

[135] Hansard, 3rd ser., vol. 30, col. 1003, 26 August 1835.
[136] Hansard, 3rd ser., vol. 30, col. 1006, 26 August 1835.
[137] Russell to Mulgrave, 3 September 1835, MC, Mulgrave MSS, M/792.
[138] Theodore Martin, *A Life of Lord Lyndhurst: From Letters and Papers in Possession of His Family* (London: John Murray, 1883), 340–4.
[139] Hansard, 3rd ser., vol. 31, cols. 533–4, 18 February 1836.

stressed that it was true that the government would officially have the power of appointment, although he argued it 'would be practically in the hands of the Inspector-General', a point Morpeth praised on account of the future inspector general's ability to appoint men without bias whereas the magistracy, 'without ascribing to them any other political feeling ... would in most cases be very desirous to appoint their own friends'.[140] As proof that the Whig government was committed to creating an impartial force, Morpeth proposed the appointment of Col. James Shaw Kennedy as the first inspector general. Russell, Morpeth, and Mulgrave had agreed on Shaw Kennedy because he was well respected by both Whig and Tory and had been approached years earlier by Peel to head London's police force, but had declined the offer. Furthermore, the Irish office triumvirate believed that Shaw Kennedy, as a distinguished army veteran, possessed the experience to instil discipline and an *esprit de corps* in the nascent body.[141]

Just as in 1835, Anglo-Irish Tories rose in opposition to the bill, and their objections were the same. They stoutly opposed placing patronage of the force in the hands of the lord lieutenant rather than local magistrates. Sir Robert Bateson, MP for Co. Londonderry, argued that government-appointed law officials were much more likely to act as political partisans, which precluded him from supporting the transfer of more power to the lord lieutenant. Bateson relayed an incident that occurred in which he had reported a sub-constable of improper conduct to the Inspector General of Ulster, Sir Frederick Stovin. Stovin allegedly agreed with Bateson that the constable in question was a man of bad character, but, because the constable was a Catholic, Stovin 'could not remove him' without losing his position as inspector general of the province, thus illustrating the political nature of police appointments and the protected status of Catholics in the force, regardless of alleged impropriety in their conduct.[142] However, Robert Peel, as leader of the Conservatives, undercut Bateson and his fellow Anglo-Irish Tory colleagues when he rose in support of Shaw Kennedy's appointment and the principle of government control over all appointments.[143]

On the bill's third and final reading in the Commons, Anglo-Irish members attempted a last-ditch effort to derail the bill by offering an amendment. Objecting to the cost of the measure and the fact that it placed the pecuniary burden on the national Consolidated Fund rather

[140] Ibid.
[141] Russell to Mulgrave, 13 December 1835, MC, Mulgrave MSS, M/812; Mulgrave to Russell, 12 January 1836, TNA, Russell Papers, PRO 30/22/2A/74–6.
[142] Hansard, 3rd ser., vol. 31, 537–8, 18 February 1836.
[143] Hansard, 3rd ser., vol. 31, 542–5, 551, 18 February 1836.

than locally, Tories proposed that Irish grand juries should approve the costs locally and have the power to audit accounts regularly. Up until the bill's introduction, Irish grand juries had voted locally on the rates necessary to pay for the maintenance of law and order. Concerned about giving up further local authority, Anglo-Irish MPs argued that placing the cost on the national Consolidated Fund would mean there was no incentive to keep costs low, which might induce corruption or financial inefficiencies. Afraid of the lord lieutenant 'putting his hands in the pocket of the people', Tory MPs claimed they simply wished to maintain some accountability. Rebuffing those arguments, Morpeth stressed the unreliability of local institutions in administering law and order in Ireland and argued 'that the judges of Ireland are not as fit persons to confide the peace of the country to as the Government, nor are the grand juries ... such competent auditors of accounts as the Lords of the Treasury'.[144] The Tories lost their motion for an amendment (60/18) and the bill passed the Commons without a vote.

In the House of Lords, however, the Whigs remained at a distinct disadvantage. Tory peers outnumbered the Whigs and a number of the most influential ultra-Protestants belonged to the upper house. When the bill was moved into committee in May 1836, to discuss and propose amendments to the Commons' version, Roden led the attack against the immense power of patronage that the bill entrusted to the government. Arguing that the bill created an autocrat out of the lord lieutenant, giving him the power to send his 'troops' (i.e., police) anywhere throughout the country on a whim at the country's expense, Roden appealed to the British constitution and the ideals of local representation. More revealing was Roden's acknowledgement that 'we are living in times of great change', as he attempted to appeal to fearmongering to kill support for the bill. By alluding to the 'deplorable ... situation of his Majesty's local subjects' who were subject to 'the machinations of a priesthood who were endeavouring to enslave the nation', Roden argued that 'we know not who may be called to rule over the destinies of our country', and implored his fellow Lords to vote against the Whigs' bill.[145] Other ultras appealed to similar sentiments. The Marquess of Londonderry, while praising the Whigs' presumptive appointee as Inspector General, Col. Shaw Kennedy, also pondered how long Shaw Kennedy would keep his job. 'Looking at the appointments made by the present Government since they came into office ... he did not know but that in six weeks Mr Maurice

---

[144] Hansard, 3rd ser., vol. 32, 521–31, 23 March 1836.
[145] Hansard, 3rd ser., vol. 33, 2 May 1836, 479–83. More on Roden, and his rhetorical flair, in Chapters 4 and 5.

O'Connell might be appointed head of the police in Ireland. Having no confidence in the Government, he should protest any Bill passing into law.'[146] With the support of moderate Conservatives, including Peel as leader of the party, the protests of Roden and his fellow ultras did not go far. Nevertheless, the bill did receive further amendments from the Lords that included stripping out language many Tory peers thought invested the lord lieutenant with the power to command the police contrary to an order from the court, as well as curtailing the cost of the measure by reducing the number of officers commissioned by the bill. With the support of moderate Tories and all the Whig peers the bill passed without a vote and became law in early May 1836.

The passage of the Irish Constabulary Act of 1836 was an achievement with lasting long-term impact as well as an immediate payoff. The bill's passage underscored how the Whig government had recognised long-standing Irish injustice, partiality and favouritism in the administration of law and order and attempted to rectify it. With the support of moderate Tories, the bill also implicitly conceded the fact that Ireland's magistracy were tainted with the stain of Orangeism and should be divested of the responsibility of appointing police officers, especially after Morpeth referred in his floor speech to sixty-nine constables and sub-constables appointed by local magistrates who had been forced to resign from the force due to their membership of the Orange Order.[147] The bill also embodied the governing philosophy of Russell, Mulgrave, and Morpeth, who believed that reforms placing more power in the hands of the central government offered the best remedy for dealing with Irish wrongs. Crucially, by creating a uniform command structure under the control of one inspector general appointed by the lord lieutenant, the bill also created a force that was readily adaptable and responsive to the demands of Irish countryside. The power vested in the inspector general to create the rules and regulations of the force, and to change them whenever necessary, proved a vital asset as the force attempted to suppress Irish agrarian violence. The bill also expanded the size of the force to 8,335 rank and file by the beginning of 1839, an increase of roughly 10 per cent from 1835.[148]

However, this episode also demonstrated, in stark relief, how constrained the Whigs found themselves politically. As alluded to earlier, by dealing with a matter of law and order – a topic firmly within the traditional remit and sensibilities of the Tory Party – the Whigs could find

---

[146] Ibid., 488–9. Maurice O'Connell was MP for Tralee and Daniel O'Connell's eldest son.

[147] Hansard, 3rd ser., vol. 33, cols. 488–9, 2 May 1836.

[148] 'Abstract Statement of Constabulary Force in each County, City, and Town in Ireland, January 1839', P. P. (1839, vol. 47), 302.

common purpose with some Conservative MPs and peers. But even that did not insulate the Whigs from opposition, including the defeat of the bill initially in 1835. The opposition demonstrated by Roden, Winchilsea, and Anglo-Irish MPs highlighted the power ultras could wield and demonstrated the kind of questions Peel would be forced to weigh in the years to come – whether to give support to Whig measures and frustrate the fringe element of his party, or to let loose the dogs of war. As the next chapters will demonstrate, he often chose the latter.

### Legislative Failure: Whigs and the Irish Railway Commission

If legislative victory articulates Whig priorities, what about their failures? One gets a glimpse of just how innovative some of their ideas were, as well as the way their programmatic endeavours centred on solving the twin problems of Irish poverty and agrarian violence, by examining the failed attempt to build Irish railways in this period with state funds. While historians have long recognised the value of the Irish Railway Commissions' work, which culminated in an incredibly detailed report with attendant maps and loads of statistical information, until recently few have attempted to examine the legislative attempt for its political significance in terms of demonstrating a peculiarly Whig agenda.[149] As Peter Hession has recently observed, the Irish Railway Commission (IRC) relied on a model of governance that emphasised 'the impact of technology' and the supposed impartiality of expert opinion as a method to counter partisan-tinged opposition.[150] In this way, the material presented by the IRC fits neatly alongside the standardised Outrage Reports (discussed in Chapter 2), which attempted to make levels of Irish outrages comprehensible to policymakers; it also fits with the way the government took data compiled from Outrage Reports to make statistical 'scientific' arguments about the level of violence to ward off critics of their Irish policy (discussed in Chapter 5). However, a close examination of the

---

[149] Peter Solar called it 'a remarkably all-embracing and systematic survery of the Irish economy'; see Peter M. Solar, 'The Agricultural Trade Statistics in the Irish Railway Commissioners' Report', *Irish Economic and Social History* 6 (1979): 24. On the ways the IRC attempted to upset the British railway development paradigm, see Philip Lloyd, 'The Irish Railway Commission (1836–1839): Aiming to Reform Railways in the United Kingdom and to Improve the Governance of Ireland', *The Journal of Transport History* 49, no. 1 (2019): 123–40.

[150] Peter Hession, 'Imagining the Railway Revolution in Pre-Famine Ireland: Technology, Governance, and the Drummond Commission, 1832–39', in *Dreams of the Future in Nineteenth Century Ireland*, ed. Richard J. Butler (Liverpool: Liverpool University Press, 2021), 247.

Whigs' focus on railway development demonstrates how many of the Whigs' ideas proved mutually reinforcing.

The immediate context to the IRC's formation had a surprisingly ecumenical orientation considering its eventual failure. In early July 1836 a number of prominent noblemen and gentlemen met at London's Thatched House Tavern to discuss the 'best Lines of Railway in Ireland' and to prevent 'the interference of mere private or local interests ... and a wasteful expenditure of money'. The list of attendees included ultra-Tories like Lord Westmeath; the leader of the Irish conservatives in the House of Commons, Sir Frederick Shaw; and Whig grandees like the Duke of Leinster; as well as Daniel O'Connell. The meeting proposed a number of resolutions that emphasised the 'national' over the 'local' and focussed on the adoption of a systematic approach, thus wishing to avoid the rampant speculation and financial disaster experienced in Britain.[151] Within weeks Lord Lansdowne had proposed the creation of a commission in the House of Lords to 'appoint proper persons to inquire and report upon the most advantageous lines of railways in Ireland', which he argued would prevent confusion over development, and the Lords adopted the motion without debate.[152] The Limerick landlord and chancellor of the exchequer, Thomas Spring Rice, decided the make-up of the commission, which included Thomas Drummond as chairman; John Burgoyne, the chairman of the Board of Works; Richard Griffith, an engineer intimately involved in the Irish Ordnance Survey; and Peter Barlow, a professor of mathematics from the Royal Military Academy.[153] The IRC produced two reports. The first, a ten-page report delivered in 1837, laid out the various modes of inquiry the commissioners had undertaken and pleaded for more time to complete their work. Nevertheless, the commissioners did reveal their preliminary conclusions, stressing that Ireland lacked the robust economic development necessary to make 'distinct lines from town to town' profitable, and therefore urged the development of 'a well-combined and judicious system of Railways, in which the joint traffic of many places ... should be made to pass ... over one common line, and where the greatest general accommodation should be attained at the smallest outlay [of capital]'.[154] In other words, the commissioners highlighted the necessity of coordinated central state planning rather than

---

[151] 'Irish Railroad Projects', *Dublin Evening Post*, 6 July 1836.
[152] Hansard, 3rd ser., vol. 35, 686, 1 August 1836.
[153] Hession, 'Imagining the Railway Revolution in Pre-famine Ireland', 248.
[154] 'First report of the commissioners appointed to inquire into the manner in which railway communications can be most advantageously promoted in Ireland', P. P. (1837, vol. 33, no. 75), 7.

throwing the development of railways open to private speculation, competition, and potential failure, which they believed would 'deprive the country for many years to come of advantages now within its reach'.[155] The commissioners published their celebrated second report in 1838; the main body of the report was in three parts and consisted of roughly 130 pages, along with about 600 pages of appendixes consisting of witness statements, maps, and an array of statistical data.[156] The commission's work, including a significant amount of surveying carried out in Ireland, cost just north of £13,500, with an additional £11,000 for printing the report's maps and plans.[157]

The commissioners' recommendations in the second report offered a bold, innovative strategy of state-led investment as a means to secure Ireland's 'modernisation' while also offering stable permanent employment to its surplus labour force. The commission proposed the creation of a central trunk line from Dublin to Cork financed by the state, which would ultimately be paid for by the Irish public. The desire to pursue state-sponsored development had both practical and political rationales. At various points in the report the commissioners argued a state-sponsored approach was the most cost-effective; that it protected the project from the parliamentary delays experienced by English projects; that it protected the public interest from the corrupting influence of private interests; that proprietors would offer land concessions to government at lower rates than to private firms; and, simply, that the potential return on investment was too low to entice the necessary risk from a large enough group of capitalists to finance the project.[158] Highlighting the overlap between various Whig priorities, Drummond privately espoused the idea of financing railways through the appropriation of tithe payments, writing a multiple-page report to Russell and suggesting it would transform tithes from 'a source of the most violent agitation into a powerful stimulant to industry and inducement to tranquillity', which Drummond believed 'could scarcely be over-estimated'.[159] Not surprisingly, Russell thought that mixing it with the thorny problem of the Irish church would only make Irish railway development more difficult and the

[155] Ibid., 8.
[156] 'Second report of the commissioners appointed to consider and recommend a general system of railways for Ireland' [hereafter 'Railway Commission Report'], P. P. (1837–8, vol. 35), 145.
[157] 'Return of Expenditure by Railway Com. In Ireland', P. P. (1839, vol. 46), 88.
[158] 'Railway Commission Report', passim., especially parts II & III.
[159] Drummond to Russell, 22 February 1838, TNA, PRO 30/22/3A/165. Mulgrave supported the proposal, writing to Russell that it would garner 'so much active support from all parties as to overbear the opposition … from the Church', Mulgrave to Russell, 23 February 1838, MC, M/901.

idea was dropped, but the suggestion underscores a holistic thinking about Irish 'problems' and creative solutions.[160]

The report also highlighted the moral effects that railway development would bring to Ireland. The commissioners located agrarian violence as an outgrowth of dire economic circumstance rather than a lack of moral character. Railway construction and the concomitant economic development brought by trains, therefore, opened a way to reform 'habits of intemperance, and that proneness to outrage ... which unhappily distinguish them [Irish peasants]'.[161] An increase in employment and subsequent decrease in crime, the commissioners believed, would allow for a reduction in military and constabulary spending as 'the moral results ... from an improvement of its [Ireland's] social condition' took hold.[162] In a bid to assuage the law-and-order crowd, however, the commissioners also argued for the security benefits railroad development would bring to a vulnerable Irish countryside: 'The facility of moving troops in large bodies, hundreds of miles within a few hours ... either to oppose foreign aggression or repress domestic outrages, must be apparent; and its influence upon the security of the public peace can scarcely be overrated.'[163] Above all, however, the report embodied a Whig approach that wanted to further integrate Ireland into the United Kingdom – in the words of the commissioners to 'cement this union, by drawing their inhabitants closer together in the bonds of mutual intercourse and knowledge'.[164] The political idealism expressed by Drummond and his colleagues was often effusive, and fitted into the wider 'justice to Ireland' paradigm:

The policy of rendering assistance is unquestionable. It is acknowledged to be necessary towards a colony, and must be considered more so in the case of a part of the United Kingdom, comprehended within its domestic boundaries. ... But there are other considerations equally importing the general welfare ... as being more worthy of a great and enlightened nation – considerations of justice, of generosity – of liberal concern for the improvement and civilization of our country.[165]

Morpeth would offer a similar vision on the duties of an enlightened British government towards one of its constituent portions seven months later when he ventured that the government 'propose[d] to employ the credit of England for the benefit of Ireland'. He went on: 'We propose, not as in the case of private companies ... that profit shall go into our own pockets, but that whatever does arise ... shall be applied to the general

[160] Russell to Mulgrave, 28 February 1838, MC, M/902.
[161] 'Railway Commission Report', 84.    [162] 'Railway Commission Report', 85.
[163] 'Railway Commission Report', 93.    [164] 'Railway Commission Report', 92.
[165] 'Railway Commission Report', 85.

benefit of the Irish people'.[166] Regrettably for the government, and for Ireland, the majority of the House of Commons did not share in this magnanimous sentiment.

With such effusive rhetoric about binding the Union closer together, and within the wider political context of other contentious Irish issues like the poor laws, education, and tithe reform it is little wonder that the Railway Commission's bold plans went nowhere. Within a day of the report's publication, the *Times* published a series of letters by Eneas MacDonnell (a frequent correspondent who attacked the hierarchy of the Irish Catholic Church)[167] who linked the report to allegations of Irish 'jobbing', referring to the Whig platform of 'justice for Ireland' as little more than 'a scheme of lottery ... [for] their patron and protector, Mr O'Connell'.[168] The more phlegmatic *Quarterly Review* praised the abstract purpose of the commission in a meandering essay on railways, but outlined what became the popular mode of attack in the House of Commons: that political economy dictated that energetic and enlightened development could only come from private capital: 'a wise government should encourage, rather than presume to contend with, that daring spirit which has so remarkably characterized British capitalists ... to check, to suppress, or to compete with this enterprising spirit, would not only involve the government in difficulty, but the nation in ruin'.[169]

Peel followed suit. 'The very progress of this debate', he stated in March 1839, when the government brought forward the motion to adopt the report, 'afforded an illustration which confirmed the doubts he had always entertained of the policy of departing from the great public principle of non-interference of government with private enterprise.'[170] In an argument that presaged the Famine-era maxim that 'Irish property should pay for Irish poverty', Peel suggested that Irish property owners and other investors had the responsibility to 'undertake their own works and trust their own intelligence', before suggesting that state-sponsored development set a precedent for the unfair advantage of privileging one part of the country over another. Although other speakers would highlight the benefit of railway development as 'the best means for tranquillizing the country',[171] the death

---

[166] Hansard, 3rd ser., vol. 45, col. 1079, 1 March 1839.

[167] Cahill, 'Irish Catholicism and English Toryism', 69.

[168] 'To the Editor of the Times', *Times*, 30 July 1838; see also 3 September 1838, and 17 October 1838.

[169] [Francis B. Head], 'Railroads in Ireland', *Quarterly Review* 63 (January 1839), 1–60, at 51–2.

[170] Hansard, 3rd ser., vol. 45, cols. 1082, 1 March 1839.

[171] Hansard, 3rd ser., vol. 45, 1113, 1 March 1839.

knell came when the Radical Joseph Hume, MP for Kilkenny, spoke against the proposals on similar lines to Peel: 'He agreed with the right hon. Baronet [Peel] ... that as Ireland was the principal gainer, Ireland should be the guarantee against loss.'[172] Although Parliament adopted the report, any plans for its implementation were shelved as the government sleepwalked from one crisis to another in the session of 1839.[173] Five days after the conclusion of the debate, Drummond wrote bitterly to Morpeth about party feeling getting in the way of sound legislation, attributing the plan's failure to 'a portion of the English and their mean jealousy and dislike to do any thing calculated to promote the advantage to Ireland'.[174]

## Conclusion

The Irish Constabulary Act of 1836, and the failed proposals of the IRC, embodied what one historians has identified as the 'high-political shift ... in government after 1835 ... in favour of government intervention', whereby ministers had a 'predisposition ... to appreciate the powers and blessing of good political institutions'.[175] Along with professionalising the police force by creating a bureaucracy that previously had not existed, Russell, Morpeth, and Mulgrave also attempted to replace a tarnished government reputation with a new one based on principles of equal justice that were more palatable to the majority of the Irish population. They also willingly worked with O'Connell in the wake of a generation of politicians who had been more comfortable with calling him a 'blackguard' than identifying that working with him 'would tend to moderate him & keep the country quiet'.[176] The king did not approve of such modern attitudes, and only slowly acquiesced to this new Whig vision of government in Ireland, a change that was due in part to his growing infirmity.[177] William's death in June 1836 brought with it the dissolution of Parliament and a subsequent election reducing the number of Whig MPs, which further strengthened the political hand of ultra-Tories who continued to stand in opposition to Whig reform, or who took a political paring knife to bills entering their chamber. But what else could be done? Lord John Russell summed up the attitude of

---

[172] Hansard, 3rd ser., vol. 45, 1111, 1 March 1839.
[173] Gray, *Making of the Poor Law*, 307–9; Chapter 5 below.
[174] Drummond to Morpeth, 6 March 1839, CH, J19/1/22/64.
[175] Mandler, *Aristocratic Government*, 172–3.
[176] Russell to Mulgrave, 6 January 1836, MC, Mulgrave MSS M/818.
[177] On William IV's disapproval of any concert with O'Connell, see Taylor to Russell, 8 January 1836, USSC, Broadland Papers, RC/D/1/3; Taylor to Russell, 10 January 1836; ibid., RC/D/1/16.

government as it moved forward under the reign of young Queen Victoria when he wrote to Mulgrave, encouraging him to press on: 'For your own part I can recommend nothing better than to advance in the same course, giving effect to the Catholic Relief Act, & destroying extreme parties by showing how well they can be treated under a justice Government.'[178]

[178] Russell to Mulgrave, 5 August 1836, MC, Mulgrave MSS, M/835.

# 4  Protestant Mobilisation and the Spectre of Irish Outrages

Confiding in his diary in May 1835, the 4th Duke of Newcastle, an ardent Protestant and ultra-Tory, summarised his opinion of the prevailing mood in Parliament as it reconvened by stating: 'If a man now wishes to be popular he calls himself a staunch Protestant + talks of defending his Religion + his Church – rails against Popery and advocates [the] conservative principles of the Institutions of the Country.' Just a few days earlier he had praised God for 'burying all things à *tout*' and bringing back 'a Protestant feeling ... recommencing with considerable ardour'. These statements by Newcastle seem somewhat incongruous with the political realities of British politics in 1835. While the Tories had won seats in the recent elections, these victories were not enough to sustain Peel's minority government, which fell in April. Worse still, the Whigs found parliamentary support from the most nefarious possible source – Daniel O'Connell and his 'tail' – a connection secured in the Lichfield House Compact, discussed in Chapter 3. How could Newcastle conclude that 'Right feeling [was] making wonderful progress' in the midst of such dire political realities?[1]

Historians branded the 1830s as the 'decade of reform' for good reason – both because of the political consequences launched by the Great Reform Act of 1832, and an acknowledgement of the philosophical discourse driving governing policy. Although the slogan was by no means used exclusively by Whigs and Radicals, the term's association with the Whig Party underscores the salient fact that the 1830s were dominated by Whig government and a concerted effort by government officials to modernise and centralise state apparatuses.[2] The label of 'reform' gave coherence to this period and provided an explanation for Britain's divergence down constitutional democratic paths while the Continent descended into revolution and autocracy. Historians have provided much nuance to this simplistic reading, especially those highlighting Whig

---

[1] 'Diaries of Henry Pelham-Clinton, 4th Duke of Newcastle Under Lyne [...]' [hereafter Newcastle Diaries] 3 May, 12 May 1835, UNSC, Ne2 F 3/1, 29, 31.
[2] Burns and Innes, eds., *Rethinking Age of Reform*; Mandler, *Aristocratic Government*.

186

failure and the party's eventual collapse, but the 'reform' label has endured.

I have argued that an effect of segregating Ireland from one's analysis of the overall trends of governing policy in the 1830s has been to limit the scope of our understanding concerning the project of 'reform' and one of the primary venues for implementation. Another significant problem arises when treating Ireland separately from the rest of Great Britain in this period – without an Irish dimension, the story around the Tory party's return to power in 1841 is incomplete.[3] In particular, it fails to account for the ways the reactionary wing of the party – the 'ultras' – recovering from the dizzying effects of reform, effectively organised a campaign to undermine Whig narratives of progress, and used Ireland – and all its complications and 'outrages' – as a means to stir anti-Catholic/anti-Irish sentiments among the British electorate. Ultra-Tories publicly lamented the death of the Protestant Ascendancy in Ireland as a result of Catholic Emancipation and became transfixed by a greater siege mentality that employed 'religious explanations for the rapid political flux',[4] suggesting that Whig governing policy was a harbinger of the undermining of the Protestant nature of the British Empire. Furthermore, Tories politicised the endemic violence of Ireland's countryside as a way to undermine Whig narratives of 'justice to Ireland', and to suggest a relationship between those outrages and potential violence across the empire. In this Tory rendering, therefore, the deplorable state of the Irish countryside and the corresponding rise of Catholic influence was an object lesson demonstrating what Whig government would do to the wider empire, and British dominance in the world.[5]

This chapter traces the influence Ireland exerted on Tory party thinking and its strategies to resist Whig government. First, it establishes the ways Catholic Emancipation and the Reform Act had undermined many Tories' Protestant-centric world view and created deep-seated anxieties about Catholic domination in all political, social, economic, and religious life. The chapter then demonstrates how the Lichfield House Compact pushed a group of ultra-Tories, many of whom were Anglo-Irish, to

---

[3] My approach follows the work of Andrew Shields, who has attempted to chart the role Irish Conservatives played in shaping British Conservative actions later in the century; see Andrew Shields, *The Irish Conservative Party 1852–1868: Land, Politics and Religion* (Dublin: Irish Academic Press, 2007).

[4] Jacqueline Hill, *From Patriots to Unionists: Dublin Civic Politics and Irish Protestant Patriotism, 1660–1840* (Oxford: Oxford University Press, 1997), 283.

[5] Alex Middleton has followed this theme in his excellent discussion of Tory condemnation of Whiggery and their colonial governance. See Alex Middleton, 'Conservative Politics and Whig Colonial Government, 1830–41', *Historical Research* 94, no. 265 (2021): 532–53.

prophesy Ireland's doom. The link between Protestant thinking and Tory politics was solidified in the re-establishment of the Protestant Association in 1835, along with the outpouring of pamphlets and newspaper propaganda highlighting Irish agrarian violence, O'Connell's perceived influence over Whig government, and wider imperial concerns. In particular, the chapter demonstrates how Irish violence was linked to the Canadian Rebellion and so-called 'thuggee' violence in India, and how the perceived rise of Catholic power in Ireland was more broadly tied to fears about the Protestant nature of the British Empire. Finally, the chapter concludes by demonstrating how these strategies were successful in stymieing Whig progress in reform – especially in Ireland – leading to O'Connell's frustration with his Whig partnership and the return of Tory government buoyed by the anti-Catholic rhetoric of the previous five years.

### Anxiety in the Age of Reform

By the time of Lord Grey's ascension to government benches in November 1830 many Protestants connected with Ireland had witnessed what they believed to be their greatest betrayal: the passage of Catholic Emancipation by their own party, by men now deemed 'pander[er]s to the will of the Popish Association, + the confidential intimates of their leaders'.[6] The run-up to Catholic Emancipation, however, had begun the important process of mobilising Protestant popular opinion against Catholic inclusion with the creation of Protestant clubs or the so-called 'Brunswick Constitutional Clubs'. Even though these efforts proved unsuccessful in stopping Emancipation's passage, they did demonstrate the latent level of anti-Catholic sentiment in Britain and the importance of Ireland as a focal point for contention.[7] As John Wolffe has noted in his study of anti-Catholicism, Protestant Ascendancy in Ireland had been 'part of the sacrosanct constitutional order defining a Protestant "empire" extending across the Irish Sea'.[8]

While rumours of Catholic Emancipation swirled, many concerned with the Protestant cause began both worrying about the effects of emancipation and also actively working against its passage. Tory peers met in July 1828 to form the 'Protestant Club' at Lord Longford's home, which

---

[6] Lord Clancarty to Lord Londonderry, 9 March 1829, Londonderry Papers, DCRO, D/Lo/C106(7).
[7] G. I. T. Machin, 'The No-Popery Movement in Britain in 1828–9', HJ 6, no. 2 (1963): 193–4; Suzanne T. Kingon, 'Ulster Opposition to Catholic Emancipation, 1828–9', IHS 34, no. 134 (November 2004): 137–55.
[8] John Wolffe, *The Protestant Crusade*, 24.

the Duke of Newcastle believed would prove 'an effectual banner against any Popish inroads upon the Constitution'. Newcastle's diary demonstrates the paranoia that some Protestants felt concerning Ireland and the potential effects of emancipation. Three days after the formation of the 'Protestant Club', Newcastle recounted his encounter with Robert Peel, which he believed demonstrated the government's complacency. In a letter to Newcastle, a converted Irish Protestant named Morris uncovered what he believed was a 'general + extensive plan ... for a rising in Ireland' with agents working throughout England to 'effect a cooperative force'. When Newcastle brought this information to Peel, he found him 'cold' and noted that he 'did not even thank me for bringing him the information'. A few weeks later Newcastle complained in his diary how 'the Rom. Cath. Rebels in Ireland have begun to shew themselves' and recounted a story from Co. Leitrim of a body of 500 Catholics armed with pikes attempting to resist the military. 'I have plainly foreseen all this + much more which is to come but this Govt as well as those before it seem [*sic*] blind to the danger which surrounds us.'[9]

The organisers of the Brunswick Clubs provided guidance on the practical means by which Irish Protestants could establish their own regional clubs. Leaders of the movement in Dublin sent out forms that provided a standard script of resolutions for prospective organisers to fill in and submit to their local newspapers ('AT a Meeting of the [blank] and Inhabitants of [blank] in the County of [blank]'), which included a list of resolutions to establish the organising committee and club officers. The opposite page of the resolutions offered 'hints for the formation of Brunswick Clubs', in which great pains were taken to disassociate their tactics from those of the Catholic Association. 'It should be ever retained in mind, that, the institution of the Brunswick Clubs, is intended purely as a measure of a defensive nature and that every proceeding calculated to give a contrary impression, as to the purpose of its formation ... [such as] large assemblies whose purposes could be perverted or misinterpreted, should invariably be discouraged.' Similarly, organisers stressed the importance of controlling 'the lower classes of Protestants' from potential 'wanton offence', while underscoring the absolute necessity of presenting an image of united Irish Protestant commitment to the British constitution. Defending the constitutional status quo – 'this great object' – was only possible through 'producing a confident and unanimous expression of Protestant political sentiment, or public opinion, throughout Ireland, and thereby informing the British people as to the real situation and circumstances of this country, with reference to the country ... and the

---

[9] Newcastle Diaries, UNSC, Ne2 F 3/1, 50–1, 55.

danger to the state consequent upon further concession'.[10] Some balked at the similarity in tactics between the Brunswick Clubs and Catholic Associations, while others such as Sir Thomas Chapman, Lord Longford's neighbour and fellow Westmeath gentry member, believed it too much 'milk + water' where he wanted 'overt acts and those expressed'. Notwithstanding the reservations of some individual members, the Brunswick Club, and later Protestant manifestations like the Irish Protestant Conservative Society or Conservative Registration Society, provided a constructive outlet for Irish Protestant paranoia, which culminated with electoral victory in 1841.[11]

The failure to stop Catholic Emancipation stirred ultra-Tories into political action, both at elite and popular levels.[12] To counter British perceptions of the Irish gentry's general fecklessness, Anglo-Irish grandees began contemplating means by which to spur one another to political action. 'If we could effect the moderate reform in our discipline', wrote Lord Mount Cashel to the ultra-Protestant Lord Farnham, 'certain am I that Popery could receive a blow which she little calculates on.' Thomas Lefroy, another ultra-Tory and MP for Dublin University, concurred with Mount Cashel's sentiments, and stressed in late 1830 the importance of organising a Protestant body to 'coerce any Government that might be, to do justice to Irish Protestants + prevent their former privileges being now turned into disqualifications'. Lefroy also laid out an important political strategy for Conservatives to regain power, which highlighted the importance of Anglo-Irish support in any future Conservative government. 'In order to get rid of the Whigs they [Irish Conservatives] must come to an understanding with Peel that if ever they assist his return to power he must give up his former policy as to Ireland', making him pledge 'to do equal justice to Protestants + appoint men to govern them, who will do so with fairness'. By the end of the following year he was writing to Farnham enthused by the prospects of creating an organisation 'to give direction + energy to the Protestants + unite them under those they are looking up to for guidance'.[13]

---

[10] 'Hints for the Formation of Brunswick Clubs', TC, 2nd Earl of Longford Papers, G Box 2, folder 16. It is interesting to note the insertion of the phrase 'public opinion', suggesting that while wanting to discipline their plebeian Protestants sympathisers, organisers also recognised the importance of a mobilised popular resistance, no doubt in response to the popular support energised by the Catholic Association.

[11] Alvin Jackson, *Ireland 1798–1998: Politics and War* (Oxford: Wiley-Blackwell, 1999), 60–1.

[12] Spence, 'Philosophy of Irish Toryism', 64–6.

[13] Lord Mount Cashel to Lord Farnham, 18 January 1830, NLI, Farnham Papers, MS 18,612, Folder 7; Thomas Lefroy to Farnham, 25 December 1830, MS 18,611, Folder 1; Thomas Lefroy to Farnham, 1 December 1831, MS 18,611, Folder 2.

The lead-up to and passage of the Great Reform Act further galvanised the political mobilisation of ultra-Tories in Ireland, many of whom interpreted the act as not simply a political question, but a religious and moral one.[14] Ultra-Tories Lords Lorton, Roden, and Enniskillen organised the Irish Protestant Conservative Society in 1831, and with it a 'Protestant Rent' used to register Conservative voters, shoulder the cost of campaigns, defend Protestants from 'overbearing violence' in exercising their right to vote, and in providing solicitors to challenge voter rolls. Much as newspapers reported the weekly amounts raised by O'Connell's 'Catholic Rent', some newspapers made note of the funds pouring into the Irish Protestant Conservative Society's coffers – from £302. 7s. 4d. in August 1832 to £760 for the last week of September 1832 and dropping back down to £256. 2s. 3d. in mid-December. *The Newcastle Courant* reported that Rev. Charles Boyton, fellow at Trinity College Dublin and Brunswick organiser, had moved to transfer the funds to the Grand Orange Lodge 'to organize that body, which was so necessary to the existence of Protestantism in Ireland'.[15] For Boyton, and other leaders in Ireland, the amount of money raised was almost secondary to the optics of pan-Protestant unity – 'a concentration of spirit and purpose ... [and] moral influence' – and the powerful effect that 'the contribution of one farthing' had to instil loyalty among even the poorest sections of the population.[16]

If Catholic Emancipation was not enough, Daniel O'Connell's vocal campaign for the repeal of the Act of Union, which commenced in earnest in 1832 with the demand for Repeal pledges from '"his" candidates', further threatened Irish Protestants.[17] While ascendancy may have been lost when Catholics walked through the doors of Parliament as duly elected members, Irish Protestants could console themselves with the knowledge that they still constituted a majority in the entirety of the

[14] On religious aspects of reform act, see Saunders, 'God and the Great Reform Act', 378–99.
[15] Alvin Jackson, 'The Origins, Politics and Culture of Irish Unionism, c. 1880-1916', in *The Cambridge History of Ireland: Volume 4, 1880 to the Present*, ed. Thomas Bartlett (Cambridge: Cambridge University Press, 2018), 90; 'Protestant Rent', BNL, 17 July 1832; 'Private Correspondence', FJ, 4 August 1832; 'Ireland', *The Aberdeen Journal*, 3 October 1832; 'Ireland', *The Aberdeen Journal*, 21 November 1832; 'London', *The Newcastle Courant*, 15 December 1832. On Boyton, a particularly important Irish Tory and later tutor of Isaac Butt, see Linde Lunney, 'Boyton, Charles', in James McGuire and James Quinn, eds., *Dictionary of Irish Biography* (Cambridge: Cambridge University Press, 2009), http://dib.cambridge.org/viewReadPage.do?articleId=a0864.
[16] Rev. Charles Boyton, *Speech Delivered by the Rev. C. Boyton, F. T. C. D., at a meeting of the Protestant Conservative Society, on Tuesday, the 10th July, 1832* (Dublin: J. Hoare, 1832), 8.
[17] Oliver MacDonagh, *Emancipist*, 72–3.

United Kingdom; Repeal, of course, jeopardised their majority status, rendering them vulnerable to reprisals for the domination they had exercised over their Catholic brethren. When Roden wrote to the Duke of Wellington seeking his advice on how Roden should lead the 'million of people who are ready to sacrifice anything and everything', Wellington responded by pointing to the powerful unifying effect the question of Repeal brought to Protestants on both sides of the Irish Sea. 'The protestants of Ireland by taking up the case of the union and of the connection with Great Britain amalgamate themselves with that country. They take their true and real position in the affairs of the empire, and they derive advantage from the course which they will have pursued', Wellington proposed to Roden. As O'Connell advocated Repeal and worked to grind parliamentary business to a halt, Wellington suggested that Irish Protestants would become more valuable to the British state in proportion to O'Connell's potential success: 'protestants may expect that they will be courted in proportion as apprehensions will be entertained of the persevering exertions of O'Connell and the Roman Catholics'. Finally, and arguably most consequentially for the remainder of the decade, Wellington suggested transforming the issue of Repeal from a political into a religious question: 'Let the question of repeal or no repeal be a question of protestant and Catholic, and you may rely upon it that the protestant cause will be in this country. I therefore recommend you to make your rallying point "no repeal of the union"'.[18] Of course, this was not the first suggestion by a British politician that an Irish political question should be transformed into a religious one – nor, it should be noted, did O'Connell make much of an effort to keep Repeal or his brand of Irish nationalism non-sectarian. Nevertheless, the transformation of Irish political issues into sectarian lightning rods became a potent strategy and powerful weapon for ultra-Tories throughout the latter half of the 1830s, ultimately bearing fruit in their electoral successes in 1841.

Political debate in London, or Dublin, was often accompanied with unrest or violence across the Irish countryside, a fact which tended to contribute to Irish Protestant perceptions of being under siege from a hostile majority. It is easy with hindsight to look back on fears of potential rebellion, or of the repeal of the Union, and to think they were irrational, disingenuous, preposterous, or some combination thereof. However, it seems worth keeping in mind how O'Connell's campaign for Catholic Emancipation had fundamentally upset the Protestant

---

[18] Roden to Wellington, 25 December 1832, USSC, Wellington Papers, WP1/1240/3; Wellington to Roden, 26 December 1832, WP1/1241/13.

world, and how the means by which he achieved this had ruptured social and political cohesion. Robert Peel observed in his memoirs that what was most terrifying about O'Connell's election in Clare 'was in the peaceable and legitimate exercise of a franchise, according to the will and conscience of the holder', because it was 'a revolution in the electoral system of Ireland, the transfer of political power'. Thus, for the Protestant-led social order, O'Connell's victory demonstrated the end of their rule:

> the fever of political and religious excitement – which was quickening the pulse and fluttering the bosom of the whole Catholic population, which had inspired the *serf* of Clare with the resolution and energy of *a freeman* ... had in the twinkling of an eye made all consideration of personal gratitude, ancient family connection, local preferences, the fear of worldly injury, the hope of worldly advantage, subordinate to one absorbing sense of religious obligation and public duty.'[19]

Peel's reference to the serf and the freeman is a telling one, as it denoted his perception of a transformation from a peasant population bound to their land, and therefore to their landlord's interest, into a political body with a will of its own.

As O'Connell began to advocate Repeal, and elections were on the horizon, parts of the countryside responded with violence. In counties Meath, Roscommon, Clare, Mayo, Sligo, and Cavan Dublin Castle received reports of the country 'in a very bad state' which necessitated the dispatch of moveable columns from Dublin.[20] In Galway, the land agent on the Mahon estate, Charles Filgate, complained of Ribbonmen being 'out every night', disturbing the population and amassing firearms. While Ribbonman activity certainly alarmed landlords, their clandestine activities suggested deeper foundational problems in the social order. 'I don't know what will become of us – all Landlords', Filgate wrote to Sir Ross Mahon in April 1831, 'if the Government dont immediately send troops'. A few days later, in a letter to the Anglican parson Rev. Rawdon Greene, married to one of Mahon's daughters, Filgate wrote: 'The times are such that I think the value of property here has fallen 1/4 + I fear, much worse times. Privately, it is the opinion of many of us, to leave this country altogether as no doubt the Reform Bill will pass + then the Repeal of the Union, which no government can then prevent ... you may say I cry out too soon, but I fear we shall soon see it.'[21]

Filgate, of course, did cry out too soon and Repeal never materialised as the inevitable consequence of including Catholics in the nation's polity.

[19] Peel, *Sir Robert Peel*, ed. Parker, 2: 48, 50, my emphasis.
[20] Anglesey to Melbourne, 22 February 1831, PRONI, Anglesey Papers, D619/29/B/22.
[21] Charles Filgate to Sir Ross Mahon, 17 April 1831, NLI, Mahon Papers, MS 47,835, folder 4; Charles Filgate to Rev. R. Greene, 29 April 1831.

However, Filgate's private confession of the desire to emigrate highlights a real problem for Irish Conservatives during the 1830s. Ultra-Tory grandees, including Enniskillen, Roden, Lorton, and Farnham, along with the Duke of Cumberland, established the Protestant Colonization Society of Ireland in 1830, 'a society for preventing Protestant emigration and pauperism, and for promoting scriptural religion and loyalty'. In a replaying of the plantations of the sixteenth and seventeenth centuries in miniature, with coded language implying the superiority of Protestant tenants over the Catholic majority, the society resettled Protestants onto 'unoccupied and waste lands' as a way to 'check the swelling torrent of emigration, that is year after year draining out the moral and physical energies of that country' and to 'turn back upon our native soil the streams of real wealth' produced by the 'honest enterprise' of 'industrious men'.[22] By 1832, the society had relocated Protestant tenants onto land in Co. Donegal and were actively seeking suitable land in Munster at the behest of Protestant interests in Cork, with financial support from subscriptions across the country and an influx of cash from the disbanded Brunswick Club. The report, totalling roughly forty pages, offers a window into the anxieties of Protestants across Ireland. In the report of their annual meeting, held in May 1832, speakers highlighted what they perceived as the moral and economic peril of Protestant emigration, which they estimated had totalled roughly 77,000 Protestants the previous year. Contrasting the 'Protestant north' where 'all is quiet, all is peace', with the rest of Ireland, which had descended 'into the shades of rapine and assassination', Capt. Cottingham argued that further emigration would drain 'the great mainstay of Protestant security' from the land. While appealing to the Protestants of Ireland to support the society's efforts, Cottingham also appealed to the British government by stressing the loyalty of Protestants and the short-sightedness of encouraging emigration to North American colonies with British money. Drawing on the experience of the American Revolution, Cottingham argued:

Oh, how prophetic was the reasoning of Lord Bacon, when he drew the comparison between the colonising of our then American settlements, and that of Ireland; a few short years but passed away, and those very colonies, established by British wealth, and people with Briton's sons, threw off the mother country, and were to be found in arms against her – (hear, hear). Who will be bold enough to say that such may not be the fate of our present Canadian and New Brunswick settlements. It becomes then, a matter of sound policy on the part of England, to promote our infant undertaking, to keep within the realms of England's natural

---

[22] Protestant Colonization Society of Ireland, *Transactions of the Protestant Colonization Society of Ireland: Reported at a Public Meeting of Subscribers, in the Dublin Institution &#x2026; May 24, 1832* (Dublin: J. Hoare, 2, Hawkins's-street, 1832), NLI P 438, 5–6.

boundary, here free-born, brave, and spirited sons – the descendants of those gallant men who conquered Ireland – who have kept Ireland as a part and parcel of the British dominions – and who are ready ... to devote their lives and properties in supporting British connection – (long and continued cheers).[23]

Thus, the political and social atmosphere for Irish Protestants in the early 1830s was one of profound anxiety and frenzied reaction. The manner and means by which O'Connell had secured Catholic Emancipation caused deep distress to those wishing to protect whatever waning influence the Protestant Ascendancy still held, and their response was to imitate O'Connell's tactics of uniting Protestants of differing economic and denominational backgrounds into societies with financial means and popular support. They also leaned on time-honoured tropes of Protestant loyalty, Catholic treachery, and the substitution of political considerations for sectarian divisions. These appeals to anti-Catholicism and sectarianism would become increasingly influential and successful throughout the 1830s, as Conservative political mobilisation grew, and Ireland became the central focus in the campaign to cast off the Whigs' programme of reform.

### Protestant Mobilisation

In the previous chapter I described the political manoeuvring that led to the Lichfield House Compact, an initially uneasy relationship that solidified due to the advance of Whigs within their own party who wanted to forge a new policy in Ireland. However, it bears repeating the extraordinary repercussions this partnership had in ultra-Tory circles, thus leading them to wage a decisive political war over the Whigs' Irish policy and secure political victory in 1841.

The precipitating six months only deepened the atmosphere of ultra-Tory despair in May 1835. Peel's short-lived Tory government had seemed like a political and spiritual deliverance for many ultra-Tories, especially because of the manner of Melbourne's dismissal, by the king's prerogative – a throwback to a bygone era of privilege when Protestant Ascendancy was wholly intact.[24] Writing in November 1834, Lord Roden congratulated Wellington 'on the deliverance which we have at last had from the misrule of those who had nearly overwhelm'd the country in

---

[23] Protestant Colonization Society, *Transactions of the Protestant Colonization Society of Ireland*, 30–1. Cottingham was the assistant secretary of the Orange Lodge of Cavan before its dissolution. See 'Select Committee on Orange Lodges, Associations or Societies in Ireland. Report, Minutes of Evidence, Appendix', 1835, House of Commons Papers, vol. 15, no. 377, 169.

[24] Greville, *Greville Memoirs*, 2: 292–302.

irretrievable ruin', while also congratulating himself for 'having been an instrument . . . of a great party in this country . . . accomplishing the object that now seems opening to our view'. 'God be praised, for the salvation of our homes, our firesides and our property', effused Lord Londonderry. Lord Kenyon wrote an account of a recent meeting in England addressed by the controversial Irish preacher Rev. Mortimer O'Sullivan 'calling on the assembled multitudes to testify their sense of the conduct of their "constitutional King" in dismissing the enemies of the Protestant faith and of the Union in Ireland' which, he reported, 'surpassed anything I ever heard'.[25] Nearly two weeks before the king's dismissal of Lord Melbourne, ultra-Tories organised a rally on Lord Downshire's Co. Down estate of 'not less than thirty, and probably near forty thousand' Protestants, where Tory grandees pledged that the Protestants of Ulster would 'shed the last drop of their blood' before allowing O'Connell to make them 'an appendage to Catholic France'.[26] Not surprisingly given the sequence of events, Lord Downshire's land agent, John Murray, praised Downshire for the 'Stimulus . . . that your Lordship has given . . . to many of the Landlords in Ireland: it was time to shew the Agitators that there would be a stop put to their [illegible] Politicks. God send that they may be defeated in their unwarrantable schemes.'[27]

Lord Downshire's great Protestant meeting continued a trend already under way in the 1830s, a recognition of the power of non-elite political action.[28] Narrating the end of Peel's short-lived ministry and the rise of Melbourne's Whig government, *Blackwood's Edinburgh Magazine* published an article articulating a way forward to restore conservative principles to government benches. The problem, as the magazine saw it, was the upsetting of the social order which had enabled Britain to ascend to imperial greatness. In nostalgic and starkly sectarian imagery, *Blackwood's* portrayed O'Connell and his influence over the Whig government as the chief cause threatening Britain's political stability and global influence. 'How deep and widespread are the seeds of evil',

[25] Lord Roden to Lord Wellington, 20 November 1835 in Arthur Wellesley, *Wellington II: Political Correspondence November 1834–April 1835*, eds R. J. Olney and Julia Melvin (London: Her Majesty's Stationary Office, 1986), 44; Londonderry to Wellington, 23 November 1834, ibid., 68; Kenyon to Wellington, 24 November 1834, ibid., 81.

[26] 'County of Down Protestant Meeting', BNL, 31 October 1834. This was the same infamous meeting where the hugely influential Presbyterian minister Henry Cooke suggested a Protestant alliance against 'Infidels, R. Catholics, [and] Radicals'; see Alvin Jackson, *Ireland, 1798–1998: Politics and War* (Oxford: Blackwell Publishers, 1999), pp. 64–5.

[27] John Murray to Downshire, 15 December 1834, PRONI, Downshire Papers, D671/C/214/265.

[28] Cronin, 'Popular Politics, 1815–1845, 132, 135. See also Daragh Curran, *The Protestant Community in Ulster, 1825–45: A Society in Transition* (Dublin: Four Courts Press, 2014).

*Blackwood's* opined, 'which have now ripened into the formation of an administration having a coalition of Revolutionists, Infidels, Papists, and Dissenters for its basis.' The Whigs' greed for political power had the effect:

to compel them to abandon all their original principles, eat in all their former denunciations, and coalesce with all their bitterest enemies; to reduce the descendants of the Russells and Cavendishes, who fought and bled to establish the Protestant faith, into the humble followers of a Popish agitator, whose professed aim is the overthrow of the reformed religious; and converted the haughty aristocrats who so long refused to admit the great agitator [O'Connell] to their tables ... into the obsequious followers of that overbearing demagogue, who has never ceased to proclaim his intention of dismembering and revolutionising the empire.[29]

In response, *Blackwood's* proffered a two-pronged antidote. First, the magazine proposed a concerted effort by Conservative media outlets, in which they included the *Quarterly*, *Fraser's Magazine*, *New Monthly Magazine*, and the *Dublin Magazine*, to put to rest 'the sophisms of error' and turn the country toward 'the cause of truth'; second, the magazine prioritised the recapturing of the House of Commons through the development of Conservative associations to pool financial resources and challenge registration rolls.[30] Alleging that the majority of electors shared a desire to overthrow the British constitution and plunge the country into anarchy, what was necessary was the restoration of the natural ruling class – 'holders of property and the men of education' – to legally organise to reshape the electoral rolls.

*Blackwood's* dual approach, which focussed pressure on the Whig government in the Conservative press and coupled it with the public organising of Conservative associations, proved prescient. Newspapers across Great Britain and Ireland began reporting on the creation of Conservative associations. To bolster enthusiasm for the cause, and to warn the country of the nation's impending peril, another leading ultra-Tory, the Earl of Winchilsea and Nottingham, published two letters 'to the Protestants of Great Britain' that newspapers reprinted widely and either valorised or pilloried depending on the paper's politics.[31] The letters appealed to Protestants of all denominational backgrounds to cast off their 'apathy and indifference at this awful national crisis' and

---

[29] 'Conservative Associations', BEM 38, no. 237 (July 1835), pp. 1–2.    [30] Ibid., pp. 5–9.
[31] The letters were first published in the *Standard*, and then copiously reprinted or editorialised depending on the political leanings of the newspaper. For a few examples see 'The Present Crisis', *Morning Post*, 19 May 1835; 'To the Protestants of Great Britain', *Cork Constitution*, 21 May 1835; for negative coverage see 'The Political Arena', *Public Ledger and Daily Advertiser*, 20 May 1835.

unite to work together to restore 'those barriers which were so unfortunately surrendered, and to drive from the citadel of the state those who
obtained admission by oaths which they are daily and openly violating'.
Drawing a parallel with the Old Testament narrative of the nation of
Israel, Winchilsea argued that Britain's global material prosperity related
in direct proportion to its commitment to Protestantism, warning the
state not to stray from the Established Church lest it welcome 'God's
wrath' for its 'wilful disobedience' and court national disaster. Referring
to the Lichfield House Compact as 'the most factious and disgraceful
political conspiracy which ever disgraced the public character of our
country', Winchilsea concluded his second letter by imploring the 'constitutional' and 'faithful' across political and religious spectrums to
join 'the Conservative Associations, which are day by day springing up
in [e]very quarter of the empire ... for the maintenance and defence of the
religious doctrines of the Reformation, and the political principles of the
glorious revolution of 1688'.[32] Building on this enthusiasm, the *Durham
County Advertiser*, which published both of Winchilsea's letters together,
regaled readers with the 'Triumph of the Conservative Cause in
Inverness-Shire' while editorialising on the powerful effects of a recent
speech of Robert Peel's in town. Newspapers across the country repli-
cated this strategy, connecting Winchilsea's clarion call for decidedly
Protestant action with Conservative Party politics.

Building on the growth of local Conservative associations, in June
ultra-Tories met at London's Exeter Hall to revive the Gordon-riots era
'Protestant Association'.[33] Just as Lord George Gordon had appealed to
the London crowd assembled at St George's Fields on 2 June 1780 by
telling them of the diabolical plans of popery to undo the Protestantism of
the British nation and wider empire, 5,000 members of the public, along
with roughly 400 of the gentry, both male and female, assembled in
June 1835 to hear the theological arguments concerning the 'real tenets'
of the Catholic Church in Ireland and its threat to the wider empire.[34]
Embodying the pan-Protestant union they hoped to inspire, the Anglican
evangelicals Rev. R. J. M'Ghee[35] and Rev. Mortimer O'Sullivan joined
the Presbyterian minister Henry Cooke on stage, arguing 'with the florid-
ity of colouring peculiar to Irish orators' that the object of Ireland's

---

[32] 'To the Protestants of Great Britain', *Durham County Advertiser*, 22 May 1835. This was
one of a number of newspapers that printed both letters together.
[33] On Protestant Association of 1780, see Ian Haywood and John Seed, 'Introduction', in
*The Gordon Riots: Politics, Culture and Insurrection in Late Eighteenth-Century Britain*, eds.
Ian Haywood and John Seed (Cambridge: Cambridge University Press, 2012), 1–18.
[34] Brad A. Jones, '"In Favour of Popery": Patriotism, Protestantism, and the Gordon Riots
in the Revolutionary British Atlantic', *JBS* 52, no. 1 (January 2013): 79–102.
[35] Also printed as McGhee.

Catholic hierarchy was to 'compel heretics [i.e., Protestants], by corporal punishment, to return to the faith of Popery' through 'confiscation of property, exile, imprisonment, and death'.[36] Using *Dens's Complete Body of Theology*, purportedly the handbook of instruction for priests training at the Catholic theology college at Maynooth, M'Ghee made comparisons between the state of Irish society and the volcanic effusions of Vesuvius warning that the Irish peasant's violence was 'enumerated amongst the virtues of the authoritative standard of their spiritual guide'.[37] Although Archbishop Murray denied that *Dens's* was ever used by the Catholic clergy, it mattered little as news of the meeting spread across Great Britain and Ireland, with proceedings reprinted in provincial newspapers, often re-enforced with editorials.[38] 'This most important meeting was held on Saturday last', reported the *Londonderry Sentinel*, 'and the details communicated … so momentous as fully to answer our anticipations. Vile and jesuitical as we had ever supposed the Popish imposture to be, we scarcely conceived it possible that, in the nineteenth century, it could inculcate … the same tyrannical and persecuting spirit which it did in the days of Mary and Catherine de Medici'.[39] In short, Ireland stood on the brink of destruction because Catholicism appeared to be on the ascendancy, and Irish Catholicism's brand of 'popery' exhibited an existential threat to the Protestant nature of British rule in Ireland, and by extension Great Britain and the wider empire.

The Protestant Association operated as the connective tissue tying together the religious rhetoric of Evangelical Protestantism and the political programme of ultra-Toryism. Perceived Irish problems – both religious and sociopolitical in nature – acted as a sort of centripetal force pulling diverse strands together in common political purpose. As Wolffe has noted,

> Between 1829 and 1834 Protestantism had gone through a similar process of metamorphosis to that experience by the Tory party as a whole: the points of continuity were evident, but with a new ideological framework provided by Evangelicalism, and a new cause provided by the Irish Church, it had become a dynamic and flexible movement that was not an atavistic relic of the past but an essential strand in the emergent Victorian political fabric.[40]

Seizing on this metamorphosis, ultra-Tory grandees like Lords Roden, Enniskillen, Kenyon, Farnham, and Lorton patronised the Protestant

---

[36] 'Great Protestant Meeting', *Morning Chronicle*, 22 June 1835; Protestant Association, *Authentic Report of the Great Protestant Meeting Held at Exeter Hall London* (Dublin: P. Dixon Hardy, 1835), 20–1.
[37] Ibid.     [38] Daniel O'Connell to P. V. FitzPatrick, *Correspondence*, 5:314–15, n. 3.
[39] 'Great Meeting at Exeter Hall', *Londonderry Sentinel*, 27 June 1835. The issue also included a supplement reprinting segments of the speeches from the meeting.
[40] Wolffe, *Protestant Crusade*, 84.

Association and other organisations like it, while numerous Conservative MPs openly associated with the organisation and occasionally published under its auspices. In an 1840 pamphlet penned by the Tory MP J. C. Colquhoun, and published by the association, Colquhoun argued that the primary focus of the association was to 'unite all who value the principles of our Constitution' and to disprove the 'falsities' of liberalism that threatened to change time-honoured institutions, and plunge Ireland, and consequently Britain, into 'a state of anarchy'.[41] He continued: '[The Protestant Association] would employ the pulpit, the platform, the press, and Parliamentary petitions, to inculcate sound views. They would use public meetings, to excite interest; by means of that interest they would circulate their publications.'[42] By 1840, Colquhoun could boast that the Association had organised provincial meetings across major cities in England and Scotland, had published at least thirty-five tracts and pamphlets, and was producing a monthly magazine *The Protestant Magazine* to disseminate its arguments. Publications were sold cheaply, even cheaper in bulk, and were meant for wide circulation. Many publications were republished articles from *Blackwood's Edinburgh Magazine*, the leading anti-Catholic ultra-Tory periodical in Britain, speeches of ultra-Tory MPs, or sermons that sold for anywhere from 1d. to 6d., or multiple shillings by the 100, often going through many editions and printings in the tens of thousands. The association met annually and published reports of the proceedings, which generally featured speeches on the dangers of Catholicism and the threat it posed to the Protestant nature of the State.[43]

The Protestant Association, and its numerous publications, along with the increasingly vocal Protestant press, spent the six years between 1835 and 1841 hammering the Whig government for its approach to governing Ireland. They feared the growth of Catholic influence in the apparatus of the state, but more so the influence of O'Connell on appointments; indeed, the Protestant press often labelled the lord lieutenant 'O'Mulgrave' and connected their discussions ironically to Irish violence in the countryside under article titles like 'O'Mulgrave Tranquility'.[44] In

[41] John Campbell Colquhoun and the Protestant Association, *On the Objects and Uses of Protestant Associations*, 3rd ed., Protestant Association (London: The Protestant Association, 1840), 3, 9.

[42] Ibid., 9–10.

[43] On some background of the organisation, see Gilbert A. Cahill, 'The Protestant Association and the Anti-Maynooth Agitation of 1845', *The Catholic Historical Review* 43, no. 3 (October 1957): 273–308, especially at 276–7; Wolffe, *Protestant Crusades*, 85–105.

[44] Among dozens of examples, see 'O'Mulgrave's Irish Tranquility', *Yorkshire Gazette*, 17 December 1836; 'The Irish Petition Fund, O'Mulgrave Tranquillity, &c.', *London*

one rather comical rendering, *Blackwood's* published an 'Operetta' of a fictional Whig cabinet meeting at which, confused and confounded about what policy to pursue, the party members wait for their leader's instructions. Rather than Prime Minister Melbourne or Lord John Russell speaking, O'Connell bursts into the room where they sing a song praising him: 'All hail to Dan O'Connell, the Master we obey: Who, quite content with his Irish Rent, To us leaves place and play.'[45]

Though catering to a small subset of the Conservative Party – those whose religious convictions proved particularly strident and anti-Catholic in outlook – the Protestant Association found its voice, and its power, in these turbulent years of opposition to the prevailing sentiments of 'reform' and liberalism. Polemical literature on Britain's impending doom and God's coming wrath amplified its voice and influence in and out of the halls of Westminster, as politicians across Britain and Ireland coordinated strategic plans.[46] In 1836 and 1837 the Duke of Newcastle presented petitions on behalf of the Protestant Association for the repeal of Catholic Emancipation and protection of the Protestant church from 'the danger which menaced' it.[47] Newspapers published accounts of the association's yearly meeting at Exeter Hall,[48] but leaders within the movement also found ways to attempt to influence those with power with the Conservative Party.

An important voice at the centre of the Protestant Association who promoted a vision of the Catholic Church as bloodthirsty was the Rev. Robert James M'Ghee. Educated at Trinity College Dublin, M'Ghee cut his teeth as a curate under the prominent Evangelical, and future Archbishop of Tuam, Power le Poer Trench.[49] By the 1830s M'Ghee had emerged as a particularly virulent and energetic critic of the Irish Roman Catholic Church. M'Ghee regularly sent Tory leaders letters urging them to expose the Catholic Church's true intentions publicly and protect Protestants throughout the United Kingdom from extermination. In a letter to Wellington, later published by the Protestant Association for the price of one penny, M'Ghee focussed on Whig

*Evening Standard*, 30 September 1837; 'The O'Mulgrave Tranquillity', *Dublin Evening Packet and Correspondent*, 23 November 1837.

[45] 'The Cabinet: A Downing Street Operetta', BEM 42, no. 261 (October 1837), 78–88, at 88.

[46] Arthur H. Kennedy to Farnham, 25 May 1835, NLI, Farnham Papers, MS 18,612, folder 24; Londonderry to Lyndhurst, 12 May 1835, DCRO, Londonderry Papers, D/Lo/C450(1).

[47] Hansard, 3rd ser., vol. 34, cols. 290–1, 10 June 1836; Hansard 3rd ser., vol. 39, cols. -339–42, 28 November 1847.

[48] For example, see 'Protestant Association', *London Evening Standard*, 12 May 1836; 27 May 1837; 10 May 1838; 9 May 1839.

[49] Whelan, *The Bible War in Ireland*, 241.

attempts to reform Irish municipal corporations. Changing the corporations' governing structure would not only 'annihilate the means of protection for our Protestant Institutions', M'Ghee wrote to Wellington, but it would transfer power to Catholics, 'our sworn Papal persecutors and traitors'. Concerned about the overall drift of conservative and liberal politics since the granting of Catholic Emancipation, M'Ghee believed emancipation had not served as a final settlement for Catholics but instead made them hungrier for power. He also highlighted a theme to which anti-Catholic commenters often returned – the relationship between the Catholic clergy, Irish peasants, and agrarian violence. Ever-ready to attribute bloodlust with the Catholic hierarchy, M'Ghee believed that clergy orchestrated Protestant murders by inscribing instructions to their parishioners in Bibles. Dwelling on the unique power of the Catholic priest in the lives of Irish peasants, M'Ghee worried that clergymen would serve dual roles as instigators of Protestant bloodshed, but also as absolvers: 'They have published a bull empowering certain privileged persons to grant pardons for all treasons, murders, and crime whatsoever that may be committed, public or private.'[50]

It may come as little surprise that M'Ghee turned to Irish violence, allegedly sectarian in its motivation, as a central argument in his letter to Wellington. After all, sectarianism provided a ready-made recurring trope for some Protestants in Ireland – an expression of a siege mentality formed by the perceived, and occasionally real, violence they suffered as a minority. And, to allege that Irish Catholics – those easily deluded ignorant souls[51] – might act without fearing spiritual damnation added to the gravity of the perceived threat. It also bears underlining that many Protestant commentators genuinely believed that the allocation of power and religious influence worked as a zero-sum game, and regardless of their 'better and more heavenly principles' the Catholic Church ultimately sought 'to use every endeavour for re-establishing the Roman Church.'[52] Nevertheless, the sheer volume of literature connecting the new Whig approach to governing Ireland with Daniel O'Connell's assumed political power within the Whig government, his collusion with Roman Catholic priests in coordinating the actions of Irish peasants, and supposed heightened agrarian violence in this period is striking. By 1835, ultra-Tories eager to assert their place within the Conservative Party

[50] Robert James M'Ghee, *Letter to the Duke of Wellington* ... (London: Protestant Association, 1839), 5–6.
[51] 'Address to the Finsbury Operative Protestant Association', *The Penny Protestant Operative* 1, no. 2 (May 1840): 11.
[52] George Stephens, *Political Prophecy Fulfilled; or, 'Ireland', with a New Preface*, 6th ed. (London: C. Mitchell, 1839), 5.

unleashed a propaganda campaign, which was coordinated by groups like the Protestant Association and conservative newspapers – together, they made sure to mix surging Catholic political influence, Irish agrarian violence, sectarian paranoia, and political revolution into a strong cocktail for English and Irish audiences to imbibe.

## Agrarian Violence as Political Propaganda

The endemic presence of violence across the Irish countryside demonstrated to British administrators and social commentators that Ireland in many ways was a failed state. The labelling of agrarian violence as 'outrages' and the reading of political subterfuge into these actions highlighted the perception that the state had failed in defending its claims 'to the monopoly of the legitimate use of physical force'.[53] Agrarian violence also undermined the state's ability to create an 'administrative and legal order' that could claim 'binding authority not only over the members of the state, the citizens, but to a large extent over all actions taking place within its area of jurisdiction'.[54] As argued in Chapter 2, Irish power holders and British politicians perceived agrarian violence as a countervailing sovereignty challenging their own administrative and legal order. This perception, whether or not it was justified by the facts on the ground, underscored in the words of the sociologist Daniel Béland the 'collective insecurity' of power holders who experienced 'the subjective feeling of anxiety and ... the concrete lack of protection'.[55]

This feeling of collective insecurity provided ultra-Tories with a valuable political tool in their programme to undermine Whig governance. Missives travelled with increasing intensity from Ireland to Britain highlighting the dangerous state of Irish society and linking Mulgrave's policies of 'justice to Ireland' to an increase in violence. While Tories disliked the theatrical flair that Mulgrave brought to the office, suggesting that it diminished the dignity of the office, the more substantial issue was the relationship between Mulgrave and Daniel O'Connell, and Mulgrave's executive power to appoint legal positions, magistrates, and the newly reformed constabulary.[56] Harsh criticism rang out from the

---

[53] On 'outrages', see Roszman, 'The Curious History of Irish "Outrages"', 481–504; Max Weber, *Economy and Society*, eds. G. Roth and C. Wittich (Berkeley: University of California Press, 1968), 54.

[54] Karl Dusza, 'Max Weber's Conception of the State', *International Journal of Politics, Culture, and Society* 3, no. 1 (Autumn 1989): 71–105, at 76.

[55] Daniel Béland, 'Insecurity and Politics: A Framework', *The Canadian Journal of Sociology/ Cahiers Canadiens de Sociologie* 32, no. 3 (Summer 2007), 317–40, at 320.

[56] Greville, *Greville Memoirs*, 2: 392; Holland, *Holland House Diaries*, 301; on Mulgrave's style see Grant, *Random Recollections*, 297–9; Peter Gray, 'A "People's Viceroyalty"?

conservative press when Mulgrave welcomed O'Connell to dinner in an official capacity in October 1835, a decision which also drew the attention of the king.[57] The inception of Whig government brought a bevy of requests from O'Connell on various appointments, some of which Whig ministers denied, but many of which they carried out.[58] O'Connell entertained aspiration of his eventual appointment into the cabinet, writing his trusted lieutenant P. V. Fitzpatrick in mid-September 1835 that 'prospects for Ireland brighten. I am beginning to think that I shall be a Cabinet Minister next session, with the rule of matters in Ireland officially committed to me', before reminding Fitzpatrick to 'keep *this dream* to yourself'.[59] Conservative polemists worried O'Connell might be right. 'That O'Connell, with his tail of six-and-thirty Irish Papists, is now the real ruler of this country, no one who has paid the slightest attention to public affairs for the last six months can for a moment doubt', opened BEM's December 1835 issue, with an article entitled 'The O'Connell Domination.' With hyperbole and a bit of Shakespeare, Archibald Alison mused 'Is not O'Connell the viceroy over the Ministry? Is he not like Warwick in the days of the civil wars, the knocker down and putter up of Kings?' After sufficiently demonstrating O'Connell's power, the article then turned its attention to the structures supporting his position. Highlighting the Catholic hierarchy's influence over the Irish peasantry, including mention of M'Ghee's favourite *Den's Theology*, the article stressed the violence underpinning the system:

Are not the murderer, the assassin, and the fire-raiser still the executioners of their mandates who fill the country with blood and conflagration unparalleled in any Christian land? Have not their priests declared from the altar, that if the revolutionary candidate was not elected for Carlow, 'rivers of blood should flow as broad as the waters of the Barrow?'

Assassins, murders, and radicals feature throughout the article, always simultaneously as 'Papists' and revolutionaries, and O'Connell makes an appearance as a 'wild Indian' who had 'brandished the tomahawk of savage extermination'.[60] *Frasier's Magazine* neatly summed up the

---

Popularity, Theatre and Executive Politics 1835–47', in *The Irish Lord Lieutenancy c. 1541–1922*, eds. Peter Gray and Olwen Purdue (Dublin: University College Dublin Press, 2012), ch. 8.

[57] Russell to Mulgrave, 16 October 1835, MC, Mulgrave MSS, M/801; Russell to Sir Herbert Taylor, 21 October 1835, TNA, Russell Papers, PRO 30/22/1E, f. 222.

[58] Some examples, among many in O'Connell's correspondence: O'Connell to Mulgrave, 13 August 1835, O'Connell, 5:326; O'Connell to Mulgrave, 19 August 1835, ibid., 5:328; O'Connell to Mulgrave, 4 December 1835, ibid, 5:345.

[59] O'Connell to Fitzpatrick, 11 September 1835, ibid., 5:332.

[60] [Archibald Alison], 'The O'Connell Domination', BEM 38, no. 242 (December 1835), 715–30, at 715, 716, and 717.

systematic array aligned against Irish Protestants, and it is worth quoting at length. In an article comparing 'Orangeism and Romanism' they argued that the newly reformed constabulary had led to the expulsion of 'the 22,000 Protestants now said to be contained in it' on the pretence of their being Orangemen, while keeping Ribbonmen in it to effect O'Connell's political ends:

the object which O'Connell and his Whig slaves have in view will be speedily attained, – the *pulverising* of the Protestants of Ireland, and their gradual extirpation by detail. Surrounded with implacable foes on every side – their friends excluded from every office of power or influence ... their very lives and dwellings guarded (!) [by] only Popish policemen who would delight to see their heretic souls crushed out of their bodies – with Papist sheriffs to nominate the juries, Papist assistant-barristers to try the causes [*sic*], and Papist crown-solicitors to conduct the evidence – what situation on the face of the whole earth will be so pitiably helpless and hapless as that of a poor Irish Protestant?[61]

According to many ultra-Tories, the dangerous concentration of executive power in the hands of the wrong people spelled social disaster. If Protestant preference in the appointment of magistrates could no longer be defended at a local level, then the only saving grace was a return to the Protestant ideals and blue-blooded conservatism of the Tory party.

Although many ultra-Tories resisted the passage of the Irish Constabulary Act in 1836, none had opposed the appointment of Col. James Shaw Kennedy as its inaugural inspector general. Kennedy, a Peninsular War veteran and seen as an efficient organiser, allayed Tory concerns about other potential nominees who held pro-Catholic sympathies.[62] The Irish government worked beside Shaw Kennedy in Dublin Castle as the inspector general developed the constabulary's rules and regulation, as well as its reporting system. Mulgrave praised Shaw Kennedy for moulding the police into a non-political and non-sectarian professional force that over the first year of its existence had gained the respect of both political parties.[63] Though the whole system was new, it appeared that Shaw Kennedy worked exceedingly hard to ensure the constabulary's success in the country and those in Dublin Castle were pleased with his decisions and success. Furthermore, his character and ability to organise the new force offered some political insulation from Tories using agrarian violence as a weapon in parliamentary debate. While the Tories disagreed with Whig diagnoses about the diminution

---

[61] 'Orangeism versus Romanism', *Fraser's Magazine* 13, no. 75 (March 1836), 377–93, at 392.
[62] Morpeth to Mulgrave, n.d. [February 1836], MC, Mulgrave MSS, M/513; Palmer, *Police and Protest*, 359.
[63] Mulgrave to Russell, 17 August [1837], TNA, Russell Papers, PRO 30/22/2F, f. 25.

of crime, the respect for Shaw Kennedy kept the Irish constabulary immune from criticism.

That political cover evaporated when Shaw Kennedy shocked the Irish government by tendering his resignation in March 1838. At the heart of his decision to leave the constabulary was an incident that revolved around the inspector general's powers of appointment and dismissal, and it involved a rather intricate case in Co. Carlow better described elsewhere.[64] In short, Shaw Kennedy expected one of his sub-inspectors, Thomas Gleeson, to be dismissed from the force for impropriety, which the government acceded to carrying out only to later decide to simply post Gleeson to another county. This decision precipitated Shaw Kennedy's resignation, writing to Mulgrave that he was 'in such a position as to render it inconsistent that I should retain the situation of Inspector General with a due regard to the controul [sic] which I consider that I should possess over the discipline of the Force'.[65] The circumstances surrounding Shaw Kennedy's decision to leave his position, that 'his recommendations [were] disregarded in the organisation of the Constabulary Force', and his inability to control all appointments and dismissals, opened the way for Tories to criticise the growing executive powers of the lord lieutenant that had the effect of centralising power in Dublin.[66] Ever since the passage of the Constabulary Act in 1836, Tories had stirred up fear of O'Connell's influence over patronage of the force. Even though Shaw Kennedy said nothing directly to confirm this concern, the fact that Dublin Castle had ignored his recommendation in the Carlow case offered apparent proof of the Tory view of an Irish government led by a supine lord lieutenant listening to O'Connell rather than his inspector general. Peel summed up this view, writing to Wellington that 'O'Connell and the Priests have had the real and essential direction of the Constabulary ... his [Shaw Kennedy's] recommendations have been scarcely attended to.'[67] Joseph Jackson, Tory MP for Bandon, Co. Cork, floated the idea of a committee of inquiry into the circumstances surrounding the resignation and to the overall culture of the constabulary. Though it does not appear to have ever been seriously considered by Peel or Wellington, Jackson's vision concerning the purpose of such a committee was particularly prophetic as many of his suggestions were

---

[64] Elizabeth Malcolm, '"The Reign of Terror in Carlow": The Politics of Policing Ireland in the late 1830s', IHS 32, no. 125 (May 2000): 59–74.

[65] Col. J. S. Kennedy to Mulgrave, 14 March 1838, TNA, Russell Papers, PRO 30/22/3A, f. 189.

[66] Joseph Jackson to Peel, 17 April 1838, USSC, Wellington MSS, WP2/50/104.

[67] Peel to Wellington, 22 April 1838, ibid., WP2/50/102–3.

reintroduced in March 1839 when Roden proposed his committee on Irish crime and outrage. Jackson wrote to Peel:

We know ... the sad effects of the misgovernment of this Country by Lord Mulgrave, or rather by those to whom he is Subject. It is nevertheless entirely difficult to bring forward direct proof of such a subject. But here is a tangible case, and I doubt not that were an enquiry instituted into the causes of Col. Shaw Kennedy's resignation & the general organisation & administration of the Constabulary Force, disclosures would be made which would astonish & alarm the British public ... it would appear also that a plan has been systematically acted upon, which has been to a great degree successful, to convert this Force, which is I believe 8000 strong, into a Body of Political Partizans. ... The Duke of Wellington could command such a Committee of Inquiry ... I do not think it possible that Lord Mulgrave's administration could survive the disclosures which must result from such an Inquiry.[68]

Although the government was able to recover with the appointment of Duncan MacGregor as inspector general in early April 1838, a man 'beloved by soldiers of all persuasions', the damage had already been done to the government's credibility in enforcing the law with an impartial police force.[69]

The perceived state of the Irish countryside served to confirm the hysteria and fuel the feeling of collective insecurity. Prognosticators interpreted criminal statistics or local incidents of outrage like tea leaves that corroborated their worst fears. Ultra-Tories focussed on Co. Tipperary as one area where the government's narratives of increasingly tranquillity defied credulity. In the midst of the parliamentary debate on the legality of the Orange Order, William Verner, MP for Armagh and grand master of the Orange Lodge in Co. Armagh, defended the Order by insisting that crime rates in Ulster were far lower because of the Orangemen who 'strengthen the bonds of British connexion with Ireland'. Mirroring a general reflection on the state of Ireland without the protection of Protestant Ascendancy, Verner suggested that the Order was not a problem to be rooted out from Irish soil but instead acted as an institution preserving law and order from the 'systemic disorder' of most of the west and south of the country.[70] He also requested official returns demonstrating the lawlessness of Tipperary, a move which heartened Mortimer O'Sullivan, who suggested to the Archbishop of Armagh, Lord John Beresford, that 'Perhaps when the matter becomes discussed among the Irish members, they will see the prudence and the safety of being bold.'[71] The official returns noted that in

---

[68] Jackson to Peel, 17 April 1838, USSC, Wellington MSS, WP2/50/104.
[69] Mulgrave to Morpeth, 9 April [1838], CH, Morpeth Papers, J/18/63/3.
[70] Hansard, 3rd ser., vol. 31, col. 847, 23 February 1836.
[71] M. O'Sullivan to Beresford, 23 February 1836, PRONI, T2772/2/6/24.

the first three months of 1836, sixty-three people had been 'committed to the Gaol' for murder, a number which nearly equalled the sixty-five committed for the calendar year of 1835.

As Chapter 2 illustrated, landlords and their agents had some reason to feel insecure as a small proportion of their tenants banded together and used violent means to resist the power of the state, including the prerogatives of private property holders. For ultra-Tories, what was important was to disseminate these fears as widely as possible – as a means to educate the British public on the true state of affairs in Ireland, and thus by doing so to recapture political power and restore order. An article in *Fraser's Magazine* written by the west Cork-born writer and Church of Ireland clergyman, Horatio Townshend, explained this point nearly at the inception of Whig government, reflecting in February 1836 that 'The present destructive ministry cannot stand, if the people of England be not with them', before suggesting that Conservatives should be 'up and doing' by employing 'every inlet of sound information ... for the purpose of rectifying the national judgment and enlightening the national mind'. The place to make the case on the demerits of the government, according to the magazine, was in Ireland. Characterising the English public as having been lulled into a false sense of complacency because in Ireland the social 'surface is so smooth' without the peasantry offering anything 'more formidable than the civil salutation', *Fraser's* warned of the coordinated system – a 'fearful conspiracy which has already triumphed over the laws of the land' – that lay underneath, needing exposure. As soon as England faced international uncertainty, the conspiracy would spring into action:

They have no desire to manifest themselves by any open hostility, as long as England is at leisure to direct all her energies against them. ... But they bide their time. She will not always be at peace; she will, sooner or later, get entangled in continental affairs: and when her armies are fighting battles in distant countries, and her government intent on foreign objects, *then* will be the season for action. ... There is not a joint of the Tail which does not carry a dispensation for the pillage of an heretical church, or a permission to persecute the Protestant clergy, even to extermination.[72]

Anglo-Irish gentry agreed. 'I think it highly necessary that some opportunity should be seized before the session expires', wrote Lord Hillsborough (son of Lord Downshire) to Peel, 'to mention the dreadful state in which

---

[72] [Horatio Townshend], 'The Present State of Ireland', *Fraser's Magazine* 13, (February 1836), 181–94, at 184–5. On Townshend, see Elizabeth Baigent, 'Townsend [Townshend], Horace [Horatio] (1750–1837), writer.' *ODNB*, 14 June 2019, https://doi.org/10.1093/ref:odnb/27629.

Ireland is at present both as to past murders, and outrages, & to those Gentlemen who are marked out for future slaughter, by this secret tribunal. ... For I can assure you that the Country from Armagh to Wexford is as ripe for Rebellion as it is possible & that only the match is wanting.'[73] Wellington expressed similar sentiments, writing to Peel that 'the people of Ireland generally are in a state of complete organisation for a general Rising; of which the period is entirely at the direction[?] of O'Connell and the Priests'.[74] In addition to the Protestant Association, its prolific output of quasi-theological political literature, and its regional network spreading across England, Scotland, and Wales, ultra-Tories could rely on the Conservative press to disseminate news of the 'real' state of Ireland.

Amplifying the volume and extending the readership of Irish material, the *Times* began to reprint stories that had been originally published in regional Irish conservative newspapers. By 1837, the *Times* had fully embraced a Tory outlook in politics and acted as 'the most vigorous and powerful agent' of Conservatism, publishing articles 'irresistible on the public mind'.[75] Between the new session of Parliament in November 1837 and January 1839, the newspaper pursued a campaign to undermine the Irish government's claim of increased Irish tranquillity. It did this most directly by contrasting articles from the government's official newspaper that reported Irish criminal activity and rewards, the *Dublin Gazette*, with the accounts of a variety of often-small provincial newspapers across Ireland. Under the same headline, 'GAZETTE – STATE OF THE COUNTRY', reprinted reports filled the columns of the *Times* from newspapers like the *Dublin Evening Post*, *Nenagh Guardian*, or *Limerick Standard*, criticising the *Gazette* for not reporting the grave state of affairs. 'The *Gazette* of Friday is silent, though the state of the counties of Sligo and Leitrim might have called for some notice from the Chief Governor even as paternal as our Marquizzical Viceroy', quipped the *Times* in early October 1838.[76] Less than a week later, the *Times* republished the *Dublin Evening Post*'s accusations against the government of much more than merely overlooking Irish violence:

Throughout the whole series of papers which, from week to week during the last three years, we have published under the foregoing title, we have accused the Irish Government of systematically suppressing the evidence and records of crime with the intent of imposing upon the people of England a false view of the result of its

---

[73] Hillsborough to Peel, 14 June 1839, PRONI, Downshire Papers, D671/C/12/745B.
[74] Wellington to Peel, 19 October 1837, BL, Peel Papers Add MS 40310, f. 217.
[75] Charles Greville, *The Greville Memoirs (Second Part): A Journal of the Reign of Queen Victoria from 1837 to 1852* (London: Longmans, Green and Co., 1885), 1:48.
[76] 'Gazette – State of the Country', *Times*, 4 October 1838.

policy ... in which the progressive tranquility and gradual restoration to order of the population were so gratuitously asserted.[77]

Adding embellishing descriptions of Irish violence, for example by referring to crimes that make 'the blood run cold', the *Times* played on a number of stereotypes of Irish crime that set it apart from ordinary English crime and deemed the acts of violence worthy of the title of 'outrage'. Referencing the 'savage' behaviour of a 'lawless peasantry' who 'spread terror and desolation' through the country, the *Times* provided a much larger stage for these provincial Irish newspapers and attempted to offer their readers an alternative picture of the prevalence of Irish outrage under Mulgrave's tenure.[78] In comparison, when discussing English murders (often in the column next to Irish matters) the paper provided a much more matter-of-fact tone in its reporting and refrained from the sensationalising language and colourful adjectives ascribed to Irish outrages.

These newspaper reports not only highlighted the apparent contradiction between official reports and the actual state of the country, but they also paraded before the public the ghastliest scenes of violence possible to make their case for Ireland's lawlessness. Take, for example, an article republished from the *Dublin Evening Packet* in the *Times* recounting a murder that had purportedly taken place in Co. Carlow, under the headline 'Revolting Murder'. According to the newspaper, on 9 November 1838 the family of Lawrence Nolan had departed from their home to dig potatoes, leaving their youngest daughter Bridget, aged eight, at home with her grandmother, Catherine Donehoe, aged eighty. A cousin of Bridget's, John Nolan, entered the home while the family was out and 'with a shovel, which was found in it [the home] broken and covered over with hair and blood', killed both Catherine and Bridget. Not content with having committed murder, the newspaper reported 'the monster threw them into the fire. A smell, like that of pork frying, reached Lawrence Nolan, who was two fields off.' By the time the family arrived back at their home, Bridget's body had been 'nearly consumed by fire, and nothing remaining but part of her head and neck, and about three inches over the ancle [*sic*] of each foot'. Nolan had run off with £2. 6 s., stolen from a chest in the bedroom. As if the graphic details of the case were not enough for their readers, the newspaper interpreted the event highlighting where blame lay for the outrage:

This is the district wherein Messrs. Thomas and John Watson acted as magistrates previous to their being deprived of their commissions of the peace by Lord

---

[77] 'Gazette – State of the Country', *Times*, 9 October 1838.
[78] Ibid.; 'The Gazette – State of the Country', *Times*, 21 December 1838.

Normanby. It is not unlikely that the bloodthirsty assassin was encouraged to perpetrate this revolting crime in the hope of escape, from the knowledge of the fact that the district was without an active magistrate. Wherever the magistrates have been removed the people calculate upon impunity. What a fearful system of government do we live under![79]

This story, along with others like it reprinted in the *Times*, demonstrated to English readers the senselessness of Irish violence – that such a heinous murder could be carried out for such a paltry sum of money highlighted the moral depravity of Irish actors, as did descriptions like 'bloodthirsty assassin' or 'savage'. Killing the innocent (an eight-year-old) and defenceless (an eighty-year-old) indicated the regression of Irish society under Mulgrave's tenure as lord lieutenant. Referring to the dismissed magistrates as 'active' would likely have been interpreted by many to mean Protestant and Tory, thus eager to enforce the law on the Catholic majority. If nothing else, the article implied Mulgrave replaced the Watsons with O'Connellite appointees who proved useless. Interestingly, the *Freeman's Journal* never published any story of the Nolans' death, nor any trial of John Nolan for murder, and the crime was not mentioned in the Reports of Outrage sent between Dublin Castle and Whitehall, thus casting some doubt on whether the event ever happened. Instead, it appears a propaganda campaign had developed in the press, with Conservative newspapers educating the English public with an ultra-Tory narrative of Irish society.

The *Times* also reprinted accounts of outrages spreading across the North Riding of that most 'unhappy county',[80] Co Tipperary. In early November 1838, extracts from the *Nenagh Guardian* reached *Times* readers listing fifteen different murders in the vicinity of Borrisokane between July and November, along with a subsequent articles about acts of incendiarism and the targeting of Protestant residents.[81] To counter these accounts, the *Freeman's Journal* published a letter to the editor from Arthur French, in which he accused the *Nenagh Guardian* and other conservative papers of inventing many of these outrages for their own political ends. 'My dear Sir – Knowing your readiness to expose the system of fabricated outrages, a trade which the provincial Conservative journals extensively deal in, I now beg to enclose you a copy of a letter from Mr. Purvis, a Protestant gentleman.' Purvis's letter explained how the *Nenagh Guardian* had reported that he received a threatening notice, and

---

[79] 'Revolting Murder', *Times*, 16 November 1838.

[80] This epithet regularly appeared in descriptions of Co. Tipperary, and of parts of the south and west of Ireland more generally. For example, 'The State of the Country', *Nenagh Guardian*, 6 June 1839.

[81] 'The Gazette – State of the Country', *Times*, 3 November 1838.

when he wrote asking the paper to correct the false story, the paper simply ignored him. French's letter to the editor laid blame for the state of Tipperary not at the feet of the peasantry, but rather with the son of the Anglican minister, Rev. Mr Goold, who evicted twelve families totalling roughly seventy people when he took possession of the land.[82] Regardless of what stories were accurate and which were fabricated or embellished, one thing seems clear – the Conservative press pursued a coordinated attack against the Irish government, and by extension the Whigs' claims of growing tranquillity in the wake of their policy of conciliation rather than coercion.

### Empire and Irish Outrage

Questions about the integrity of the British Empire in light of the threats posed by Catholic ascendancy and increased agrarian violence became an important undercurrent in the ultra-Tory narrative against Whig govern-ance. Generally, this took on one of two forms. The first was linking events abroad with potential unrest in Ireland, suggesting that the Irish countryside could be inspired to action because of Britain's troubles elsewhere, or more likely that Irish events might inspire violence in other colonial spaces. The second form highlighted the structural impor-tance of Ireland within the British Empire, an implicit acknowledgement of its quasi-colonial and quasi-integrated status, and the potential domino effect of Ireland striking out for 'freedom' from the British system – whether via O'Connell's vague, often muted, demands for 'Repeal' or something more sudden and violent. Along these lines Tories drafted semi-religious arguments, too, highlighting Catholics' political allegiance to papal authority and thus the potential supplanting of their Protestant and British empire of liberty for an oppressive Catholic papal empire of slavery in its place. In these visions Irish peasants were nothing more than 'vassals of the Pope' and the political unrest they stirred a means of 'subverting the ancient institutions of the Empire'.[83]

While historians have made many fruitful contributions on Ireland's role in British imperialism, as well as on the multiplicity of reactions in Ireland to imperial developments abroad, little of this literature touches on the 1830s.[84] Maybe this should not come as a surprise given the

---

[82] 'Tipperary Fabricated Outrages', FJ, 12 November 1838.
[83] 'Petition to Parliament', NLI, Brunswick MSS, MS 5017(2), f. 42.
[84] The literature here is too developed to list exhaustively, but some recent examples include Timothy McMahon et al., eds., *Ireland in an Imperial World*; Bender, 'Ireland and Empire', 343–60; Paul Townend, *The Road to Home Rule: Anti-Imperialism and the Irish National Movement*, History of Ireland and the Irish Diaspora (Madison: The University

intense historical focus on the domestic side of the Whigs' programme of reform in the 1830s, not to mention a prevailing sense in the literature of the rise of the imperialism of free trade as a dominant modus operandi for imperial action in the post-Napoleonic world.[85] However, the events of the 'age of reform' included the violent expansion of the East India Company across huge swathes of territory in the Indian subcontinent, a humiliating and tragic defeat in the first Anglo-Afghan war, the beginning of the first Opium War, conflict in New Zealand and Australia, and rebellion across Upper and Lower Canada – no quiet time for the British Empire.[86] When these are coupled with the traumatic reverberations of Catholic Emancipation in 1829 it is no surprise that Tories looking abroad did not see a stable British Empire, but a vulnerable one tossed to and fro in the turbulent seas of 'reform' and 'the spirit of the age'.

Although an imperial framework may not have been the primary lens by which commentators discussed Irish agrarian violence and Catholic ascendancy, it nevertheless became a feature in writings throughout the latter half of the 1830s, often as a stick to compel British Protestants to wake up to the danger posed by Irish Catholicism. The Protestant Association's publications, especially the *Protestant Magazine*, which was intended for a mass audience, often played on this theme. Repeal, for example, threatened 'the dismemberment of the empire' and the eventual establishment of an 'absolute dominion' over Great Britain by 'Popery' which the authors hoped would 'arouse lukewarm Protestants to a sense of duty'.[87] Writers alluded to 'Papal aggression' directed against individual Protestants at home and abroad, as well as the institution of Protestantism, thus highlighting the potential threat to church establishment.[88] *The*

of Wisconsin Press, 2016); Barry Crosbie, *Irish Imperial Networks: Migration, Social Communication and Exchange in Nineteenth-Century India* (Cambridge: Cambridge University Press, 2011); Matthew Kelly, 'Irish Nationalist Opinion and the British Empire in the 1850s and 1860s', P & P 204, no. 1 (August 2009): 127–54; Niamh Lynch, 'Defining Irish Nationalist Anti-Imperialism: Thomas Davis and John Mitchel', *Éire-Ireland* 42, nos. 1 & 2 (Spring/Summer 2007), 82–107.

[85] John Darwin, *The Empire Project: The Rise and Fall of the British World-System 1830–1870* (Cambridge: Cambridge University Press, 2009), ch. 1; John Gallagher and Ronald Robinson, 'The Imperialism of Free Trade', *The Economic History Review* 6, no. 1 (August 1953): 1–15.

[86] Antoinette M. Burton's *The Trouble with Empire* is a timely intervention here, challenging historians to grapple with all the 'trouble' that empire – both its construction and maintenance – brought rather than structuring our narratives around 'hegemony'. See Burton, *The Trouble with Empire: Challenges to Modern British Imperialism* (Oxford: Oxford University Press, 2017), especially chs. 1, 3; also John Darwin, *Unfinished Empire: The Global Expansion of Britain* (New York: Bloomsbury Press, 2012), xii–xiii, ch. 5.

[87] 'Repeal of the Union', *The Protestant Magazine* 2 (November 1840), 398.

[88] 'Popish Aggressions in Tahiti', *The Protestant Magazine* 2 (August 1840), 254–9; 'Restoration of the Protestant Constitution of Great Britain and Ireland', *The Protestant*

214 4 The Spectre of Irish Outrages

*Progress of Popery*, another Protestant Association publication written by Macleod Wylie, claimed its purpose was to demonstrate to the ill-informed how 'Popery, both at home and abroad, is in the possession of immense strength, and has been, and is now, marching forward with giant strides to its old ascendancy'; and to awaken those 'who pretend to zeal for Protestantism' to rally together.[89] The twenty-page pamphlet builds the historic case for the growth of Catholicism in Great Britain, Ireland, and its colonies beginning with an inventory of Catholic peers, wealthy gentry, and members of the House of Commons. The Whigs' decision to appoint Catholics to prominent legal offices in Ireland was noted, as was the appointment of Sir Maurice O'Connell as the Governor of New South Wales, a man 'whose very name speaks volumes . . . [of] the same gross maladministration of patronage' that prevailed in the United Kingdom.[90] Equally unnerving for Wylie was the massive increase of Catholic populations throughout the colonies and subsequent growth of the Catholic Church hierarchy.[91] The fears were twofold – first, the concern that financial support was a zero-sum game, and an increase in Catholic populations over Protestant ones would lead to the state reducing financial support for the Protestant church (as it had done in Ireland);[92] and, secondly, an existential fear that the British Empire was in the process of losing its *Britishness* with the rise of Catholicism. Crucially, Wylie put this growing Catholic influence across the Empire within the context of Catholic Emancipation, and Ireland's endemic agrarian violence.

We hope, then, that this will convince the Protestants of Great Britain, if everything else fails to excite them, that Popery is preparing for greater movements than have hitherto been made. It seems that now the Roman Catholics deem themselves strong enough to follow the course of their Irish brethren, and are preparing to consummate their intrigues by intimidation. Such was the policy adopted in Ireland. At first, nothing was heard but professions of loyalty, nothing but promises of peace; but when the time came to speak out, first for emancipation, then

*Magazine* 2 (December 1840), 369–74; 'Aggressions of Popery in Prisons', *The Protestant Magazine* 2 (December 1840), 398.

[89] The Protestant Association [ Macleod Wylie ], *The Progress of Popery in the British Dominions and Elsewhere* (London: Protestant Association, 1839), 1–20, at 3.

[90] Ibid., 6.

[91] He also references the connection between Maynooth and the exporting of Catholic clergy throughout the English-speaking world. See Colin Barr, '"Imperium in Imperio": Irish Episcopal Imperialism in the Nineteenth Century', EHR 123, no. 502 (June 2008): 611–50.

[92] This concern was powerfully expressed by the Bishop of Exeter, see Charge Delivered to the Clergy of the Diocese of Exeter/ by Henry, Lord Bishop of Exeter; at His Triennial Visitation in the Months of August, September, and October, 1839 (London: J. Murray, 1839), ECL, Phillpotts Papers, DP/PHI, C70363, at 2, 4, 14; Bishop of Quebec (George Mountain) to Phillpotts, 28 November 1838, ibid., ED11/45/2; Phillpotts to Mountain, 14 January 1839; ED11/45/3.

against tithes, and afterwards for repeal, all cloaks and coverings were cast aside, and the tremendous machinery so long preparing was suddenly unveiled to view.[93]

In short, in the eyes of Wylie and his ilk, the tolerance of Catholicism's growth in the 1830s had opened the floodgates to an active and violent Catholicism that aimed not simply to gain acceptance but to exert dominance.

The outbreak of violence in Canada in 1837–8 provided the easiest referent for those wishing to connect their paranoia about Ireland to wider imperial waters.[94] Grievances in both Lower and Upper Canada had long simmered, despite the British granting forms of representative government for both provinces in 1791. Francophones in Lower Canada complained of economic exclusion, as well as 'alien control', while those in Upper Canada objected to a range of economic issues around land grants, tariffs, and the privileges of the Anglican Church. Louis-Joseph Papineau, a committed republican, led the rebellion in Lower Canada and was supported by his Cork-born lieutenant Dr Edmund Bailey O'Callaghan, a regular correspondent with O'Connell in the 1830s, along with a sizeable number of peasants.[95] Given the somewhat analogous situation between French Canadians and Irish Catholics, Melbourne's Whig government worried how O'Connell, often compared to Papineau, might react to a colonial Catholic people demanding a republic. In late December 1837 Russell wrote to Mulgrave about the potential that 'the difficulties of the Canadian Affair' might 'stir some of the old Irish agitators to press for concessions to Ireland'.[96] Although the government received private assurances from O'Connell that he would 'do no mischief on the Canada Question', Conservative politicians, newspapers, and journals capitalised on the violence in Canada and its relationship to the Irish countryside.[97]

As word of the rebellion in Lower Canada spread, the *Times* published a series of articles attempting to shape the narrative and to indict Whig

---

[93] Ibid., 17–18.

[94] As Shane Lynn has demonstrated, Lower Canada by the mid-1830s had a vibrant political culture shaped by O'Connell's campaign for Catholic Emancipation; see Shane Lynn, 'Friends of Ireland: Early O'Connellism in Lower Canada', IHS 40, no. 157 (May 2016): 43–65.

[95] Michael J. Turner, 'Radical Agitation and the Canada Question in British Politics, 1837–41', *Historical Research* 79, no. 203 (February 2006): 90–114; Maureen Slattery, 'Irish Radicalism and the Roman Catholic Church in Quebec and Ireland, 1833–1834: O'Callaghan and O'Connell Compared', *CCHA Historical Studies* 63 (1997): 29–58, at 30.

[96] Russell to Mulgrave, 30 December 1837, MC, Mulgrave MSS, M/894.

[97] Mulgrave to Russell, 6 January 1838, TNA, Russell Papers, PRO 30/22/3A, f. 37.

colonial policy. On 23 December 1837, when 'little, if anything, [was] yet established with regard to the unfortunate state of Lower Canada', the *Times* writer began answering hypothetical questions about whether readers should consider a rebellion justified. Where the American Revolution should be understood as a justified rebellion due to 'perverse and unreasoning rulers' who pursued policies 'inconsistent with the *habitual* relations of parent state and colony', the author was quick to point out that in their estimation the Rebellion of 1798 'was not caused by any peculiar pressure of grievance or suffering upon the body of people', but was a manipulation by its leaders of the 'general sense of destitution' among Ireland's peasantry. The result of that manipulation was the attempt at 'the expulsion of the Protestant and British power out of Ireland' and a 'false rebellion'. The lesson readers should take? That if 3–4 million 'Irish fanatics' could be turned out by 'systematic and artful organisation', then the Canadian Rebellion must be crushed:

> It is very easy of belief, therefore, that the rebellion of Lower Canada may have been the exclusive workmanship of incendiaries directed by a few central chiefs … having for its materials a race of ignorant men, jealous and fearful of their British neighbours, and therefore actuated by an envenomed hatred of them, as the Irish are at all times by a vague exasperation at the wretchedness of their own physical condition.[98]

Politicians, newspapers, and social commentators made the connection between violence in Ireland and Canada explicit as word of the rebellion's spread to Upper Canada engrossed newspaper headlines. As the Whig government offered the reduction in Irish outrages as an example of the success of their 'justice to Ireland' approach, Anglo-Irish Tories presented a radically different picture of the Irish countryside. Under the headline 'The Base, Bloody, & Brutal Whigs', the *Kerry Evening Post* (one of a number of conservative Irish newspapers) tied the Whigs' relationship with O'Connell to their inability to prevent 'a civil war … bloody and brutal' in Canada, which they feared would 'spread desolation and blood over a fair portion of the domains of Britain', especially as it was clear 'the similarity of the movements in Ireland, under the direction of Mr O'Connell, and those in Canada, as regulated by the master mind of the great colonial agitator [Papineau]'.[99] Writers in the conservative journals all articulated similar points of comparison varying in degree of eccentricity based on their brand. Thus, the *Quarterly Review*, the most restrained and long established, published a long article by John Wilson Croker critiquing government policy in Canada that focussed on the

---

[98] *The Times*, 23 December 1837.
[99] 'The Base, Bloody, & Brutal Whigs', *Kerry Evening Post*, 3 January 1838.

unwillingness of Russell to acknowledge that the fundamental grievances of Lower Canada centred on republicanism and a desire to 'to throw off ... the *monarchical sovereignty of England*'.[100] Although Croker made few direct references to Irish violence, constructing his article around the alleged republican goals of Papineau put readers into a frame of reference which included O'Connell's previous demands for 'Repeal'; thus, bloodshed – in this case in the form of the Canadian Rebellion – was the logical outcome of any rhetoric of separatism. To further solidify this comparison, Croker noted that Papineau's ninety-two resolutions stating Lower Canada's grievances included praising O'Connell the '"GREAT and LIBERATOR ... of whom our fellow-countrymen entertain corresponding sentiments" for the ways he "even under Tory ministry, and before the reform of Parliament" was successful "in the emancipation of Ireland from the same bondage and the same political inferiority which menace the people of Lower Canada"'. Croker replied to these resolutions observing: 'The old pagan and popish doctrine of *sanctuary* is, it seems, in full force at Downing Street; and those who could touch the sacred images of *St. Daniel* and *St. John* [Hume], were allowed the immunities and impunity of asylum ... [by] her Majesty's – we should have said ridiculous – ministers, if the blood stain did not obliterate ridicule. But that blood!'[101]

*Blackwood's* and *Fraser's* demonstrated far less restraint. *Blackwood's* published articles on Canada in consecutive issues in February and March 1838. The first, 'A Sketch of the Canadas' written by George Croly, offered a matter-of-fact accounting of the history of the two provinces, including its natural landscape, economy, demography, and culture, before turning to the crisis. Croly argued that Papineau and his 'gang of scoundrels' presented false grievances as a mere pretext for armed rebellion, stressing that 'the history of agitation in Canada is the counterpart of agitation in Ireland. Every day fabricated its grievance. Conciliation was foolishly practiced, until grievance-making was an established trade'.[102] And, similar to Croker, Croly saw only one inevitable conclusion of conciliation and grievance-making – complete separation from the British Empire: 'it was publicly and universally declared that the subjection of the Canadas to the mother country was altogether an intolerable burden, [and] that the model of the Republic within sight was the one thing desirable'. Croly concluded the article by reciting the

---

[100] [ J. W. Croker ], 'Canada', *Quarterly Review* 61 (January 1838): 249–72, at p. 253. It should be noted that J. W. Croker was anything but restrained; see Robert Portsmouth, *John Wilson Croker: Irish Ideas and the Invention of Modern Conservatism, 1800–1835* (Dublin: Irish Academic Press, 2010).
[101] 'Canada', 263–4.
[102] [George Croly], 'A Sketch of the Canadas', BEM 43 (February 1838), 214–27, at 226.

popular characterisation of Melbourne's government as only being animated by its members' desire for place and salary before emphatically declaring 'we must have neither a Papineau Cabinet in the colonies, nor an O'Connell Cabinet at home'.[103] Macleod Wylie, in his March 1838 article 'Canada and Ireland' continued where Croly left off. 'At present, in Ireland, there are all the symptoms which preceded [the] Canadian revolt', Wylie argued, in that the government was 'yielding through fear to the majority what they had denied before to the pretended was justice, and the effects have been the same. Every thing received has been deemed an instalment; nothing has been given us in return; separation is still demanded in Canada, and repeal is expressed reserved as a *dernier resort* in Ireland.'[104] Wylie noted what he saw as O'Connell's conditional commitment to Whig government, which brought with it 'the vaunted tranquillity and peace', but that would shatter once the government fell, thus demonstrating O'Connell's true colours as the leader of a 'violent popular and general movement' requiring Britain's military might to suppress. In short, the policy of conciliation, especially if animated by any democratic spirit, inevitably brought bloodshed, as witnessed in 1640–1 and in the French Revolution. Accordingly, Wylie advocated a return to 'a firm Protestant system', which in practice sounded a lot like Protestant Ascendancy.[105] *Fraser's* was even more explicit, entitling their February 1838 article as 'The Rehearsal', which in four pages succinctly summarised the points of comparison between the plight of Protestants in Canada and Ireland, the contrived grievances of the Catholic majorities, the shared policy of conciliation, and most importantly, similar consequences in terms of bloodshed. However, *Fraser's* put the crisis in stark religious terms, and spent the article's last two pages quoting extensively from Croly's *Interpretation of the Apocalypse*, concluding with his words:

With Popery like a millstone round her neck, England has gone down, and must still go down. With Popery cut loose from her, she has strength, not merely to float, but to control the storm. With Protestantism for her principle, she might defy human casualty to the end of time; with Popery for her lawgiver, she must be prepared to see the rapid sacrifice of her freedom, her religion, and her empire. PROTESTANTISM must be the supreme rule of England, or England must be a ruin.[106]

---

[103] Ibid., 227. Immediately following Croly's article was another on the government's specific policy in Canada, which lay blame for the crisis on government procrastination and negligence. See [Alfred Mallileau], 'Ministerial Policy in the Canadas', BEM 43 (February 1838), 228–47.

[104] [Macleod Wylie], 'Canada and Ireland', BEM 43 (March 1838), 385–95, at 388 and 386.

[105] Ibid., 394–5.    [106] 'The Rehearsal', *Fraser's Magazine* 17 (February 1838), 255–8.

With newspapers and journals noting the similarities between Canada and Ireland, and the violence in both locales, it was also foremost in the minds of politicians and gentry members. Peel wrote to Wellington suggesting that Conservatives should offer the Whigs their 'cordial support' partly to protect England's 'immense colonial empire', which could be undone by a successful revolt, but also because 'our position with regard to Ireland was an additional motive for taking a decided course'.[107] As the crisis continued into February and English Radicals made the government's response in Canada a point of debate, Wellington worried about the consequences of bringing the government down on such a question. 'Suppose that O'Connell should, as he has threatened, avail himself of that opportunity [war in Canada] to agitate Repeal! What does he mean by agitating Repeal? . . . Have we the means of enforcing good order in Ireland?'[108] Newcastle confessed similar sentiments to his journal, writing in his concluding entry for the year 1837 that while he could take solace in the fact that 'The vile O'Connell is fast-falling', thus opening the potential for 'a chance of salvation amidst a chaos of destructive Events', events in Canada mitigated his optimism. 'As Canada has openly rebelled, it is of the utmost conse-quence that Ireland Should not be Excited to follow the Example of the Colony – a rising in Ireland & in Scotland in aid of the Canada insurrec-tion would place us in a Situation of imminent danger'.[109] Gentry members in Ireland echoed what they read in the journals. Charles Fox, the recently defeated Conservative MP for Co. Longford and cousin to the ultra-Tory Farnham family, wrote his cousin Henry (the future 7th baron) in 1838 that 'this Canada business ought to open the eye of everyone . . . to the consequence of that policy which treats enemies of the Constitution + British connexion as men to whom every concession is to be made . . . till they take up arms'.[110]

Working hand in hand with the rhetoric aiming to dispel the government's claims of tranquillity in Ireland were the references to the political system of Ribbonism, and the violence of Ribbonmen. By 1839 Roden was contending that Ribbonism had found inspiration in the Canadian Rebellion, and that Ribbonmen, in conjunction with O'Connell, were planning a rebellion of their

---

[107] Peel to Wellington, 7 January 1838, in Peel, *Peel Correspondence*, 2:355.

[108] Wellington to Peel, 22 February 1838, BL, Peel Papers Add MS 40310, f. 222.

[109] Newcastle Diaries, 31 December 1837; Henry Pelham Fiennes Pelham-Clinton of Newcastle, *Unrepentant Tory: Political Selections from the Diaries of the Fourth Duke of Newcastle-under-Lyne, 1827–38*, ed. Richard A. Gaunt (Woodbridge: Boydell & Brewer, 2006), 331.

[110] Charles Fox to Henry Maxwell, 1 January 1838, NLI, Farnham MSS, MS 18,613, folder 20.

own.[111] Roden successfully established a committee to inquire into Irish crime (discussed in Chapter 5), which heard the testimony of magistrates, landlords, and constables, some of whom explicitly referred to the alleged connection between the importance of rebellion in Canada and Ribbonmen in Ireland. H. W. Rowan, a magistrate in Co. Westmeath, testified to the wide influence of Ribbonism as a 'political Object ... to overturn the Government in Ireland' that had gathered momentum throughout 1838, 'perhaps [from] the Impulse given to it by the Rebellion in Canada'.[112] Constables and magistrates seized passwords from alleged Ribbonmen that took the form of riddles like: 'Q: I hope your Irish Sons will gain their Freedom. A: Yes, when the Canadas conquer' or 'Q: Have you got any news? A: We hear they are doing well in Canada'.[113] In another case in Co. Armagh, constables arrested a man named John Carroll at a fair; in addition to carrying a weapon, he had in his possession a paper referring to the 'Liverpool Hibernian Benevolent Burial Society' along with passwords referring to Canada's oppression and how 'Lord Durham will alleviate their grievances'.[114] Officials found these benevolent societies incredibly suspicious, especially in towns with large Irish populations like Glasgow and Liverpool, because they believed they operated as a front for clandestine Ribbon organising. Maj. George Warburton, a long-standing stipendiary magistrate generally sympathetic to the Whigs' reform programme, nevertheless testified to an organised plot in Co. Meath to post notices from Derry to Dublin 'calling upon the People to imitate the Friends of Liberty in Canada, and to rise and shake off the Yoke that had so long oppressed them'.[115]

The arrest of alleged Ribbon secretary Richard Jones and his subsequent trial in 1840 produced seemingly endless fodder for Tory newspapers to speculate on the alleged connections between Ribbon men, the Canadian Rebellion, and other colonial contexts. The *Nenagh Guardian*, sometimes cutting and pasting from the *Dublin Evening Post*, made particular hay of the revelations at Jones's trial, in particular the interpretation that 'Ribbonism is a universal system, acting upon one uniform principle ... a political,

---

[111] Hansard, 3rd ser., vol. 45, col. 764, 22 February 1839; ibid., vol. 46, col. 963, 21 March 1839.

[112] 'Report from the Select Committee of the House of Lords, appointed to enquire into the state of Ireland in respect of crime, and to report thereon to the House; with the minutes of evidence taken before the committee, and an appendix and index' [hereafter Select Committee on State of Ireland], P. P. (1839, vol. 11, no. 486), 140, 158.

[113] Ibid., 168, 210.

[114] 'Reports on Ribbonism', 4 May 1838, NAI, CSO/RP/1838/20/67. On Ribbonism's transnational connections in this period see Hughes and MacRaild, *Ribbon Societies*, chs. 3 and 4.

[115] 'Select Committee on State of Ireland', 79.

seditious and revolutionary system'.[116] By 1840, O'Connell was wavering on his commitment to the Whigs and had returned to vague threats of repeal; he had also created the Precursor Society in August 1838, which threatened to agitate for repeal if further reforms were not enacted.[117] Newspapers seized the opportunity to tie O'Connell's threats to Ribbon subterfuge, and by proxy, to tarnish a politically weak Whig government still receiving political life support from O'Connell's votes at Westminster. 'The political aspirations for Daniel's favourite project, the dismemberment of the British empire, were directly inculcated on the Ribbonmen', the *Nenagh Guardian* argued. The paper referenced passwords found on Jones's person at the time of his arrest, which included statements such as 'Will we have a repeal of the Union? I think we will – when we are united we shall be righted – what a glorious sight to see the North and South combined', which likely referred to an internecine feud between Ribbon societies in Belfast and Dublin. However, the article also noted the movement's transnational connections, commenting on how, during a trial of an accused Ribbonman, the judge 'mentioned that Irish Ribbonism has recognised and sympathised with the rebellion in Lower Canada! *Loyal* fellows these O'Connellites', concluding with complaints about the lack of attention other newspapers had paid to Ribbonism's influence in Whig government and those 'Irish *Thugs*' associated with O'Connell.[118]

The appellation of 'thug' by the *Nenagh Guardian* was no accident. Captain Philip Meadows Taylor published his bestselling novel *Confessions of a Thug* in 1839 and Conservative outlets quickly adapted the novel's storyline for their own political purposes. Joseph Lennon and Luke Gibbons have both demonstrated ways in which the Orient, and Orientalist discourses, were prominent in nineteenth-century literature, often either as an allegory for Irish writers to work out anti-colonial struggle, or in the words of Gibbons, because they represented 'an internal struggle ... between constitutional nationalism and a dissident, insurrectionary tradition'.[119] Anglo-Irish Tories also employed Orientalist discourse as a way to mark Catholic Ireland's political and social position as akin to the wilds of untamed portions of India – and in need, therefore, of British discipline. For that reason, Tory writers and newspapers were quick to appropriate 'thuggee' and deploy it as a term to undermine the Whigs' argument of Irish tranquillity.

[116] 'Ribbonism', *Nenagh Guardian*, 22 July 1840.     [117] Geoghegan, *Liberator*, 106.
[118] 'Ribbonism', *Nenagh Guardian*, 22 July 1840; on the Ribbon feud see Hughes and MacRaild, *Ribbon Societies*, 79–80, and on 'localism', Garvin, 'Defenders, Ribbonmen and Others', 133–55.
[119] Joseph Lennon, 'Irish Orientalism: An Overview', in *Ireland and Postcolonial Theory*, eds. Clare Carroll and Patricia King (South Bend, IN: Notre Dame Press, 2003), 144–5.

In January 1840 the *Dublin University Magazine* published an article by the Rev. Samuel O'Sullivan, entitled 'Thuggee in India, Ribandism in Ireland, compared.' In it, O'Sullivan reviewed Taylor's bestselling novel, comparing the Thuggee cult described in it to the 'ribbon system' witnessed around Ireland. As was rather common for a literary journal, O'Sullivan excerpted Taylor's novel at length, attentively noting the religious elements of the Thugs' initiation, in which the protagonist Ameer Ali places his hand on the Koran to swear 'an oath, a fearful oath' to 'pursue to destruction every human being ... thrown in thy power'.[120] Detailing Ali's first ritualistic murder and the accompanying religious service, O'Sullivan noted how 'no devotees of the Romanish communion ever worshipped their patron saint with more devotion, than the Thugs ... exhibited towards their goddess Bhowanee'. After a good bit of sermonising on the universal depravity of humanity and the powerful benefits of 'true religion', O'Sullivan reaches his purpose – the comparison between Thugs in India and Ribbonmen in Ireland. 'What is ribandism ... but a species of political Thuggee, in which the conspirators are of one religion, and bind themselves, by an oath of blood, to the extermination of all from whom opposition to their evil designs might be apprehended?' He continued:

The system of Irish Thuggee is *political* as well as *religious*. It is by acting upon the temporal power, that it is enabled to accomplish its ecclesiastical objects. The party [referring to the Whigs] in power have sold themselves to work the will of the great agitator, to whom the Irish Thugs look up as their Magnus Apollo.[121]

Whereas in the case of India both Tory and Whig agreed on the depravity of Thug violence and the need to root it out, O'Sullivan argued that the Whigs actively propagated a narrative that turned a blind eye to the Ribbonmen's violence and O'Connell's involvement in its orchestration, despite its danger to 'the integrity of the empire'. In short, O'Sullivan used a colonial context not simply to demonstrate the potential dangerous similarities between India and Ireland, but also as a contrast between the political forces working to end Thug violence in India versus those in Ireland whom in O'Sullivan's estimation were using ribbon violence for political ends (O'Connell) or actively ignoring the problem to keep their place in power. The consequence of this political opportunism or laziness was the sacrifice of Ireland's Protestant population to the whims of 'popery', as well as the undermining of Britain's Protestant constitution and the stability of the Empire as a whole. Samuel's brother Mortimer echoed these sentiments, stressing in a letter to the Archbishop of Armagh

---

[120] [Rev. Samuel O'Sullivan], 'Thuggee in India, Ribandism in Ireland, Compared', DUM 15, no. 85 (January 1840), 50–65, at 55.
[121] Ibid., 59–60.

the dangers of Ribbonism as a system that 'weakens the strength of the British empire, and . . . keeps a large mass of people in a state of readiness for any enterprise by which the empire may be shaken'.[122]

As the concept of the 'thug' spread, Conservative Irish newspapers found similar political uses, adapting O'Sullivan's more scholarly approach. When O'Connell shifted his attention back to Repeal, newspaper editors referred to 'O'Connellite thugs' and their 'hell-born confederacy . . . to dismember the British Empire', or the 'Papistico-Thug Society' of Ribbonism (also known as 'O'Connell Thugs') demonstrating 'the real nature of the "Mulgrave tranquillisation of Ireland"'.[123] Others made note of 'the system of Irish Thuggism', as trials of alleged Ribbonmen commenced in the 1840s.[124] Still others compared the 'thug' of the east (India) to that of the west (Ireland), noting how while the Indian thug 'wanders the country, as a tinker or a tailor would do mending kettles or making coats', the Irish thug sees his action 'in the light of a public execution, which somebody must perform for the good of the country'. In other words, those perpetrating Irish outrages followed a political programme aimed at undermining the social order:

This monstrous system is very erroneously designated by the term 'WILD JUSTICE.' . . . when the Neophyte Thug, of the western school, can be worked up to these deeds of death by the throw of a die, the feeling of security from detection, and some hell-born phantom of patriotism . . . this is the unerring sign of a disorganization in the framework of civilized life that must tear up the very roots of society, and bring chaos back again, unless some remedy be found to check the downward march of religion, morality, philosophy – of humanity itself![125]

## Conclusion

By the latter half of the 1830s, the Duke of Newcastle had good reason to confide in his diary that 'a general feeling is beginning to pervade the country against Popery & in favour of our Protestant Church'.[126] Seizing on the real and perceived fears of Protestants in Ireland, ultra-Tories mobilised Protestants to a common defence using a repertoire of rhetoric that recalled Catholic treachery and enumerated daily assaults on Ireland's minority population and its interest. However, mobilising Protestants across Ireland

---

[122] Mortimer O'Sullivan to Archbishop Beresford, 28 July 1839, PRONI, T2772/2/6/28.
[123] 'The Repeal Agitation', *Nenagh Guardian*, 29 July 1840; 'Ribbonism', *Bucks Herald*, 4 July 1840; 'State of the Country: State of the County of Carlow', *Wexford Conservative*, 25 August 1841. See also 'State of Ireland', *John Bull*, 7 June 1841.
[124] 'Extraordinary Trial for Ribbonism', *London Evening Standard*, 5 March 1844.
[125] James Johnson, *A Tour in Ireland: With Meditations and Reflections* (London: S. Highley, 32, Fleet Street, 1844), at 145.
[126] Newcastle, *Unrepentant Tory*, 346.

was not enough to return the British government to the firm footing of Tory rule. Ultra-Tories realised soon after the loss of Protestant Ascendancy that they need to mobilise popular opinion across the whole of the United Kingdom. New associations large and small, national and regional, political and religious, sprang up across Great Britain and Ireland that focussed their critique on the relationship between Whig government, O'Connell's political influence, apparent Catholic ascendancy, and Irish agrarian violence. The re-established Protestant Association was one important voice directing this campaign, with its prolific output of pamphlets and the creation of new periodicals that communicated a mixture of Protestant news and propaganda. Other media organs, including *The Times*, participated in disseminating stories highlighting the disjuncture between Irish outrages and government reports of increased tranquillity.

This chapter has also demonstrated that wider imperial concerns – especially around Whig colonial policy, Catholic preferment, and colonial violence – proved useful political tools in the ultra-Tory campaign to unseat the Whigs. Whether they focussed on the apparent analogous relationship between French Catholic rebels in Lower Canada and Ireland's peasantry, or the similar practices of Indian thugs and Irish Ribbonmen, Tory commentators and politicians found reason to cast their eyes abroad to emphasise the grave risk that would be posed to the British Empire if the Whigs were allowed to continue their programme of 'reform' at home. Dwelling on the alleged political aspirations of the Catholic Church underscored the potential disloyalty of Catholics domestically. Many ultra-Tories, and even some more moderate Conservatives, believed that the Catholic hierarchy did not view emancipation as some sort of final settlement but a decisive step towards the complete undermining of the Protestant establishment, and as a result the British characteristics of liberty and freedom. In the place of that establishment, argued many, popery intended to bring about slavery and tyranny. What is more, the Catholic Church, or Daniel O'Connell's, role in *establishing* a new order was the problem to which Tory commentators habitually returned. Agrarian violence was not spasmodic, episodic, or unintelligible; rather, outrages were the means to establish 'a reign of terrorism in Ireland ... to paralyse the government' and to undermine the integrity of the British Empire.[127] The dysfunction of the Irish countryside shone brightest in the political sky at that time, and operated as a point by means of which Tory commentators and politicians could chart their course back to government benches.

---

[127] [William Sewell], 'Romanism in Ireland', *Quarterly Review* 67, no. 133 (December 1840), 118–71, at 160.

# 5    Ireland and the Tory Imagination

In early March 1839 Lord Roden, the ultra-Tory and de facto leader of the Irish peers, proposed the formation of a select committee to inquire into Irish outrages. The start date of the proposed committee's purview – 1835 – conspicuously corresponded with the beginning of Lord Mulgrave's tenure as lord lieutenant, a period Roden identified with 'tears of sorrow and streams of blood'. The committee, discussed in greater detail below, was the culmination of the Tories' strategic effort to make Ireland – and particularly Irish agrarian violence – a rallying point to topple the Whig government of Lord Melbourne. Speaking before the House of Lords, Roden noted the 'conspiracy in Ireland – a conspiracy systematic, organised, and secret ... which was directed against the life and property of all who would not join it and support the treasonable objects which its members had in view'. Highlighting the alleged role of Ribbonism in coordinating a campaign for 'the annihilation of the Protestant faith', Roden peddled sectarian narratives stoking anti-Catholic sentiment and that connected Irish outrages to the political programme of O'Connell, which Roden argued received support from the Whigs in power.[1] The motion cleared the House of Lords and the committee eventually produced a 1,600-page report full of witnesses' testimony that reflected on the state of Ireland, the accuracy of criminal statistics, and the effectiveness of Whig government in the country.[2]

This chapter picks up where Chapter 4 left off by following the Tory propaganda campaign from the pages of periodicals and newspaper articles to the Houses of Parliament. It begins with an examination of the run-up to Roden's motion for a select committee on Irish crime, the formation of which demonstrated the collective insecurity shared by Protestants across Great Britain and Ireland as regarded the Whig government's policy of 'justice to Ireland'. If the episode was, in part, a confirmation of the growing influence of ultra-Tories in forging a strategy to regain

---

[1] Hansard, 3rd ser., vol. 46, cols. 955–6, 21 March 1839.
[2] 'Select Committee on State of Ireland', P. P. (1839, vol. 11, no. 486).

political power, it was also an illustration of the unifying effect Ireland had in bringing together the government's disparate political coalition. Lord John Russell's spirited defence of the government's Irish policy reshaped the question into a confidence vote at a time when the government was politically anaemic. The chapter then turns to chart the undoing of the Lichfield House Compact and O'Connell's return to a more ambivalent parliamentary approach, which ultimately led to the collapse of Whig government in 1841 and enabled a resurgent Conservative Party to capture a majority of parliamentary seats thanks to a strategy based on the anti-Catholic/anti-Irish rhetoric discussed in Chapter 4. Finally, the chapter highlights how Robert Peel's government in 1841 attempted a return to the governing norms that had been in place prior to the 'decade of reform', a move which would contribute to his government's collapse in 1846.

### The House of Lords and Ireland

Tory strategy within Parliament since the Whigs came to power had been largely defensive in posture. The pattern was well established. The government would introduce legislation in the House of Commons that contained controversial clauses but would sail through its first and second readings. The House of Lords would then either reject the legislation outright or would dramatically alter it to the point where it hardly resembled the original bill, thus leaving the government with the choice of accepting the alterations or abandoning the legislation until a future session of Parliament. Peel and Wellington worked hard to keep members unified despite the wide array of political opinions and lingering distrust among some of their number that was a legacy of the way Catholic Emancipation had been passed. Strategy sessions with either leader would often include both Irish MPs and peers so as to coordinate the policy between both houses.[3] On the issue of Irish tithes, for example, Peel confessed to the Archbishop of Armagh, John Beresford, his concern regarding the optics of rejecting the Whigs' proposal for reform rather than amending the bill in line with Tory preference. Changing tactics and throwing out the bill would give 'the Enemies of the Church ... particularly [of] the Church in Ireland' the means to represent the Tories as intransigent and unwilling 'to reform any real abuse in the Church'.[4] This cautious strategy often infuriated the

---

[3] Earl of Rosslyn to Wellington, 9 February 1836, USSC, Wellington MSS, WP2/38/23; Peel to Wellington, 12 March 1836, WP2/38/130.

[4] Peel to Beresford, 10 May 1836, RCBL, MS 183, folder 1, f. 42. On the resolution of the Tithe Question see Macintyre, *Liberator*, ch. 5.

ultra-Tory peers who preferred purity in political principles to any attempt at compromise.[5]

Nevertheless, Tories wishing to flex their constitutional muscle looked to the House of Lords as the venue in which to do so. Lord Londonderry wrote to his fellow Conservative Lord Lyndhurst early in Melbourne's government about the importance of the House of Lords as the place of 'Conservative Power that if boldly wielded will assuredly arrive at an ultimate Triumph', thus hoping to spur more open confrontation of obnoxious Whig proposals.[6] And, by 1839, tensions were mounting. Outside the walls of Parliament, the Conservative press had grown increasingly strident in its opposition to Whig government, especially in Ireland. Regional Protestant organisations had grown across the country, and the Protestant Association continued to publish treatises on the dangers of Irish Catholicism while also hosting its annual meeting at Exeter Hall and organising petitions to present to Parliament. In Ireland, Roden galvanised Anglo-Irish gentry members to organise a 'Great Protestant Meeting' in January 1837 after strategising with their 'best English friends' on the importance of cooperation in their struggle 'against the Revolutionary Spirit of the Day'.[7] Roden continued to organise Protestants with signature campaigns for petitions concerning an Irish conspiracy, while newspapers continued to report on the growing number of Irish outrages.

The elections following King William IV's death demonstrated the success of the Tory strategy linking Whig government with Ireland and agrarian crime. The elections brought an increase in Tory members from English counties, though these were somewhat offset by O'Connellite and Whig victories in Ireland. O'Connell campaigned relentlessly in Ireland and as a testimony to his commitment to the Whig alliance demanded between £4,000 and £6,000 from the Whigs' election funds to help support the government's 'friends': 'Do something for us and we will do well for you.'[8] While monetary support came slowly from the Whigs to Ireland, the association with O'Connell proved detrimental to Whig

---

[5] The Duke of Newcastle frequently lamented to his journal about Wellington and Peel's strategy, while congratulating himself on his resolution to take 'the only proper, dignified & noble course'. See Newcastle, *Unrepentant Tory*, ed. Gaunt, 16 April 1836, 298 for one of many examples.

[6] Londonderry to Lyndhurst, 12 May 1835, DCRO, Londonderry Papers, D/Lo/C450(1).

[7] Roden to Downshire, 2 December 1836, PRONI, Downshire Papers, D671/C/17/633a; on the meeting itself see *Saunder's News-Letter*, 25 January 1837.

[8] O'Connell to Edward Ellice, 12 July 1837, O'Connell, *Correspondence*, 6:62. On the subject of money and elections more broadly, see Michael J. Keyes, 'Money and Nationalist Politics in Nineteenth Century Ireland: From O'Connell to Parnell' (PhD dissertation, NUI Maynooth, 2009), http://eprints.maynoothuniversity.ie/2899/1/MJK_Money_and_nationalist_politics.pdf, especially chapters 1–3.

prospects with the English electorate. John Allen, a friend of Lord Holland, confided that the Whigs had lost ground, due in part to their government 'deriving its support from the Irish members. Many merchants and country gentlemen feel indignant that England should be governed, as they say, by Ireland.' Allen also suggested that a rabid fear of Catholicism had swept through much of the country, and he disclosed his surprise at reports that 'Dissenters and even Quakers declar[e] that they look to the established Church as the only security against the Papists!'[9] Concerned with the optics of O'Connell raising money for the Whigs in Ireland, Russell and Mulgrave implored him to shutter his General Association, which had operated as a fundraising association throughout the elections.[10]

Inside Parliament, some Tory peers and MPs grew restless with what they perceived as Wellington's policy of moderation and delay.[11] In reply to the Queen's Speech, which opened the new parliamentary session with claims that the government had brought about 'external peace and domestic tranquillity' in November 1837, Lord Roden brought a motion demanding documents demonstrating the state's ability to garner convictions, the number of criminal offences that had been reported to the constabulary, and the number of rewards that had been offered by the state to witnesses for their cooperation. Roden argued that rather than being more tranquil '[in] some districts at no period had property, had life, had the exercise of the Protestant religion in Ireland, been in greater danger than at the very moment when he had the honour of addressing their Lordships'.[12] The confrontation did not go well for Roden. Lord John Russell raised concerns with Lord Mulgrave in October 1837 about the alarming rise in particular types of crime – such as incendiary fires and murders – between September 1836 and September 1837, and Mulgrave had dutifully studied the statistics produced by the Outrage Reports discussed in Chapter 2.[13] Mulgrave gained legal advice from the crown solicitor for Munster, Matthew Barrington, about how increasing committals for crimes could be understood as the result of a successful policing strategy and a decrease in overall criminal activity.[14] In debate Mulgrave

[9] Holland, *Holland House Diaries*, 373.
[10] Russell to Mulgrave, 13 August 1837, MC, Mulgrave MSS, M/875; Keyes, 'Money and Nationalist Politics', 88. O'Connell obliged the government's request. See O'Connell to Arthur French, 23 August 1837, *Correspondence of Daniel O'Connell*, 6: 83.
[11] Newcastle, *Unrepentant Tory*, ed. Gaunt, 18 November 1837, 327.
[12] Hansard, 3rd ser., vol. 39, cols. 212–14, 27 November 1837.
[13] Russell to Mulgrave, 19 October 1837, MC, Mulgrave MSS, M/885; Mulgrave to Russell, 23 October 1837, TNA, PRO 30/22/2F, f. 159.
[14] Matthew Barrington to Mulgrave, 7 November 1837, NLI, Monteagle Papers, MS 13,357/18.

brought these statistics to bear, quoting from the Outrage Reports, and noting the positive reaction among Ireland's population at the government's attempts to 'induc[e] a reciprocal feeling of confidence between the governors and the governed' based on the idea that 'the English will unite in procuring for Ireland that justice which she has not formerly experienced'.[15] Lord Holland, writing in his diary shortly after this exchange, reflected on how Mulgrave had 'vindicated himself triumphantly' while 'every accusation [in the House of Commons] recoiled on the Orangemen, and the whole terrifick apparatus which No Popery declaimers had vowed they would exhibit on the grandest edge fell flat at once and shamed its worshippers'.[16] Holland was wrong in his analysis of anti-Catholicism's strength, and though Roden's attack on Mulgrave's government did not lead to the revelation of some grand political conspiracy between the government and insurrectionary forces, it did provide the public with statistical accounts of Irish outrages between 1835 and 1837.[17] The debate previewed the arguments that Roden would deploy in 1839 as he took up Mulgrave's challenge to 'prove that [Mulgrave was] censurable for the existing state of things in Ireland'.[18]

Matters got no better for the government in 1838, as ultra-Tories continued their campaign in the press linking the alleged growth of Irish outrage to the government's relationship with O'Connell and its 'promotion' of Catholicism. The violence reported in Tipperary caused the greatest problems for the government and highlighted the growing division between the administration of Dublin Castle and the local apparatus of law and order exercised by magistrates. Rumour and intrigue went part and parcel with reports of violence. 'Upwards of three or four thousand people were addressed by one of the priests ... and immediately after the Mob attacked several Protestant Houses ... and demolished all the Windows', wrote Richard Molley, a postmaster from Tipperary. 'I have heard several Gentlemen say today that the whole was countenanced and put forward thro' emmissaries [sic] from the Government [acting on O'Connell's orders]', Molley continued, implicating O'Connell and by extension the British government in the targeting of Protestants for reprisals, including the local vicar and a landlord by the name of Mr Andrews.[19] Other landlords, or their agents and employees, found

[15] Hansard, 3rd ser., vol. 39, col. 226, 27 November 1837.
[16] Holland, *Holland House Diaries*, 378.
[17] 'Outrages (Ireland). Return of rewards offered by proclamation of Lord Lieutenant, &c., and of all crimes and outrages reported by the stipendiary magistrates and officers of police in Ireland', P.P., 1837–38, vol. 46, no. 157.
[18] Hansard, 3rd. ser., vol. 39, col. 242, 27 November 1837.
[19] Richard Molley to Irish Office, 1 August 1837, TNA, HO 100/251/3.

themselves the target of anonymous missives, rocks, or bullets, such as Denis Murphy, who was murdered in 1836, or Richard Jackson, who pleaded to the government for police protection because of 'a conspiracy formed to murder me', but who had to pay 5s. per day for the pleasure of two policemen's' company.[20] Sectarian narratives were also well established, such as reports that Captain Rock was sending notices to tenants in Tipperary and targeting them with threats because of their Protestantism. James Cronin received a letter in July 1835 and in a sworn affidavit claimed he had been targeted *'to intimidate him, being a Protestant, from locating on said land, in order to prevent him and other Protestants from making up the number of a Protestant Congregation'*, while the notice from 'Captin iou Rock [*sic*]' bade him 'stay where you are or else go to where you came from, I wish the devil swep [*sic*] all the Orangmen [*sic*] out of this, not to be troublin['] us'.[21] Similar notices instructed the tenantry around parts of Thurles not to pay their rents, claiming to draw their authority from 'the advice of OConnell and of your Priests'; these were further evidence of the existence of a political conspiracy between the Irish Catholic hierarchy and the Irish Catholic statesman.[22]

Agrarian violence in Tipperary had caused previous governments problems over the decade, including during Peel's stint as home secretary in 1830. The Duke of Northumberland, then lord lieutenant, attributed the violence in Tipperary to 'a disposition amongst the resident Gentry, to let their lands upon imprudent & impossible conditions & to demand prices which reckless peasant covenant, without a reasonable hope on their part ... that the pecuniary stipulation can ever be fulfilled'. Evictions, seizure of property, and 'that sanguinary hostility between Proprietor and occupant' most often were the result.[23] Peel criticised the inability of the local gentry to quell the collective action of peasants and planned to send in stipendiary magistrates whenever 'the Local Gentry shall appear to be inadequate to their duty'.[24] By 1835, one local magistrate was writing to Dublin Castle requesting, '[for] the future tranquillity of this Country', to hang three men convicted of conspiring to murder their landlord, and to display their remains in the centre of their home village or outside the hospital where the remaining conspirators resided. In doing so he hoped their very public deaths may 'ward off from this Country that terrific

[20] 24 July 1837, Outrage Reports, NAI, 1837/27/442; 20 February 1837, ibid., 1837/27/661.
[21] Information of James Cronin, 21 July 1835, NAI, CSORP 1835 Box 44, 2/45/1/2.
[22] [?] to Morpeth, 15 December 1835, ibid., 29/52.
[23] Northumberland to Peel, 23 January 1830, BL, Peel Papers MS 40327, f. 94.
[24] Peel to Northumberland, 14 July 1829, BL, Peel Papers MS 40327, f. 34.

system of assassination, which for so many years continues to prevail'.[25] Nevertheless, in a letter replying to the magistrates of Tipperary, Mulgrave refused to apply the Coercion Act in the county and instead stressed 'the generally improved tranquillity' there, all of which came to light after the Tory MP Col. Verner demanded the government publish its correspondence with the magistrates, along with the coroner's verdict for every death in the county between 1832 and 1836.[26]

By early April 1838, a group of magistrates assembled at Cashel wrote to Mulgrave to express their deep concern at the attempted assassination of three landlords, which left one of them dead and the other two seriously wounded. 'There are circumstances connected with these horrible facts illustrative of the state of society in this country', wrote the magistrates, declaring 'that in that district neither life nor property is safe; we therefore respectfully trust that your Excellency will put in force the strongest powers which the laws of the land permit in those districts'. The magistrates alleged that it had been widely known throughout the district that these assassinations were planned, but that the serious 'state of intimidation' in the area prevented the jury from bringing convictions.[27] The former Tory MP and judge, John Leslie Foster, confirmed to the Duke of Wellington that crime was markedly higher than the Whig government insisted; the discrepancy was in part due to the fact that the government sent all possible cases to the quarter sessions, 'so that a Calendar of 212 Prisoners at present indicates a much greater degree of Criminality'.[28]

The government responded with urgency to the magistrates' attacks. Thomas Drummond, the undersecretary, drafted a letter with the assistance of the solicitor general and a final revision by Mulgrave, defending government policy. In it, Drummond systematically contradicted the claim that juries had been intimidated at prior quarter sessions and assizes by quoting the stipendiary magistrates stationed throughout the county, all of whom denied that 'juries had ceased to be capable of discharging their important functions, from the apprehension of danger'. Using statistical data drawn from the previous five years, Drummond argued that trials and convictions of murder cases were above average. As Tipperary was often used as a cipher for the state of the country as a whole, Drummond was implying that increasing convictions signified a better

---

[25] J. P. Vokes to Gosset, 8 April 1835, NAI, CSORP 1835 Box 44, 4/48/17.

[26] 'Return of Number of Persons committed to Prison in County of Tipperary, 1832–35; Police Reports and Coroners' Inquests; Letter from Lord Lieutenant to Magistrates of Tipperary on Application for Coercion Act', P. P. (1836, vol. 42, no. 226).

[27] 'Tipperary County. A copy of correspondence which has recently taken place between Her Majesty's government and the magistrates of the county of Tipperary, relative to the disturbed state of that county', P. P. (1837–8, vol. 46, no. 735).

[28] Leslie Foster to Wellington, 21 March 1838, USSC, Wellington Papers, WP2/50/11.

working judiciary. What was most significant about the letter, however, was Drummond's insistence on the role that the landed gentry were playing in creating an environment where peasants responded with such violent collective action. As the great majority of serious outrages occurred as a result of issues related to land tenure, Drummond argued, it was not surprising that the peasantry acted violently when ejections per year had doubled in number between 1833 and 1837. Drummond continued:

> Property has its duties as well as its rights; to the neglect of those duties in times past is mainly to be ascribed that diseased state of society in which such crimes take their rise; and it is not the enactment or enforcement of statutes of extraordinary severity, but chiefly in the better and more faithful performance of those duties, and the more enlightened and humane exercise of those rights, that a permanent remedy for such disorders is to be sought.[29]

Although 'property has its duties' became the aphorism that gave this letter its fame, what arguably was more offensive to Tories, and more illustrative of Whig ideology concerning the party's Irish policy, was its suggestion that Irish outrage did not stem from the moral depravity of the peasantry but rather from the moral shortcomings of their landlords whose neglect of duty all but guaranteed the disorder of Irish society.[30] Much to the chagrin of their Tory opponents, the government's Irish administration did not believe harsher laws would fix Irish society or quell Irish outrage; only the development of a relationship born of mutual respect and trust between landlord and tenant would ultimately secure tranquillity.

The fracas that ensued after the publication of this letter was predictable, but it afforded conservative newspapers another opportunity to cast the government as not simply inept, but as wilfully ignoring the information provided by local magistrates on the 'real' state of affairs in Ireland.[31] The murder of Lord Norbury in January 1839, discussed at the beginning of Chapter 2, further propelled narratives of Irish depravity and government inaction. It operated as an ideal backdrop for Lord Roden to stage his direct confrontation with the Whigs over their Irish policy.

Robert Jocelyn, the third earl of Roden, has not been a subject of major study but is arguably the most important ultra-Tory of this period. His involvement with the Dolly's Brae incident in 1849, which saw the largest

---

[29] 'Copy of a letter to Lord Donoughmore', 22 May 1838, NLI, Larcom MSS, 645, emphasis added.

[30] This language also featured prominently in IRC's second report; see 'Railway Commission Report', 79–82.

[31] 'The Late Murder in Ireland', 4 May 1838, *Lincolnshire Chronicle*; 'Captain Drummond's Reply to the Tipperary Magistrates', *London Evening Standard*, 17 September 1838.

open confrontation between Orangemen and Catholics since the 1790s, led to his dismissal from the magistracy and his retreat from public affairs, which may go some way to explaining his relatively low profile; a lack of a clearly organised collection of his political papers does not help, either.[32] Nevertheless, in the 1830s and 1840s he was the leader of Anglo-Irish peers and a force for the maintenance of Protestant privilege. His family owned considerable land in counties Louth and Down. Religiously devout, Roden was the president of the Sunday School Society of Ireland and a benefactor of a number of proselytising organisations. He joined the Orange Order in 1831 in an attempt to create a united Protestant opposition to the effects of Catholic Emancipation, driven by his fear of the rising political power of Ireland's Catholics and their growing resistance to the collection of tithes.[33] When Wellington and Peel took over government after the dismissal of Melbourne's first government in 1834 by William IV, Roden seized the opportunity to rebuild a Protestant Ascendancy. Writing to Wellington, Roden fawned over the duke's return to power and 'the deliverance which we have at last had from the misrule of those who had nearly overwhelm'd the country in irretrievable ruin', while stressing the need for the duke to bring in 'firm and decided measures' to break agrarian unrest, and to appoint Protestants to key positions to demonstrate 'that their institutions will be preserved'.[34] When the Tory government moved forward with a non-sectarian Irish education plan, Roden wrote to Wellington as the defender of Protestantism in Ireland: 'In consequence to the answer which Sir Henry Harding[e] is reported to have given ... I shall be *obliged* to put a similar question to you ... trusting I shall receive a reply more likely to calm the minds of the Protestants of Ireland'.[35] By 1835, Roden was panicked at the thought of O'Connell's influence on Melbourne's government and believed Ireland had little to protect itself with but for the loyalty of 'our Protestant people'.[36] Consistently anti-Catholic and desirous of a return to the Protestant Ascendancy into which he had been born, Roden was a natural spokesman for Toryism's deepest fears concerning Ireland. And, while he was not wholeheartedly supported,[37] Roden's

---

[32] According to the tenth Earl, all of Roden's papers have been deposited at PRONI, and only exist in the form of worn and poorly reproduced reels of microfilm, MIC 147.

[33] Bridget Hourican, 'Robert Jocelyn, Third Earl of Roden', *Irish Dictionary of National Biography* (Dublin: Royal Irish Academy, 2009), http://dib.cambridge.org/viewReadPage.do?articleId=a4284.

[34] Roden to Wellington, 20 November 1835, *Wellington, Political Correspondence*, 44.

[35] Roden to Wellington, n. d. [3 March 1835], ibid., 489.

[36] Roden to Londonderry, 16 April 1835, PRONI, T3438/1.

[37] Wellington was sceptical of Roden's plans; see Wellington to Westmeath, 6 March 1839, USSC, Wellington MSS, WP2/57/64.

committee was the culmination of years of fear, criticism, and hyperbole about Irish outrages and their potential to destroy Ireland, Great Britain, and the British Empire.

### Roden and the Battle over Irish Outrages

Tempers in the House of Lords in the period leading up to Roden's motion had been particularly hostile. The ultra-Tory members assailed Mulgrave's use of the lord lieutenant's prerogative of mercy for prisoners. Peers raised the issue on five different occasions between the first sitting of Parliament on 5 February and Roden's motion on 21 March 1839.[38] Roden, Westmeath, the Earl of Charleville, Lord Lyndhurst, and even Lord Brougham (now no friend of the Whigs) challenged Mulgrave to defend his use of pardons in Ireland and raised a number of particular cases demonstrating its imprudence. In one case, Mulgrave granted a pardon to John Coughlan, a man sentenced to transportation for life, when the surgeon suggested that Coughlan was medically unfit for the journey. Within a short period of his commutation, however, Coughlan had allegedly raped a woman and had been rearrested.[39] While Mulgrave asserted that his use of the prerogative of mercy was no different than that of his predecessors, the ultra-Tory faction continued to harass him over individual cases that came to their attention and required Mulgrave to furnish official documentation from Dublin to support his arguments.[40]

Perhaps more problematically for the government, the Tories also attacked the appointment of Lord Ebrington as Ireland's incoming lord lieutenant. At the beginning of the year, Melbourne and Russell determined the necessity of reshuffling ministerial portfolios, which resulted in Lord Ebrington's appointment, as well as Mulgrave's as colonial secretary.[41] While a member of the House of Commons, during the debate on Irish tithe reform Ebrington raised his qualified support for the bill because he thought the transfer of payments from tenant to landlord might entice further reforms: 'the burden would be on those who were much better able to bear it, and who, he hoped, would carry on

---

[38] Hansard, 3rd ser., vol. 45, cols. 842–4, 25 February 1839; 907–16, 26 February 1839; 1261–2, 5 March 1839; vol. 46, cols. 10–25, 7 March 1839; 789–90, 18 March 1839.

[39] Hansard, 3rd ser., vol. 45, cols. 842–4, 25 February 1839.

[40] For example, see Normanby to Drummond, 27 February [1839], MC, Mulgrave MSS, M/267; Normanby to Drummond 10 March [1839], M/268; Drummond to Normanby, 14 March 1839, M/269.

[41] Other candidates were suggested for lord lieutenant, including Lord John Russell's brother, Lord Tavistock, and Lord Charlemont. See MacDonald to Morpeth, 17 February 1839, CH, Morpeth MSS, J19/1/22/85, f. 56.

the war with effect'.[42] On learning of Ebrington's appointment Lord Lyndhurst seized on this statement, which he changed to '"to render the war that was then against the Protestant church in Ireland more formidable"', in order to use it as proof that the government's avowed policy in Ireland was 'to wage war against the Established Church in Ireland, and ... against the Protestant Church of this country'.[43] Roden and other ultras piled on, and as a result Ebrington was required to defend his appointment on the day he took his seat in the Lords.[44]

Roden proposed his committee in the House of Lords on 21 March 1839, after considerable deliberation about when to make his case and with great secrecy. Despite his anxiety, Roden expressed his hope that if the vote carried it would reveal 'the most marvellous facts and proofs of the Iniquity of Lord Mulgrave's administration'.[45] In the House, Roden argued that matters in Ireland had never been worse, and that the tranquillity that the government trumpeted was 'but the tranquillity of death'. He continued:

[There is] a conspiracy in Ireland – a conspiracy systematic, organised, and secret, and which was directed against life and property of all who would not join it and support the treasonable objects which its members had in view. .... The Riband conspiracy was exactly the same as those of the Precursor Association ... separation from England, in which was involved the annihilation of the Protestant faith.[46]

Roden offered anecdote after anecdote of murder, assaults on Protestants, incendiary fires, and political violence. In his estimation, and in the opinion of his fellow Tory colleagues, the violence demonstrated that the Catholic population had organised itself into so-called 'Riband' or 'Ribbon' societies, which were secret, oath-bound, avowedly sectarian, and politically hostile to the political union with Britain. By connecting Ribbon conspiracies with O'Connell's newly created Precursor Association, a political society meant to encourage further concessions to Ireland, Roden underscored the widely asserted connection between O'Connell and popular violence on the one hand, and the Whigs' political connection to O'Connell on the other. Implicitly, Roden connected the Whigs to Irish outrages through this O'Connellite connection, while explicitly Roden condemned Mulgrave for his lax enforcement of law and order that benefitted O'Connell's political ends. Although

[42] Hansard, 3rd ser., vol. 44, col. 656, 26 July 1838.
[43] Hansard, 3rd ser., vol. 45, cols. 950–1, 28 February 1839.
[44] Hansard, 3rd ser., cols. 1144–9, 4 March 1839.
[45] Roden to Londonderry, 6 March 1839, PRONI, T3438/1.
[46] Hansard, 3rd ser., vol. 46, cols. 949, 964, 21 March 1839. The Precursor Association was O'Connell's new public association, which sought to put pressure on the government for further reform through the threat of advocating repeal.

a long debate followed Roden's accusations and motion for a committee, the result was essentially a foregone conclusion – the Lords had occupied a conspicuous position over the last four years as the champion of Conservatism in all Irish policy matters and the enduring muscle of Tory opposition to Melbourne's government. While it is questionable whether all Tories thought the motion a wise one, Wellington's support for the committee quashed any doubt.[47] Writing in a triumphant mood after the motion carried, Roden expressed his belief to his fellow ultra, Lord Londonderry, that the committee had the potential to strike 'the first Reel [*sic*] Blow' against the government, while Newcastle confided in his diary that he believed the committee 'will no doubt bring to light the Popish conspiracy + all its hideous <u>machinations</u>' and had the power to bring down the government.[48]

In the midst of the debate, Mulgrave combatted Roden's anecdotes of wanton violence with government statistics. Relying on the official returns of outrage sent from Drummond that 'show[ed] the constant attention of the government to the means of enforcing the law', Mulgrave demonstrated that both committals and convictions had proportionally increased during his time in office. Although it would seem that more committals to prison suggested an increase in criminal activity, Mulgrave countered that it rather demonstrated the positive effect the new constabulary force had had by carrying out more arrests. Additionally, the rate of convictions had increased dramatically in spite of the increase in committals. Whereas convictions in murder and manslaughter cases had only been at 27 per cent in 1832, by 1838 they had risen to 47 per cent. A similar increase was witnessed in the aggregate rate of convictions in all cases involving the endangering of life between 1832 and 1838, from roughly one in four cases reaching a guilty verdict in 1832, to one in every two cases by 1838. Mulgrave also referred to the most immediate returns of outrages to point out the gradual success of the government's policy of 'justice to Ireland'. Comparing the final three months of the calendar years 1837 and 1838, Mulgrave noted that outrages had dropped from 1,254 to 769, respectively. Although murders in the same period had increased slightly, from fifty-two to fifty-eight, the remaining outrages cited by Mulgrave showed a marked decline.

---

[47] Wellington to Peel, 23 March 1839, BL, Peel Papers, Add MS 40310, f. 259; Peel to Wellington, 25 March [1839], USSC, Wellington Papers, WP2/58/38–9; Hansard, 3rd. ser., vol. 46, cols. 1012–16, 21 March 1839. It is ironic that Roden's motion carried on such a small majority – only five votes – and seems to have been the result of Roden's ardent desire for secrecy. The Conservatives did not whip votes on the night of the motion and many Tories were not present. See Greville, *Greville Memoirs*, 1:152.

[48] Roden to Londonderry, n. d. [March 1839], DCRO, D/Lo/C/84 (12); Newcastle Diary, 23 March 1839, UNSC, Ne2 F 6/1, 19; emphasis in the original.

Although the Duke of Wellington complained that any time that Mulgrave could 'command the official documents ... [he] always had the best of the discussion', the impressive display of statistics made no difference in the vote, and the select committee was duly established.[49]

The Whigs needed to decide how best to respond. They considered four different options. First, they could submit to Roden's committee but remain in office. This option proved impossible because during the debate Mulgrave and Melbourne both framed the motion as a censure on the government's Irish administration, and therefore were unwilling to roll over and concede that their policies were damaging to Irish tranquillity. The second option was to resign. Not surprisingly, Mulgrave favoured this idea, as did some members of the cabinet. From his point of view it would be an advantage if ministers were to resign on a question – Ireland – that had been their great strength in office; as Greville put it, 'Ireland is the great strength of the present Government as it is the weak point of the Tories'.[50] Resigning over an Irish question would make things particularly difficult for the Tories to govern, lest Ireland break out in serious unrest. The majority of the cabinet, however, deemed this course too dangerous and worried how Tories might twist their own intentions to demonstrate that they never intended the committee as a question upon which the government should resign. Ministers considered a third option of creating a large number of liberal peers, thus fundamentally changing the political disposition of the upper house, but knew that the public would not acquiesce to such a radical step. Finally, the government could subject its Irish policy to the scrutiny of the House of Commons, which it considered the proper venue in which to determine the country's confidence in the government. Cabinet considered this the most attractive option, but also recognised it carried the greatest potential risk as it essentially challenged the Tories to throw them out of office. While ministers believed they could rely on the support of O'Connell and his Irish members, they felt less certainty with their position vis-á-vis English Radicals and even some English Whigs. Nevertheless, Russell determined to equate the Whigs' Irish policy with their overall fitness for government, and in so doing, demonstrated the centrality of Ireland to their overall governing ethos.[51]

In preparation for its defence, the government's Irish administration brought its case to the public. In Dublin, Drummond helped to organise a 'Grand National Meeting of the Friends of Liberal Government in Ireland', held at the Royal Theatre in Dublin on 11 April 1839.

[49] Wellington to Westmeath, 5 March 1839, USSC, Wellington MS, WP2/57/63.
[50] Greville, *The Greville Memoirs*, 1:153.    [51] Holland, *Holland House Diaries*, 393–4.

Attended by prominent members of the Irish aristocracy, as well as a number of Members of Parliament, the meeting was an opportunity to pass a resolution 'to support them [the Whigs] in a declaration of principle which they have made as regards Ireland'. Lord Fingal, one of the most popular of Ireland's aristocrats due in part to his Catholicism, remarked at length on the unifying effect Roden's motion had on Irish society. 'The move on the 21st of last month has had a good effect; it has brought forward that which sometimes lies dormant, namely, the energies of those of the highest rank . . . [and] has placed them at their proper place; it has brought them forward to support the people, and they no doubt will support them.' In the midst of one of the speeches a number of Orangemen tried to disrupt the meeting but were expelled from the venue by the constabulary – a symbolic acting-out of the promise of Whig government and the danger of the reintroduction of Conservative government on Orange principles.[52] The government also celebrated O'Connell's attendance, and his restrained speech, which oscillated between poking fun at the Conservatives trying to heckle him from the audience to affirming his commitment to the Whigs' agenda of 'equality and justice' towards Ireland.[53] O'Connell's Precursor Society had been stirring up unrest at the government's inability to adopt further reform. However, Ebrington had a close relationship with O'Connell and was convinced the latter would give up his newly formed society if the liberals publicly demonstrated that they shared a common cause in 'promoting Liberal government in Ireland'.[54] Although the meeting was a one-off event, it was ostensibly the kind of response O'Connell wanted from the government and he praised the Whigs 'repeating several times with emphasis: "I am a Ministerialist, I am a Ministerialist, I am an uncompromising Ministerialist."'[55] The meeting passed a petition to Parliament that affirmed the principles of Mulgrave's government, and called on the Commons to resist 'the attempts of any party to regain an ascendancy'.[56]

Inside Parliament, Lord John Russell prepared a motion of his own that would require the Commons to affirm the principles of the Whigs' Irish

[52] 'Great National Meeting', FJ, 12 April 1839.
[53] Drummond to Morpeth, April 1839, CH, Morpeth MSS, J19/1/23/2; 'Great National Meeting', FJ, 13 April 1839. In a letter before the meeting, O'Connell wrote to Mulgrave to encourage him to 'enlist once again the Reform force in order to be *able*, as you are willing, to add to the security of the Throne the *active* gratitude of the Irish people'. O'Connell to Normanby, 6 April 1839, in O'Connell, *Correspondence*, 6:229.
[54] Ebrington to Morpeth, 7 April 1839, CH, Morpeth MSS, J19/1/22/90; on Ebrington's friendship with O'Connell, see Morpeth to Mulgrave, 30 October 1835, MC, Mulgrave MSS, M/490; Geoghegan, *Liberator*, ix.
[55] Hugh Fortescue to Morpeth, n.d. [13 April 1839?], CH, Morpeth MSS, J19/1/23/4.
[56] 'Grand National Meeting', FJ, 13 April 1839.

policy. Initially, ministers debated among themselves how best to craft a resolution; whether to expand from Roden's initial purview of examining Irish agrarian violence to cover the last fifteen years, and thus provide a wider context for the fluctuation in Irish outrages under both parties, or whether to focus solely on the soundness of the Whigs' policy.[57] Russell opted for the latter course. Using a familiar narrative, he argued that the government had begun to undo the damage wrought on Ireland by Protestant Ascendancy and by the partiality of law and order that had alienated Ireland's population from British systems of justice. In the place of coercion, he argued, Mulgrave had brought about conciliation and equality in an attempt to bring the privileges of the British constitution to Irishmen, and while this work moved at a glacial pace, Russell argued that popular sentiment in Ireland and government statistics confirmed the positive effect it had had on society. Unsurprisingly, Russell articulated a very Whiggish narrative of steady movement towards greater liberty and progress in extending Ireland's equality in matters of law and order with Great Britain. He noted:

We have endeavoured to introduce a friendly relation between this country and that part of the United Kingdom … to unite by affection, to unite by feelings of good will and love, the people of this country and the people of Ireland – to make the whole United Kingdom stronger against all its enemies – to found the government of Ireland, as the Government of England has long been founded, upon opinion, upon affection, upon good will; and that if the Ministry should fail, it will fail in an attempt to knit together the hearts of her Majesty's subjects.[58]

Robert Peel's response to Russell's motion was complicated. Soon after Roden's motion, Peel identified the political trouble the Conservatives found themselves in. By 1839 the Whigs had grown politically weak, and the press were satirising their desire to hold onto 'place and power' without the real support of the country. The Radicals had grown frustrated with the unwillingness of the government to advance further concessions on electoral reform.[59] Still, Peel recognised that an Irish question could work at 'rallying their [Whig] friends on some totem on which they

---

[57] Ebrington to Morpeth, 7 April 1839, CH, Morpeth Papers, J19/1/22/90; Ebrington to Morpeth, 10 April 1839, J19/1/22/94. Somewhat ironically, Peel had thought Roden had originally intended a general committee on Irish crime over the past decade and he was none too pleased when he found out about the focus on Mulgrave's tenure; see Peel to Wellington, 25 March [1839], USSC, Wellington MSS, WP2/58/38–9.

[58] Hansard, 3rd ser., vol. 47, col. 39, 15 April 1839.

[59] Hilton, *Mad, Bad, and Dangerous?*, 500–2; Ian Newbould, 'Sir Robert Peel and the Conservative Party', 544. I disagree with a number of the arguments in Newbould's analysis, but he is right to identify this episode as particularly important in Tory policy moving forward.

agree'.[60] However, on Irish matters the Tory Party had a problem. On the one hand, they benefitted politically from the Whigs solving Irish questions while labouring under the current political constraints. Partially restricted by the Lords' obstruction, Russell had been forced to moderate his Irish bills if they stood any chance of passing – evidenced by the tithe bill, which had been passed without an appropriation clause, and the passage of a bill of municipal reform that had included a much higher threshold for enfranchisement than had been originally intended. If the roles had been reversed, however, Peel's ability to deal with Irish grievances would have been hamstrung by a vocal ultra-Tory minority – still sore from his 'betrayal' over Catholic Emancipation and therefore unwilling to allow moderation in Irish matters – and by O'Connell, who would mobilise Irish popular opinion. Charles Greville noted this; how it was in 'Peel's interest that Irish questions should assume a shape, and make such a progress, before he returns to office, as should render their final adjustment inevitable'.[61] On the other hand, Peel found agreeing with Russell's motion politically impossible lest he lose the confidence of his own party. Thus, Peel was in the unenviable position of wanting to stand against the government while also seeing the potential consequences of attempting to throw out the government on an Irish question. As a result, Peel compromised and pursued a third way, offering an amendment to Russell's motion for an up-or-down vote on Irish policy that instead took a principled stand against the propriety of the House of Commons expressing its opinion on a legislative decision of the House of Lords.[62] In other words, he did what many politicians do and answered a different question than the one being asked.

The debate stretched on for five days in the House of Commons, which demonstrated just how much was at stake for the Whigs. With a razor-thin majority, a complicated relationship with O'Connell, and an even more fraught one with English Radicals, the ministry needed everyone to rally behind it. Considering the speeches of many English Radicals, it seems that an Irish question was the only one that could rally the disparate parties together. Joseph Hume argued that 'the vote which was to be given this night, was no vote of confidence in the Ministry … [but] was confined exclusively to the policy they had pursued in Ireland'.[63] Fellow Radical George Grote complained that he expected further reform from Peel as much as he did from 'finality Jack', but in the end agreed to vote with the government, 'believing sincerely, that it deserves the esteem and

[60] Peel to Wellington, 25 March [1839], USSC, Wellington MSS, WP2/58/38–9.
[61] Greville, *The Greville Memoirs*, 1:153.
[62] Hansard, 3rd ser., vol. 47, col. 39–77, 15 April 1839.
[63] Hansard, 3rd ser., vol. 47, col. 262, 18 April 1839.

imitation, and that it has worked beneficially for the Irish people'.[64] Lord Holland lamented in his diary about the pains Radicals took to distinguish their approval of Mulgrave's policy in Ireland from their view of the general policy of Melbourne's government by hurling political insults along the way.[65] Even the ministry's daily, *The Morning Chronicle*, praised the Radicals' rhetoric, pushing for greater reform: 'The victory will be fruitless – even as to Ireland it will be eventually fruitless – unless it be followed up by decisive adoption of a policy ... the banner of progressive reform ... [which is] the only banner round which the country can be rallied for the discomfiture of Toryism'.[66] Radicals had identified Russell's weakness and hoped that their support on Irish affairs (which they had always given) would extract some movement towards greater reform in the future, such as on the issue of the ballot or shorter parliaments.[67] O'Connell thought this possible, too, writing to FitzPatrick that Russell's success in the Commons had resulted in 'talk of a change in the detail of the Ministry, now in its principle sure to radicalise it a little'.[68] Though Radicals would be disappointed in the future, their votes of confidence in Russell led to a majority in favour of the government of twenty-four, which proved much higher than originally expected. The Whigs commanded the House of Commons, and although this did not stop Roden's committee from meeting, it did undermine its ability to deliver any decisive blows against the Whigs.

## The Lords' Committee on Irish Crime and Outrage

The Lords' Committee on Irish Crime and Outrage called over forty witnesses across forty-three days of meetings between April and July 1839. The product of its labour was a 1,600-page document of compiled witness testimony, along with copies of official returns of outrage, correspondence between magistrates, landlords, and Dublin Castle, and pages of evidence concerning the early release of Irish prisoners in all thirty-two counties by the lord lieutenant between 1835 and 1839.[69] Those looking for the opinion of the committee concerning Irish crime and outrage would be sorely disappointed with this document, as the chairman, Lord Wharncliffe, made clear that the committee '[thought] it

---

[64] Hansard, 3rd ser., vol. 47, col. 183. Lord John Russell earned the moniker 'finality Jack' when he opposed efforts by English Radicals to amend the 1832 Reform Act, describing it as a 'final measure'. See Hansard, 3rd ser., vol. 39, col. 70, 20 November 1837.

[65] Holland, *Holland House Diaries*, 394.

[66] 'The Morning Chronicle', *The Morning Chronicle*, 19 April 1839.

[67] Newbould, 'Study in Failure?', 543–4.

[68] O'Connell to FitzPatrick, n.d. [c.20 April 1839], O'Connell, *Correspondence*, 6:233.

[69] 'Select Committee on State of Ireland'.

desirable that the Evidence given by those Witnesses should be submitted to the House ... unaccompanied by any Comment or Opinion upon the Part of the Committee'.[70] Instead, the committee suggested that the House of Lords should consider whether 'the Committee shall resume its labours in the next Session of Parliament'.[71] The evidence presented is chock-full of rumour, insinuation, and defensive testimony, and the evidence is presented in a raw and disjointed state. This dissonance reflects the composition of the committee, roughly divided between the two parties, with a majority in favour of the Tories. The document presents the committee's questions anonymously, giving the impression of a disembodied, internally coherent, singular voice asking each witness questions. The questions themselves, however, are far from congruous in their tone, which suggests that individual members from both parties may have followed up each other's questions by attempting either to reset a witness's testimony to fit their own agenda, undermine a previous Lord's question, or call into question the evidence of a witness. Therefore, when referring to the report it is vital to assess the content of the testimony as well as the context and tone of the anonymous inquisitors.

Although the House of Commons had already passed a vote of confidence in the Whigs' Irish administration, for the majority of the committee its aim was a rather simple one – it was an opportunity to air all the miscues and missteps in Irish policy over the last four years, along with a chance to call witnesses whose evidence could undermine the government's narrative of increased tranquillity. In short, the committee was intended to embarrass the government and lay the groundwork for a reversion to patterns of governance in accordance with Tory predilections. As a result, the committee attempted to exploit Col. Shaw Kennedy's resignation from the constabulary, confrontations between government-appointed constables and local magistrates, the targeting of Protestants, the intimidation of jurors, the unwillingness to pay tithes to the Church of Ireland, and the existence of a countrywide conspiracy of oath-bound Catholic secret societies, especially the Ribbonmen/Riband men.

Members of the committee were particularly keen to establish a narrative that described the development of an oath-bound secret society that had been allowed to run wild throughout the country. Although the idea of a nationwide conspiracy seems rather fanciful, the

[70] Lord Wharncliffe, draft report, 'Select Committee on the State of Ireland in Respect of Crime', WSRO, Goodwood Collection, MS 681.

[71] 'Select Committee on State of Ireland', iii. See also, Hansard, 3rd ser., vol. 49, cols. - 1275–1385, 6 August 1839.

country's history of both agrarian and political secret societies was evidence enough to justify the committee's insinuations, which were only bolstered by the idea that O'Connell controlled both the ministry and Ireland's peasantry, aided by the hierarchy of the Catholic Church. To demonstrate that the government had fallen asleep at the wheel (or worse) and allowed a grassroots secret society to develop throughout the country, members of the committee pressed the issue with most of their witnesses. And, with many of those witnesses, the evidence was rather damning. Even those with a generally positive disposition towards the government testified to the rising influence of Ribbonism in the countryside. George Warburton, a veteran of the constabulary, a magistrate, and most recently a deputy inspector of the reformed constabulary, would not concede that the government was withholding aid that would expose Ribbonism; however, he did confess that that organisation's membership was continually increasing in number, and that it was politically motivated and centrally organised. When pressed as to whether there was a central body controlling the local societies, Warburton could see it no other way: 'They must have emanated from some Head. There have been several Times mentioned to me different Places for the Head Quarters; Belfast ... Armagh ... Dublin ... but the Truth is, that the Matter was so mysteriously conducted that I believe the Parties themselves knew nothing of the Source from whence the System sprang or the Orders emanated.'[72] When pressed on the political aspirations of the society, and whether its members shared O'Connell's enthusiasm for Repeal, Warburton referred to a case in Co. Meath in which a man had been arrested while on a mission to post notices from Navan to Derry 'calling upon the People to imitate the Friends of Liberty in Canada, and to rise and shake off the Yoke that had so long oppressed them'.[73] The new inspector general, Duncan McGregor, though reticent about Ribbonism's scope and aim, also believed that the organisation was probably spread across much of the country, and that its subscribers willingly took orders from some authority, whether locally or nationally.[74]

Behind the scenes Roden worked to gather intelligence on Ribbon activity that he could bring before the committee with examples of the society's insurrectionary purpose. In late April Roden, along with more than a dozen other Anglo-Irish ultra-Tories, agreed to pay up to £50 each for a professional agent to gather information and 'prepare the business which must be brought before the Committee'.[75] Rev. J. M. Charlton, an

[72] 'Select Committee on State of Ireland', 58.
[73] 'Select Committee on State of Ireland', 79.
[74] 'Select Committee on State of Ireland', 129.
[75] 'Sub List, Ex Committee', April 20, 1839, PRONI, MIC 147/7, f. 281.

Anglican curate in Kingscourt, Co. Cavan, replied to a letter Roden had sent out in early May 1839, apparently soliciting information about Ribbon activity in Ulster. Rev. Charlton reported on intelligence from a recent convert, Arthur Brannigan, who had previously been a deputy county master of Ribbonism in Monaghan before becoming 'a Scripture Reader and a man of sound Christian principles and conduct'. Allegedly, Brannigan had observed provincial meetings in Armagh and county and parish meetings at which new members had been initiated, and had witnessed 'plans [being] concerted for threatening, beating and assassinating Protestants and others, obnoxious to this Society', and the collection of funds for 'the purpose of buying arms'.[76] Another correspondent with Roden, Rev. C. Beaufort, wrote with news that two prominent farmers in counties Leitrim and Monaghan had been arrested in connection with their Ribbonism, one of whom had a brother employed as a 'clerk of the crown', as well as the arrest of a man in Co. Tyrone who had been found in possession of papers demonstrating 'a conspiracy of great extent, reaching beyond Ireland to Liverpool Manchester + Glasgow'. Beaufort lamented that Roden's committee had already finished gathering evidence and hoped they would resume meeting, because 'this is a matter that ought to be sifted to the bottom'.[77] While it may be easy to attribute these stories to tinfoil-hat conspiracy theories, in fact they are indicative of a focussed political narrative that received the wide support of the Anglo-Irish gentry members who were at the head of the nineteenth-century social order. These narratives, which represent probably only a fraction of what Roden received, stressed points that he clearly believed to be true and wanted to publicise – the existence of a widespread violent political conspiracy that was spread across Ireland and into Great Britain and that targeted Protestants, had revolutionary aspirations, and had enmeshed people employed in low-level state bureaucracy. At the end of the committee's summer meetings taking testimony, Roden believed their work had barely scratched the surface and the committee should meet again the following session to continue inquiries into 'many most material Branches of the greatest Importance to the Elucidation of the State of Ireland in respect of Crime'.[78]

Resident magistrates and landlords who testified before Roden's committee were unabashed in their concern about Ribbonism's influence, and the committee provided a platform for fearmongering. Henry Wilson Rowan, a resident magistrate of Co. Down who had previously served in

[76] Rev. J. M. Charlton to Roden, 27 May 1839, ibid., f. 285–7.
[77] Rev. C. Beaufort to Roden, n. d. [c. October 1839], ibid., f. 343–4.
[78] Roden, draft report, 'Select Committee on the State of Ireland in Respect of Crime', WSRO, Goodwood Collection, MS 681.

a number of other counties, provided ample material about the dangers of Ribbonism and the way in which the government's negligence was allowing the society to flourish. When asked about the objective of the organisation, Rowan gave a list that included the overthrow of the British government, an end to Protestantism in Ireland, the expropriation of all estates previously forfeited, and the eventual establishment of a Catholic king of Ireland. Although the notion of a Catholic king reigning in Ireland belonged more to the 1730s than the 1830s, Rowan's testimony confirmed many of the worst fears of men like Roden. Worse still, Rowan believed the Catholic Church's hierarchy was orchestrating the secret society, and questioned the veracity of the clergy's opposition: 'I should say that that [a denouncement] is considered by the society to be a superficial Denunciation'.[79] Other witnesses testified to the characteristic difference between the priests of the older generation, who had been educated abroad, and the younger generation from lower-class backgrounds and who had been educated at Maynooth, who were considered politically radical and had spread out across parishes in Ireland.[80] Members of the committee referred to cases in which the prisoner charged for an outrage was a priest, or had been assisted by the priesthood, attempting to connect the clergy to the pernicious influence of Ribbonism.[81] Although many witnesses, especially those connected with the constabulary, testified that the clergy had always aided in discovering potential Ribbonmen in their parishes as well as ostracising those enrolled in the society by refusing them confession, absolution, or the Eucharist, many on the committee continued to put stock in the clergy's duplicity.

The threat of Ribbonmen infiltrating the ranks of the constabulary arguably unnerved committee members more than any other danger. This worry was nothing new – politicians and Ireland's gentry had long objected to Catholics owning guns and worried about the loyalty of the largely Catholic militia leading up to, during, and after the rebellion of 1798.[82] Whereas in the past Catholics may have been armed, for example in the Volunteer movement of 1782, this was at the discretion of their landlords. Therefore, even if conservative or sectarian landlords were opposed to their fellow landlords arming Catholics, at the very least those Catholics were well known to their landlords and were rooted

[79] 'Select Committee on State of Ireland', 140, 145.
[80] 'Select Committee on State of Ireland', 522. More on the Maynooth controversy in the section 'Conclusion: Betrayal of the Irish Protestants and the End of Peel's Party'.
[81] 'Select Committee on State of Ireland', 616.
[82] Allan Blackstock, 'The Irish Yeomanry and the 1798 Rebellion', in *1798: A Bicentenary Perspective*, ed. Thomas Bartlett (Dublin: Four Courts Press, 2003), 334.

within the community. Similarly, local magistrates had appointed constables prior to 1836, and again, if any Catholics were admitted to the constabulary, it was assumed they must be of good standing in their community to garner a magistrate's patronage. Now, however, all responsibility for appointments lay with the government, a point exploited by members of the committee. According to its testimony, the class of persons enrolled in the constabulary ensured its corruption:

2042. Have you ever know any Policemen in Riband Societies? – It has been stated to me by a Ribandman, that there were a good many among those recently introduced who are Ribandmen. I refer to some who have been appointed within those Six or Eight Months.

2050. Did you not report it to the Government? – I did not. I have no Doubt there are many Ribandmen in the Police; I cannot see how it can be otherwise.

2051. Why do you consider it hardly possible it can be otherwise? – I think, from the Class of Persons now introduced into the Police, and from the Number of Individuals who are Ribandmen throughout the Country, there must be some occasionally appointed Members of the Police who were previously Ribandmen.

2262. You only state, from the Information of other Persons, that there were Ribandmen in the Police? – Their names and Residences have been stated to me; the Persons who recommended them (*almost all Priests*), and the Grounds of their being recommended.[83]

Other witnesses told similar stories of Ribbon infiltration into the constabulary, and that the men now appointed 'are inferior to what we used to get'.[84]

These answers highlight two important criticisms of the government's Irish administration ultra-Tories were keen to advance. First, as the responsibility for all appointments now lay with officials in Dublin Castle, they should also be held responsible for allowing the riff-raff of Irish society into the constabulary. Second, the testimony implicated the government in seeking the counsel of the wrong members of Irish society for prospective appointments by listening to the suggestions of priests. The decision to seek the advice of Ireland's Catholic clergy rather than Ireland's Protestant gentry signified all that was wrong with the government – replacing the long-standing and time-honoured role of the propertied in favour of religious leaders who were considered by many Anglo-Irish as compromised proponents of a superstitious religion. More practically, the government's Irish administration's embrace of the Catholic clergy, as well as of Ireland's Catholic propertied and middle classes, signified a betrayal by the British government, as it replaced the Protestant Ascendancy with a Catholic one.

[83] 'Select Committee on State of Ireland', 168–9, 188, emphasis added.
[84] 'Select Committee on State of Ireland', 247.

Those committee members intent on smearing the government's Irish administration did all they could to steer witnesses towards conclusions that condemned Mulgrave's government. Had crime increased? According to these witnesses it had, and in fact was worse now than in any time in recent memory. When asked by a member whether outrage was more or less prevalent than four years ago, William Fausset, a magistrate in Co. Sligo, stated: 'It has been far worse for the last Four Years than it has been for Twenty Years.' Another witness, John Hatton, chief constable of Co. Meath, believe the Ribbon conspiracy worse in the past five years. The Earl of Donoughmore, the lord lieutenant of Co. Tipperary, considered his county in a far worse state than it had been in previous years, too, and believed the rights of property holders were being impeded.[85]

Other witnesses simply disagreed. Arthur Moore, a judge in the Court of Common Pleas, drew on his twenty years of experience and testified that he perceived 'a general Tendency to moral and a manifest physical Improvement in the Appearance of the Country'. A stipendiary magistrate in Co. Wexford described the last four years as 'very peaceable', while numerous other government officials, including those connected with the constabulary, believed the increase in government vigilance had resulted in a significant decrease in criminal activity.[86] Both sets of witnesses relied on their own opinions and observations, or worse, on second-hand accounts and hearsay. Thus, while the whole ordeal of taking testimony that exposed potential conspiracies and government blunders was not positive for the government's Irish administration, Roden's committee could not produce any definitive testimony to prove that crime and outrage had increased during Mulgrave's tenure as lord lieutenant.

The instrument the government possessed that trumped hearsay, rumour, or mere opinion was the numerical data drawn from the Outrage Reports, which they argued demonstrated a picture of Irish society where outrage was declining rather than increasing. Tories remained sceptical of the veracity of the data that government quoted, but the general effect of 'scientific' data in shaping debate was crucial.[87]

---

[85] 'Select Committee on State of Ireland', 217, 240, 940; James Hill to Lord Donoughmore, 25 March 1839, TCD, Donoughmore Papers, G/27/5.

[86] 'Select Committee on State of Ireland', 1240, 1249; Matthew Barrington's memorandum 'Committee on the State of Ireland' offers a compelling narrative about the non-political nature of outrages and an interpretation of the reduction in criminal activity as a result of government activity. See Matthew Barrington, 'Committee on the State of Ireland', NLI, Monteagle Papers, MS 13,357/21.

[87] Jefferies Kingsley to Wellington, 15 March 1839, USSC, Wellington MS, WP2/58/8; 'Morning Chronicle', *Morning Chronicle*, 5 August 1839.

The task of compiling and deploying this data was left to Undersecretary Thomas Drummond. Drummond's central position in the bureaucratic machinery of Dublin Castle, where he touched nearly every paper that entered or exited the building, meant that not only could he refute the tall tales of other witnesses, but he could also command the official returns to prove the positive effects of government activity. Some questioned the propriety of allowing Drummond to appear before the committee. Ebrington worried about Drummond having to subject himself to 'the ordeal of any questions that the ardent malignants of Lyndhurst, Philpotts, Brougham can get at for purposes of ... embarrassment', but admitted that Drummond was eager to refute the assertions made by other witnesses and to present the strengths of Mulgrave's government 'before the public'.[88] Prior to appearing, Inspector General McGregor wrote Drummond urging him to refute all of H. W. Rowan's claims about Ribbon infiltration of the constabulary. Drummond also corresponded with the Catholic Archbishop of Dublin, Daniel Murray, concerning the clergy's response to the potential presence of Ribbonmen in various parishes, and received assurances that the priests would report any nefarious activity in their congregations.[89]

Drummond's testimony, corroborated by table after table of statistics, demonstrated three separate points. First, and most straightforwardly, his testimony highlighted that many of the most serious crimes had diminished year to year since 1835 (see Table 5.1). Second, taking a more longitudinal view, Drummond tried to establish a decline in crime over the previous ten years by comparing mean averages of committals to gaol in 1826, 1827, and 1828 with 1836, 1837, and 1838. Third, Drummond showed how the government was now more successful in securing convictions than it had been in any previous period.

Drummond's first and most important task was to refute the entire premise of the committee by demonstrating that crime had decreased rather than increased during Mulgrave's tenure as lord lieutenant. Using Outrage Reports for the period 1836–8 and the constabulary returns from previous periods, Drummond's statistics showed that major crimes like murder, firing at persons, serious assault, and rape had declined since 1835, many of them consistently year over year. Although members of the committee could point to the alarming number of homicides and the relatively stable number in the robbery of arms as causes for serious

---

[88] Ebrington to Morpeth, 28 May 1839, CH, Morpeth Papers, J19/1/23/53. Drummond himself was not happy with the course taken by the government regarding Roden's committee, but was now focussed on how 'to make the best of a bad business'. Drummond to Morpeth, 30 May 1839, ibid., J19/1/23/56.

[89] McGregor to Drummond, 8 June 1839, TNA, CO 904/7/255; Archbishop Murray to Drummond, 9 June 1839, ibid., CO 904/7/257.

Table 5.1 *Number of serious offences, 1835–9*

| Crime | 1835 | 1836 | 1837 | 1838 | 1839 | Percentage difference 1835/1839 % |
|---|---|---|---|---|---|---|
| Homicide | 266 | 235 | 231 | 215 | 245 | −8 |
| Firing at persons | 90 | 81 | 65 | 81 | 55 | −39 |
| Serious or aggravated assault | 1229 | 1235 | 967 | 945 | 855 | −30 |
| Rape or intent to commit rape | 309 | 209 | 119 | 106 | 108 | −65 |
| Robbery | 889 | 901 | 748 | 534 | 548 | −38 |
| Incendiary fires | 564 | 539 | 327 | 518 | 489 | −13 |
| Demand or robbery of arms | 184 | 196 | 173 | 202 | 196 | 7 |
| Illegal meetings | 239 | 232 | 34 | 62 | 74 | −69 |
| Firing into dwellings | 102 | 107 | 28 |  | 63 | −38 |

Source: 'Select Committee on State of Ireland', P. P. (1839, vols. 11–12, no. 486), 1076

concern and evidence of a violent and politically motivated conspiracy, significant reductions in every other category made that argument rather unconvincing. Even though crime in those two categories may not have decreased from levels in 1835, Drummond underscored that over a ten-year period they had fallen considerably. Using population data collected from Ireland's recent railway commission, which had estimated Ireland's population at 8,523,000 in 1839, Drummond controlled for the population difference between the two data sets by increasing the number of committals in the 1826–8 period in proportion to the rate of population increase, which he conservatively estimated at roughly 15 per cent. Table 5.2 shows these comparative figures. Murder and manslaughter both decreased over that period, by 10 and 46 per cent respectively, while other serious offences such as arson also declined. On the other hand, the rates of a number of other categories of crime, most prominently assaults, attacking homes, and riots increased dramatically. Drummond argued that the increase in these crimes, 'minor Offences', demonstrated the vigilance of the new police force acting throughout the Irish countryside and also in the city of Dublin. 'It will be seen that in all the minor Classes of Crime to which I have alluded there is a large Increase, but a Decrease upon the aggravated Offences, proving most clearly that the Increase upon the former Heads arises from the Vigilance of the Police.'[90] Drummond concluded that not only were the police more attentive in their apprehension of criminals for minor offences but that the crown

[90] 'Select Committee on State of Ireland', 1079.

Table 5.2 *Comparative rates of various outrages between 1826 and 1838*

| Crime | Average 1826–1828 | Average with addition of one seventh for population between 1827 and 1837 | Average of 1836, 1837, 1838 | Column 3 compared to Column 2 | | Percentage increase or decrease % |
|---|---|---|---|---|---|---|
| | | | | Increase | Decrease | |
| Murder | 505 | 577 | 521 | | 56 | −10 |
| Manslaughter | 81 | 93 | 50 | | 43 | −46 |
| Assault with intent to murder | 71 | 38 | 115 | 27 | | −31 |
| Conspiracy to murder | 21 | 24 | 17 | | 7 | −29 |
| Sexual offences | 302 | 345 | 304 | | 41 | −12 |
| Abduction | 53 | 61 | 32 | | 29 | −47 |
| Assaults | 4,763 | 5,443 | 6,533 | 1,090 | | 20 |
| Burglary | 256 | 293 | 129 | | 164 | −56 |
| Arson | 64 | 73 | 32 | | 41 | −56 |
| Killing and maiming cattle | 13 | 15 | 13 | | 2 | −13 |
| Robbery of arms | 24 | 27 | 36 | 9 | | 33 |
| Administering oaths | 50 | 57 | 52 | | 5 | −9 |
| Attacking homes | 72 | 82 | 142 | 60 | | 73 |
| Riot, breach of the peace | 861 | 984 | 1958 | 974 | | 99 |
| Appearing armed | 14 | 16 | 20 | 4 | | 25 |
| Housebreaking, sacrilege & c. | 559 | 638 | 90 | | 548 | −86 |
| Taking forcible possession | 142 | 162 | 178 | 16 | | 10 |
| Cattle, horse, pig stealing | 767 | 877 | 578 | | 299 | −34 |
| Larceny | 3,311 | 3,784 | 5,624 | 1,840 | | 49 |

Source: 'Select Committee on State of Ireland', P. P. (1839, vols. 11–12, no. 486), 1099

prosecutors were now more successful in convicting those accused of aggravated offences.

Figure 5.1 shows the conviction rates for murders, assaults, house attacks, riots, and burglaries between 1831 and 1838. It shows that a number of serious crimes saw increased conviction rates, as

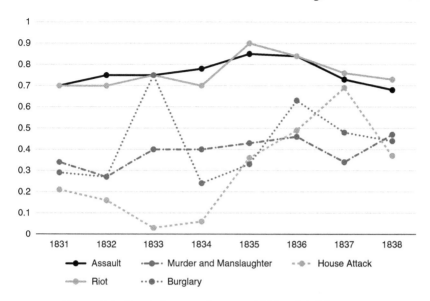

Figure 5.1  Conviction rates between 1831 and 1838

Drummond argued, especially crimes like house attacks. Convictions for murder and manslaughter also saw a slight increase from 37 per cent in 1831 to a high of 46 per cent in 1836 and 1838. Figure 5.2 reproduces the number of committals, which confirmed Drummond's argument concerning the increased activity of the police in arresting offenders for minor offences, with a proportional decline in major crimes such as murder and manslaughter.[91] Drummond's statistics supported the evidence of many of the crown solicitors and judges called before the committee. They stressed that generally crime had decreased because the government had been more vigilant in prosecuting faction fights at fairs (categorised as 'riots'), while also reporting that they had witnessed a marked decrease in the number of major crimes, such as murders, on their calendars.

The committee called Drummond to testify on three separate occasions, which included an extensive examination of the supposed Ribbon conspiracy, which he dismissed, and the above-referenced testimony on

---

[91] The figure excludes 'assaults' because these numbered in the thousands, which would skew the scale of the figure. Additionally, in 1837 the constabulary office decided to reclassify some assaults, removing them from the 'outrages' designation; thus, committals in assaults dropped from 6,533 in 1836 to 3,136 in 1837. The government was criticised for manipulating the figures. See 'Select Committee on State of Ireland', 1092–3 for data.

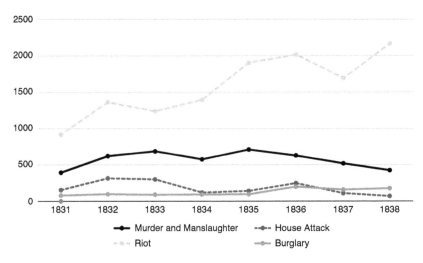

Figure 5.2   Number of committals between 1831 and 1838

comparative levels of outrages. His testimony was thoroughly praised by the government and celebrated in the popular press once the Lords' report was published in August 1839. Lord Spencer, who had previously employed Drummond as his private secretary, wrote to Drummond after his testimony concluded and informed him of how the testimony before the committee had raised his reputation 'immensely'.[92] The *Morning Chronicle* characterised Drummond's testimony as decisive, evidence 'which shatters into atoms the whole of the Tory case against the Irish government, and establishes ... the fact of the improvement of Ireland in every respect, moral and social; that improvement being mainly owing to the exertions of the libelled administration of Lord Normanby'.[93] Similarly, in Ireland, the *Freeman's Journal* believed Drummond's testimony invaluable because 'it shivered all the lies and calumnies of the Tories in fragments, whilst it afforded the best proof of the wisdom of the present ... policy of our rulers'.[94] Both the *Morning Chronicle* and the *Freeman's Journal* printed extensive excerpts of Drummond's testimony, including his refutation of Ribbon conspiracies in the constabulary and on the increase of agrarian outrages.

[92] O'Brien, *Thomas Drummond*, 354.
[93] 'Morning Chronicle', *Morning Chronicle*, 5 August 1839.
[94] 'The Lord's Committee – Mr Drummond's Evidence', FJ, 7 August 1839. See also 'Mr Drummond's Evidence', FJ, 16 August 1839.

Nevertheless, as convincing as Drummond's evidence may have been in favour of government policy, it did little to arrest the parliamentary political theatre of the House of Lords. Lord Brougham moved that the House of Lords censure Mulgrave's Irish government in spite of attempts to dissuade him. The vote was a foregone conclusion in a venue that for the previous four years had operated as the centre of organised opposition to the Whig's Irish policy, carrying by a margin of over thirty votes (86–52).[95] The *Leeds Intelligencer*, the conservative newspaper of record in Yorkshire, noted 'the blow inflicted upon Ministers by this motion is a severe one'. Their verdict on the implicit conclusions of the committee highlighted just how dependent Melbourne's government had become on O'Connell:

No doubt, then, that *in Ireland*, under O'Connell's reign, the principle laid down by Lord Brougham, and affirmed by the House of Peers, would be highly '*inconvenient*' to a Minister [Mulgrave] who looks to the Agitator for support, and who dare not offend a Romish Priest. . . . O'Connell, who threatens to dismember the empire, who keeps the United Kingdom in a fever, and extorts pence from the poor through his agents the priests, on pain of punishment here and hereafter, is cherished and petted, admitted to state secrets, and set above the law of the land.[96]

### The End of Whig Government

The Whig government hobbled along for another two years, but a variety of circumstances demonstrated its lack of parliamentary power and waning popular support. Shortly after Roden's motion and the subsequent debate in the House of Commons, the government brought forward a measure to suspend the constitution of Jamaica. The ensuing debate and vote left the government with a majority of five, and included the defection of the English Radical Joseph Hume, MP for Kilkenny, along with a couple other Irish members.[97] The Whigs considered this majority too small to govern effectively and tendered their resignation to the Queen.[98] The Queen sent for Wellington, who advised her to ask Peel to form a government. Although the Queen ultimately prevented Peel from forming a government due to the so-called 'bedchamber crisis', when she refused him the right to change some of her ladies-in-waiting, the intervening few days of uncertainty suggest how a new Conservative

---

[95] Hansard, 3rd ser., vol. 49, col. 1382, 6 August 1839.
[96] 'The Intelligencer', *Leeds Intelligencer*, 10 August 1839. Emphasis in the original.
[97] Hume's defection left O'Connell raging and plotting to run for Kilkenny himself; see O'Connell to FitzPatrick, 7 May 1839, O'Connell, *Correspondence*, 6: 237–8.
[98] Holland, *Holland House Diaries*, 394–6.

254    5 Ireland and the Tory Imagination

government would have changed course in its Irish policy. In an undated memorandum Peel appeared to be uncertain about his Irish appointments, but noted the need to 'Remove Drummond at all events' as undersecretary.[99] On 9 May, Stanley wrote Peel with suggestions for Drummond's replacement – 'After I left you last night in thinking of Drummond's situation, the name of my late Private Secretary, Jas. Earle occurred to me'.[100] Although it is unsurprising that Peel would want to get rid of the civil servant who had been so influential in implementing the Whigs' political programme in Ireland, this nevertheless underscores Drummond's influence in Dublin. Peel also listed Thomas De Grey, the second Earl De Grey, as the Conservative government's designate for lord lieutenant. Although Peel's thinking is not entirely clear regarding this appointment, De Grey's marriage to Lady Henrietta Frances Cole, the daughter of the first Earl of Enniskillen – a prominent ultra-Tory 'Orange' scion – would have reassured the right wing of Peel's party into thinking their position was safe after the Mulgrave–O'Connell onslaught of the past four years.[101]

The Whigs came back to office after the Queen refused Peel the right to change some of her ladies-in-waiting, but their reliance on English Radicals and Irish MPs was now more apparent than ever. In the midst of the ministerial chaos, Russell wrote a rather telling letter to O'Connell at once praising him for 'the constant & disinterested support which [he had] given to the Ministry' and also warning O'Connell not to press for repeal of the Union. More suggestively, Russell highlighted the effects that Tory anti-Catholic/anti-Irish sentiment had achieved throughout England, and that O'Connell's push for Repeal had only inflamed such sentiment:

It is my opinion that there is not as you sometimes allege any hostility among the people of England to their fellow subjects in Ireland. But so much pains have been taken to persuade them that the Roman Catholics wish to subvert the Protestant Religion, that they act in ignorance of the real question in dispute. It has been my anxious wish to diffuse by calm Argument more sound ways of thinking on the subject of Ireland & to oppose freedom of conscience to the religious bigotry of Exeter Hall.[102]

Although in the onslaught carried out by Roden in order to organise his committee O'Connell had declared himself an unapologetic 'ministerialist',

[99] 'List of Cabinet Appointments' [n. d.], BL, Peel Papers, Add Ms 40426, ff. 254–5.
[100] Stanley to Peel, 9 May 1839, BL, Peel Papers, Add Ms 40426, ff. 318–19.
[101] 'List of Cabinet Appointments', [n. d.], BL, Peel Papers, Add Ms 40426, f. 333. Lady de Grey tried to use her '<u>Orange</u> connexions' as a reason to dissuade Peel from appointing her husband Lord Lieutenant; see [Lady?] de Grey to Peel, [n. d.], BL, Peel Papers, Add Ms 40426, f. 278.
[102] Russell to O'Connell, 9 May 1839, TNA, Russell Papers, PRO 30/22/3C/277.

by mid-1838 he had grown frustrated with the relationship. Outside pressure from the press and from some within the Catholic hierarchy had O'Connell questioning his alliance with the Whigs.[103] Archbishop MacHale complained to O'Connell about 'the unreserved confidence' placed in the Whigs and thought it was a 'baneful influence on the interests of Ireland'.[104] O'Connell's Precursor Society, intended to place outside pressure on the government to enact further reforms, was seen by the Whigs as a threat to the continuance of their government. The Irish Solicitor General David Pigot wrote in no uncertain terms about the damaging effects the Precursor Society's call for 'Justice or Repeal' would have for Ireland's future, as it nearly guaranteed a return of Tory government and with it 'Hardinge [as] Chief Secretary for Ireland, a military lord lieutenant, the troops garrisoning, the police patrolling, spies at every meeting, an indictment for every speech'. In Pigot's eyes, a rupture between the Whigs and O'Connell meant that O'Connell must bid 'adieu for our generation to a liberal government in Ireland'.[105] O'Connell countered that agitation in Ireland would motivate Whigs to unify in addressing more of Ireland's grievances, which would have the added benefit of demonstrating that the Tories were unfit to rule Ireland because they would be unwilling to solve any Irish issues. In other words, O'Connell wanted to place more emphasis on the Whigs' Irish policy as both a motivation for continuing reform and as an insurance policy against the return of Peel and Wellington.[106] Ultimately, O'Connell disbanded the Precursor Society, in part to appease the government, who continued to argue it had proved a significant political liability.

O'Connell's shifting political calculations can be seen in the editorialising of the *Pilot*, which was essentially the O'Connellite newspaper in Dublin. During the first half of 1839, the newspaper focussed its attention on attacking the Tories, especially the Roden committee, and defending the government. As rumours swirled about the impending collapse of the administration during the bedchamber crisis, the *Pilot* published O'Connell's letter to T. M. Ray, one of O'Connell's main organisers, stressing the need to revive the Precursors as a rallying point against Peel's incoming administration but not to rush to the rhetoric of Repeal: 'The moment has not exactly come to raise the Repeal cry . . . we must not, just now, give the Orange party, or even the milk-and-water Reformers, the excuse, or the advantage of too sudden or too violent a Repeal cry.'[107] In another public letter, O'Connell revived the Byron couplet he regularly

---

[103] Geoghegan, *Liberator*, 110–12.
[104] MacHale to O'Connell, 26 September 1838, in O'Connell, *Correspondence*, 6:179.
[105] Pigot to O'Connell, [*c.* 27 September 1838], in O'Connell, *Correspondence*, 6:181.
[106] O'Connell to Pigot, 30 September, in O'Connell, *Correspondence*, 6: 183–6.
[107] 'O'Connell's Letter to T. M. Ray, Esq.', *The Pilot*, 10 May 1839.

used to incite popular agitation – 'Heredity Bondsmen! Know ye not? Who would be free, themselves must strike the blow' – while also advocating for the grand alliance of reforms that had come to effect in April.[108] In other words, O'Connell and the *Pilot* primed the pump for popular agitation in the event of a return to Tory government. When the crisis had passed and the Queen had reinstated Melbourne's government, *The Pilot* proceeded to defend the ministry. In a series of editorials, the newspaper stated its belief in the sincerity of the government's plans for further reforms in Britain and Ireland. Picking up on the anger expressed by English Radicals at Russell's 'finality' comments, the *Pilot* turned the phrase on its head to describe a potential Conservative government: 'There are two parties before us, the one holding to finality, the other to *non*-finality – the one, therefore, to corruption, sustained by tyranny – the other to reform, free discussion, and improvement.' The paper went on to describe the characteristics of the Whig non-finality government: 'A government founded on the principles of non-finality, on the contrary, is founded on the *principle of reform*. It may not move forward fast enough for the wants or wishes of the public, but it, at least, protects the public in discussing [further reforms], and permits the power to grow up and strengthen to which it must itself finally yield.'[109] A week later, the paper praised the cabinet's decision to make the ballot question, a key Radical and O'Connellite desire, open to the individual consciences of its members.[110] Implicitly condemning the English Radicals' impatience for further reform, the *Pilot* stressed that a return to Tory government would ensure the 'finality' of the Reform Act and end any possibility for new reforms in Ireland.

However, by September the *Pilot* and O'Connell had changed their tune. The Lords' 'desire to do mischief . . . towards Ireland . . . was never so strong', according to O'Connell, which left him anxious to 'animate them [the Irish people] to the [voters'] registry . . . and quietly and cautiously for the Repeal'.[111] In early September 1839, the National Trades' Political Union passed a resolution condemning the British government for its failure to enact a variety of reforms and pledged its commitment to O'Connell leading Ireland forward in the initiative of Repeal. In the words of the first speaker, Mr O'Brien:

Seven years ago they [the Irish people] were told if they gave up Repeal agitation, justice would be done them. Was that promise realised? No. He did not blame the

---

[108] 'O'Connell's Letter to the People of Ireland', *The Pilot*, 10 May 1839.
[109] 'Finality or No Finality', *The Pilot*, 1 July 1839.
[110] 'Non-Finality – Open Questions – the Ballot', *The Pilot*, 8 July 1839.
[111] O'Connell to Fitzpatrick, 21 August 1839, in O'Connell, *Correspondence*, 6:276–7.

government for that. Some of them certainly deserved blame; but, upon the whole, they were entitled to the gratitude of Ireland for having placed over them such men as Lords Normanby and Morpeth (cheers). However, they could do nothing. Repeal was their only remedy (cheers) . . . They were convicted they could not get justice for Ireland. The manner in which that man who would always be dear to the hearts of Irishmen, Lord Normanby, had been treated, was a proof of that (hear, hear).[112]

For the remainder of the month the *Pilot* editorialised on the necessity of repealing the Union by continually citing the government's failure to obtain justice for Ireland and appealing to the history of past Irish parliamentary successes for inspiration. 'People of Ireland – old men, who look back with mournful pride on the glories of '82 . . . read O'Connell's reply to the honest Trades' Union, and learn to hope – to fight – to conquer.'[113] The newspaper operated as a voice of popular dissatisfaction at the parliamentary process O'Connell had adopted, pressing him to seize the Repeal banner, and pledging its assistance in disseminating his message of 'loyal[ty], of liberty, and of the universal rights of man' to the entire country.[114]

O'Connell's correspondence largely reflects this shift in tactics away from 'justice to Ireland' towards the threatening demand for 'justice or Repeal', followed simply by his campaign for Repeal. O'Connell complained to Richard Lalor Sheil about the Whigs' breaking their promise to make his son-in-law, Charles O'Connell, a stipendiary magistrate because of O'Connell's decision to agitate for Repeal, hoping that Sheil might be able to do something to influence the government on his behalf.[115] Further rejection of his claims for patronage along with the inability of the government to produce effective legislation for Ireland resulted in O'Connell's formal organisation of the National Association for Justice or Repeal in April 1840. Having spent the previous five years supporting the Whigs, O'Connell found it difficult to muster financial support for his new endeavour but hoped that the dire political circumstances would spur the Irish professional classes to see the benefits of a domestic legislature.[116] In spite of the challenges, however, O'Connell saw Repeal as the only option that offered him freedom to manoeuvre and a way to win back the support of the Irish people, who he feared had abandoned him due to his inability to produce further reforms.[117] In O'Connell's estimation, the Tories were gaining strength and would return to power – O'Connell needed to be

---

[112] 'National Trades' Political Union', *The Pilot*, 4 September 1839.
[113] 'O'Connell on Repeal', *The Pilot*, 25 September 1839.
[114] 'Extraordinary Meeting of the Trades' Political Union', *The Pilot*, 27 December 1839.
[115] O'Connell to Sheil, 29 October 1839, in O'Connell, *Correspondence*, 6:285–6.
[116] Keyes, 'Money and Nationalist Politics', 95–7; O'Connell to John O'Connell, 29 April 1840, in O'Connell, *Correspondence*, 6:326.
[117] O'Connell to Fitzpatrick, 8 August 1839, *Correspondence*, 6:267.

ready for that eventuality and his unequivocal commitment to Repeal offered an opportunity to make sure this was so. By July 1840, O'Connell had renamed his association the 'Loyal National Repeal Association' and succeeded in enlisting the support of Archbishop MacHale to begin organising his Repeal efforts in Connacht.[118]

The general election of 1841 decisively ended the decade of reform, ushering in Peel's Conservative government with a majority that would not be surpassed until 1886. In the words of Boyd Hilton, the election was the first since 1708 'to [have brought] about the fall of a government enjoying majority support' and thus constituted a 'foretaste of "democracy" in so far as the electorate decided who should run the country'.[119] The legacy of the election is somewhat disputed. Not surprisingly, given the future split brought about by Peel's decision to repeal the Corn Laws, some historians have interpreted the result of the 1841 election on economic lines as either demonstrating the electorate's surprising lack of interest in the question of such duties, or as demonstrating that most voters were motivated to register as voters because of the question of duties.[120] Others have highlighted the important role played by provisions in the 1832 Reform Act in politicising the voter registration process and the centrality of local party organisation in it, and the subsequent rise in 'partisan loyalties' with the emergence of national issues.[121] Although some historians mention the role of Irish issues in the election, this Whig liability has been significantly underemphasised. Given the work of the Protestant Association, local Conservative Associations, and the press in publicising Irish agrarian violence, stoking anti-Catholic sentiment, and vilifying the Whig government for their active role in promoting the political interests of O'Connell and the Catholic Church, it is worth exploring to what extent these issues featured in the 1841 election.

In Tory journals, Whig complicity in Irish crime stood as one example among many that writers used to promote the prudence of returning to Tory government. In the July issue of *Blackwood's Edinburgh Magazine*, written after the dissolution of Parliament and during the elections, Archibald Alison presented a comprehensive overview of Whig government that focussed on the divide between their rhetoric while in opposition and the reality of Whig governance, and demonstrated the increases in the national

---

[118] MacDonagh, *Emancipist*, 185–91.    [119] Hilton, *Mad, Bad & Dangerous?*, 517.

[120] Betty Kemp, 'The General Election of 1841', *History* 37, no. 130 (June 1952): 146–57; Edwin Jaggard, 'The 1841 British General Election: A Reconsideration', *Australian Journal of Politics & History* 30, no. 1 (April 1984): 99–114.

[121] Philip Salmon, *Electoral Reform at Work: Local Politics and National Parties, 1832–1841*, Royal Historical Society Studies in History New Series, vol. 27 (Woodbridge: Boydell and Brewer, 2002), www.jstor.org/stable/10.7722/j.ctt81f7k.16; Cragoe, 'The Great Reform Act'; Hilton, *Mad, Bad & Dangerous?*, 516.

debt, in crime, and in overseas blunders using an array of statistical data. Irish crime featured prominently in his critique. Alison noted that while they were in opposition, the Whigs had condemned the Tory's Irish policy for its 'neglect of the moral cultivation' of Ireland's population, but that during 'the blessings of Romish ascendancy and Whig conciliation, the number of capital and atrocious crimes has increased in a degree at once fearful and alarming', which demonstrated 'the total inadequacy of Whig legislation ... to ameliorate it or prevent its steady increase'.[122] In a long article discussing mostly economic matters, J. W. Croker spent very little time on Irish affairs, but noted that the Whigs had tried to distract the public with rhetoric about cheap bread when their real problems were '*the disorder of our finances*, and their *subserviency to Mr. O'Connell*' before appealing to readers' patriotism to rid themselves of O'Connell's influence: 'And, finally, *every lover of his country*, every heart that feels for the safety, honour, and integrity of the British empire, will exert his voice and his influence against the allies – the patrons or more truly the clients and *protégés* – of the Irish Repealers.'[123] *Fraser's Magazine*, true to its preference for the hyperbolic, praised the 'no-popery cry' exhibited in Great Britain, writing that 'The leading newspapers of England see this anti-social superstition in its true light, as treason to the constitution and enmity to the church', before proceeding to list the 'lately persecuted or murdered Protestant Clergy'; the author considered this 'but a tithe of the monuments of papal cruelty – the victims of that savage and superstitious faith which can extinguish home, and country, and relationship'.[124] In another issue, just after the elections, the author drew on published articles in *The Times* noting the 'terrorism' of the Irish countryside that 'intimidate[d] Protestants and Conservatives' from voting and suppressed the strength of Conservatism in the country.[125] All the important groundwork of linking Irish violence, O'Connell and the Catholic clergy, and Whig government together over the previous five years had paid off, with partisans praising 'the Sovereign Ruler of the Universe' for their deliverance from Whig rule and papal domination.[126]

A focus on Ireland also featured in local elections. Arguably, the most emblematic sign of Whig failure in the 1841 election campaign was the defeat of Lord Morpeth in the West Riding of Yorkshire. In the run-up to the election the *Leeds Intelligencer*, the leading Conservative newspaper in

---

[122] [Archibald Alison], 'The Whig Dissolution', BEM 50, no. 309 (July 1841), 1–31 at 9.
[123] [J. W. Croker], 'The Budget and the Dissolution', *The Quarterly Review* 68 (June 1841), 238–80, at 280.
[124] 'The Literary Labours of Daniel O'Connell Esq., MP', *Frasier's Magazine* 23 (May 1841), 528–46, at 533, 544. The list was republished in the *Protestant Magazine*; see 'The Persecuted Clergy of Ireland', *Protestant Magazine* 3, 207–8.
[125] 'The "Felo de se" of the Whigs', *Frasier's Magazine* 24 (August 1841), 237–52, at 250.
[126] 'The Late Election', *Protestant Magazine* 3 (August 1841), 249–52, at 249.

Yorkshire, offered a continuous critique against the Whig government and Lord Morpeth, much of it referring to Irish issues. In early June the newspaper published a letter signed 'A politician on Christian Principles' that listed six reasons why churchmen should not vote for Morpeth. It began: 'Since the last West-Riding Election, his Lordship has sanctioned Popery, by carrying about a begging-box in a Popish place of worship in Ireland', and referred to Morpeth's support for appropriation of church revenue in Ireland for 'the education of Papists, Socinians, & c.'.[127] In early July, when candidates gave their election statements, the Conservative candidate Edmund Beckett Denison reminded voters that the Melbourne government was 'a Government only in name; continually obliged to bow to its Irish supporters'.[128] As news began to unfold of the significant Conservative gains across England and Scotland, the editors again noted that the public was punishing the Whigs for their close alliance with O'Connell. 'It is high time to get rid of a Government that blushes not to appear in close alliance with semi-traitors and open violators of the law', they declared, before concluding that it was Morpeth's 'slavish leanings to O'Connell that has [sic] prepared the way for his crushing defeat in the West Riding'.[129] Another letter to the editor after Morpeth's defeat warned electors against being deceived by Morpeth's concession speech, which had received some praise in *The Times* for its conciliatory tone:

> Lord Morpeth is a joint of the backbone of the present reckless Ministry. His bland manners and winning address have only made him a more effective tool for working out Whig treachery; for instance, against the suffering Protestants of Ireland during his tenure in office. . . . He went to work out Mr Daniel O'Connell's Popish policy and purposes, against the Protestant church and its members. He, to pay the price which that bad man demanded, found it necessary to pull down and heap insult upon the estate gentry of that country, and to immolate the peace and comfort of their civilized families at the shrine of Maynooth in every locality.[130]

The local liberal newspaper also pinpointed the influence of Irish matters and anti-Catholic sentiments in the mobilisation of Conservative voters. In an eight-point list highlighting the causes that brought about the Tory majority, which began with 'the prejudices of the Agricultural, Colonial, and other Monopolists', the paper continued by noting 'the revival of

---

[127] 'Reasons Why a Churchman Should Not Vote for Lord Morpeth', *Leeds Intelligencer*, 5 June 1841.

[128] 'To the Electors of the West-Riding Yorkshire', *Leeds Intelligencer*, 3 July 1841.

[129] 'Triumphant Progress of the Elections', *Leeds Intelligencer*, 17 July 1841.

[130] 'To the Freeholders of the West Riding of Yorkshire', *Leeds Intelligencer*, 24 July 1841. O'Connell, and others in Ireland, attempted to persuade Morpeth to take a seat in Ireland or to contest for one in Dublin, both of which he refused. See R. More O'Ferrall to Morpeth, 24 July 1841, CH, Morpeth MSS, J19/1/32/74.

High Church feeling in the country the last eight or ten years is one of the most striking features of the Age'. It continued:

An Establishment is a Religious Monopoly ... The Religious Monopolists have been disturbed, offended, and alarmed by a series of measures favourable to Religious Liberty – measures which are an honour to the age, such as the Repeal of the Corporations and Test Acts, Catholic Emancipation, Irish Church Reform, the Irish Tithe Bill ... appropriating the funds of ecclesiastical sinecures in Ireland ... The lowering of the political Ascendancy of the Protestants in Ireland, by a firm and equitable administration of the Government, was another cause of offences. These excellent measures stirred up the pride and bigotry of the Church party.[131]

Politicians offered similar analyses. When renominating Peel for his seat at Tamworth, Peel's brother, the Conservative MP William Yates Peel, questioned what Whigs meant when they talked about 'justice to Ireland'. 'If it meant the Established Church should be robbed of its revenues – if it meant that Irish Noblemen and their agents should be murdered, the assassination being witnessed by many, and yet the assassin being allowed to escape', then it was no justice at all. While challenging speculations that future Tory policy in Ireland would be based on religious discrimination, the speech also highlighted the inherent difference from, and implicit superiority of English noblemen and labourers in comparison to their Irish counterparts.[132] The new Home Secretary Sir James Graham argued that the Conservatives had proved so successful because of the Whigs' Irish policy, especially on the question of church appropriation. 'Were I asked to place my finger upon one act of the late Government which had more than any other destroyed all public confidence in them ... I should point out their conduct on the appropriation clause,' Graham argued, and after enumerating multiple other Whig follies, stressed that he had parted company with Melbourne in 1835 because he 'saw Mr O'Connell exercising a most pernicious influence in Ireland, and [...] saw no disposition on the part of those in authority to put a stop to the evil (Great cheering)'.[133] William Wilberforce, eldest son of the abolitionist, castigated the Whigs for exploiting Irish unrest for their political gain, arguing that even magistrates appointed by the Whig government testified to the depravity of Ireland – 'no country in civilized society was ever reduced [to such a] state that Ireland [has been], by the agitation carried on there to return the supporters of the Whig government, by Mr O'Connell and the Roman Catholic priests. (Hears and cheers).'[134]

---

[131] 'Inquiry into the Causes Which Have Given the Tories a Majority at the General Election', *Leeds Mercury*, 24 July 1841.

[132] 'The Re-election of Ministers', *Leeds Intelligencer*, 18 September 1841.

[133] 'Return of Sir J. Graham Without Opposition', *Leeds Intelligencer*, 18 September 1841.

[134] 'Electioneering Proceedings at Bradford: Speech of Mr Wilberforce', *Leeds Intelligencer*, 28 August 1841.

This is not to say that the 1841 general election revolved around the state of the Irish countryside – it didn't. Nevertheless, considering the radically different portrayals of Ireland constructed for public consumption by Whigs and ultra-Tories throughout the latter half of the 1830s it should come as little surprise that Irish issues, whether circling around agrarian violence or church appropriation, managed to creep into the rhetoric of politicians at the hustings, or into newspapers pontificating on electoral prospects or results. On reflection it is striking, too, just how often politicians or the press levelled personal criticism and attack against O'Connell, and how effective that strategy proved to be. An election song of 1841 found in Peel's papers gives as good an indication as any of how the Whig–O'Connell alliance could be animated for political ends:

> Like a plain dealing soldier has Wellington spoke
> Ere the crown shall go down there are crowns to be broke;
> Ere we give up the game we must have a new deal,
> So stand fast with me round the banner of Peel,
> Now fill up your cups and I'll fill up my can;
> A fig for the Whigs and their master King Dan;
> We shall soon see them both to the right-about wheel,
> If we only are true to brave Arthur and Peel,
> God bless them, God bless them
>
> . . .
>
> It is useless to murmur for what is now past,
> The Conservative flag must be nail'd to the mast,
> The ship is still sound from the deck to the keel,
> And will weather all storms when she's guided by Peel,
> So fill up your cups and I'll fill up my can;
> A fig for the Whigs and the Big Beggarman!
> For trust me they both in due season shall feel,
> That they've not seen the last of brave Arthur & Peel.[135]

## Back to the Beginning?

The country, or at the very least Great Britain, was 'true to brave Arthur and Peel', and Peel returned to government benches in command of a comfortable majority in the Commons, and (at least theoretically) a friendly majority of Conservative peers. Considering the role that anti-Irish rhetoric had played in the election, many wondered what Peel's Irish policy would entail. Whigs believed that 'above all' Ireland would prove to be Peel's nightmare, as 'O'Connell's influence will now be successfully

[135] 'A Song for the Election', [c. July 1841], BL, Peel Papers, Add MS 40429, f. 450.

exerted to render the government of Ireland impossible'.[136] Speculation swirled concerning what influence the ultra-Tory faction might have on Peel and the character of the government's new Irish administration. In Ireland, the popular press lambasted Peel's pledge of toleration and equal justice, pointing to his legal appointments as evidence of his singular agenda of 'persecuting our country ... and following the principles of Orangeism'.[137] Peel moved forward with his appointment of Thomas De Grey as lord lieutenant, which did little to revise liberals' perception that Ireland was returning to Orange-dominated government. However, the Orange press voiced considerable doubts when learning of Peel's appointments, noting that only one of them had voted against Catholic Emancipation, as well as remarking on the paucity of offices for 'the leaders of the Irish Protestants', and voicing concern about Lord Eliot, the new Chief Secretary of Ireland, because of his 'inordinate love of popularity'.[138] Thomas Drummond had died in 1840 and had been replaced as undersecretary by Norman MacDonnell. However, Peel decided to replace MacDonnell with Edward Lucas, a Conservative MP and County Monaghan landowner whose father had been High Sheriff of Monaghan during the 1798 rebellion. Peel thought Lucas, as a conservative and 'an Irishman', would give much satisfaction to the population, and his appointment was received by Conservative newspapers with approbation as that of a man committed to the 'endeavours to improve and tranquillise Ireland'.[139] Naturally, opinion in Ireland differed. According to the liberal *Dublin Review*, reflecting on the first months of Peel's government in February 1842, 'every measure which they have since adopted, has tended to justify the evil omens at first formed by the Irish people of the new Lord Lieutenant's policy'.[140] In matters of patronage, Peel's government reversed the trend towards appointing Catholics and, regardless of any genuine desire on Peel's part for impartiality, the Irish office resembled that of 1835. The government's Irish administration lacked internal coherence, as Peel attempted to straddle a moderate line but placed those with reactionary principles, if not decidedly Orange ones, in places of prominence. In many ways, it was a turning back of the clocks.[141]

---

[136] Greville, *Greville Memoirs*, 2: 22.
[137] 'How Is Ireland to Be Governed?', *The Pilot*, 6 September 1841.
[138] 'The New Ministry', *Wexford Conservative*, 8 September 1841; 'The New Ministry', *The Standard*, 8 September 1841.
[139] Peel to Lucas, 1 September [1841], BL, Peel Papers, Add MS 40, 487. Emphasis in the original.
[140] 'Peel's Government', *The Dublin Review* 12, no. 23 (February 1842), 258.
[141] Kerr, *Peel, Priests and Politics*, ch. 2. Charles Read has argued against the view of De Grey as a reactionary or as being in any way influenced by his wife's Orange connections. Although one can find significant points to disagree with in Read's analysis, what is clear

The ways in which the government chose to deal with Irish outrages and the subsequent task of administering law and order also underscored the end of any Whig experiment of 'justice to Ireland'. Liberal or nationalist newspapers complained heavily about the reintroduction of very conservative law officials, many of them intimately involved with the ultra-Tory politics of the 1830s, including the appointment of Conservative MP Joseph Jackson as solicitor general, Francis Blackburne as attorney general (and later Chief Justice of the Queen's Bench), and Abraham Brewster as law advisor; O'Connell questioned the new government's pledge to administer the law impartially as he considered Brewster an avowed Orangeman.[142] De Grey announced many of these appointments as the Queen's representative in Ireland, which left room for great confusion between him and Peel. While Peel stressed caution in the government's appointments, De Grey rushed ahead. The retirement of Lord Chief Justice Bushe from the Queen's Bench caused the government to promote then Solicitor General Edward Pennefather, which left his position vacant. In a letter dated 22 October, De Grey stressed to Peel his desire to fill the post as fast as possible, and assuming that Peel wanted to promote Joseph Jackson, De Grey offered Jackson the post. Peel, however, wrote to De Grey on 24 October (before De Grey's letter had reached him in London) that he was 'afraid that Jackson is weak in point of Law', and worried he would attempt to seek further promotion to attorney general, which would open claims to higher positions to which 'he might not be fully qualified'. De Grey responded to Peel's letter that it was too late, and that Jackson had already been offered the position of solicitor general.[143] Peel was angry. The Queen wrote to her prime minister, having heard about Jackson's appointment through the newspaper; she was concerned because 'she had always understood Jackson to belong to the violent Orange Party, and she doubted the Policy of his appointment'. Peel, forced to defend Jackson, stressed to the Queen that while he was 'a man of decided opinions in politics' he was not an Orangeman, though he 'offered an able and uncompromising resistance in and out

---

is that De Grey was considered by many contemporaries as tainted by Orange influence, which undoubtedly cast a shadow over government policy. Charles Read, 'Peel, De Grey, and Irish Policy, 1841–1844', *History* 99, 334 (January 2014): 1–18.

[142] 'Government of Sir Robert Peel', *The Pilot*, 15 September 1841; 'The Humbug Ministry', *The Pilot*, 22 September 1841; 'Counsel to the Chief Secretary', *Morning Chronicle*, 22 September 1841; 'Appointments in Ireland', *Morning Chronicle*, 5 October 1841.

[143] Peel to De Grey, 19 October 1841, BL, Peel Papers, Add MS 40477, f. 35; De Grey to Peel, 22 October 1841, ibid., f. 39; Peel to De Grey, 24 October 1841, ibid., f. 45 (emphasis in the original); De Grey to Peel, 26 October [1841], ibid., 49.

of Parliament to Mr O'Connell and his projects'.[144] Though the Queen ultimately acceded to Jackson's appointment, the fact she saw him through the lens of sectarianism serves as an apt example of how perceptions of Peel's motives contrasted with the government's rhetoric of moderation and impartiality. It also demonstrated the divisions within Peel's Irish administration.

By July of the following year, Peel was writing to De Grey, deeply concerned at what he had heard in respect to the operation of law courts. That month, in the House of Commons, Richard Sheil called into question the supposed principles of 'equal justice' professed by Peel and De Grey, again pointing to the appointment of officials who were 'so conspicuous for the part which [they] had acted on every question by which Ireland has been agitating, for the last twenty years'. According to Sheil, the fact these appointments had been made on the basis of sectarian principles was made manifest in two separate religiously motived murder cases in Ulster. One case involved the government challenging and expelling all potential Catholic jurors from the jury panel, and the other centred on the actions of the attorney general, who had prevented a prisoner's counsel from seeing the legal brief.[145] Peel spelled out in detail the embarrassment to the government in a letter to De Grey:

We had a debate last night on Irish affairs ... some points, in respect to which the conduct of your Law Advisers (after all the Explanations we could offer) did not appear in so satisfactory a light as I could have wished. The constitution of the Jury by which Hughes was convicted – discrepancies between the states [statements] of Mr O'Hogan the Counsel for the next of Kin, and the Attorney Genl. as to the service of the right of challenge, the indiscriminate challenge of all the R. Catholics on the panel, the conviction of the Prisoner by an exclusively Protestant Jury after two preceding failures to convict, did I think notwithstanding the explanatory circumstances leave rather an unfavourable impression ... The Irish Law Officers ought to bear in mind that there [*sic*] prosecutions ... will be [the] subject of discussion in the House of Commons, and that they will be judged [...] by a great majority accustomed to English principles & Rules of proceeding.[146]

Law appointments continued to vex the government's Irish administration, as De Grey favoured 'firm, bold' men of the type that many in Ireland identified with the bygone days of Protestant privilege, while Lord Eliot as Chief Secretary proposed more conciliatory candidates. De Grey stressed the fitness of the men he favoured, complaining in October 1842 to the Home Secretary Sir James Graham about

[144] Peel to De Grey, 26 October [1841], ibid., f. 51.
[145] Hansard, 3rd ser., vol. 65, cols. 253, 255–7, 18 July 1842.
[146] Peel to De Grey, 19 July 1841 [actually 1842], BL, Peel Papers, Add MS 40477, f. 250.

prospective appointments to the bench: 'I cannot see how it can be regarded as packing the Bench, to put the fittest man in the places best suited to their respective qualities ... so far from shaking publick confidence, if that change ensured the placing a better man in the station, it would in my opinion be likely to increase the publick confidence.'[147] In another letter, responding to pressure to find Catholics to appoint, De Grey continued his insistence on 'fitness', opining that he 'wished very much to have found any Catholick of standing, and professional repute who could have been made Serjeant[.] But there is not one fit!!'[148]

Eliot and De Grey also clashed over the appointment of stipendiary magistrates; this was a position which carried immense symbolic importance because it was appointed by the government and, during Mulgrave's tenure, had been seen as a counterweight to that of the more reactionary or inactive resident magistrates. Eliot proposed reappointing a number of stipendiary magistrates whom De Grey had previously deselected early in their administration due to cost-cutting.[149] Eliot believed that reinstating magistrates previously appointed by Melbourne's government would provide good optics in Ireland. De Grey disagreed with Eliot's strategy, though he did reappoint one formerly dismissed magistrate who had originally been appointed by the Melbourne government, a Mr Gray, who happened to be a Conservative in politics, thus undermining any positive effects at his reinstatement. However, De Grey also appeared to feel far less concern about any optics in Ireland, writing to Graham that 'if we were within 10 or 15 votes in the H. Of Commons, there is no calculating upon what meanness one might be obliged to submit to ... but that is luckily not our case'.[150] Instead, he pledged to form his own opinions and chart his own course, which further grated on his relationship with Eliot.[151] De Grey's own course did not necessarily mean choosing reactionaries, and he made it explicitly clear to Graham that while their political allies in Ireland could rely on his support, it was always qualified by whether they chose 'fit men' for the job at hand, which itself was an open question.[152]

The question of Irish outrages did not recede from government minds, either. Tipperary, once again, proved the most problematic place in the country as peasants rallied together to resist the absolute rights of private

---

[147] De Grey to Graham, 5 October 1842, BARS, De Grey Papers, L30/18/93.
[148] De Grey to Graham, 31 October 1842, ibid., L30/18/102. Emphasis in the original.
[149] 'Memorandum Respecting the Stipendiary Magistrates', 20 January 1842, ibid., L30/18/18/17.
[150] De Grey to Graham, 4 December 1842, ibid., L30/18/18/110.
[151] Eliot to Peel, 26 December 1842, BL, Peel Papers, Add MS 40480, f. 209–10.
[152] De Grey to Graham, 4 December 1842, BARS, De Grey Papers, L30/18/18/110.

property in matters related to land and employment. The crimes of these 'blood-stained lawgivers' were standard fare – threatening notices, assaults on those that occupied land, and attacks on landlords – and the remedy, as proposed by one resident magistrate, was time-honoured, too: 'The first Remedy which the writer would suggest for the suppression of "agrarian crimes" in Tipperary is, to make the Peasantry *respect* the Law of the land. Not that *moral respect* which flows from loyalty, for that could not be inculcated; but that *physical respect* which operates by a fear of punishment.'[153] 'There is no better lesson for the Irish people to be taught', wrote the undersecretary Edward Lucas, 'than that if they are convicted of murder they are pretty sure to be hanged.'[154] De Grey likely agreed with this sentiment, though he noted that in Tipperary the government was struggling to make arrests, let alone convictions. The remedy for such problems offered some challenges. While it seems clear that De Grey would have preferred more executive power, as under previous governments, that impulse was somewhat stymied by disagreements among the cabinet, as we will see. Nevertheless, he wrote to Graham on the merits of 'keeping our very large (and I am bound to say) active and vigilant Force, both magistrates and constabulary on the alert', pursuing the establishment of special commissions, and reforming an arms bill.[155] In the House of Lords, Lord Wharncliffe reported that while two murders had recently occurred in the county, peers could rest assured knowing that the government had increased the number of constabulary in the area from 800 to 900 and that over 1,700 troops were stationed throughout the county, in addition to the presence of seven stipendiary magistrates 'to guard against any extensive outbreak'.[156]

The level of Irish outrage – the point raised so effectively by Lord Roden in 1839 – was raised again this time by Whigs aiming to discredit the Tory policy of reverting to old governing practices of coercion. While the law courts were failing to function impartially, the problem of Irish outrages did not recede into the background, either. Possibly remembering the effect that Irish outrages had had on impugning Mulgrave's government, Ireland's former Lord Lieutenant Earl Fortescue (formerly Viscount Ebrington) raised the question in the House of Lords in August 1842 and demanded the constabulary returns for all outrages during the government's tenure. Fortescue highlighted the general diminution of outrages during his service as lord lieutenant, as well as how

---

[153] [Thomas George Stoney], *The Present State of Tipperary, as Regards Agrarian outrages . . .*, NLI (Dublin, May 1842), 1, 18.
[154] Lucas to De Grey, 23 April 1842, BARS, De Grey Papers, L29/700/29/19.
[155] De Grey to Graham, 24 December 1842, ibid., L30/18/18/120.
[156] Hansard, 3rd ser., vol. 63, cols. 882, 27 May 1842.

outrages 'in these graver offences' had increased during the second half of 1841, when De Grey had taken over. He noted that the government had failed to renew eight stipendiary magistrates on their ascension into office, opting instead for their duties to be performed by resident magistrates. Furthermore, Fortescue brought to light the government's Irish administration's employment of an agent provocateur named Hagan who had previously been arrested as a Ribbonman and had subsequently been set loose by the state to infiltrate Ribbon lodges under the direction of local magistrates. According to Fortescue, 'If true, the magistrates who could so act were utterly unworthy to hold their commissions.'[157] In short, Irish outrages continued to be the measure by which each party evaluated the other's success, as well as Ireland's state of civilisation and security.

Daniel O'Connell's proclamation that 1843 would be 'the Repeal year' prompted significant agitation among Ireland's population, as well as consternation among landlords and government officials. O'Connell's actual intentions regarding Repeal – whether he really believed it was a desirable goal or rather a means to exact concessions from the British government – is of secondary importance to the ways the disciplined mobilisation of Irish people caused landlords to feel under threat and to persuade Dublin Castle to interpret these activities as a threat to the state's power.[158] With tens or hundreds of thousands assembling across the countryside to hear O'Connell rail against the injustice on offer from Westminster, landlords increased the volume of their entreaties for Dublin Castle to act. Confessing their 'deepest anxiety' and concerned that 'rebellion and anarchy must shortly overwhelm our Country', magistrates in Fermanagh wrote to De Grey pleading for 'speedy and decided measures to put down' O'Connell's monster meetings.[159] Others wrote asking the government to grant special dispensations to arm Protestants for mutual protection or to revoke permits to own firearms from officials of the Repeal Association, so-called repeal wardens.[160] Within Dublin Castle itself, the undersecretary worried about the potential for rebellion and the inability of O'Connell to control the public, while also blaming the Chief Secretary for 'the apathy of the Government'.[161] A memo from the Duke of Wellington included explicit reference to the events of 1798

---

[157] Hansard, 3rd ser., vol. 65, cols. 1112–14, 8 August 1842.

[158] MacDonagh, *Emancipist*, ch. 9, especially 221, 236–41.

[159] 'Resolutions of the Magistrates of County Fermanagh', 16 June 1843, BARS, De Grey Papers, L29/700/13/8.

[160] De Grey to Farnham, 17 November 1843, BARS, De Grey Papers, L29/700/14/2; Saunderson to Farnham, 21 November 1843; BARS, De Grey Papers, L29/700/14/4; Lord Bandon to De Grey, 26 December 1843, ibid., L29/700/1/7.

[161] Lucas to De Grey, 18 May 1843, BARS, De Grey Papers, L29/700/29/49; Peel to De Grey, 9 May [1843], BL, Peel Papers, Add MS 40,480, f. 50.

and the need for gentlemen to reinforce their homes and induce their loyal tenants to do the same. It also included military suggestions, including for military officials to secure 'the line from Dublin, by Mullingar to Athlone' as it was 'the shortest across the Island, and it cuts it in two', and for the government to stock food and ammunition at key military depots, such as Charles Fort in Kinsale, Spike Island in Cork, and Carrickfergus in the north.[162] Lucas, on behalf of De Grey, wrote to all the stipendiary magistrates across Ireland requesting they furnish Dublin Castle with a list of names of all those who held a government office and supported the Repeal movement. This led to the removal of over eighty-five commissions to the magistracy and twelve deputy lieutenants of the county, the majority of whom were Catholic, a symbolic but powerful display that turned back the clocks on the progress that had been made in incorporating Catholics into the apparatus of the state just a few years earlier.[163]

How did the government justify their decision? Naturally, they referenced 'outrage', a convenient shorthand that drew on the prevailing anxieties, fears, and paranoia about the potential for political subversion and violent rebellion. Thus, in the Lord Chancellor Edward Sugden's letters to Lord Ffrench, a magistrate of Galway, Sugden admitted that while the Repeal meetings were not themselves illegal, they had an 'inevitable tendency to outrage' that made a magistrate's support of such a meeting inconsistent with their legal duties. 'A magistrate who presides over or forms part of such a meeting can neither be prepared to repress violence', wrote Sugden, 'nor could he be expected to act against a body for whose offence he would himself be responsible.'[164] A few days earlier in the House of Lords, Lord Roden, with characteristic calmness, had stressed how his peers 'could not conceive the extent of the conspiracy, nor the violence and intimidation which at present prevailed in every part

---

[162] 'Memorandum', 27 May 1843, BARS, De Grey Papers, L29/700/28/9. This document is attributed to Wellington, but it could also conceivably have come from Lord Wellesley; this is especially likely as it is part of Wellesley's correspondence with De Grey, Wellesley had extensive knowledge of Ireland as a former lord lieutenant, and it was only signed 'W'.

[163] De Grey Journal, May 1843, BARS, De Grey Papers, L31/114, 77; Edward Lucas to Stipendiary Magistrates (Circular 6970), 23 May 1843, NAI, CSORP 3/617/18; 'A list of the Deputy Lieutenants who have been deprived of their commission . . . and whether they are Protestant or Catholic', ibid. Some magistrates held multiple commissions in different counties. Ó Faoláin states that twenty-three gentlemen lost their commission, see Ó Faoláin, *King of the Beggars* (London: Thomas Nelson and Sons, 1938), 333.

[164] Edward Sugden to Lord Ffrench, 23 May 1843, 'Letters Respecting Superseding of Magistrates from Com. of Peace in Ireland, since May 1843', P. P. (1843, vol. 51, no. 403). In O'Connell's own correspondence with Sugden, he noted the ridiculousness of the government's appeal to the propensity towards violence, in light of the fact that not one meeting had led to any violence whatsoever. He also called the government's legal justifications into question.

of Ireland', before appealing to the government to show its determination to prevent 'a civil war', or worse, 'the dismemberment of the empire'.[165] Lord Brougham agreed, casting the importance in wider imperial waters. Reflecting on the history of the past nine years since 1834 across Britain, Ireland, and Europe, Brougham felt convinced that the repeal of the Union actually would have global consequences:

The severance of the Legislative union ... meant in reality the disruption of the empire itself, and the entire dissolution of the integrity of that empire; and no man could doubt that to prevent such a catastrophe, which would be the ruin of one of the greatest (if not the greatest) monuments of civilisation which human wisdom has ever reared – to prevent that grievous catastrophe ... the uttermost exertions of the power of this country[,] its moral force, its legislative force, and its physical force, would be put forward cheerfully and anxiously and heartily, at the first intimation on the part of her Majesty's Government, that any such extraordinary exertion was by them deemed necessary for a purpose of such paramount importance.[166]

In another symbolic turning back of the clocks, for their policy of 1843, Peel's government reached back to the King's Speech of 1834, another time when O'Connell had been campaigning (rather half-heartedly) for Repeal. On the same day that Roden referenced civil war in Ireland in the upper house, in the lower house Peel promised Viscount Jocelyn – MP for King's Lynn, and Roden's son – that 'there is no influence, no power, no authority, which the prerogatives of the Crown and the existing law give to the Government, which shall not be exercised for the purpose of maintaining the Union – the dissolution of which would involve, not merely the repeal of an act of Parliament, but the dismemberment of this great empire'.[167]

The details of the struggle between O'Connell and the British government concerning the repeal of the Union have been discussed in great detail elsewhere and only merit a brief summation here.[168] O'Connell's organisation and continual meetings throughout the summer of 1843 led to a government reaction within Parliament that contemplated coercive legislation and placed the means and methods of governing Ireland centre stage. When O'Connell used language that suggested subversive intent and the potential remit for violence, the government used it as a pretext to outlaw the Repeal Association, which culminated in O'Connell calling off

---

[165] Hansard, 3rd ser., vol. 69, col. 3, 9 May 1843. Roden also referenced the Rebellion of 1798.

[166] Hansard, 3rd ser., vol. 69, col. 9, 9 May 1843.

[167] Hansard, 3rd ser., vol. 69, col. 24, 9 May 1843.

[168] MacIntyre, *Liberator*, pp. 266–84; Geoghegan, *Liberator*, ch. 9; MacDonagh, *Emancipist*, ch. 9.

his meeting at Clontarf in October 1843. O'Connell, along with some of his Repeal compatriots, would be put on trial in 1844 and convicted of a number of offences, a decision that the House of Lords invalidated in September 1844 when they ruled he should be released; O'Connell spent a little over three months in Dublin's Richmond penitentiary.

However, an Irish crisis – the Repeal movement – had again returned the precarity of Irish society to the spotlight. Did the crisis bring about the need for additional powers to adequately ensure the safety of the state? While Protestant leaders like Roden pressed the government to enact for more active measures to undermine O'Connell, whether outlawing the Repeal meetings or allowing landlords to arm their loyal tenants for mutual defence, the issue divided cabinet. De Grey emphasised the need for additional powers similar to the coercive legislation favoured during times of need over the previous three decades to deal with O'Connell, arguing that if he had recourse to them it would almost guarantee he did not need to use them, but without them 'we are left to the mercy of the mob'.[169] Appealing to the cabinet in June, De Grey argued that all of Irish life – from interpersonal relationships to economic matters – hung on the whims of O'Connell. In the meantime, the government's friends, and by extension the security of the country, dangled in the wind:

Is not the peace, + prosperity of the whole country now in jeopardy? Is not distrust + dread of each other ... already such that the casual[?] transactions of life are impeded? Are not money transactions + purchases + sale of property, banking affairs + advance of money upon Irish security, if not stopped, at all events suspended? Is not in short the whole fabric of society dependent upon the will of one man? And is not that man becoming daily more daring + exciting in his language? to such an extent that even he may not be able to survive the passions he has roused? ... The Protestant party are in the greatest alarm + dread + so many place [sic] under serious apprehensions of midnight massacre. They ask for Troops, which we cannot in all cases grant. They ask for arms, which we invariably refused. They ask for power to organise + arm themselves, which we equally refused. They ask for protection of the Law, which we are obliged to acknowledge is not adequate: + finally they ask that we will in such case endeavour to obtain an increase of powers, which as yet we have not attempted.[170]

Peel, articulating the feelings of cabinet after its long deliberations, set out its conclusions on the reasons why coercive legislation would not do. First, O'Connell would deftly outmanoeuvre any attempt to outlaw the Repeal Association with an Act of Parliament, much as he had in the 1820s with the Catholic Association. Second, the cabinet feared that

[169] De Grey Journal, May 1843, BARS, De Grey Papers, L31/114, 75.
[170] De Grey Journal, 18 June 1843, 126–7.

coercive legislation would only further inflame passions in Ireland, 'giving a new Stimulus to Repeal Agitation'. Here, Peel and the cabinet concluded – it turns out, incorrectly – that Repeal agitation had a short life span and would soon peter out. Third, thinking in holistic United Kingdom terms, the cabinet noted the significant constitutional challenges that would be presented by passing coercive legislation to outlaw Irish petitioning of Parliament by the repeal movement on the one hand, while simultaneously allowing the Anti-Corn Law League and the Chartists to organise in Great Britain. In Parliament, this would mean the arraying of all forces of opposition in unity against the government, while outside, 'a very powerful and very inflamed party ... [that] confederated with Repealers against the practical measure directed against Repeal' would create much deeper problems than Repeal presented in its current form.[171] De Grey did not buy these arguments and protested that the Protestants to whom the government in Ireland needed to look to for support increasingly believed Peel was contemplating selling them down the river, implicitly recalling his fatal betrayal in 1829.[172] Writing in his journal, De Grey believed opposing Repeal by using coercion was a hill worth dying on:

[I]f the Government is to be overthrown by a want of confidence, it would go out of office upon much higher + better grounds if a denial of power to suppress a rising Rebellion in Ireland were the cause, than upon any other question. If the information [being received by Dublin Castle] comes up to what I fear it may, I would suspend all other measures, + would put the documents on the table of the House + I would declare, that until I was able to save this branch of the empire, I would attend to nothing else. If the Government falls there, it falls gloriously + honorably: but I do not believe that it would![173]

While Peel, his Home Secretary Sir James Graham, and Lord Eliot maintained their commitment to a policy of general non-intervention, Protestant popular opinion in Ireland shifted against the government. The *Dublin Evening Mail*, arguably the most influential Conservative newspaper in Ireland, hammered Peel, Graham, and Eliot for their inaction while simultaneously ratcheting up the threat of the insurrectionary rhetoric ascribed to the Repeal movement. Reviving long-standing tropes of English neglect or betrayal, the *Dublin Evening Mail* accused the government of 'cold aversion',[174] 'culpable supineness',[175] and acting as a 'ministry who has deceived and betrayed you'.[176] The newspaper

[171] Peel to De Grey, 12 June 1843, BL, Peel Papers, Add MS 40, 480, ff. 79–84, at 82.
[172] De Grey to Peel, 17 June 1843, ibid., ff. 87–93.
[173] De Grey Journal, 19 May 1843, BARS, De Grey Papers, L31/114, 90.
[174] 'Policy Toward Ireland', *Dublin Evening Post*, 9 June 1843.
[175] 'The Protestant Anniversaries', *Dublin Evening Post*, 26 June 1843.
[176] 'Anti-repeal Meeting', *Dublin Evening Post*, 12 June 1843.

highlighted what they perceived as the consistent failure of conciliation with Ireland's Catholic majority as O'Connell and the Catholic hierarchy wanted nothing less than Protestantism's elimination, the severance of the British connection, and 'a general confiscation of every species of property now held by Protestants'.[177] 'Determined upon carrying out concession and conciliation of the enemies of British connexion, they *have* incurred the displeasure of the only friends of that connexion existing in Ireland', lamented one article, as it underscored that the dangerous consequences of conciliation had already included 'the movement into Ireland of five-and -twenty thousand soldiers; the filling of her arsenals with military stories; the beleaguering of her coasts with a fleet of war steamers and seventy-fours'.[178] The newspaper wanted government action to meet the challenge of popery's 'insurrectionary movement', whose aims included 'the cutting of the throats of us – the Protestants of Ireland'.[179] Recalling recent history, the *Dublin Evening Mail* noted that Lord Grey's Whig government had passed a coercion bill in February 1833, which included clauses granting the lord lieutenant power to suppress popular meetings, roughly three weeks after King William IV had denounced O'Connell from the throne as the head of 'disturbers of the public peace'; the *Mail* then asked rhetorically whether it was 'necessary to draw the parallel between the vigour of the Whig Earl GREY and the perplexed torpor of the nondescript politician who now holds the helm of British affairs?'[180]

While Protestants in Ireland waited for government action, a number of leading Anglo-Irish families assembled in the London home of the Earl of Wicklow to draft resolutions pledging their support in case the government ever got its act together.[181] Meanwhile, the Protestant Association resolved to organise a national day of 'especial prayer to God'. Worried that government apathy encouraged O'Connell and the Catholic hierarchy, the Association's magazine, *The Protestant Magazine*, evoked memories of sectarian bloodshed:

[I]f the Papists are to be permitted in this manner to arm and organise themselves, whilst the Protestants remain inactive, there is great danger that the latter may fall defenceless victims to one of those horrible massacres which have been perpetrated so repeatedly by the Papists, both in Ireland and other countries. And all history bears witness that concession to the Church of Rome has ever been followed by some violent outbreak, or dreadful effusion of blood. Surely all our

[177] 'The Condition of Ireland Question', *Dublin Evening Post*, 10 July 1843.
[178] 'Conciliation', *Dublin Evening Post*, 5 June 1843.
[179] 'Anti-repeal Protestant Meetings', *Dublin Evening Post*, 7 June 1843.
[180] 'Facts for Sir Robert Peel', *Dublin Evening Post*, 5 June 1843.
[181] 'Most Important Meeting of Irish Peers and Commoners at the Earl of Wicklow's', *Dublin Evening Post*, 19 June 1843.

sympathies should be awakened, and our most earnest prayers should be offered up in behalf of the Protestants of Ireland, who do not seem to be sufficiently protected at this critical juncture by the aegis of the executive government.[182]

Since the government would not protect them, Irish Protestants believed they had themselves alone to rely upon, but this presented its own challenges. Lord Roden, and other prominent Protestants implicitly connected with Orange societies, worried that the annual Twelfth of July demonstrations might lead to confrontations that would torpedo the British public's sympathy for Irish Protestants, with damning consequences within the context of Repeal. Roden published letters in the newspapers imploring Protestants to demonstrate their loyalty to the government by not marching illegally, advice that De Grey also endorsed in his correspondence with members of the gentry.[183] Secretly, the government also sent an emissary to meet the Protestant communities locally to dissuade them from their annual displays of dominance, which often ended in sectarian riot and bloodshed. Working with Lord Roden, the government official (likely a stipendiary magistrate) was introduced to local loyalist communities, printed materials dissuading any marching, and attempted to take the pulse of the community across counties Down, Armagh, and Antrim.[184] The anniversary largely passed without any disturbance that year, but the tranquillity belied the deep frustration and scepticism felt among many Protestants. The Protestant controversialist and then-rector of Killyman parish in Tyrone, Revd. Mortimer O'Sullivan, wrote to De Grey that 'altho' the Protestants were obedient + tranquil yesterday ... they were far from feeling satisfied'. Col. Blacker, a former grand master in Co. Armagh, relayed complaints of one-sided concessions to O'Connell and warned that 'if the Repeal processions are tolerated much longer it will be difficult to persuade our people that it is proper or just to interfere with them', thus suggesting that the sectarian kettle was reaching boiling point. In an earlier letter, T. M. Reilly, deputy lieutenant of Co. Down, wrote: 'You cannot conceive the state the country is in of alarm, disgust, despair + indignation. We meet at every turn those who think a demonstration of strength ... would be useful for self defence + who fancy they are totally abandoned by the Govt.'[185]

[182] 'The Present Crisis – Resolution of the Committee', *The Protestant Magazine* 5 (July 1843), 223.

[183] De Grey to Erne, 24 April 1843, BARS, De Grey Papers, L29/700/13/3. De Grey wrote to Lord Erne in Fermanagh that 'the tranquillity of the Protestant Party, if the influence of their gentry can effect it, will be the heaviest blow that their enemies can receive'.

[184] 'Journal, June – July 1843', BARS, De Grey Papers, L29/700/36/12.

[185] 'Extracts from very recent private letters on the state of the country and the policy of the Government', BARS, De Grey Papers, L29/700/36/11, emphasis in the original. Although newspapers reported on the tranquillity of the Twelfth of July, sectarian rioting

## Conclusion: Betrayal of Irish Protestants and the End of Peel's Party

The Conservative government, in the end, did not abandon the Protestants of Ireland over the matter of Repeal; they chose other issues to abandon them on, instead. As O'Connell continued to organise Ireland's population, government opinion hardened in proportion to its fears that an eruption of violence was inevitable.[186] The government procured legal pretexts to force a showdown with O'Connell before the Clontarf meeting and subsequently to arrest him, grinding Repeal to a halt. O'Connell proceeded to seek aid from his old friends, the Whigs, while quarrelling with new elements in his own camp, embodied in the Young Ireland movement. Crucially, however, O'Connell's campaign had only further convinced Peel of the need to change the way Ireland was governed, what McIntyre calls Peel's 'second and constructive phase'.[187] Peel continued to spar with De Grey about finding Catholics to appoint to various positions within the Irish government's bureaucracy, writing that while a policy of only picking the man 'superior in point of qualification' seemed sound in practice, in reality it led to systematic discrimination against Catholics and 'a monopoly in favour of the Protestant just as complete as it was before the removal of Disability'.[188] With O'Connell's general weakness, both inside and outside Parliament, in the aftermath of the Repeal campaign's collapse, and taking into account the relative calm of the countryside, Peel believed the time was right to provide significant Irish reforms that might win over moderate Catholic views. Along with Eliot and Graham, Peel proposed legislation that would indirectly support the Catholic clergy; he pledged himself to reform the franchise on equal terms with Great Britain; he suggested his support for reform in educational policy; and he endorsed Eliot's proposal to significantly boost the support of the Catholic college of Maynooth – all measures that Peel framed, at least in part, in terms of the advantage a stable Ireland offered to the security of the British Empire.[189] While the Whigs generally questioned Peel's sincerity – 'how is he to be for equality who governs for Inequality + by Inequality?', Russell mused to his former Chancellor of the Exchequer, Thomas Spring Rice – the Whigs found themselves in a difficult political situation, needing to distance themselves from O'Connell's Repeal movement

---

immediately followed the anniversary in Belfast; 'Rioting in Sandy-Row and Barrack Street', BNL, 18 July 1843; also, see Farrell, *Rituals and Riots*, 141–3.
[186] MacDonagh, *Emancipist*, 238–43.   [187] Macintyre, *The Liberator*, 277–82, at 280.
[188] Peel to De Grey, 22 August [1843], BL, Peel Papers, MS Add 40,478, f. 166.
[189] Kerr, *Peel, Priests, and Politics*, ch. 3; on imperial security see 118.

while also finding ways to distinguish their Irish policy from that of the Tories.[190]

For the evangelical Protestants in both Britain and Ireland who had used Irish agrarian outrage to stir up anti-Catholic sentiments so effectively in 1841, Peel's shift to more conciliatory approaches was yet another betrayal. At the beginning of 1844, the *Protestant Magazine* bemoaned the 'traitors [who] have been at work, some who have dared to call themselves Conservatives, professing to be the firm supporters of the Protestant throne, faithful Protestants, have so undermined the foundations ... which were cemented by the blood of our martyred forefathers'. Rather than 'wait for *any* Government', the author argued that Protestants individually had only one course to pursue: 'we must cry aloud, disregarding the coldness of professed friends, or the scoffs of open enemies'.[191] The *Times* offered a similar reflection on the dangerous consequences of Peel's actions. Reflecting on the two main sources of Conservative Party support – agriculture and Protestantism – the paper argued that although agriculturalists might tolerate 'the radical reforms which he has introduced into the tariffs', Protestants would not be placated. 'Sir Robert Peel might revolutionise the laws which protected the great proprietors and farmers ... but at present *he places a sacrilegious hand on the religious Constitution of England, and he will see the consequences; and let him be assured that he will pay the penalty.*'[192]

Peel's penalty was his fall from office and the fracture of his political party. While it is unlikely that the orthodox interpretation of Peel's downfall centring on the Corn Laws will be radically altered, the rhetoric of his Protestant base from the Repeal crisis through the debate over Maynooth does suggest the importance of both Ireland and religion in the backlash he suffered. Disraeli's speech stating that Peel 'bamboozles one party, and plunders the other' was not a reference to the debate over agricultural policy but that over the Maynooth grant; and the oft-quoted rhyme, 'How wonderful is Peel!/He changeth with the Time/Turning and twisting like an eel/Ascending through the slime' was prefaced with the lines 'He gives whatever they want/To those who ask with Zeal/He yields the Maynooth Grant.'[193]

---

[190] Russell to Lord Monteagle, 1 October 1843, NLI, Monteagle Papers, MS 13,394/3; on the Whigs' difficulties see Palmerston to Russell, 22 December 1843, TNA, Russell Papers, PRO 30/22/4C, ff. 102–3.

[191] 'A Word to Protestants', *Protestant Magazine* 6 (January 1844), at 10, 13.

[192] *The Times*, quoted in A. S. Thelwall, *Proceedings of the Anti-Maynooth Conference of 1845: With a Historical Introduction, and an Appendix.* Compiled and Edited (at the Request of the Central Anti-Maynooth Committee) by the Rev. A. S. Thelwall (London: Seeley, Burnside and Seeley, 1845), at lvi; emphasis in the original.

[193] Both quoted in Simon Skinner 's excellent chapter, 'Religion', in *Languages of Politics in Nineteenth-Century Britain*, ed. David Craig and James Thompson (Houndmills: Palgrave Macmillan, 2013), 93–117, at 104–5.

Massive electoral victories built on the back of an extremely effective anti-Irish/anti-Catholic campaign allowed Peel the freedom to treat the ultra-Tory faction with disdain. However, the dogged refusal of Irish problems to subside, culminating with the instability brought about by O'Connell's campaign for Repeal, exposed the distance between Anglo-Irish politicians and the Conservative Party led by Peel. When ultra-Tories in Ireland wanted a return to the hard-and-fast application of former coercive powers they were met with indecision, or indeed conciliation. The backlash over Maynooth, therefore, was a culmination of the disjointed pursuit by Peel to travel some *via media*, which convinced neither side in Ireland.

# 6    Conclusion

This book has argued that Irish agrarian violence – 'outrages' – emerged as a significant point of contention in British politics during the decade of reform, which conditioned how that decade unfolded. In Ireland itself, some of the country's rural poor adopted tactics to resist the imposition of British legal and social norms and the emergence of a capitalist regime regulating aspects of their very existence – like access to land, the value of their labour, or their exclusion from an increasingly export-oriented agricultural market. British and Irish elites interpreted this collective action as a subversive threat to the structure of the state, and notwithstanding differing points of emphasis, deployed its coercive power to assert the British state's dominance in Irish life. The experience of violence, but also the spectre of that violence, bred the insecurity that led to a tendency to read political revolution into every backyard brawl, further muddying the historical waters and leading historians to ponder whether conservatives were justified in their perception that 'a Rebellion, as in 1798, again threaten[ed] to overwhelm' them, that 'treasonable societies' were 'arming and organising themselves for the coming event', and that they were 'again threatened with the massacre of 1641'.[1] The easy answer, of course, is no; however, the focus of this book on Irish outrage has been on how perceptions and hyperbolic rhetoric could be just as effective at influencing political outcomes as the pikemen of '98 and the memories of 1641.

The question remained, how to deal with Irish outrages? This book has answered that question by exploring the shift in governing culture that took place across the 1830s and the ways opponents mobilised to thwart its impact. The politics of ministers connected with the government of Ireland was animated by their commitment to the enlightenment principles of the French Revolution and a firm aristocratic conviction that government could act as a constructive force to alleviate peoples'

---

[1] Anon. , *The Address of the Metropolitan Conservative Society of Ireland to the Protestant of Great Britain* [...] (Dublin: W. Warren, 1840), 16.

grievances. Rather than relying on coercive legislation to rule Ireland by force, Russell, Mulgrave, and Morpeth attempted to pacify it by means of centralising reforms and opening up positions of political power to an aspirant Catholic professional class. In this project, they found a political ally in Daniel O'Connell, who saw the new Whig government in 1835 as 'a brain blow to the Orange faction' and believed he could do the most good for Ireland by keeping 'what control [he] possibly [could] *over* the new Government instead of being under *their* control'.[2] O'Connell's alliance with the Whigs was more than a marriage of convenience; in fact, it was a relationship born of mutual respect. The Whigs recognised O'Connell's tremendous power in Ireland, and rather than scorn that influence they sought to harness it. Though O'Connell never had as much power in the Whigs' government as opponents ascribed to him, the fact Mulgrave offered him a post within the government serves as ample testimony both to the novelty of the Whigs' approach and their recognition of his pre-eminence. Had the House of Lords been a more cooperative body and accepted more Whig reform efforts early in their time in office it is entirely possible, if not probable, that O'Connell would have maintained his alliance and never returned to 'simple repeal'.

Reliance on O'Connell, however, proved a double-edged sword. The reality is that the Lichfield House Compact soured not so much because of discord between the participants but rather as a result of the growing frustration on O'Connell's side and their eventual intolerance of the lack of legislative progress. Catholic Emancipation did not dampen religious animosity; rather, it acted as an accelerant. Ultra-Tories saw the world crumbling before their eyes, and rather than resign themselves to their fate they weaponised the Protestant identity of the British state – and wider empire – in a bid to mobilise the electorate to vote out Whigs who were dependent on their political positions, from 'the Burly Beggarman and *County-monger* … the Master of the Whig-Radical-Papist-Repeal-Cabinet, and virtual Ruler of the Empire'.[3] Their most successful weapon turned out to be the rhetoric of Irish violence, which they dressed up in sectarian, revolutionary, or cultural motives to suit their purposes. The anti-Catholic/anti-Irish sentiments they stirred up throughout the later 1830s produced the electoral conclusion they hoped for – a massive Conservative majority. What did not follow, however, was the wider Protestant deliverance or a rebirth of Protestant Ascendancy. Instead,

---

[2] O'Connell to FitzPatrick, 10 April 1835, O'Connell, *Correspondence*, 5:288; O'Connell to FitzPatrick, 14 April 1835, ibid., 5:289.
[3] *Reflections on the O'Connell 'Alliance', or Lichfield House Conspiracy: From a Letter to a Friend* (London: Roake and Varty, 1836), 8.

freed from his reliance on ultra-Tory support, Peel plodded along a *via media* that appeased no one in Ireland.

The early 1840s witnessed the coming apart of political parties as Whigs transformed into Liberals, Conservatives ignored the anti-Catholic wing their 1841 electoral campaign had unleashed, and O'Connell lost his singular grip on Irish nationalism. In Ireland, the rise of Young Ireland as a cultural nationalism that appealed to a shared – or invented – national identity that was 'racy of the soil' chafed with O'Connell's vision of an explicitly Catholic nationalism.[4] Where O'Connell advocated 'moral' force to press the Irish people's demands for repeal, Young Ireland increasingly advocated the potential necessity of physical violence. This underlying tension came to the surface when Peel outlawed O'Connell's meeting at Clontarf, forcing the latter to choose between constitutionalism and the potential for violent unrest. However, the tensions between the movements extended beyond tactics and identity and included a fundamental division between Young Ireland's ethno-racial vision, which employed 'the racial language of Celts and Saxons', and O'Connell's utilitarianism, which embraced British political, economic, and legal systems, provided that men like O'Connell could control these processes within Ireland.[5]

Neither Young Ireland nor O'Connell were able to bring about repeal and the debate between constitutional moral suasion and a separatist (and potentially violent) cultural nationalism would continue to swirl throughout the nineteenth and twentieth centuries. Instead, the Great Famine in Ireland would interrupt these arguments and plunge the country into its darkest years. The Famine became the defining event of the modern era; it characterised Irish identity, hastened the country's global diaspora, and became the trump card in the hands of Irish nationalists describing their long oppression at the hands of the British government.[6] The Famine, in its tragic way, alleviated the pressure on Ireland's land

---

[4] O'Connell wrote to Rev. Paul Cullen, at that time the rector of the Irish College in Rome, with a sixteen-point treatise on the benefits of repeal for Catholicism, which included his belief that 'a legislature devoted to Religion, to Catholic truth in doctrine' would have a profound 'moral effect' on the people. See O'Connell to Cullen, 9 May 1842, in O'Connell, *Correspondence*, 7:160. On Young Ireland, see Cian T. McMahon, *The Global Dimensions of Irish Identity: Race, Nation, and the Popular Press, 1840–1880* (Chapel Hill: University of North Carolina, Press, 2015), ch. 1; on the role of civic republican traditions rather than 'romanticism', see David Dwan, 'Civic Virtue in the Modern World: The Politics of Young Ireland', *Irish Political Studies* 22, no. 1 (2007): 35–60.

[5] McMahon, *Global Dimensions of Irish Identity*, 30.

[6] This debate recently entered back into popular discourse with the publication of Tim Pat Coogan's *The Famine Plot: England's Role in Ireland's Greatest Tragedy* (New York: Palgrave Macmillan, 2013), which resurrects the 'genocide' debate and the intentionality of British policymakers in perpetuating mass deaths in Ireland. On the merits of the book, and Coogan's scholarship, see 'Was the Famine a Genocide?', https://drb.ie/was-the-famine-a-genocide/.

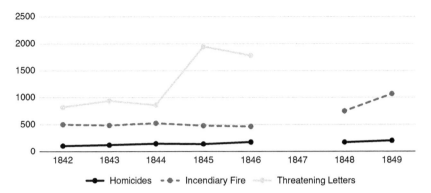

Figure 6.1 Numbers of homicides, incendiary fires, and threatening letters between 1842 and 1849
Source: Compiled from 'Outrages (Ireland). A return of outrages specially reported to the Constabulary Office in Ireland, during the year 1842, 1843, 1844 and 1845', P. P. (1846, vol. 35, 217); 'Outrages (Ireland). Returns of the number and description of outrages specially reported by the constabulary throughout Ireland, in each of the years 1845 and 1846', P. P. (1847, vol. 56, 64); 'Outrages (Ireland). Number of outrages reported by the constabulary in Ireland during the periods of six months, ending respectively the 30th June 1848, 31st December 1848, 30th June 1849, 31st December 1849, and 30th June 1850, classified under five heads', P. P. (1850, vol. 51, 639)

holdings as the most vulnerable died, emigrated, or were pushed into Ireland's cities and workhouses. In the process, however, outrages continued across the Irish countryside. Between 1842 and 1849, homicides in Ireland nearly doubled.[7] Similarly, crimes like incendiary fires and threatening letters also saw remarkable increases between the early 1840s and the beginning of the Famine. Figure 6.1 gives an indication of the rise in homicides, incendiary fires, and threatening notices from an array of different parliamentary sources.[8]

As is clearly evident, the beginning of the Famine marked an increase in violence. The increase in evictions pushed peasant actors to rally together to defend local land ownership and to protect their families and larger communities from landlords and their agents who wished to consolidate holdings and make estates profitable in the

[7] McMahon, *Homicide in Pre-Famine and Famine Ireland*, 20.
[8] Figure 6.1 is compiled from three different parliamentary papers, none of which include statistics for 1847, hence their absence. Similarly, no data exist concerning threatening letters in 1848 and 1849.

future.[9] The increase in violence prompted Peel's government to propose a new coercion bill – the Protection of Life (Ireland) Bill – which
vested the lord lieutenant with increased powers, including the authority
to impose martial law and pre-emptively arrest those deemed
suspicious.[10] Secret societies continued to operate in some localities,
targeting landlords who ejected tenants and responding to the evolving
crisis.[11] In the wake of O'Connell's death, the worsening Famine crisis,
callous actions of land agents, and failed government policy spurred
Young Ireland to action as they staged a rebellion in 1848 – farcical in
its execution, but a touchstone for later generations of Irish nationalists
carrying the flame of revolutionary nationalism.[12]

While outrages in Ireland continued to increase in 1845 and the beginning
of 1846, Peel's government returned to the age-old solution of coercion. The
Chief Secretary, the Earl of St. Germans (Lord Eliot's title after his father's
death in 1845), proposed in March 1846 to pass the Protection of Life
(Ireland) Bill, which would increase the powers of the lord lieutenant,
enabling him to proclaim districts and impose strict curfews, transgression
of which would be punishable by transportation. Referencing the Coercion
Bill passed by Lord Grey's government in 1834, St. Germans made a strong
appeal for the necessity of 'arbitrary power' because 'There were official
reports made to the Executive Government daily of the outrages committed
in every part of Ireland'. Referring to the 'systematic course [of the
violence] ... utterly defying all the powers of the law', St. Germans highlighted the wanton acts of violence, especially murders, being carried out
across Ireland, which had convinced him that the only remedy lay in the
application of force.[13] St. Germans found interesting allies in his task,
including Lord Monteagle (formerly Thomas Spring Rice), the former
chancellor of the exchequer in Melbourne's government and a lifelong
Whig. Monteagle rallied those on his side of the House by appealing again
to history and reminding his colleagues of all the great Irish patriots and
liberal lords who had supported the Insurrection Act of old, an act 'infinitely
stronger, more unconstitutional, and more repulsive to all the doctrines

---

[9] On the process of 'squaring' and its traumatic effects see Mac Suibhne, *The End of
Outrage*, 89–96; W. E. Vaughan, *Landlords and Tenants in Mid-Victorian Ireland*
(Oxford: Oxford University Press, 1994), 20–6.
[10] Enda Delaney, *The Curse of Reason: The Great Irish Famine* (Dublin: Gill & Macmillan,
2012), 108–9; 'Bill, intituled, Act for Better Protection of Life, and to facilitate
Apprehension and Detection of Persons guilty of certain Offences in Ireland',
P. P. (1846, vol. 3, no. 132).
[11] Mac Suibhne, *The End of Outrage*, 61–2.
[12] Christine Kinealy, *Repeal and Revolution: 1848 in Ireland* (Manchester: Manchester
University Press, 2009), ch. 6.
[13] Hansard, 3rd ser., vol. 84, col. 687, 6 March 1846.

wisely laid down for ordinary occasions' than the one St. Germans proposed.[14] For a brief period, even Lord John Russell supported Peel's efforts to pass this legislation and put an end to the violence witnessed across the Irish countryside, before coming to his senses and using it as the means by which to topple Peel's government.[15]

Here the Conservative government stood in March 1846 – on the very same precipice where thirteen years earlier the Whigs had stood, dealing with the same problems of Irish agrarian violence, coming to the same conclusions as before, and using the same rationales to justify their actions. What is more, though Peel's government collapsed after the division over the bill, it mattered little – the Whigs who would take Peel's place would not be the same as those who had entered Parliament triumphantly in 1835 on the basis of the principle of Irish church appropriation or the desire to do 'justice to Ireland'. Rather, Lord John Russell headed a government not of young Whig interventionists convinced in the capability of good govern-ance to solve public grievances, but of liberals who put their faith in the workings of the free market, and moralists placing their faith in the assur-ance of God's providence. The application of these principles would bring with them horrifying consequences in the form of a massive number of deaths in Ireland over the subsequent five years.[16] They would also bring about the end of the Whig Party and the beginning of the new Liberal one.

Although the Famine did temporarily alleviate the heavy burden of popu-lation on Irish land, it did not solve the structural problems inherent in Ireland's landholding system.[17] Instead, government policy attempted to reinforce the landlord system by enticing new capital investment from Britain into old bankrupted estates under the Encumbered Estates Act, which between 1849 and 1855 facilitated the sale of roughly 2.5 million acres of land.[18] As Peter Gray has noted, the British government's unwilling-ness to modify its understanding of the relationship between landlord and

---

[14] Hansard, 3rd ser., vol. 84, cols. 710–11, 6 March 1846.

[15] Greville, *Greville Memoirs*, 2: 375, 382.

[16] Mark McGowan, '*The Famine Plot* Revisited: A Reassessment of the Great Irish Famine as Genocide', *Genocide Studies International* 11, no. 1 (December 2017): 87–104; Peter Gray, 'Ideology and the Famine', in *The Great Irish Famine*, ed. Cathal Póirtéir (Dublin: Mercier Press, 1995). For a more charitable view of the Whigs' Famine policy based on their economic priorities, see Charles Read, 'Laissez-Faire, the Irish Famine, and British Financial Crisis', *The Economic History Review* 69, no. 2 (May 2016): 411–34.

[17] Ó Gráda notes that after the Famine farmers had greater access to land, labourers worked in a tighter labour market, and landlords received a higher proportion of rent due to them. Nevertheless, these were temporary results of the famine rather than fixed outcomes. See Cormac Ó Gráda, *Black '47 and Beyond: the Great Irish Famine in History, Economy, and Memory* (Princeton, NJ: Princeton University Press, 2000), ch. 4.

[18] Willie Nolan, 'Land Reform in Post-Famine Ireland', in *Atlas of the Great Irish Famine, 1845–52*, eds. John Crowley, William J. Smyth, and Mike Murphy (Cork: Cork University Press, 2012), 571.

tenant, and an insistence on a laissez-faire approach to regulating that relationship, ended up driving the land question and the national question onto one common road.[19] Not surprisingly, the new 'improving' landlords who were eager to turn a profit on their investment looked to sheep and cattle as a source of substantial revenue, and in the process continued large-scale land clearances in the 1850s and 1860s.[20] Before the economic downturn of the late 1870s, landlords were living in what some historians have deemed the 'Indian summer of landlordism'.[21] This Indian summer quickly ended during the economic downturn of the 1870s, with the unprecedented rise in collective action by Irish tenants to protect themselves against landlord evictions and economic immiseration.[22]

Even during the Famine, however, tenants fought for the introduction of the three Fs – fair rent, fixity of tenure, and free sale – on surprisingly ecumenical lines with the formation of the Tenant League in 1850. Though the League never reached the level of support of O'Connell's Monster Meetings, the fact that Presbyterian and Catholic clergy members agreed on the necessity of land reform ensured that the issue would remain on the nation's consciousness until adequately addressed.[23] Irish peasants and a growing number of small farmers latched onto the words of James Fintan Lalor, who in leading a tenant meeting in Tipperary in September 1847 said: 'That of natural right, on the grant of God, the soil of Ireland belongs to the people of Ireland ... which never could or can be parted with, pass, or perish; and which no power on earth, nor any length of adverse possession can take away, annul, bar, or diminish'.[24] Lalor's insistence on the Irish people's right as 'land-owners and law-maker of this island'[25] neatly encapsulated the inspiration for the collective action carried out by Michael Davitt's Land League during the Land Wars between 1879 and 1881, which had, for the first time fused the revolutionary tradition of agrarian violence with parliamentary politics, and had

[19] Gray, *Famine, Land and Politics*, 329–30, 332.
[20] Donald E. Jordan, *Land and Popular Politics in Ireland: County Mayo from the Plantation to the Land War* (Cambridge: Cambridge University Press, 1994), 116.
[21] Cormac Ó Gráda, *Ireland Before and After the Famine: Explorations in Economic History, 1800–1925*, 2nd ed. (Manchester: Manchester University Press, 1993), 152.
[22] Clark, *Social Origins of the Irish Land War*, 321–2.
[23] Paul Bew, *Ireland: The Politics of Enmity, 1789–2006* (Oxford: Oxford University Press, 2009), 234–5.
[24] 'The Meeting at Holycross', FJ, 20 September 1847.
[25] Lalor's letter to the *Irish Felon* contained his most enduring lines to Irish nationalist rhetoric: 'The principle I state ... is this, that the entire ownership of Ireland, moral and material, up to the sun, and down to the centre, is vested of right in the people of Ireland; that they, and none but they, are the land-owners and law-maker of this island.' See L. Fogarty, *James Fintan Lalor: Patriot and Political Essayist, 1807–1849* (Dublin: Talbot Press, 1919), 60–1, www.archive.org/stream/jamesfintanlalor00lalouoft/jamesfintanla lor00lalouoft_djvu.txt.

made terms like 'boycotting' famous. It also invoked the legacy of much of the types of Irish outrage that had been so prevalent in pre-Famine society. This fusion of agrarian violence and revolutionary politics only continued during the early twentieth century as a vital nexus developed between political revolutionaries, like the members of the Irish Republican Brotherhood (IRB) and later, of Sinn Féin, an organisation intent on the redistribution of Irish land and on peasant proprietorship.[26]

How did segments of the British press understand this dangerous fusion? Not surprisingly, they understood it in terms of Irish outrages. Gladstone's Liberal Party received the scorn of *The Times* during the Land War because of Gladstone's relationship with the Irish parliamentary leader Charles Stewart Parnell, whose power base was largely comprised of Land League activists. These men, who participated in agrarian violence for distinctly political ends – in this case for the settlement of the land question – were described with the neologism 'outrage-monger', a linguistic legacy produced by the fusion between land politics and revolutionary politics in an Irish context.[27] Land reform would continue to animate the relationship between Irish politics, the British government, and a potentially violent and at times revolutionary countryside, whose issues were addressed after Irish independence and produced their own bitter legacies.[28]

For a brief window of six years, a group of interventionist Whigs had occupied ministerial benches, determined to do 'justice to Ireland'. Supported by one of the greatest politicians of the nineteenth century, Daniel O'Connell, these men brought new modes of thinking to government policy and attempted to enact meaningful reforms. Their legacy was mostly one of failure. The anger and hostility that had been generated by governing Ireland as an equal part of the United Kingdom brought about one of the largest Conservative parliamentary victories, as a minority of the Conservative Party wielded an exaggerated influence over the party's trajectory and deployed Irish outrages as a political wedge to drive English voters to back Robert Peel. Thus, this episode in Whig failure is a good reminder of the fact that Ireland was not simply John Bull's other island, adrift across the Irish Sea; instead, it played an important, at times decisive role in shaping, constraining, and frustrating the politics, culture, and function of the United Kingdom as a whole. We still hear those historical echoes today.

[26] Fergus J. M. Campbell, *Land and Revolution: Nationalist Politics in the West of Ireland, 1891–1921* (Oxford and New York: Oxford University Press, 2005), chs. 4, 6.

[27] 'Outrage, n.', *OED Online*, June 2020, Oxford University Press, www.oed.com/view/Entry/133856.

[28] Terence Dooley, *The Land for the People: The Land Question in Independent Ireland* (Dublin: University College Dublin Press, 2004); Anne Dolan, 'Politics, Economy and Society in the Irish Free State, 1922–1939', in *The Cambridge History of Ireland vol. 4*, ed. Thomas Bartlett (Cambridge: Cambridge University Press, 2018), 323–48.

# Bibliography

## Primary Sources

### Archives and Private Collections

Belfast: Public Records Office of Northern Ireland (PRONI)
  Anglesey Papers
  Downshire Papers
  Gosford Papers
  Roden Papers (MIC 147)
Chichester: West Sussex Record Office (WSRO)
  Goodwood Collection
Dublin: National Archives of Ireland (NAI)
  Chief Secretary's Office: Official Papers Miscellaneous Assorted (OPMA)
  Chief Secretary's Office Registered Papers (CSROP)
  Outrage Papers (OP)
  Rebellion Papers (RP)
Dublin: National Library of Ireland (NLI)
  Farnham Papers
  Larcom Papers
  Mahon Papers
  Monteagle Papers
  O'Hara Papers
Dublin: Representative Church Body Library (RCBL)
  Beresford Papers
Dublin: Trinity College Dublin
  Donoughmore Papers
Durham: Durham County Records Office (DCRO)
  Londonderry Papers
Exeter: Exeter Cathedral Library (ECL)
  Phillpotts Papers

Kew: The National Archives (TNA)
    Colonial Office, Dublin Castle Records
    Home Office Papers
    Irish Office Papers
    Russell Papers
Liverpool: Liverpool Public Library (LPL)
    Derby Papers
London: British Library (BL)
    Broughton Papers
    Peel Papers
London: University College London (UCL)
    Chadwick Papers
Nottingham: University of Nottingham Special Collections (UNSC)
    Newcastle Papers
Pakenhamhall: Tullynally Castle (TC)
    Lord Longford Papers
Southampton: University of Southampton Special Collections (USSC)
    Broadlands Papers
    Palmerston Papers
    Wellington Papers
Whitby: Mulgrave Castle (MS)
    Mulgrave MSS
York: Castle Howard (CH)
    Morpeth Papers


*Official Publications*

*Hansard's Parliamentary Debates*, 1st, 2nd, and 3rd series.


*Contemporary Books*

Anon. *The Address of the Metropolitan Conservative Society of Ireland to the Protestant of Great Britain* [...]. Dublin: W. Warren, 1840.
    *Addresses Presented to His Excellency the Earl of Mulgrave, from the Different Parts of Ireland, During the Years 1835 and 1836, with His Excellency's Answers.* Dublin: William Fredrick Wakeman, 1836.
    *The Assembled Commons; or, Parliamentary Biographer, with an Abstract of the Law of Election, by a Member of the Middle Temple.* London: Scott, Webster, and Geary, 1838.
    *Popery in Power, and Britain Betrayed* .... London: J. F. Shaw, 1854.
Boyton, Charles. *Speech Delivered by the Rev. C. Boyton, F. T. C. D., at a Meeting of the Protestant Conservative Society, on Tuesday, the 10th July, 1832.* Dublin: J. Hoare, 1832.

Carleton, William. *Traits and Stories of the Irish Peasantry*. London: Routledge, 1877.

Colquhoun, John Campbell, and the Protestant Association. *On the Objects and Uses of Protestant Associations*. 3rd ed. London: The Protestant Association, 1840.

Curwen, John Christian. *Observations on the State of Ireland, Principally Directed to Its Agriculture and Rural Population; in a Series of Letters Written on a Tour through That Country*, 2 vols. (Vol. 1). London: Baldwin, Cradock, and Joy, 1818.

Disraeli, Benjamin. *Vindication of the English Constitution in a Letter to a Noble and Learned Lord*. London: Saunders and Otley, 1835.

Dixon, James. *Letters of the Duties of Protestants with Regard to Popery*. Sheffield: G. Chaloner, 1840.

Dixon, Richard Watson. *The Life of James Dixon, D. D., Wesleyan Minister*. London: Watson and Hazell, 1874.

Doyle, James Warren. *Letter to Thomas Spring Rice, Esq. M.P. &c: On the Establishment of a Legal Provision for the Irish Poor, and on the Nature and Destination of Church Property*. Dublin: R. Coyne, 1831.

Drummond, Thomas. *Memoir of Thomas Drummond*. Edited by John Ferguson McLennan. Edinburgh: Edmonston and Douglas, 1867.

Ellenborough, Edward Law, Earl of. *A Political Diary, 1828–1830*. London: R. Bentley & Son, 1881.

Fogarty, L. *James Fintan Lalor: Patriot and Political Essayist, 1807–1849*. Dublin: Talbot Press, 1919. www.archive.org/stream/jamesfintanlalor00lalouoft/ja mesfintanlalor00lalouoft_djvu.txt.

Godwin, William. *An Enquiry Concerning Political Justice: And Its Influence on General Virtue and Happiness*. London: G. G. J. and J. Robinson, 1793.

Grande, James. *William Cobbett, the Press and Rural England: Radicalism and the Fourth Estate, 1792–1835*. Basingstoke: Palgrave Macmillan, 2014.

Grant, James. *Random Recollections of the House of Lords: From the Year 1830 to 1836, Including Personal Sketches of the Leading Members*. London: Smith, Elder, & Co., 1836.

Greville, Charles. *The Greville Memoirs: A Journal of the Reigns of King George IV and King William IV*. Edited by Henry Reeve. 2 vols. New York: D. Appleton and Company, 1886.

Greville, Charles. *The Greville Memoirs (Second Part): A Journal of the Reign of Queen Victoria from 1837 to 1852*. Edited by Henry Reeve. London: Longmans, Green & Co., 1885.

Hatherton, Baron Edward John Walhouse Littleton. *Memoir and Correspondence Relating to Political Occurrences in June and July 1834*. Edited by Henry Reeve. London: Longmans, Green and Co., 1872.

Holland, Henry Richard Vassall. *The Holland House Diaries 1831–1840: The Diary of Henry Richard Vassall Fox, Third Lord Holland, with Extracts from the Diary of Dr John Allen*. Edited by Abraham D. Kriegel. London: Routledge & Kegan Paul, 1977.

Inglis, Henry D. *A Journey Throughout Ireland, During the Spring ... of 1834.* London: Whittaker & C., 1834.

Johnson, James. *A Tour in Ireland: With Meditations and Reflections.* London: S. Highley, 32, Fleet Street, 1844.

Lewis, George Cornewall, Sir. *On Local Disturbances in Ireland: And on the Irish Church Question.* London: B. Fellowes, 1836.

Lewis, Samuel. *A Topographical Dictionary of Ireland: Comprising the Several Counties, Cities, Boroughs, Corporate, Market, and Post Towns, Parishes, and Villages, with Historical and Statistical Descriptions,* 2 vols. (Vol. 1.) Baltimore, MD: Genealogical Pub. Co., 1984.

*A Topographical Dictionary of Ireland: Comprising the Several Counties, Cities, Boroughs, Corporate, Market, and Post Towns, Parishes, and Villages, with Historical and Statistical Descriptions,* 2 vols. (Vol. 2.) Baltimore, MD: Genealogical Pub. Co., n.d.

M'Ghee, Robert James. *Letter to the Duke of Wellington [upon the Roman Catholic Question].* 2nd ed. London: Protestant Association, 1839.

*A Sermon Preached in Harold's Cross Church [. . .].* Dublin: Grant and Bolton, 1843.

Martin, Theodore. *A Life of Lord Lyndhurst: From Letters and Papers in Possession of His Family.* London: John Murray, 1883.

Mitchel, John. *The History of Ireland: From the Treaty of Limerick to the Present Time.* Vol. 1. 2nd ed. Dublin: James Duffy, 1869.

O'Brien, Richard Barry. *Thomas Drummond: Under-Secretary in Ireland, 1835–40; Life and Letters.* London: Kegan Paul, Trench, & Co., 1889.

O'Connell, Daniel. *The Correspondence of Daniel O'Connell.* Edited by Maurice O'Connell. 8 vols. Dublin: Irish Manuscripts Commission, 1972–80.

*Daniel O'Connell: His Early Life, and Journal, 1795 to 1802.* Edited by Arthur Houston. London: Sir I. Pitman & Sons, 1906.

Peel, Robert. *Sir Robert Peel: From His Private Papers.* Edited by Charles Stuart Parker. 3 vols. London: John Murray, 1899.

Phillpotts, Henry. *Charge Delivered to the Clergy of the Diocese of Exeter / by Henry, Lord Bishop of Exeter; at His Triennial Visitation in the Months of August, September, and October, 1839.* 4th ed. London: J. Murray, 1839.

Protestant Association, The. *Authentic Report of the Great Protestant Meeting Authentic Report of the Great Protestant Meeting Held at Exeter Hall London.* 3rd ed. Dublin: P. Dixon Hardy, 1835.

[Macleod Wylie]. *The Progress of Popery in the British Dominions and Elsewhere.* London: Protestant Association, 1839.

Protestant Colonization Society of Ireland. *Reflections on the O'Connell 'Alliance', or Lichfield House Conspiracy: From a Letter to a Friend.* London: Roake and Varty, 1836.

*Transactions of the Protestant Colonization Society of Ireland: Reported at a Public Meeting of Subscribers, in the Dublin Institution, ... May 24, 1832.* Dublin: J. Hoare, 2, Hawkins's-street, 1832.

Russell, John. *Recollections and Suggestions, 1813–1873*. Boston, MA: Roberts Brothers, 1875.

Sanders, Lloyd C., ed. *Lord Melbourne's Papers*. 2nd ed. London: Longmans, Green, 1890.

Stephens, George. *Political Prophecy Fulfilled; or, "Ireland," with a New Preface*. 6th ed. London: C. Mitchell, 1839.

[Stoney, Thomas George ]. *The Present State of Tipperary, as Regards Agrarian Outrages, Their Nature, Origin, and Increase, Considered, with Suggestions for Remedial Measures; Respectfully Submitted to the Right Hon. Lord Eliot, MP, Chief Secretary to the Lord Lieutenant*. Dublin: G. R. Tracy, 1842.

Thelwall, A. S. *Proceedings of the Anti-Maynooth Conference of 1845: With an Historical Introduction, and an Appendix. Compiled and Edited (at the Request of the Central Anti-Maynooth Committee) by the Rev. A. S. Thelwall*. London: Seeley, Burnside and Seeley, 1845.

Torrens, W. M. *Memoirs of William Lamb, Second Viscount Melbourne*. London: Ward, Lock, and Co., 1890.

Tucker, Robert C., ed. *The Marx-Engels Reader*. 2nd ed. New York: W. W. Norton & Company, 1978.

Vaughan, W. E., and A. J. Fitzpatrick, eds. *Irish Historical Statistics: Population, 1831–1971*. Dublin: Royal Irish Academy, 1978.

Wellesley, Arthur Wellesley, 1st Duke of Wellington. *Wellington II: Political Correspondence, November 1834–April 1835*. Edited by R. J. Olney and Julia Melvin. Vol. 2, 1st ed. Prime Ministers' Papers Series. London: Her Majesty's Stationery Office, 1986.

Wellesley, Richard Colley. *The Wellesley Papers: The Life and Correspondence of Richard Colley Wellesley, Marquess Wellesley, 1760–1842*. Vol. 2, 1st ed. London: Herbert Jenkins Limited, 1914.

### Newspapers and Journals

*The Aberdeen Journal*
*Belfast News-Letter*
*Blackwood's Edinburgh Magazine*
*Bucks Herald*
*Cheltenham Chronicle*
*Cobbett's Weekly Political Register*
*Cork Constitution*
*Dublin Evening Packet and Correspondent*
*Dublin Evening Post*
*The Dublin Review*
*Dublin University Magazine*
*Durham County Advertiser*
*Edinburgh Review*
*Fraser's Magazine*
*Freeman's Journal*
*Kerry Evening Post*
*Leeds Intelligencer*

*Leeds Mercury*
*Limerick Evening Post*
*Lincolnshire Chronicle*
*London Evening Standard*
*Londonderry Sentinel*
*Mail*
*Mayo Constitution*
*Morning Chronicle*
*Morning Post*
*Nenagh Guardian*
*The Newcastle Courant*
*The Penny Protestant Operative*
*The Pilot*
*The Protestant Magazine*
*Public Ledger and Daily Advertiser*
*The Quarterly Review*
*Sligo Champion*
*The Standard*
*The Times (London)*
*Wexford Conservative*
*Yorkshire Gazette*


*Parliamentary Papers*

ProQuest's online database UK Parliamentary Papers contains every paper referenced in this book: http://parlipapers.proquest.com.


## Secondary Sources

Akenson, Donald H. *Discovering the End of Time: Irish Evangelicals in the Age of Daniel O'Connell*. Montreal: McGill-Queen's University Press, 2016.

Archer, John E. *Social Unrest and Popular Protest in England, 1780–1840*. Cambridge: Cambridge University Press, 2000.

Armitage, David. 'Greater Britain: A Useful Category of Historical Analysis?' *The American Historical Review* 104, no. 2 (April 1999): 427–45.

Aspinall, Arthur. 'The Irish "Proclamation" Fund, 1800–1846'. *The English Historical Review* 56, no. 222 (April 1941): 265–80.

'The Use of Irish Secret Service Money in Subsidizing the Irish Press'. *The English Historical Review* 56, no. 224 (October 1941): 639–46.

Baigent, Elizabeth. 'Townsend [Townshend], Horace [Horatio] (1750–1837), Writer.' *ODNB*. Oxford: Oxford University Press, 2019. https://doi.org/10/1093/ref:odnb/27629

Barr, Colin. '"Imperium in Imperio": Irish Episcopal Imperialism in the Nineteenth Century'. *The English Historical Review* 123, no. 502 (June 2008): 611–50. https://doi.org/10.1093/ehr/cen161.

Bartlett, Thomas. 'An End to Moral Economy: The Irish Militia Disturbances of 1793'. *Past & Present*, no. 99 (May 1983): 41–64.

'Defenders and Defenderism in 1795'. *Irish Historical Studies* 24, no. 95 (1985): 373–81.

*The Fall and Rise of the Irish Nation: The Catholic Question, 1690–1830*. Savage, MD: Barnes & Noble, 1992.

Beames, Michael. 'The Ribbon Societies: Lower-Class Nationalism in Pre-Famine Ireland'. *Past & Present* 97, no. 1 (1982): 128–43.

'Rural Conflict in Pre-Famine Ireland: Peasant Assassinations in Tipperary, 1837–1847'. In *Nationalism and Popular Protest in Ireland*, edited by C. H. E. Philpin, 264–83. Cambridge: Cambridge University Press, 1987.

Beckett, J. C. *The Making of Modern Ireland: 1603–1923*. New York: Alfred A. Knopf, 1966.

Beiner, Guy. *Forgetful Remembrance: Social Forgetting and Vernacular Historiography of a Rebellion in Ulster*. Oxford: Oxford University Press, 2018.

Béland, Daniel. 'Insecurity and Politics: A Framework'. *The Canadian Journal of Sociology/Cahiers Canadiens de Sociologie* 32, no. 3 (Summer 2007): 317–40.

Bender, Jill C. 'Ireland and Empire'. In *The Princeton History of Modern Ireland*, edited by Richard Bourke and Ian McBride, 343–60. Princeton, NJ: Princeton University Press, 2016.

Bew, Paul. *Ireland: The Politics of Enmity, 1789–2006*. Oxford: Oxford University Press, 2009.

Biagini, Eugenio. *British Democracy and Irish Nationalism, 1876–1906*. Cambridge: Cambridge University Press, 2007.

Bielenberg, Andy. 'Exodus: The Emigration of Southern Irish Protestants during the Irish War of Independence and the Civil War'. *Past & Present*, no. 218 (2013): 199–233.

'The Irish Economy, 1815–1880: Agricultural Transition, the Communications Revolution and the Limits of Industrialisation'. In *The Cambridge History of Ireland*, edited by James Kelly, vol. 3. Cambridge: Cambridge University Press, 2018.

Blackstock, Allan. *An Ascendancy Army: The Irish Yeomanry, 1796–1834*. Dublin: Four Courts Press, 1998.

'The Irish Yeomanry and the 1798 Rebellion'. In *1798: A Bicentenary Perspective*, edited by Thomas Bartlett. Dublin: Four Courts Press, 2003.

'Tommy Downshire's Boys: Popular Protest, Social Change and Political Manipulation in Mid-Ulster 1829–1847'. *Past & Present* 196 (2007): 125–71.

Bottigheimer, Karl S. Review of The Irish in Europe, 1580–1815, Thomas O'Connor, ed. *The Sixteenth Century Journal* 33, no. 1 (Spring 2002): 264–6.

Bourke, Richard. 'Pocock and the Presuppositions of the New British History'. *The Historical Journal* 53, no. 3 (August 2010): 747–70.

Boyce, D. George, and Alan O'Day, eds. *The Making of Modern Irish History: Revisionism and the Revisionist Controversy*. London: Routledge, 1996.

Bradshaw, Brendan. 'Nationalism and Historical Scholarship in Modern Ireland'. *Irish Historical Studies* 26, no. 104 (November 1989): 329–51.

Brady, Ciaran. *The Chief Governors: The Rise and Fall of Reform Government in Tutor Ireland 1536–1588*. Cambridge: Cambridge University Press, 1994.

*Interpreting Irish History: The Debate on Historical Revisionism 1938–1994*. Dublin: Irish Academic Press, 1994.

Brent, Richard. *Liberal Anglican Politics: Whiggery, Religion, and Reform: 1830–1841*. Oxford: Clarendon Press, 1987.

Bric, Maurice J. 'Priests, Parsons and Politics: The Rightboy Protest in County Cork 1785–1788'. *Past & Present*, no. 100 (August 1983): 100–23.

'The Tithe System in Eighteenth-Century Ireland'. *Proceedings of the Royal Irish Academy. Section C: Archaeology, Celtic Studies, History, Linguistics, Literature* 86C (1986): 271–88.

Broeker, Galen. 'Robert Peel and the Peace Preservation Force'. *The Journal of Modern History* 33, no. 4 (December 1961): 363–73.

*Rural Disorder and Police Reform in Ireland, 1812–36*. London: Routledge and Kegan Paul, 1970.

Brown, Stewart J. *Providence and Empire: Religion, Politics and Society in the United Kingdom, 1815–1914*. Religion, Politics and Society in Britain. Harlow: Pearson Longman, 2008.

Burns, Arthur and Joanna Innes. 'Introduction'. In *Rethinking the Age of Reform: Britain 1780–1850*, edited by Arthur Burns and Joanna Innes, 1–70. Cambridge: Cambridge University Press, 2003.

Burns, Arthur, and Joanna Innes, eds. *Rethinking the Age of Reform: Britain 1780–1850*. Cambridge: Cambridge University Press, 2003.

Burton, Antoinette M. *The Trouble with Empire: Challenges to Modern British Imperialism*. Oxford: Oxford University Press, 2017.

Butler, Richard J. *Building the Irish Courthouse and Prison: A Political History, 1750–1850*. Cork: Cork University Press, 2020.

'Rethinking The Origins of the British Prisons Act of 1835: Ireland and the Development of Central-Government Prison Inspection, 1820–1835'. *The Historical Journal* 59, no. 3 (September 2016): 721–46.

Cahill, Gilbert A. 'Irish Catholicism and English Toryism'. *The Review of Politics* 19, no. 1 (January 1957): 62–76.

'The Protestant Association and the Anti-Maynooth Agitation of 1845'. *The Catholic Historical Review* 43, no. 3 (1957): 273–308.

Campbell, Fergus J. M. *Land and Revolution: Nationalist Politics in the West of Ireland, 1891–1921*. Oxford and New York: Oxford University Press, 2005.

Chaffin, Tom. *Giant's Causeway: Frederick Douglass's Irish Odyssey and the Making of an American Visionary*. Charlottesville, VA: University of Virginia Press, 2014.

Chase, Malcolm. *1820: Disorder and Stability in the United Kingdom*. Manchester: Manchester University Press, 2013.

Clark, Gemma. 'Arson in Modern Ireland: Fire and Protest Before the Famine'. In *Crime, Violence and the Irish in the Nineteenth Century*, edited by Kyle Hughes and Donald M. MacRaild, 212–26. Liverpool: Liverpool University Press, 2018.

*Everyday Violence in the Irish Civil War*. Cambridge: Cambridge University Press, 2014.

Clark, J. C. D. *English Society 1688–1832: Ideology, Social Structure, and Political Practice During the Ancien Regime*. Cambridge Studies in the History and Theory of Politics. Cambridge: Cambridge University Press, 1985.

Clark, Samuel. 'The Importance of Agrarian Class: Agrarian Class Structure and Collective Action in Nineteenth-Century Ireland'. *British Journal of Sociology* 29, no. 1 (March 1978): 22–40.

*Social Origins of the Irish Land War*. Princeton, NJ: Princeton University Press, 1979.

Close, David. 'The Formation of a Two-Party Alignment in the House of Commons between 1832 and 1841'. *The English Historical Review* 84, no. 331 (1 April 1969): 257–77.

Colley, Linda. *Britons: Forging the Nation, 1707–1837*. New Haven, CT: Yale University Press, 1992.

Connolly, S. J. 'The Houghers: Agrarian Protest in Early Eighteenth-Century Connacht'. In *Nationalism and Popular Protest in Ireland*, edited by C. H. E. Philpin, 139–62. New York: Cambridge University Press, 1987.

*Religion, Law, and Power: the Making of Protestant Ireland 1660–1760*. Oxford: Oxford University Press, 1992.

Coohill, Joseph. *Ideas of the Liberal Party: Perceptions, Agendas and Liberal Politics in the House of Commons, 1832–52*. Parliamentary History : Texts & Studies vol. 5. Chichester: Wiley-Blackwell for The Parliamentary History Yearbook Trust, 2011.

Cragoe, Matthew. 'The Great Reform Act and Modernization of British Politics: The Impact of Conservative Associations, 1835–1841'. *Journal of British Studies* 47 (July 2008): 581–603.

Cronin, Maura. 'Popular Politics, 1815–1845'. In *The Cambridge History of Ireland*, edited by Thomas Bartlett, vol. 3 edited by James Kelly, 128–49. Cambridge: Cambridge University Press, 2018.

Crosbie, Barry. *Irish Imperial Networks: Migration, Social Communication and Exchange in Nineteenth-Century India*. Cambridge: Cambridge University Press, 2011.

Crossman, Virginia. 'Emergency Legislation and Agrarian Disorder in Ireland, 1821–41'. *Irish Historical Studies* xxvii, no. 108 (1991): 309–23.

*Politics, Law and Order in Nineteenth-Century Ireland*. Dublin: Gill & Macmillan, 1996.

Cullen, L. M. 'The Political Structures of the Defenders'. In *Ireland and the French Revolution*, edited by Hugh Gough and David Dickson. Dublin: Irish Academic Press, 1990.

Cunningham, John. 'Popular Protest and a "Moral Economy" in Provincial Ireland in the Early Nineteenth Century'. In *Essays in Irish Labour History: A Festschrift for Elizabeth and John W. Boyle*, edited by Francis Devine, Fintan Lane, and Niamh Puirséil, 26–48. Dublin: Irish Academic Press, 2008.

Curran, Daragh. *The Protestant Community in Ulster, 1825–45: A Society in Transition*. Dublin, Ireland: Four Courts Press Ltd, 2014.

Dangerfield, George. *The Strange Death of Liberal England*. New York: Perigee Books, 1980.

*The Damnable Question: A Study of Anglo-Irish Relations.* London: Little, Brown, 1976.

Darwin, John. *The Empire Project: The Rise and Fall of the British World-System, 1830–1970.* Cambridge: Cambridge University Press, 2009.

*Unfinished Empire: The Global Expansion of Britain.* New York: Bloomsbury Press, 2012.

Delaney, Enda. *The Curse of Reason: The Great Irish Famine.* Dublin: Gill & Macmillan, 2012.

Dolan, Anne. 'Politics, Economy and Society in the Irish Free State, 1922–1939'. In *The Cambridge History of Ireland*, edited by Thomas Bartlett, vol. 4:323–48. Cambridge: Cambridge University Press, 2018.

Donnelly, James S. *Captain Rock: The Irish Agrarian Rebellion of 1821–1824.* Madison, WI: Wisconsin University Press, 2009.

'Hearts of Oak, Hearts of Steel'. *Studia Hibernica* 21 (1981): 7–73.

'Pastorini and Captain Rock: Millenarianism and Sectarianism in the Rockite Movement of 1821–4'. In *Irish Peasants: Violence and Political Unrest 1780–1914*, edited by Samuel Clark and James S. Donnelly, 102–36. Madison, WI: Wisconsin University Press, 1983.

*The Land and the People of Nineteenth-Century Cork: The Rural Economy and the Land Question.* London: Routledge & Kegan Paul, 1975.

'The Rightboy Movement, 1785–8'. *Studia Hibernica*, no. 17–18 (1977/78): 7–73.

'The Terry Alt Movement 1829–31'. *History Ireland* 2, no. 4 (Winter 1994): 30–5.

'The Whiteboy Movement, 1761–5'. *Irish Historical Studies* xxi, no. 81 (1978): 20–54.

Dooley, Terence A. M. *The Land for the People: The Land Question in Independent Ireland.* Dublin: University College Dublin Press, 2004.

*The Murders at Wildgoose Lodge: Agrarian Crime and Punishment in Pre-Famine Ireland.* Dublin: Four Courts Press, 2008.

Durey, Michael. 'Abduction and Rape in Ireland in the Year of the 1798 Rebellion'. *Eighteenth-Century Ireland* 21 (2006): 27–47.

Dusza, Karl. 'Max Weber's Conception of the State'. *International Journal of Politics, Culture, and Society* 3, no. 1 (Autumn 1989): 71–105.

Dwan, David. 'Civic Virtue in the Modern World: The Politics of Young Ireland'. *Irish Political Studies* 22, no. 1 (2007): 35–60.

Eastwood, David. '"Amplifying the Province of the Legislature": The Flow of Information and the English State in the Early Nineteenth Century'. *Historical Research* 62, no. 149 (October 1989): 276–94.

Ellis, Steven G., and Christopher Maginn. *The Making of the British Isles: The State of Britain and Ireland, 1450–1660.* Harlow: Routledge, 2007.

Ertman, Thomas. 'The Great Reform Act of 1832 and British Democratization'. *Comparative Political Studies* 43, no. 8–9 (August 1, 2010): 1000–22.

Farrell, Elaine. '"Infanticide of the Ordinary Character": An Overview of the Crime in Ireland, 1850–1900'. *Irish Economic and Social History* 39 (2012): 56–72.

'*A Most Diabolical Deed': Infanticide and Irish Society, 1850–1900.* Manchester: Manchester University Press, 2015.

Farrell, Sean. *Rituals and Riots: Sectarian Violence and Political Culture in Ulster, 1784–1886*. Lexington: University Press of Kentucky, 2000.

Fisher, Jess Lumsden. '"Night Marauders" and "Deluded Wretches": Public Discourses on Ribbonism in Pre-Famine Ireland'. In *Crime, Violence and the Irish in the Nineteenth Century*, edited by Kyle Hughes and Donald MacRaild, 53–66. Liverpool: Liverpool University Press, 2017.

Fitzpatrick, David. 'Class, Family and Rural Unrest in Nineteenth-Century Ireland'. In *Ireland: Land, Politics and People*, edited by P. J. Drudy, Irish Studies, vol. 4: 37–75. Cambridge: Cambridge University Press, 1981.

Fontana, Biancamaria. 'Founders of the Edinburgh Review (act. 1802–1829)'. *Oxford Dictionary of National Biography*. Oxford: Oxford University Press, 2008. https://doi.org/10.1093/ref:odnb/95409.

Foster, R. F. 'Introduction'. In *Nationalism and Popular Protest in Ireland*, edited by C. H. E. Philpin, 1–15. Cambridge: Cambridge University Press, 1987.

Gallagher, John, and Ronald Robinson. 'The Imperialism of Free Trade'. *The Economic History Review* 6, no. 1 (August 1953): 1–15.

Garvin, Tom. 'Defenders, Ribbonmen and Others: Underground Political Networks in Pre-Famine Ireland'. In *Nationalism and Popular Protest in Ireland*, edited by C. H. E. Philpin (1982): 133–55.

Gash, Norman. *Mr Secretary Peel – The Life of Sir Robert Peel*. New York: Longmans, Green and Co., 1961.

'Peel and the Party System 1830–50'. *Transactions of the Royal Historical Society* 1 (December 1951): 47–69.

Geoghegan, Patrick. 'The Impact of O'Connell, 1815–1850'. In *The Cambridge History of Ireland: Volume 3: 1730–1880*, edited by James Kelly, The Cambridge History of Ireland. vol. 3:102–27. Cambridge: Cambridge University Press, 2018.

*Liberator: The Life and Death of Daniel O'Connell, 1830–1847*. Reprint edition. Dublin: Gill & MacMillan, 2013.

Gibbons, Stephen Randolph. *Captain Rock, Night Errant: The Threatening Letters of Pre-Famine Ireland, 1801–1845*. Dublin: Four Courts Press, 2004.

Gillespie, Raymond. 'Explorers, Exploiters and Entrepreneurs: Early Modern Ireland and Its Context, 1500–1700', 147–53. In *An Historical Geography to Ireland*, edited by B. J. Graham and L. J. Proudfoot. London: Academic Press, 1993.

Graham, A. H. 'The Lichfield House Compact, 1835'. *Irish Historical Studies* 12, no. 47 (March 1961): 209–25.

Gray, Peter. *Famine, Land and Politics: British Government and Irish Society, 1843–50*. Dublin: Irish Academic Press, 1999.

'Ideology and the Famine'. In *The Great Irish Famine*, edited by Cathal Póirtéir. Dublin: Mercier Press, 1995.

*The Making of the Irish Poor Law, 1815–43*. Manchester: Manchester University Press, 2009.

'A "People's Viceroyalty"? Popularity, Theatre and Executive Politics 1835–47'. In *The Irish Lord Lieutenancy c. 1541–1922*, edited by Peter Gray and Olwen Purdue, 158–78. Dublin: University College Dublin Press, 2012.

Gray, Peter, and Olwen Purdue, eds. *The Irish Lord Lieutenancy c. 1541–1922*. Dublin: University College Dublin Press, 2012.

Gribben, C., and A. Holmes, eds. *Protestant Millennialism, Evangelicalism and Irish Society, 1790–2005*. Houndmills: Palgrave Macmillan, 2006.

Griffin, C. J. 'The Violent Captain Swing?' *Past & Present* 209, no. 1 (November 15, 2010): 149–80.

Harling, Philip. 'Parliament, the State, and "Old Corruption": Conceptualizing Reform, c. 1790–1832', in *Rethinking the Age of Reform: Britain 1780–1850*, edited by Arthur Burns and Joanna Innes, 98–113. Cambridge: Cambridge University Press, 2003.

Hawkins, Angus. *Forgotten Prime Minister: The 14th Earl of Derby: Volume I: Ascent, 1799–1851*. Oxford: Oxford University Press, 2009.

Haywood, Ian, and John Seed. 'Introduction'. In *The Gordon Riots: Politics, Culture and Insurrection in Late Eighteenth-Century Britain*, edited by Ian Haywood and John Seed, 1–18. Cambridge: Cambridge University Press.

Haywood, Ian, and John Seed, eds. *The Gordon Riots: Politics, Culture and Insurrection in Late Eighteenth-Century Britain*. Cambridge: Cambridge University Press, 2012.

Hession, Peter. 'Imagining the Railway Revolution in Pre-Famine Ireland: Technology, Governance, and the Drummond Commission, 1832–39'. In *Dreams of the Future in Nineteenth Century Ireland*, edited by Richard J. Butler, 245–70. Liverpool: Liverpool University Press, 2021.

Higgins-McHugh, Noreen. 'The 1830s Tithe Riots'. In *Riotous Assemblies: Rebels, Riots and Revolts in Ireland*, edited by William Sheehan and Maura Cronin, 80–95. Cork: Mercier Press, 2011.

Hill, Jacqueline. *From Patriots to Unionists: Dublin Civic Politics and Irish Protestant Patriotism, 1660–1840*. Oxford: Oxford University Press, 1997.

Hilton, Boyd. *A Mad, Bad, and Dangerous People? England, 1783–1846*. Oxford: Oxford University Press, 2006.

'The Ripening of Robert Peel'. In *Public and Private Doctrine: Essays in British History Presented to Maurice Cowling*, edited by Michael Bentley, 63–84. Cambridge: Cambridge University Press, 1993.

'Whiggery, Religion and Social Reform: The Case of Lord Morpeth'. *The Historical Journal* 37, no. 4 (December 1994): 829–59.

Hinde, Wendy. *Catholic Emancipation: A Shake to Men's Minds*. Oxford: Blackwell, 1992.

Hobsbawm, E. J. *Primitive Rebels: Studies in Archaic Forms of Social Movement in the 19th and 20th Centuries*. New York: W. W. Norton, 1965.

Hobsbawm, E. J., and George F. E Rudé. *Captain Swing*. New York: Pantheon Books, 1968.

Holton, Karina. 'A Turbulent Year: Lord Anglesey's First Viceroyalty and the Politics of Catholic Emancipation, 1828'. *Studia Hibernica* 43 (September 2017): 53–93.

Hoppen, K. Theodore. *Governing Hibernia: British Politicians and Ireland, 1800–1921*. Oxford: Oxford University Press, 2016.

'An Incorporating Union? British Politicians and Ireland 1800–1830'. *English Historical Review* 123, no. 501 (1 April 2008): 328–50.

'Ponsonby, John William, Fourth Earl of Bessborough (1781–1847)'. *ODNB*, https://doi.org/10.1093/ref:odnb/22500

'Riding a Tiger: Daniel O'Connell, Reform, and Popular Politics in Ireland, 1800–1847'. In *Reform in Great Britain and Germany, 1750–1850*, edited by Timothy Charles William Blanning and Peter Wende. Proceedings of the British Academy vol. 100: 121–43. Oxford: Oxford University Press for the British Academy, 1999.

Hourican, Bridget. 'Robert Jocelyn, Third Earl of Roden'. *Irish Dictionary of National Biography*. Dublin: Royal Irish Academy, 2009. http://dib.cambridge.org/viewReadPage.do?articleId=a4284

Howe, Stephen. *Ireland and Empire: Colonial Legacies in Irish History and Culture*. New York: Oxford University Press, 2000.

Huggins, Michael. *Social Conflict in Pre-Famine Ireland: The Case of Roscommon*. Dublin: Four Courts Press, 2007.

'Whiteboys and Ribbonmen: What's in a Name?' In *Crime, Violence and the Irish in the Nineteenth Century*, edited by Kyle Hughes and Donald M. MacRaild. Liverpool: Liverpool University Press, 22–37.

Hughes, Kyle, and Donald M. MacRaild. 'Introduction'. In *Crime, Violence and the Irish in the Nineteenth Century*, edited by Kyle Hughes and Donald M. MacRaild, 1–20. Liverpool: Liverpool University Press, 2018.

*Ribbon Societies in Nineteenth-Century Ireland and Its Diaspora: The Persistence of Tradition*. Liverpool: Liverpool University Press, 2018.

Innes, Joanna. 'What Would a "Four Nations" Approach to the Study of Eighteenth-Century British Social Policy Entail?' In *Kingdoms United? Great Britain and Ireland since 1500: Integration and Diversity*, edited by Sean J. Connolly, 181–99. Dublin: Four Courts Press, 1999.

Innes, Joanna, Mark Philp, and Robert Saunders. 'The Rise of Democratic Discourse in the Reform Era: Britain in the 1830s and 1840s'. In *Re-Imagining Democracy in the Age of Revolutions: America, France, Britain, Ireland 1750–1850*, edited by Joanna Innes and Mark Philp, 114–28. Oxford: Oxford University Press, 2013.

Jackson, Alvin. *Ireland, 1798–1998: Politics and War*. Oxford: Wiley-Blackwell, 1999.

'The Origins, Politics and Culture of Irish Unionism, c. 1880–1916'. In *The Cambridge History of Ireland: Volume 4, 1880 to the Present*, edited by Thomas Bartlett, 4:89–116. Cambridge: Cambridge University Press, 2018.

*The Two Unions: Ireland, Scotland, and the Survival of the United Kingdom, 1707–2007*. Oxford: Oxford University Press, 2011.

Jaggard, Edwin. 'The 1841 British General Election: A Reconsideration'. *Australian Journal of Politics & History* 30, no. 1 (April 1984): 99–114.

Jeffery, Keith, ed. *'An Irish Empire'? Aspects of Ireland and the British Empire*. Manchester: Manchester University Press, 1997.

Jenkins, Brian. *Era of Emancipation: British Government of Ireland, 1812–1830*. Kingston: McGill-Queens University Press, 1988.

Jones, Brad A. '"In Favour of Popery": Patriotism, Protestantism, and the Gordon Riots in the Revolutionary British Atlantic'. *Journal of British Studies* 52, no. 1 (January 2013): 79–102.

Jones, Emily. *Edmund Burke and the Invention of Modern Conservatism, 1830–1914: An Intellectual History*. Oxford: Oxford University Press, 2017.

Jones, Peter Daniel. 'Captain Swing and Rural Popular Consciousness: Nineteenth-Century Southern English Social History in Context.' (PhD dissertation, University of Southampton, 2002). http://ethos.bl.uk/OrderD etails.do?did=1&uin=uk.bl.ethos.270386.

Jones, Wilbur Devereux. 'Lord Mulgrave's Administration in Jamaica, 1832–1833'. *The Journal of Negro History* 48, no. 1 (January 1963): 44–56.

Jordan, Donald E. 'The Irish National League and the "Unwritten Law": Rural Protest and Nation-Building in Ireland 1882–1890'. *Past & Present*, no. 158 (February 1998): 146–71.

*Land and Popular Politics in Ireland: County Mayo from the Plantation to the Land War*. Cambridge: Cambridge University Press, 1994.

Joyce, Patrick. *The State of Freedom: A Social History of the British State since 1800*. Cambridge: Cambridge University Press, 2013.

Kanter, Douglas. 'The Campaign Against Over-Taxation, 1863–65: A Reappraisal'. In *Taxation, Politics, and Protest in Ireland, 1662–2016*, edited by Douglas Kanter and Patrick Walsh. Cham: Springer, 2019.

'The Politics of Irish Taxation, 1842–53'. *English Historical Review* 127, no. 528 (October 2012): 1121–55.

Katsuta, Shunsuke. *Rockites, Magistrates and Parliamentarians: Governance and Disturbances in Pre-Famine Rural Munster*. Abingdon: Routledge, 2020.

'The Rockite Movement in County Cork in the Early 1820s'. *Irish Historical Studies* 33, no. 131 (May 2003): 278–96.

Kearney, Hugh. *The British Isles: A History of Four Nations*. Cambridge: Cambridge University Press, 1989.

Kelly, James. *Food Rioting in Ireland in the Eighteenth and Nineteenth Centuries: The 'Moral Economy' and the Irish Crowd*. Dublin: Four Courts Press, 2017.

'Infanticide in Eighteenth-Century Ireland'. *Irish Economic and Social History* 19 (January 1992): 5.

'"An Unnatural Crime": Infanticide in Early Nineteenth-Century Ireland'. *Ireland Economic and Social History* 46, no. 1 (2019): 66–110.

Kelly, Matthew. 'Irish Nationalist Opinion and the British Empire in the 1850s and 1860s'. *Past & Present* 204, no. 1 (August 1, 2009): 127–54.

Kemp, Betty. 'The General Election of 1841'. *History* 37, no. 130 (June 1952): 146–57.

Kenny, Kevin, ed. *Ireland and the British Empire*. Oxford: Oxford University Press, 2005.

Kerr, Donal A. *Peel, Priests and Politics: Sir Robert Peel's Administration and the Roman Catholic Church in Ireland, 1841–1846*. Oxford: Oxford University Press, 1982.

Keyes, Michael J. 'Money and Nationalist Politics in Nineteenth Century Ireland: From O'Connell to Parnell'. National University of Ireland Maynooth, 2009. http://eprints.maynoothuniversity.ie/2899/1/MJK_Money_and_natio nalist_politics.pdf.

Kinealy, Christine. *Repeal and Revolution: 1848 in Ireland*. Manchester: Manchester University Press, 2009.

King, Peter. *Crime and Law in England, 1750–1840: Remaking Justice from the Margins*. Cambridge: Cambridge University Press, 2006.

Kingon, Suzanne T. 'Ulster Opposition to Catholic Emancipation, 1828–9'. *Irish Historical Studies* 34, no. 134 (November 2004): 137–55.

Knott, John William. 'Land, Kinship, and Identity: The Cultural Roots of Agrarian Agitation in Eighteenth and Nineteenth-Century Ireland'. *Journal of Peasant Studies* 12, no. 1 (October 1984): 93–108.

Kriegel, A. D. 'The Irish Policy of Lord Grey's Government'. *English Historical Review* 86, no. 338 (January 1971): 22–45.

Laird, Heather. *Subversive Law in Ireland, 1879–1920: From 'Unwritten Law' to the Dáil Courts*. Dublin: Four Courts Press, 2005.

Lee, Joseph. 'The Ribbonmen'. In *Secret Societies in Ireland*, edited by T. D. Williams, 26–35. London: Gill and MacMillan, 1973.

Lennon, Joseph. 'Irish Orientalism: An Overview'. In *Ireland and Postcolonial Theory*, edited by Clare Carroll and Patricia King, 129–57. South Bend, IN: Notre Dame Press, 2003.

Lindsey, Kiera. '"The Absolute Distress of Females": Irish Abductions and the British Newspapers, 1800 to 1850'. *The Journal of Imperial and Commonwealth History* 42, no. 4 (2014): 625–44.

Lloyd, Peter. 'The Irish Railway Commission (1836–1839) aiming to reform railways in the United Kingdom and to improve the governance of Ireland'. *The Journal of Transport History* 49, no. 1 (2019): 123–40.

Luddy, Maria. 'Abductions in Nineteenth-Century Ireland'. *New Hibernia Review/Iris Éireannach Nua* 17, no. 2 (2013): 17–44.

Lunney, Linde. 'Boyton, Charles'. In James McGuire and James Quinn, eds., *Dictionary of Irish Biography*. Cambridge: Cambridge University Press, 2009, http://dib.cambridge.org/viewReadPage.do?articleId=a0864.

Lynch, Niamh. 'Defining Irish Nationalist Anti-Imperialism: Thomas Davis and John Mitchel'. *Éire-Ireland* 42, nos. 1 & 2 (Spring/Summer 2007): 82–107. https://doi.org/10.1353/eir.2007.0020.

Lynn, Shane. 'Friends of Ireland: Early O'Connellism in Lower Canada'. *Irish Historical Studies* 40, no. 157 (May 2016): 43–65.

Mac Suibhne, Breandán. *The End of Outrage: Post-Famine Adjustment in Rural Ireland*. Oxford: Oxford University Press, 2017.

MacDonagh, Oliver. *The Emancipist: Daniel O'Connell 1830–47*. New York: St. Martin's Press, 1989.

'O'Connell's Ideology'. In *A Union of Multiple Identities: The British Isles, c. 1750–c. 1850*, edited by Laurence Brockliss and David Eastwood, 147–61. Manchester: Manchester University Press, 1997.

Machin, G. I. T. 'The No-Popery Movement in Britain in 1828–9'. *The Historical Journal* 6, no. 2 (1963): 193–211.

Macintyre, Angus. *The Liberator: Daniel O'Connell and the Irish Party, 1830–1847*. London: Hamish Hamilton, 1965.

Maddox, Neil P. '"A Melancholy Record": The Story of the Nineteenth-Century Irish Party Processions Acts'. *The Irish Jurist* 39 (2004): 243–74.

Magennis, Eoin. 'In Search of "Moral Economy": Food Scarcity in 1756–57 and the

Crowd'. In *Crowds in Ireland, c. 1820-1920*, edited by Peter Jupp and Eoin Magennis, 189–211. New York: St. Martin's Press, 2000.

'A "Presbyterian Insurrection"? Reconsidering the Hearts of Oak Disturbances of July 1763'. *Irish Historical Studies* xxxi, no. 122 (1998): 165–87.

Malcolm, Elizabeth. '"The Reign of Terror in Carlow": The Politics of Policing Ireland in the Late 1830s'. *Irish Historical Studies* 32, no. 125 (May 2000): 59–74.

Mandler, Peter. *Aristocratic Government in the Age of Reform: Whigs and Liberals, 1830–1852*. Oxford: Oxford University Press, 1990.

McBride, Ian. *Eighteenth-Century Ireland: The Isle of Slaves*, New Gill History of Ireland, vol. 4. Dublin: Gill & MacMillan, Limited, 2009.

'The Shadow of the Gunman: Irish Historians and the IRA'. *Journal of Contemporary History* 46, no. 3 (1 July 2011): 686–710.

McCabe, Desmond. 'Social Order and the Ghost of Moral Economy in Pre-Famine Mayo'. In *A Various County: Essays in Mayo History, 1500–1900*, edited by Raymond Gillespie and Gerard P. Moran, 91–112. Westport: Foilseacháin Náisiúnta Teoranta, 1987.

McDowell, R. B. *The Irish Administration, 1801–1914*. Studies in Irish History, Second Series, No. 2. London: Routledge & Kegan Paul, 1964.

McEldowney, John F. 'Legal Aspects of the Irish Secret Service Fund, 1793–1833'. *Irish Historical Studies* 25, no. 98 (November 1986): 129–37.

McGauran, John-Paul. 'George Cornewall Lewis, Irish Character and the Irish Poor Law Debate, 1833–1836'. *Journal of Historical Geography* 57 (July 2017): 28–39.

McGowan, Mark G. '*The Famine Plot* Revisited: A Reassessment of the Great Irish Famine as Genocide'. *Genocide Studies International* 11, no. 1 (December 2017): 87–104.

McGraw, Sean, and Kevin Whelan. 'Daniel O'Connell in Comparative Perspective, 1800–50'. *Éire-Ireland* 40, no. 1 & 2 (2005): 60–89.

McMahon, Cian T. *The Global Dimensions of Irish Identity: Race Nation, and the Popular Press, 1840–1880*. Chapel Hill: University of North Carolina Press, 2015.

McMahon, Richard. *Homicide in Pre-Famine and Famine Ireland*. Liverpool: Liverpool University Press, 2013.

McMahon, Timothy, Michael de Nie, and Paul Townsend, eds. *Ireland in an Imperial World: Citizenship, Opportunism, and Subversion*. London: Palgrave Macmillan, 2017.

McNally, Patrick. 'Rural Protest and "Moral Economy": The Rightboy Disturbances and Parliament'. In *Politics and Popular Culture in Britain and Ireland 1750-1850: Essays in Tribute to Peter Jupp*, edited by Allan Blackstock and Eoin Magennis, 262–82. Belfast: Ulster Historical Foundation, 2007.

Middleton, Alex. 'Conservative Politics and Whig Colonial Government, 1830–41'. *Historical Research* 94, no. 265 (2021): 532–53.

Miller, David W. 'The Armagh Troubles, 1784–95'. In *Irish Peasants: Violence and Political Unrest 1780-1914*, edited by Samuel Clark and James Donnelly, 155–91. Madison, WI: Wisconsin University Press, 1983.

'Irish Christianity and Revolution'. In *Revolution, Counter-Revolution and Union: Ireland in the 1790s*, edited by Jim Smyth, 195–210. Cambridge: Cambridge University Press, 2000.

*Peep O'Day Boys and Defenders: Selected Documents of the County Armagh Disturbances 1784–1796*. Belfast: Public Records Office of Northern Ireland, 1990.

'Radicalism and Ritual in East Ulster'. In *1798: A Bicentenary Perspective*, edited by Thomas Bartlett, 195–211. Dublin: Four Courts Press, 2003.

'Soup and Providence: Varieties of Protestantism and the Great Famine'. In *Ireland's Great Famine and Popular Politics*, edited by Enda Delaney and Breandán Mac Suibhne, 59–80. New York: Routledge, 2016.

Mirala, Petri. 'Law and Unlawful Oaths in Ireland: 1760–1835'. In *Politics and Popular Culture in Britain and Ireland 1750-1850: Essays in Tribute to Peter Jupp*, edited by Allan Blackstock and Eoin Magennis, 209–22. Ulster Historical Foundation, 2007.

Mitchell, L. G. *Lord Melbourne, 1779–1848*. Oxford: Oxford University Press, 1997.

Mooney, Desmond. 'The Origins of Agrarian Violence in Meath, 1790–1828'. *Records of Meath Archaeological and Historical Society* 8, no. 1 (1987): 45–67.

Murphy, Kathleen S. 'Judge, Jury, Magistrate and Soldier: Rethinking Law and Authority in Late Eighteenth-Century Ireland'. *The American Journal of Legal History* 44, no. 3 (July 2000): 231–56.

Murray, A. C. 'Agrarian Violence and Nationalism in Nineteenth-Century Ireland: The Myth of Ribbonism'. *Irish Economic and Social History* 13 (1986): 56–73.

Nelson, Ivan F. *The Irish Militia, 1793–1802: Ireland's Forgotten Army*. Dublin: Four Courts Press, 2007.

Newbould, Ian. 'Sir Robert Peel and the Conservative Party, 1832–1841: A Study in Failure?' *The English Historical Review* 98, no. 388 (1983): 529–57.

'Whiggery and the Growth of Party 1830–1841: Organization and the Challenge of Reform'. *Parliamentary History* 4, no. 1 (December 1985): 137–56.

*Whiggery and Reform, 1830-1841: The Politics of Government*. Stanford, CA: Stanford University Press, 1990.

Newcastle, Henry Pelham Fiennes Pelham-Clinton of. *Unrepentant Tory: Political Selections from the Diaries of the Fourth Duke of Newcastle-under-Lyne, 1827–38*. Edited by Richard A. Gaunt. Parliamentary History Record Series 3. Woodbridge: Boydell & Brewer, 2006.

Nolan, Willie. 'Land Reform in Post-Famine Ireland'. In *Atlas of the Great Irish Famine, 1845–52*, edited by John Crowley, William J. Smyth, and Mike Murphy, 570–9. Cork: Cork University Press, 2012.

Ó Ciosáin, Niall. '"114 Commissions and 60 Committees": Phantom Figures from a Surveillance State'. *Proceedings of the Royal Irish Academy, Section C* 109 (1 January 2009): 367–85.

*Ireland in Official Print Culture, 1800–1850: A New Reading of the Poor Inquiry*. Oxford: Oxford University Press, 2014.

O'Donoghue, Patrick. 'Causes of the Opposition to Tithes, 1830–1838'. *Studia Hibernica* 5 (1965): 7–28.

Ó Faoláin, Seán. *King of the Beggars: A Life of Daniel O'Connell, the Irish Liberator, in a Study of the Rise of the Modern Irish Democracy (1775–1847)*. London: Thomas Nelson and Sons, 1938.

O'Ferrall, Fergus. *Catholic Emancipation: Daniel O'Connell and the Birth of Irish Democracy 1820–30*. Dublin: Gill and Macmillan, 1985.

Ó Gráda, Cormac. *Black '47 and Beyond: The Great Irish Famine in History, Economy, and Memory*. Princeton, NJ: Princeton University Press, 2000.

   *Ireland Before and After the Famine: Explorations in Economic History, 1800–1925*. 2nd ed. Manchester: Manchester University Press, 1993.

   *Ireland: A New Economic History 1780–1939*. Oxford University Press, 1995.

Ó Luain, Kerron. '"Craven Subserviency Had Vanished. Bitter Hostility Had Arrived": Agrarian Violence and the Tenant League on the Ulster Borderlands, 1849–52'. *Irish Historical Studies* 43, no. 163 (May 2019): 27–54.

Ó Tuathaigh, M. A. G. *Thomas Drummond and the Government of Ireland, 1835–41*. O'Donnell Lectures 21. Dublin: National University of Ireland Dublin, 1978.

Ohlmeyer, Jane. 'Seventeenth-Century Ireland and the New British and Atlantic Histories'. *The American Historical Review* 104, no. 2 (April 1999): 446–62.

Owens, Gary. '"A Moral Insurrection": Faction Fighters, Public Demonstrations and the O'Connellite Campaign, 1828'. *Irish Historical Studies* xxx (1997): 513–41.

Palmer, Stanley H. *'Drummond, Thomas'*. ODNB. https://doi.org/10.1093/ref:odnb/8084.

   *Police and Protest in England and Ireland, 1780–1850*. Cambridge: Cambridge University Press, 1988.

Parry, Jonathan. *The Rise and Fall of Liberal Government in Victorian Britain*. New Haven, CT: Yale University Press, 1993.

Philips, David. 'A Weak State? The English State, the Magistracy and the Reform of Policing in the 1830s'. *English Historical Review* 119, no. 483 (2004): 873–91.

Phillips, John A., and Charles Wetherell. 'The Great Reform Act of 1832 and the Political Modernization of England'. *The American Historical Review* 100, no. 2 (1995): 411–36.

Pocock, J. G. A. 'British History: A Plea for a New Subject'. *Journal of Modern History* 47 (December 1975): 601–28.

   'Deconstructing Europe'. In *The Discovery of Islands: Essays in British History*, 269–88. Cambridge: Cambridge University Press, 2005.

   'History and Sovereignty: The Historiographical Response to Europeanization in Two British Cultures'. *Journal of British Studies* 31, no. 4 (October 1992): 358–89.

   'The Limits and Divisions of British History: In Search of the Unknown Subject'. *The American Historical Review* 87, no. 2 (April 1982): 311–36.

   'The New British History in Atlantic Perspective: An Antipodean Commentary'. *The American Historical Review* 104, no. 2 (April 1999): 490–500.

'The Union in British History'. *Transactions of the Royal Historical Society*, Sixth Series, 10 (2000): 181–96.

Portsmouth, Robert. *John Wilson Croker: Irish Ideas and the Invention of Modern Conservatism, 1800–1835*. Dublin: Irish Academic Press, 2010.

Powell, Martyn J. 'Ireland's Urban Houghers: Moral Economy and Popular Protest in the Late Eighteenth Century'. In *The Laws and Other Legalities of Ireland, 1689–1850*, edited by Michael Brown and Seán Patrick Donlan, 231–53. Farnham: Ashgate, 2011.

Prest, John. *Lord John Russell*. Columbia: University of South Carolina Press, 1972.

Quinault, Roland. 'The French Revolution of 1830 and Parliamentary Reform'. *History* 79, no. 257 (October 1994): 377–93.

Read, Charles. 'Laissez-Faire, the Irish Famine, and British Financial Crisis'. *The Economic History Review* 69, no. 2 (2016): 411–34.

'Peel, De Grey and Irish Policy, 1841–1844'. *History* 99, no. 334 (January 2014): 1–18.

Reid, Colin W. '"An Experiment in Constructive Unionism": Isaac Butt, Home Rule and Federalist Political Thought during the 1870s'. *English Historical Review* 129, no. 537 (1 April 2014): 332–61.

Reid, David Patrick. '"The Tithe War" in Ireland, 1830–1838' (PhD dissertation, Trinity College Dublin, 2013).

Ridgway, Christopher, ed. *The Morpeth Roll: Ireland Identified in 1841*. Dublin: Four Courts Press, 2013.

Roberts, Matthew. 'Daniel O'Connell, Repeal, and Chartism in the Age of Atlantic Revolutions'. *The Journal of Modern History* 90, no. 1 (March 2018): 1–39.

Roberts, Paul E. W. 'Caravats and Shanavests: Whiteboyism and Faction Fighting in East Munster, 1802–1811'. In *Irish Peasants: Violence and Political Unrest 1780-1914*, edited by Samuel Clark and James S. Donnelly. Madison, WI : University of Wisconsin Press, 1983.

Rodgers, Nini. *Ireland, Slavery and Anti-Slavery: 1612–1865*. Basingstoke: Palgrave Macmillan, 2007.

Roszman, Jay R. 'The Curious History of Irish "Outrages": Irish Agrarian Violence and Collective Insecurity, 1761–1852'. *Historical Research* 91, no. 253 (August 2018): 481–504.

Ryan, David. '"Ribbonism" and Agrarian Violence in County Galway, 1819–1820'. *Journal of the Galway Archaeological and Historical Society* 52 (2000): 120–34.

Salmon, Philip. *Electoral Reform at Work: Local Politics and National Parties, 1832-1841*, Royal Historical Society Studies in History, New Series, vol. 27. Woodbridge: Boydell & Brewer, 2002. www.jstor.org/stable/10.7722/j.ctt81f7k.

Samuel, Raphael. 'British Dimensions: "Four Nations History"'. *History Workshop Journal*, no. 40 (Autumn 1995): iii–xxii.

Saunders, Robert. 'God and the Great Reform Act: Preaching against Reform, 1831–32'. *Journal of British Studies* 53, no. 2 (April 2014): 378–99.

Scott, James C. *Seeing Like a State: How Certain Schemes to Improve the Human Condition have Failed*. New Haven, CT: Yale University Press, 1999.

Shaw, Daniel J. 'An Economic Perspective on the Irish Tithe War of 1831–1838'. *The Journal of European Economic History* 44, no. 3 (2015): 91–140.

Shields, Andrew. *The Irish Conservative Party 1852–1868: Land, Politics and Religion.* Dublin: Irish Academic Press, 2007.

Simmons, Dana. 'The Weight of the Moment: J. G. A. Pocock's Politics of History'. *History of European Ideas* 38, no. 2 (June 2012): 288–306.

Skinner, Simon. 'Religion'. In *Languages of Politics in Nineteenth-Century Britain*, edited by David Craig and James Thompson, 93–117. Houndmills: Palgrave Macmillan, 2013.

Slattery, Maureen. 'Irish Radicalism and the Roman Catholic Church in Quebec and Ireland, 1833–1834: O'Callaghan and O'Connell Compared'. *CCHA Historical Studies* 63 (1997): 29–58.

Smith, D. A. 'Lewis, Sir George Cornewall, Second Baronet (1806–63)'. In *Oxford Dictionary of National Biography.* Oxford: Oxford University Press, 2004. www.oxforddnb.com/view/article/16585

Smyth, Jim. 'Introduction: The 1798 Rebellion in Its Eighteenth-Century Contexts'. In *Revolution, Counter-Revolution and Union: Ireland in the 1790s*, edited by Jim Smyth, 1–20. Cambridge: Cambridge University Press, 2000.

*The Men of No Property: Irish Radicals and Popular Politics in the Late Eighteenth Century.* Houndmills: Macmillan, 1992.

Solar, Peter M. 'The Agricultural Trade Statistics in the Irish Railway Commissioners' Report'. *Irish Economic and Social History* 6 (1979): 24–40.

'Occupation, Poverty and Social Class in Pre-Famine Ireland, 1740–1850'. In *The Cambridge Social History of Modern Ireland*, edited by Eugenio F. Biagini and Mary E. Daly, 25–37. Cambridge: Cambridge University Press, 2017.

Spence, Joseph. 'The Philosophy of Irish Toryism, 1833–52: A Study of Reactions to Liberal Reformism in Ireland in the Generation between the First Reform Act and the Famine, with Especial Reference to Expressions of National Feeling among the Protestant Ascendancy' (PhD dissertation, Birkbeck College, University of London, 1990).

Thompson, E. P. *Customs in Common.* New York: New Press, distributed by W. W. Norton, 1993.

*The Making of the English Working Class.* New York: Pantheon Books, 1964.

'The Moral Economy of the English Crowd in the Eighteenth Century'. *Past & Present* 50 (1971): 76–136.

Tilly, Charles. *Contentious Performances.* Cambridge: Cambridge University Press, 2008.

Townend, Paul A. *The Road to Home Rule: Anti-Imperialism and the Irish National Movement.* History of Ireland and the Irish Diaspora. Madison: The University of Wisconsin Press, 2016.

Tucker, Robert C. *The Marx-Engel Reader.* New York: W. W. Norton & Co., 1978.

Turner, Michael J. 'Political Leadership and Political Parties, 1800–1846'. In *A Companion to Nineteenth-Century Britain*, edited by Chris Williams, 125–39. Blackwell Companions to British History. Oxford: Blackwell, 2004.

'Radical Agitation and the Canada Question in British Politics, 1837–41'. *Historical Research* 79, no. 203 (February 2006): 90–114.

Vaughan, W. E. *Landlords and Tenants in Mid-Victorian Ireland*. Oxford: Oxford University Press, 1994.

Wall, Maureen. 'The Whiteboys'. In *Secret Societies in Ireland*, edited by T. Desmond Williams. London: Gill and MacMillan, 1973.

Weber, Max. *Economy and Society: An Outline of Interpretive Sociology*. Edited by Guenther Roth and Claus Wittich. Berkeley: University of California Press, 1978.

Whelan, Irene. *The Bible War in Ireland: The 'Second Reformation' and the Polarization of Protestant–Catholic Relations, 1800–1840*. Madison: University of Wisconsin Press, 2005.

Whelan, Kevin. 'The Revisionist Debate in Ireland'. *Boundary 2* 31, no. 1 (2004): 179–205.

Williams, Leslie, and William H. A. Williams. *Daniel O'Connell, the British Press and the Irish Famine: Killing Remarks*. London: Routledge, 2016.

Williams, Raymond. *Keywords: A Vocabulary of Culture and Society*. New York: Oxford University Press, 1983.

Wolffe, John. *The Protestant Crusade in Great Britain, 1829–1860*. Oxford: Clarendon Press, 1991.

# Index

For EU product safety concerns, contact us at Calle de José Abascal, 56–1°,
28003 Madrid, Spain or eugpsr@cambridge.org.

www.ingramcontent.com/pod-product-compliance
Ingram Content Group UK Ltd.
Pitfield, Milton Keynes, MK11 3LW, UK
UKHW020359140625
459647UK00020B/2561